LEARNING TO SCHOOL

Federalism and Public Schooling in Canada

Among countries in the industrialized world, Canada is the only one without a national department of education, national standards for education, and national regulations for elementary or secondary schooling. For many observers, the system seems impractical and almost incoherent. But despite a total lack of federal oversight, the educational policies of all ten provinces are very similar today. Without intervention from Ottawa, the provinces have fashioned what amounts to a *de facto* pan-Canadian system.

Learning to School explains how and why the provinces have achieved this unexpected result. Beginning with the earliest provincial education policies and taking readers right up to contemporary policy debates, the book chronicles how, through learning and cooperation, the provinces gradually established a country-wide system of public schooling. A rich and ambitious work of scholarship, it will appeal to readers seeking fresh insights on Canadian federalism, education policy, and policy diffusion.

(Studies in Comparative Political Economy and Public Policy)

JENNIFER WALLNER is an assistant professor in the School of Political Studies at the University of Ottawa.

Studies in Comparative Political Economy and Public Policy

Editors: MICHAEL HOWLETT, DAVID LAYCOCK (Simon Fraser University), and STEPHEN MCBRIDE (McMaster University)

Studies in Comparative Political Economy and Public Policy is designed to showcase innovative approaches to political economy and public policy from a comparative perspective. While originating in Canada, the series will provide attractive offerings to a wide international audience, featuring studies with local, subnational, cross-national, and international empirical bases and theoretical frameworks.

Editorial Advisory Board

For a list of books published in the series, see page 411.

JENNIFER WALLNER

Learning to School

Federalism and Public Schooling in Canada

UNIVERSITY OF TORONTO PRESS
Toronto Buffalo London

© University of Toronto Press 2014
Toronto Buffalo London
www.utppublishing.com
Printed in the U.S.A.

ISBN 978-1-4426-4781-7 (cloth)
ISBN 978-1-4426-1589-2 (paper)

Printed on acid-free, 100% post-consumer recycled paper with vegetable-based inks.

Library and Archives Canada Cataloguing in Publication

Wallner, Jennifer, 1977–, author
Learning to school: federalism and public schooling in Canada /Jennifer Wallner.

(Studies in comparative political economy and public policy)
Includes bibliographical references and index.
ISBN 978-1-4426-4781-7 (bound). – ISBN 978-1-4426-1589-2 (pbk.)

1. Public schools – Canada.   2. Public schools – Canada – History.
3. Education and state – Canada.   4. Education and state – Canada – History.
5. Education – Standards – Canada.   6. Education – Standards – Canada –
History.   I. Title.   II. Series: Studies in comparative political economy
and public policy

LA412.W24 2014   371.010971   C2014-900317-X

This book has been published with the help of a grant from the Federation for the
Humanities and Social Sciences, through the Awards to Scholarly Publications
Program, using funds provided by the Social Sciences and Humanities Research
Council of Canada.

University of Toronto Press acknowledges the financial assistance to its publishing
program of the Canada Council for the Arts and the Ontario Arts Council.

University of Toronto Press acknowledges the financial support of the Government of
Canada through the Canada Book Fund for its publishing activities.

For my parents, John and Lydia,
and for my mentor, Richard

Contents

List of Tables

List of Appendices

Acknowledgments

Although only my name is on the cover, writing this book was far from a solitary venture. While I cannot hope to be exhaustive in thanking everyone who helped me, I can try.

From the outset, I owe a major debt of gratitude to all the politicians, public servants, and members of the provincial education policy communities who agreed to speak with me and participate in this project. The interviews allowed me to understand how people manage to work within what seems to outsiders to be a chaotic and fragmented world and produce what is a remarkably coherent policy system. Without their time and contributions, this project would not have been possible.

This book started off as a PhD dissertation as I pursued my doctorate in political science at the University of Toronto. There I was lucky enough to fall under the influence of Richard Simeon. My mentor and friend, Richard sparked my interest in federalism and pushed me to build bridges while he supervised my research. I also benefited enormously from my other committee members, Grace Skogstad and Linda White. They provided me with insightful and incisive feedback on all my work and encouraged me to keep soldiering through the seemingly never-ending process of researching and writing a dissertation. Rod Haddow and Kathryn Harrison were my external evaluators on the original project. Their comments and questions helped me move my thesis into new territory.

Beyond the immediate sphere of my dissertation committee, a number of other professors at the University of Toronto were instrumental in my development as a scholar. Joe Wong, Graham White, Rob Vipond, Phil Triadafilopoulos, Susan Solomon, David Rayside, Neil

Nevitte, Jeff Kopstein, Ran Hirschl, and David Cameron – thank you all for your comments and advice over the years.

In addition to the faculty, I benefited immensely from my fellow students in the program. It is an honour and a privilege to have them as my friends and colleagues. Jorg Wittenbrink, Steve Trott, Leah Soroko, Reuven Shlozberg, Vincent Pouliot, Mike Painter-Main, Celine Mulhern, Juan Marsiaj, Petr Kafka, Genevieve Fuji Johnson, Josh Hjartarson, Marc Hanvelt, Victor Gomez, Erica Fredericksen, Bill Flanik, Jim Farney, Jan Erk, Essyn Emurla, Seb Daillaire, Wayne Chu, Antoine Bilodeau, Sebastian Baglioni, Cheryl Auger, Chris Alcantara, and others made the experience of doing a PhD unforgettable.

Special thanks also go to both deb thompson and Elisabeth King, who not only read the initial dissertation but also commented on revised chapters as I worked to turn my research into a manuscript.

The book evolved from a dissertation into a completed book thanks to the guidance and support of a number of people. However, to quote Richard Simeon, "as the traditional caveat goes, the responsibility for errors of fact and interpretation are mine alone."

My colleagues at the Johnson Shoyama Graduate School of Public Policy were extremely supportive as I embarked on this adventure. Daniel Béland provided many substantive comments, and Greg Marchildon offered the necessary strategic advice to keep me moving forward. I finished revising this book as a member of the School of Political Studies at the University of Ottawa. Michael Orsini forced me to be much clearer and more explicit about my analytical approach ("Don't make me wait till the end of the intro!"). Luc Turgeon let me burst into his office and helped me puzzle through things as if we were back at CHASS. Martin Papillon's comments and reflections on various chapters were crucial in moulding the argument into its current form.

I am grateful for my association with the University of Toronto Press. Daniel Quinlan, my primary contact, has been wonderful, always willing to provide comments on drafts of chapters while helping me navigate the waters of external reviews, SSHRC, and editorial boards. The other members of the UTP team, including Wayne Herrington, have been amazing as they turned the manuscript into a book. A major debt of gratitude is also owed to the external reviewers of the manuscript – you took my arguments seriously and gave me the comments to make my work better.

Finally – where would I be without Steve? You have been with me through it all, and I could not have done it without you.

Abbreviations

ACDE	Association of Canadian Deans of Education
AIP	Agreement in Principle
AIT	Agreement on Internal Trade
APEF	Atlantic Provinces Education Foundation
ATA	Alberta Teachers' Association
BCCT	British Columbia College of Teachers
BCSTA	British Columbia School Trustees Association
BCTF	British Columbia Teachers' Federation
CAMET	Council of Atlantic Ministers of Education and Training
CAP	Canada Assistance Plan
CEA	Canadian Education Association
CEGEP	*Collège d'enseignement général et professionnel*
CERI	Centre for Educational Research and Innovation
CHST	Canada Health and Social Transfer
CICS	Canadian Intergovernmental Conference Secretariat
CMEC	Council of Ministers of Education Canada
CMP	Council of Maritime Premiers
CNEA	Canada and Newfoundland Education Association
CSBA	Canadian School Boards Association
CSE	*Conseil supérieur de l'éducation*
CST	Canadian Social Transfer
CSTA	Canadian School Trustees' Association
CTF	Canadian Teachers' Federation
DEA	Dominion Education Association

EPF	Established Program Financing
EQAO	Education Quality and Accountability Office
ESEA	Elementary and Secondary Education Act
GDP	Gross Domestic Product
IMF	International Monetary Fund
IOSCO	International Organization of Securities Commissions
MTS	Manitoba Teachers' Society
NACER	National Advisory Committee on Educational Research
NCLB	No Child Left Behind
NDP	New Democratic Party
NEP	National Energy Program
NPM	New Public Management
NWP	New West Partnership
OBE	Outcomes-Based Education
OCT	Ontario College of Teachers
OECD	Organisation for Economic Co-operation and Development
OEEC	Organisation for European Economic Co-operation
PCAP	Pan-Canadian Assessment Program
PEI	Prince Edward Island
PISA	Program for International Student Assessment
SAIP	School Achievement Indicators Project
TILMA	Trade Investment Labour Mobility Agreement
TVTA	Technical and Vocational Training Assistance Act
UK	United Kingdom
UN	United Nations
UNESCO	United Nations Educational, Scientific, and Cultural Organization
WCP	Western Canadian Protocol for Collaboration in Education

LEARNING TO SCHOOL

Federalism and Public Schooling in Canada

Introduction: An Unexpected Policy Framework

In 1976, the Organisation for Economic Co-operation and Development (OECD) conducted a review of elementary and secondary education in Canada. This was the first time that all ten provincial education systems had been assessed simultaneously, and the results were less than glowing:

> The fact that there is, and apparently can be, no Federal Department of Education has created a kind of vacuum in education policy at the higher federal decision-making level ... There is to date no sign of a coherent federal policy for education emerging, nor much evidence of success in ironing out inconsistencies and even outright contradictions among various parts of the total federal effort in education.[1]

The reviewers decried the lack of national goals and unified standards and issued a clear warning to Canadian educational authorities:

> The lack of generally binding propositions concerning the socio-political goals of education has the effect of producing a damaging uncertainty about the meaning and purpose of the vast Canadian educational enterprise. This uncertainty may be noted in other countries too, but probably nowhere as openly evident and unchallenged as in Canada.[2]

The message was clear. The absence of central intervention in education overseen by federal decision makers was translating into dramatic inconsistencies that were compromising the school system as a whole. The reviewers were no less blunt in their prescribed remedy – Ottawa needed to establish a national department of education, empowered with the binding authority to standardize provincial policy choices and institutionalize a national policy framework for elementary and secondary education.

Fast-forward to elementary and secondary education today. In contrast to this image presented by the OECD, there is extensive evidence of consistency and certainty flowing across the ten jurisdictions. This is not to imply that the provincial education systems are mirror images of one another. In fact, interesting variations in strategies and practices continue to demarcate the systems, and many of these will be discussed in this book. In the main, however, elementary and secondary schooling is similarly configured across the country. As a result, Canadian children from coast to coast have access to reasonably commensurate systems of public education regardless of where they reside. But how do we know that the provincial education systems are reasonably commensurate?

Provinces invest in elementary and secondary education at comparable levels with similar amounts of per pupil funding and similar student–teacher ratios. On international tests, Canadian students perform remarkably well, and furthermore, Canada receives top marks on inter-regional and inter-school equity, which means that school location is not an important determinant of educational achievement (see Appendix 1). Peering into the substance of education policy itself, moreover, the administration of public schooling is comparably organized across the country; most provinces finance their systems with the same arrangements; regional initiatives in curriculum have become the norm; a pan-Canadian consensus on learning objectives in science has been ratified; a pan-Canadian assessment program that provides comparable data from coast to coast is executed annually; and a formal agreement on teacher mobility may be coming into view on the horizon. Put together, this suggests that an active policy framework is at work in Canadian elementary and secondary education.

I am not arguing that the provincial education systems are free from defects, shortcomings, or blemishes.[3] Because I focus exclusively on the provincial education systems, this book does not grapple with the massive and tragic disparity between the schooling provided by the federal government to on-reserve Aboriginal Peoples and that provided by the provinces.[4] Nevertheless, even when we look within the provincial systems, at 71 per cent, the high school non-completion rate for registered Aboriginal Peoples who have attended provincial schools continues to far exceed that of the non-Aboriginal population. An additional concern is that outside of Quebec, francophone students tend to underperform relative to their anglophone counterparts, which indicates the presence of a persistent disparity between the language groups. In a number of urban centres, certain groups of immigrants and visible minorities are failing to complete high school at alarming rates. Educators are also becoming increasingly aware of a growing gender gap, with females consistently outperforming males: boys earn lower grades and trail in reading and writing, and more of them fall at the bottom of standardized tests. And, somewhat anecdotally, educational opportunities for rural students continue to lag behind those afforded to students in urban areas. Policy makers in each of the ten jurisdictions must address all of these problems.

Yet those problems do not diminish the fact that when we compare the provincial education systems to one another, all ten show remarkably strong similarities in investments, achievements, and substantive policies. The evidence therefore indicates that the provinces have defied the odds and found a way to develop and maintain similar policy activities and fashion a *de facto* pan-Canadian policy framework for elementary and secondary education without the direct intervention of the federal government.

This book seeks to answer a critical question: How did the provinces manage to establish this overarching system of education? Answering this question requires us to re-examine core assumptions in the federalism literature regarding the plausibility, reliability, and effectiveness of substate policy interactions, while simultaneously reconsidering the processes that are presumed to underpin the formulation of policy frameworks. The prevailing wisdom suggests that the achievement of interjurisdictional policy similarity is unlikely without direct interventions by a central government that has the necessary authority and capacity to hierarchically impose or compel common behaviour by the substate jurisdictions. Furthermore, using the concept of policy diffusion, federal scholars often implicate coercion and competition as the primary motors that drive the establishment of policy frameworks in federations. The central findings of this book, however, are first, that substate governments can and often do collaborate without the proverbial Leviathan as embodied by the central government directly intervening in their affairs, and second, that the processes of learning and cooperation can generate interjurisdictional policy similarity.

I argue that while the federal government can – and in fact did – play an important albeit indirect role in crafting policy frameworks, the provinces can work together to craft coherent policy systems. Provincial policy decisions are made not in isolation but rather in consideration of the decisions and actions taken by other jurisdictions. Captured by the concepts of interdependence and connectivity, actors such as provincial leaders, education officials, schooling professionals, and other members of the policy community are linked together through formal and informal channels that influence the transmission of policy ideas among them. The economic and legal interdependence created under a federal union and organizational and cultural bonds that can evolve within a federation furnish conduits for disseminating policy ideas and offer varying incentives and opportunities for policy activity. These bonds, by their nature and intensity, generate a structural environment in which ideas move among the jurisdictions. Swirling around and throughout this environment, moreover, are the policy ideas themselves, including programs, public sentiments, and paradigms, which tend to prevail at particular points in time. Put together, these structural and ideational components constitute the active policy climate within which decisions are made. And, like the meteorological term from which it is derived, a policy climate is not immutable – it can transform over time.

While the diffusion of ideas across the porous borders of a federation is inevitable, the causal processes and mechanisms that propel the movement of ideas are contextually contingent. This means that the processes of diffusion can be altered when the bonds of interdependence and connectivity change. Certain configurations of the policy climate may privilege coercion or competition within a federation while others favour learning and cooperation. Furthermore, contrary to what some studies of diffusion imply,[5] the movement of policy ideas across territorial borders neither immediately nor automatically translates into the implementation of similar practices that are gradually transformed into a shared policy framework. I argue that the implementation and adaptation of policies is influenced by the internal policy context of the receiving jurisdiction. Specifically, the existing policy legacies and the active policy regimes at work within the various provinces influence the likelihood that they will introduce similar policies. Moreover, the probability that an idea will be adopted and the degree to which it is adjusted as it is translated into a novel setting both turn on the relevance of that idea to an identified problem, its compatibility with existing administrative structures, the political promise of the idea, and the ways in which advocates demonstrate its potential utility and appropriateness in the receiving jurisdiction. This study thus enriches our appreciation for the dynamics of policy making in federal settings and contributes to a fuller understanding of substate policy activity by explaining these perplexing results in the crucial case that is Canadian elementary and secondary education.

In the course of explaining how the provinces formed the policy framework, it is clear that other questions need to be addressed. Was the policy framework in elementary and secondary education recently achieved due to external forces such as globalization, or can the development of the framework be traced back through past decisions by the provincial decision makers themselves? If that framework evolved over time, did its emergence occur systematically, through purely rational processes of decision making based exclusively on material interests, or did other normative and ideational factors play a role? Were similar policies adopted consistently across all the provinces, or did varying patterns of policy activity occur? Which factors and conditions encouraged the adoption of common policies or, alternatively, the preservation of certain variations that continue to subtly differentiate the provincial systems? Finally, recognizing that education is not a monolithic sector, did choices in particular dimensions of the education sector shape the overall character of the system both within and beyond provincial borders? These questions require us to systematically identify and explore the factors that influence the processes of policy diffusion and the likelihood of substate similarity – or the achievement of policy convergence – while also considering the reverberating and ricocheting effects that choices in the individual dimensions of a policy arena can have on the configuration of a sector as a whole.

At its heart, this is a book about institution building and institutional change. To unravel these processes and mechanisms, I have grounded this study in an institutionalist approach. In its contemporary formulation, institutionalism is divided into three streams or traditions: rational choice institutionalism, sociological institutionalism, and historical institutionalism. Each on its own offers certain pertinent advantages while simultaneously suffering from a series of well-known defects.[6]

Rooted in methodological individualism, rational choice institutionalism focuses on how individuals build and modify institutions to achieve their interests, making decisions based on the logic of consequences.[7] Both formal rules and informal norms are said to limit the range of choices an individual is likely to make as he or she weighs potential outcomes relative to anticipated costs. Actors, moreover, are bounded by cognitive constraints that further limit their capacities to gather and digest information and make informed decisions, which means that choices may not result in the most efficient outcome. Institutional development is said to occur through path-dependent mechanisms of increasing returns, feedback, and choices made within prevailing constraints. What is more, different polities may be encouraged to make similar institutional choices based on competitive pressures to secure the best results. However, with their focus on how individual choices drive institutional change, rational choice institutionalists tend to study short time frames that are poorly suited to examining long-term historical developments. Furthermore, when the concept of path dependence is applied, the mechanisms that drive institutional change are often underspecified and opaque. Finally, the emphasis on self-interest and the logic of consequences assumes that actors make decisions based on only one type of logic. Yet researchers are increasingly attuned to the fact that people are influenced by other types of ideas and logics, which need better integration into our analytical frameworks than what rational choice conventionally offers.

Emerging from organizational theory, sociological institutionalists emphasize the importance of cognitive scripts and of cultural ideas, assessing the ways in which informal conventions and non-codified practices shape human behaviour and meso-level institutional development.[8] Rather than seeing institutions as attempts to find efficient means to realize official goals through a cost–benefit calculus, they view organizations like education systems as shaped by culturally specific practices and codes of appropriateness that become embedded and self-reinforcing over time. These codes of appropriateness can gradually be diffused through policy fields and industrial sectors and even across countries via the processes of emulation, normative professionalization, and coercion. John Meyer and others argue that to ensure their survival, institutions seek legitimacy from their environment, moulding themselves to conform to these informal and shared cultural values, norms, and cognitive schema.[9] However, it is not always entirely clear who or what confers "legitimacy" or how "appropriateness" comes to be defined. Also, the roles of actors and that of agency tend to be marginalized as structures come to occupy the prominent place that drives accounts of institutional development. Finally, sociological institutionalists are often unclear about how values or practices can be transformed as they move among environments, for they assume that imported ideas are simply replicated by the receiving community, generating greater homogeneity over time, even though such outcomes are rarely given.

Lastly, historical institutionalists focus on the ways in which macro-level structures of the polity and the economy privilege certain interests over others, influence collective behaviour, and propel certain outcomes over time.[10] Defining institutions as formal or informal procedures, routines, norms, and conventions, scholars working within this tradition take exception to behaviouralism, which emphasizes the role of interest groups, policy makers, and individual political leaders as the drivers of politics with little consideration of how the institutional context shapes the interests and behaviours of these agents. Instead, they move context to the forefront of the analytical framework accompanied by the importance of timing and sequencing. Historical institutionalists try to specify the order of action and trace processes to identify the factors that shape institutional development; to explain institutional stability, like their rational choice counterparts, they implicate the mechanism of path dependence with its self-reinforcing processes and increasing returns that prioritize certain options on the political menu. Rather than seeing action as driven either by the interest-based logic of instrumentality or by the ideationally based logic of appropriateness, however, many of them see behaviour as a result of interplay between the two. Historical institutionalists are nevertheless often criticized for under-specifying the ways in which path dependence works and the factors that shape its activity. Furthermore, they are unclear about the role of ideas, offering them only a backseat to other structural features of the context. Finally, some historical institutionalist accounts, like those of their sociological counterparts, leave little room for agency, as the trajectory for institutional development is seemingly preordained.

To explain and understand the development of policy frameworks in federations, in this book I craft an analytical architecture that seeks to bridge these three institutionalist terrains. John Campbell's recent work on globalization has led him to assert that despite the "bickering ... institutionalists should see that they have much more in common and at stake together than they thought previously." He further advocates "a sustained three-way dialogue in institutionalist analysis."[11] It is through a constructive dialogue that we can resolve some of the problems that have beset institutionalism and further its explanatory capacity.

My interests in the historical development of a policy system led me to start from the base of historical institutionalism, which draws our attention to the importance of timing and sequencing in a particular context made up of formal rules and informal practices. Here the actions of education policy makers nested within a temporally and structurally bound context take centre stage. My interest in the meso-level policy development of the provincial education systems draws inspiration from sociological institutionalism's focus on organizational evolution and the ways in which institutions can become infused with values that subsequently affect their configuration and evolution. Normative and cultural factors are woven into my analytical architecture as I argue that cultural bonds influence the processes of diffusion and that the implementation and adaptation of new policies is shaped by the active features of the internal educational regime at work within each provincial system. Finally, to correct for the determinist and structuralist tendencies of historical and sociological institutionalism, I integrate insights from rational choice institutionalism without relying exclusively on rational choice theory to understand institutional change. Specifically, I work to identify the ways in which actors are influenced by one another and by their environments when making decisions as well as how these decisions in turn reshape or adjust the prevailing policy context, the choices that subsequent actors make, and the wider policy climate.

The contributions of this study on Canadian education policy are therefore threefold. First, empirically, I will demonstrate that direct intervention by the central government is not necessary to the creation of overarching policy frameworks in federal systems and that intergovernmental learning and cooperation can play a vital and meaningful role shaping substate policy activity. Second, working inductively with a comparative historical approach to institution building, I will determine with greater clarity the factors that enable or privilege certain processes of policy diffusion over others, identify the scope conditions that encourage substate governments to either enact similar policies or pursue alternative practices, and show how seemingly disparate policy choices can have considerable effects that subsequently resonate not only within a specific dimension of the education system but also throughout the system as a whole. Third and finally, I will endeavour to make broader theoretical contributions by synthesizing aspects from the three traditions of institutionalism, thereby advancing the "second movement" in institutional analysis while concomitantly injecting an "ideational turn" into the study of federalism, a field that heretofore has been largely dominated by mainly rationalist approaches.

The remainder of this introduction unfolds in five parts. I open with a discussion of the literature on federalism and social policy. The second section addresses why education is an important field for study and the types of insights that can be drawn from its investigation. Moving into a series of more technical discussions, the third section explains why Canadian elementary and secondary education is a crucial case for assessing the need for central intervention for policy frameworks in federations, while the fourth section outlines my methodology. The final section provides a roadmap of the book to help readers navigate their way through the pages that follow.

Federalism and Social Policy

Federalism involves a division of powers between a central authority and constituent political units; it manifests itself in an arrangement of shared rule and self-rule. Ruminating on this arrangement, observers of federal systems have long been vexed by a fundamental question: What effects does the logic of diversity, which is embedded in the federal principle of self-rule, have on the abilities of actors to create policies and programs that are reasonably consistent across the constituent jurisdictions, a crucial element of achieving shared rule? There are rival interpretations regarding the reconciliation of these seemingly opposing principles that we can loosely (and albeit imperfectly) divide between federal sceptics and federal optimists.

Harold Laski penned perhaps the staunchest condemnation of federalism in his provocatively titled article, "The Obsolescence of Federalism." In this brief but influential piece, written in the immediate aftermath of the Great Depression, he declared that "the epoch of federalism is over."[12] He argued that by dividing power and authority among different orders of government, federalism creates weak governments and prevents the emergence of critical standards of policy uniformity that are necessary for a society to flourish. Years later, Jeffrey Pressman and Aaron Wildavsky recorded similar concerns: "If the federal principle maintains its vitality, then it means precisely that state and local organizations must be able to oppose, delay, and reject federal initiatives."[13] Furthermore, since Mancur Olson's seminal work on group dynamics, *The Logic of Collective Action*, it has been generally accepted that autonomous actors rarely work well together in the pursuit of common interest, particularly if they lack a strong central leader.[14] Olson's own reflection on "federal"-type groups, moreover, specifically identified the crucial role for the central government. Olson suggested that if the central organization "provides some service to the small constituent organizations, they may be induced to use their social incentives to get the individuals belonging to each small group to contribute toward the achievement of the collective goals of the whole group."[15]

Olson's logic, which resonates through many studies of federations, is clearly reflected in Anthony Welch's analysis of the Australian welfare state, in which he opined: "It is hard to imagine how the current levels of social and economic infrastructure could have been achieved without conscious, large-scale and ongoing intervention by the [national] state."[16] According to the various studies that are sceptical about effective policy making in federations, the key risks include intergovernmental bickering, pre-empted policy space that restricts government action, incoherent policy activities as substate governments pursue different pathways, suboptimal outcomes, and the possibility of a "race to the bottom" – a variant of destructive competition drawn from welfare economics – as jurisdictions cut corners or agree to standards set by the weakest member.[17]

What do education policy scholars themselves think of federalism? While few in number, those working exclusively in the field of education policy who consider how political institutions may influence schooling systems tend to regard federalism with a high degree of uncertainty. Milbrey McLaughlin explains that substate education sectors are likely to exhibit considerable differences due to variations in such factors as size, commitment to broader objectives, and the relative capacities of the respective jurisdictions.[18] Following a detailed investigation of the pitfalls of the American Elementary and Secondary Education Act, Jerome T. Murphy concluded: "The federal system – with its dispersion of power and control – not only permits but encourages the evasion and dilution of federal reform, making it nearly impossible for the federal administrator to impose program priorities."[19] Others maintain that substate governments could use their authority to manipulate proficiency standards and threaten the performance of the system as a whole, or limit the access of certain groups to educational programs, thereby compromising the realization of national equity for the population as a whole.[20] And, in their evaluation of lifelong learning policy in Canada, Tara Gibb and Judith Walker bluntly state: "That responsibility lies with provincial governments creates challenges for the federal government in developing coherence in implementing policies consistently across Canada."[21] In general, then, it seems that the division of powers and fragmentation of authority over schooling is not well regarded by those who work in the education field.

Not all evaluations of federalism's impact on social policy are as grim, however. Since Justice Louis Brandeis's famous declaration in *New State Ice Co. v. Liebmann*, the division of powers has been valued as a means to encourage policy innovation, in the sense that substate governments can act as "laboratories of democracy" by testing new strategies without risk to the country as a whole.[22] The formal division of powers between a central government and constituent units affords territorially based groups room for autonomous decision making to create distinctive policy packages. "A federal state," writes Réjean Pelletier, "rests on the idea of a division of sovereignty between two orders of government, with each maintaining legislative autonomy in their respective spheres of competence."[23] And in this instance, perhaps expressing more support for the division of powers, Wildavsky declared: "Uniformity is antithetical to federalism. The existence of states free to disagree with one another and with the central government inevitably leads to differentiation."[24] For the economist Charles Tiebout, the advantages of federalism are clear. The governments of substates have the opportunity to put forward unique policy packages that are carefully tailored to the needs of their own citizens. Conjuring up an image of disgruntled consumers, Tiebout then says that citizens in turn have the opportunity to "vote with their feet" and exit to a different jurisdiction should the programs on offer there prove more appealing.[25] Tiebout and his followers thus present an optimistic interpretation of federalism, one in which effectiveness and efficiency are driven by the forces of interjurisdictional competition; this enhances public welfare and the provision of what are likely to be diverse programs.[26]

The significance of substate legislative autonomy is also heightened in federations with multinational polities, like Canada, where policy innovation and experimentation take on new meaning. The division of powers enables political leaders to use public policies as tools for identity building and mobilization.[27] Furthermore, drawing from more normative arguments that social groups are the providers of culture, federalism opens the door for a substate government to assume leadership and further the historical continuity of a certain culture that is distinct from the national body politic. "It is argued," notes Alain-G. Gagnon, "that there is a collective good in the preservation of languages, traditions, institutions and symbols of previous generations, and the members of a political community such as Quebec, Catalonia,

or Wales should act not only as inheritors but as trustees of their respective cultures and political legacies."[28] For many scholars, then, the
potential flexibility of the federal bargain allows multilingual and multinational communities to coexist under the rubric of a shared state;
the desirability of interjurisdictional policy similarity is not assumed.
Where Laski was concerned about achieving uniformity, Charles Taylor instead calls for recognition of the "deep diversity" of federal polities, a diversity that eschews notions of a "nationalizing project, since
this process tends to subsume differences, or at least relativize them in
status in their relationship to the 'national' state."[29] Those working in
this area of the federalism field thus appear to de-emphasize the importance of interjurisdictional comparability, prioritizing instead the value
of local creativity and substate autonomy, and applaud federalism's
potential for achieving these.[30]

The long-term success of any state nevertheless requires a certain degree of internal parity to cultivate equity for the citizenry as a whole.
Why is this the case? For the answer to this question we can look to
the writings of British sociologist T.H. Marshall and the idea of social
citizenship, which posits that all citizens should "live the life of a ci-
vilised being according to the standards prevailing in the society."[31] Using this concept of social citizenship, Keith Banting affirms that "the
promise of social citizenship is the equality of treatment of citizens, to
be achieved through common social benefits." Banting nevertheless immediately draws our attention to the fact that "the promise of federalism is regional diversity in public policies, reflecting the preferences
of regional communities and cultures."[32] There is a clear tension here
that flows from the two ends that federalism is trying to achieve: "One
end is always found in the reason why the member units do not simply
consolidate themselves into one large unitary country; the other end
is always found in the reason why the member units do not choose
to remain simply small, wholly autonomous countries."[33] The logic of
diversity could overpower the logic of social citizenship as constituent
governments pursue distinctive paths in ways that subsequently undermine social cohesion in a state. Policy making in federations is thus
somewhat akin to finding the balance point on a teeter-totter: tilting too
much in favour of policy similarity risks smothering the diversity principle; tilting too much towards diversity could compromise the integrity of the state itself. Federations, Bruno Théret notes, therefore need to
institutionalize "self-preservation mechanisms ... which permanently
regulates its constitutive contradiction between unity and diversity."[34]

One solution to this dilemma lies in the formulation of policy frameworks. While the term has become ubiquitous, policy frameworks are rarely defined – a problem I will try to remedy. A policy framework can act as a kind of umbrella that instils a particular type of logic to manage the systems and programs at work within a country. While the scope, components, and details of frameworks vary considerably, their hallmarks include: certain identified objectives and goals, stipulations of programs, specifications of preferred instruments and methods of administration, and the criteria for citizens to access particular programs. These frameworks constitute a foundational scaffolding that can guide decision makers, filtering (but not determining) their activities and initiatives in various policy areas and concomitantly overcoming some of the challenges that beset policy making in federal systems.[35] It must be stated that policy frameworks do not require complete uniformity of practices and procedures across the participating jurisdictions. Rather, they can help ensure a modicum of commensurability in order to reconcile the tensions between federalism and social policy. How then are these frameworks constructed? Or, more specifically, who drives their formulation, and what processes?

Some researchers implicate factors beyond the domestic arena as the crucial determinants. Those working in the field of globalization studies, for example, suggest that increasing capital mobility is driving countries to adopt common policies, which subsequently trickle down and impose degrees of uniformity on substate practices in federations. "If globalization represents the decay of national borders," ask Mark A. Luz and C. Marc Miller, "how can internal borders in federal states remain unaffected?"[36] Here, substate policy similarity is achieved almost as an unintended consequence of the inexorable homogenizing pressures of globalization, which force governments to adopt neoliberal practices, reduce welfare state spending, and generally shrink the scope of the state. Taking a more ideational approach, others have implicated the emergence of a "world culture" as a driver of policy homogeneity. John Meyer and his colleagues, for example, have argued that a rationalistic world culture has shaped the characteristics of national states and societies and that this accounts for the structurally similar configuration of most states around the world.[37] Transferring these insights into a federation itself, it can be anticipated that such monolithic pressures exerted by the rationalistic world culture will generate similarities among substates and result, unintentionally, in an active policy framework.

Alternatively, and with a clearer sense of agency, those working in the area of internationalization highlight the significance of transnational actors that can encourage the installation of their preferred programs that shape both central and substate policy choices, potentially generating increased policy similarity. In addition, domestic commitments to international bodies can encourage the adoption of common strategies and regulations within a federation, furthering the creation of a shared policy framework. Momentarily stepping away from the social policy arena, Grace Skogstad's work on agricultural policy concludes that Canadian policy makers have been supportive of internationalization as a "rule-based regional and multilateral trading regime with authoritative dispute settlement patterns."[38] She finds that participation in these international regimes has had discernible effects on the development of Canadian agricultural policy and has shaped the selection of policy instruments to align Canadian practices with international standards and thereby maintain Canada's legitimacy on the international stage. Meanwhile, in education, Anja P. Jakobi has examined the global dissemination of the principle of "lifelong learning" and determined that international organizations have helped drive the gradual emulation of this idea by countries around the world.[39] Internationalization can thus create conditions that foster the formulation of policy frameworks in federations through the mechanisms of soft coercion and normative suasion.

Moving into the domestic realm, an interesting point of agreement appears between federal pessimists and federal optimists regarding the significance of the central government in framework formulation, although the perceived desirability of such intervention varies dramatically. At one end of the spectrum we find scholars who welcome the central government's engagement in social policy and who scarcely question the implications of such activity. Ken Battle and Sherri Torjman write that Ottawa must "awaken fully from its Rip Van Winkle slumber and reassert its crucial role in helping the provinces and territories reform and finance social employment and health programs that fall under their jurisdiction."[40] Addressing specifically the area of education, James Alexander Corry once declared:

If there is indeed a nation to be spoken for and protected, then the federal government must speak for the nation, take steps to ensure its survival, and nourish its growth ... If there are national needs and objectives that require concerted educational policy in two, several or all provinces, no provincial legislature is itself competent in the matter ... The British North America Act makes it clear that Parliament is competent.[41]

Others, however, hotly contest central intervention in areas of substate competency, arguing that such activity is anathema to the federal principle, for it can stymie creativity, prioritize inappropriate goals (thus drawing attention away from problems that actually beset the respective jurisdictions), or mandate practices that do not accurately reflect substate conditions.[42] In multinational federations, the complexity of central intervention is further amplified and the issues become even more thorny, for the engagement of the "national" government may be viewed as an instrument to assimilate local allegiances, marshal splintered loyalties, and overwhelm alternative identities in the name of imposing a one-size-fits-all model of integration.[43]

This propensity to implicate the central government in the formulation of policy frameworks has analytical and normative roots. Based on the tenets derived from rational choice theory, including Olson's *Logic of Collective Action*, there is a presumption that actors (here, substate policy makers) often lack the motivation to contribute to a joint effort and will free-ride on the efforts of others. Using those theories that emphasize instrumental rational calculation based on the logic of consequences where actors are autonomous and independent, a consensus thus emerges. Absent strict standards, hierarchical monitoring, and enforcement mechanisms, substate policy makers are unlikely to contribute to collective institution building. In an effort to mitigate this pathology, the recommendation that policy sectors be managed by an authority with coercive powers takes centre stage.[44] In federations, the central government is the actor most likely to have the necessary capacity to pull all the substate decision makers into line, due to its greater fiscal capacity and bureaucratic resources, as well as its capacity to deploy levers of authority – such as conditional grants, common standards, and legal mandates – to install a shared policy framework that covers the entire country.

Moving into the more normatively grounded arguments, should local experiments and innovations prove successful, it is the central government that seemingly possesses the legitimacy to universalize these strategies on behalf of the country as a whole in order for all to reap collective benefits. Indeed, this interpretation of the value of the central government lies at the heart of one of the iconic stories of the Canadian federation: the initiation of hospital insurance by the Province of Saskatchewan and its subsequent universalization by the federal government through conditional grants. The legitimacy of the central government to universalize programs expands from the pursuit of a liberal and uniform conception of the state where "citizens are individually and equally incorporated into the political community."[45] In federations, the central – or national – government is typically regarded as the governing authority capable of intervening to encourage, direct, persuade, coax, cajole, or entice the installation of somewhat similar policy practices in the quest to build a shared common identity for the country as a whole.

Nevertheless, a strong word of caution is required here. In multinational federations, the reification of the central or "national" government is likely to be deeply contested, and intrusions by one government on behalf of a so-called "common identity" could drive further wedges between the majority and minority national communities. As Christian Dufour writes: "Federalism is a system that provides for the *sharing* but also the *separation* of powers between two levels of government … The very nature of the federal principle implies a fundamental degree of separation that has always been vital for Quebec. That is why federalism should not be confused, as it often is, with subsidiarity partnership or decentralization."[46] Consequently, such normatively rooted arguments in favour of central intervention in the name of a single political community may not be universally accepted depending on the nature of the federal system in question.

There is also a strong propensity in this literature to view the emergence of frameworks as a result of two types of diffusion processes: central coercion and intergovernmental competition.[47] The emphasis on coercion flows naturally from the image of the central government as the primary actor in framework building. Coercion, as Beth Simmons and her co-authors describe it, occurs when powerful actors intentionally influence others to adopt a preferred policy, either through direct action such as conditional grants or through indirect influence such as ostracization.[48] Applying this to federations, the central government is the natural coercer, capable of influencing the substate governments to introduce preferred policies by offering selective incentives for certain behaviours. Reviewing US state policy activity in human services, Andrew Karch determined that Washington's intervention affects the probability that state lawmakers will adopt a particular strategy; it does so by either reducing the barriers that prevent implementation or offering resources to help overcome those barriers.[49] Policy frameworks thereby emerge as a result of the central government acting as a coercive enforcer driving policy activity.

The highlighting of competition as a driver of interjurisdictional policy frameworks evolves from Tiebout's seminal article, which argued that if citizens and capital were mobile, the various jurisdictions would compete to offer goods and services to collectively maximize welfare with packages that best satisfied their preferences.[50] Interestingly, it seems that while competition has the potential to encourage diversification, it can also compel homogenization and harmonization as substate decision makers battle for valuable resources and choose to adopt comparable policies. The problem with competition, however, as Kathryn Harrison and others have succinctly pointed out, is that it can generate negative consequences if substate governments engage in a destructive race to the bottom or harmonize their practices to the lowest common denominator.[51] Once again we find ourselves back at the feet of the central government, for it often falls to that body to mitigate the potential for such destructive competition by establishing certain minimum standards, which substate governments must then meet.

Another thread that runs through much of this work questions the willingness or capacity of substate actors to pursue progressive policies and invest in social programs. William Riker once boldly declared that "if in the United States one approves of Southern white racists, then one should approve of American federalism."[52] While this is a dramatic assertion, the concern it raises is that certain interests – to use a less radical example, corporations – can capture substate governments and thereby drive policies that are beneficial to them and not the wider population. Alexis Bélanger, for one, suggests that certain groups see the provinces as "ignoramuses and have demonstrated greater confidence in the federal government. This point of view appears to be based on the assumption that the Canadian federal government is synonymous with progressive public policy."[53] Empirically testing this argument, Barbara Carroll and Ruth Jones tracked the trajectory of provincial housing policies after Ottawa scaled back its role in the field and found that, after devolution, variations in provincial spending increased, with the general trend being towards reduced support for provincial housing.[54] Similarly, much of the research on pensions, health care, and social security – all areas that have seen the direct intervention of a central government – concludes that the division of powers tends to delay the establishment and expansion of social programs until a central authority steps in and encourages activity, acting as an external harmonizer.[55] The implication seems clear: the central government is necessary to the construction of viable and effective policy frameworks.

The dominant narrative of the federalism literature thus indicates that central intervention is the crucial catalyst and that coercion or competition drives the diffusion of policies across the constituent units of a federation. However, a small but growing number of scholars are beginning to challenge this narrative. Tackling the supposition that the division of powers favours conservative, less generous policy orientations, Alain Noël suggests that there is no necessary connection between centralization and progressivism, or decentralization and conservatism.[56] A key implication of Noël's argument is that substate policy autonomy is not necessarily antithetical to the expansion of social programs. Nicole Bolleyer, moreover, recently avowed that students of federalism have long overlooked the interactions *among* substate governments, privileging instead the hierarchical dynamics at work when the central government directly engages with the constituent units of a federation.[57] I wholeheartedly agree with her observation, and this work represents a determined effort to begin filling in this glaring gap in the field.

Where many scholars of federalism rest their analyses on the ideas of Mancur Olson, Elinor Ostrom has worked to explain how communities manage and govern common resources through "self-organizing and self-governing forms of collective action."[58] Ostrom does not see actors as trapped in static situations they are incapable of altering; indeed, she shatters the notion that external authorities must hierarchically impose universal institutional frameworks in order to resolve problems of collective action. The key lies in recognizing that the prevailing theories fail to sufficiently acknowledge the incremental and self-transforming characteristics of human interactions, the importance of the characteristics of external political regimes, how internal variables affect the collective provision of rules, and the need to include both transaction costs and the availability of information in the analysis. In various circumstances, to manage common resources, Ostrom argues that actors can craft their own regulatory frameworks and design effective monitoring systems to ensure adequate compliance. Ostrom's research remains firmly embedded in the rational choice theory of individual action; nevertheless, it offers a new lens through which to view substate policy activity, one that emphasizes the importance of interactions and cooperative commitments as drivers of viable policy frameworks.

Instead of seeing substate jurisdictions as independent and autonomous units, an alternative view, applying insights from sociological institutionalism, would see jurisdictions as interconnected and – perhaps more significantly – as interdependent. Seen through this lens, policy development in federations is not "a one-shot strategic game but an ongoing process in which governments meet with regularity."[59] Furthermore, it may be that policy frameworks can emerge from forces other than coercion and competition. For example, common problems, parallel influencers, and social learning have all been identified as crucial drivers of policy exchanges.[60] How might these apply to our case here? Finally, the federalism literature has demonstrated a strong propensity to favour "rational self-interest and strategic calculation to the exclusion of cognitive and normative processes,"[61] with the result that formal laws, economic incentives, and political institutions have long been the prominent explanatory variables. To fully understand what drives substate jurisdictions to adopt policies, in this book I endeavour to supplement rational actor accounts by considering other aspects of the policy climate – aspects that stretch beyond material interests to encompass normative and ideational factors – while assessing how features of the policy climate interact with the attributes of the individual policy context that shapes (and in turn is shaped by) the choices people make.

Education Policy

Why study education? First, even though education is one of the state's largest activities, it has taken a back seat to investigations of other areas of social policy. This has led to a serious gap in our knowledge of the political dynamics that characterize this policy field. Second, where most studies have focused on areas that are redistributive, education is an area of developmental policy, meaning that different incentives may be at play for those working in the field, incentives that should be explored. Finally, while education is ubiquitous, country-specific particularities persist: the sector is saturated with complicated policy options that amount to a cornucopia of choices for decision makers to select from. This makes it an ideal sector for our project of considering how shared goals and ideas from a broader policy climate can be interpreted and operationalized differently as they are integrated into a particular context and policy system. I examine each of these reasons in greater detail below.

For more than one hundred years, governments have taken an increasingly active role in the education of their citizenry. In part, we can attribute this interest to three ends that education is thought to achieve: critical thinking, individual self-actualization, and social integration.[62] Under Platonic thinking, education was recognized as a means to develop critical thinking skills that would enable individuals to think objectively about the situations around them. Rousseau later observed that education can also be a means to develop the individual, to help her see herself as an independent being capable of achieving her own goals and aspirations. Finally, schooling is an agent of socialization that transmits shared social values and norms from one generation to the next while simultaneously preparing individuals to participate in the workforce. Education today is viewed as a tool for securing cohesion – as one newspaper headline put it, education is "the glue that can fix cracks in our society."[63] Indeed, elementary and secondary education is one of the most significant activities of the modern state and plays a vital role in the "modern drive towards social equality."[64]

Despite the critical role played by education, this sector is rarely included in studies of social policy. The sectors traditionally identified with social policy – or "the policy of governments with regard to action having a direct impact on the welfare of the citizens by providing them with services and income"[65] – have included health care, pensions, and employment insurance. Some analysts, such as Daniel Béland and André Lecours, have gone so far as to pointedly exclude education from their investigations on the grounds that it does not fit within the defined parameters of social policy.[66] However, Carsten Jensen writes that the exclusion of education "may be more a matter of convention than anything else."[67] Peter Flora and Arnold Heidenheimer note that a crucial task of the welfare state is to interact with the labour market so that individuals using public programs can maintain or elevate their social status. For them, the "essence of the welfare state"[68] thus includes education. This book therefore helps fill the void in this policy area.

The field also offers a new opportunity for researchers grappling with the dynamics of policy making in federated states. It is fair to say that, with some important exceptions, most of the existing research has focused on redistributive policy.[69] Redistributive policies are those that reallocate or restructure resources within a given population or across regions; they all, however, transfer wealth from the taxpaying rich to the dependent poor – or "from the 'haves' to the 'have nots.'"[70] Substate governments often have compelling reasons to shun redistributive policies: to avoid attracting poorer populations to their territory, they make sure they are less generous than their neighbours. The incentives to take this policy course can generate a vicious race to the bottom as governments ratchet down their spending to remain competitive relative to their counterparts in other parts of the country.

A poignant example of such a race to the bottom materialized in Alberta during the 1990s. The provincial government decided to retrench its welfare programs, reducing its spending and tightening eligibility requirements in a number of areas. Neighbouring provinces reported a spike in the number of displaced Albertans who had crossed the border to receive the more generous benefits that were available. Anecdotal stories suggested that Alberta was spurring this out-migration by issuing one-way bus tickets to destinations outside the province.[71] As a result, neighbouring provinces felt pressured to reduce their own welfare benefits to better synchronize with Alberta's practices.

Redistributive policies, however, are only one form of state action. Governments also engage in developmental policies that are intended to enhance the overall capacity of both state and society. Rather than ameliorating resource discrepancies within a country, developmental policies invest in the general well-being of the community as a whole. They "provide the physical and social infrastructure necessary to facilitate a country's economic growth"[72] – thus, they are the bricks and mortar of the state and include the institutions designed to educate the polity as it plays a decisive role in strengthening the state's overall capacity.

Focusing on education thus allows us to explore whether different incentives and mechanisms are at play in an area of developmental policy in a federated state. Substate governments, driven by competitive pressures, may have incentives to avoid redistributive policies and undercut one another's programs and benefits, potentially generating a race to the bottom, but they may be more motivated to invest in developmental policies and to look to one another for reasons other than competition. Only by exploring education can we begin to uncover these alternative mechanisms and unravel the factors that may lead to sustained intergovernmental collaboration and the emergence of policy frameworks through seemingly unconventional routes.

Finally, as an acknowledged linchpin of egalitarian policies, schooling-for-all is a widely accepted goal worldwide.[73] Schooling carries a powerful socialization function, transmitting shared norms and values across generations.[74] What is more, the connection between education and the knowledge economy, which has been recognized since the 1970s, has undoubtedly contributed to the expanding scope of educational programming in the industrialized and developing worlds. Organizations such as the OECD and the United Nations (UN) have underscored the importance of education to countries' economic success and have encouraged governments to invest more heavily in it. As a consequence, governments are no longer content to simply provide the basics of reading, writing, and arithmetic, and public schools now offer a wider range of curricular choices designed to prepare children for their entry into the labour market, where they will be active contributors to society. It would be perilously detrimental for a federation to maintain an incoherent education system with gross disparities across substates and inconsistencies in the programs available to the respective polities, for this would undermine social cohesion, compromise collective identity, hinder the labour market, and probably contribute to the erosion of the federation.

The state's prominence in elementary and secondary schooling today masks the considerable conflict involved in establishing that role. Before the late eighteenth century, education in the Western world was reserved for the elite and was provided primarily by private tutors or religious institutions. In the eighteenth century in Canada, for example, it was religious orders that created the educational scaffolding, and they developed a strong foothold on it. The emergence of the nation-state led eventually to public universal education, but only after protracted and divisive battles between elected politicians and religious clerics that often involved the public at large.[75] Even today, education is still noteworthy for the intense negotiations it generates among state officials, client groups, educators, and the public, all of whom jockey to craft public schooling. Impassioned debates occur over every aspect of education, including the legitimacy of requiring all children to attend schools, the content of curriculum, the role of organized religion in public education, the financing of schools, the legitimacy of mandatory exams, the form of teacher education, and even the means of transporting students to and from schools. Put succinctly by Ronald Manzer, public schools are:

> stakes in struggles for political power. Educational politics and policy-making are rent by conflicting political, economic, and cultural interests that seek to organize schools to fit particular conceptions of a good

community and a good life and to teach knowledge skills serving particular interests.[76]

Conflicts over education policy thus provide a window into the battles within and across political communities, and between interests and ideas mediated by institutions. These are central concerns for those interested in political science and public policy.

Canadian Elementary and Secondary Education as a Crucial Case

If you are interested in the dynamics of substate policy making in federations and the circumstances that allow coordination and collaboration to flourish, Canada is a crucial case to study and elementary and secondary education is the ideal sector to explore. The reasons are threefold: the institutionalized policy autonomy of the provinces; the federation's internal political and economic diversity; and Canada's multinational polity.

Few would dispute that Canada is one of the most decentralized countries in the world, with provincial governments enjoying greater autonomy than their substate counterparts in other federations.[77] For example, in her comparison of Canada and Australia, Gwendolyn Gray observed that "political, financial, and constitutional powers are far more decentralized in Canada than in Australia … Canada is thus a 'more federal' nation than Australia."[78] This means that provinces have considerable independent capacities as policy makers, which heightens the potential for policy differences to appear among them. Observers of education policy, moreover, classify Canadian education as one of the most decentralized policy sectors, given that the provinces exercise almost complete legal, administrative, and financial responsibility for elementary and secondary education.[79] Since the country's inception, the federal government has never maintained an authoritative body capable of imposing overarching standards in the field – something that does not go unnoticed on the international stage. "When I travel abroad," one education official reported, "international leaders are frequently flabbergasted by the institutional framework of Canadian education. In Russia, for example, educational officials were shocked when I told them that there are 18 ministers responsible for education in Canada."[80] Provincial decision makers are thus essentially masters of their own educational domains, free to make policy choices of their own devising.

The organization of Canadian education is quite simple to contrast with that of other federations, illustrated here by Australia and the United States. The Australian federation demonstrates a remarkable pattern of central intervention in elementary and secondary education. Early in Australia's history, the national government began exerting strong guidance to encourage the development and chart the direction of schooling across the country.[81] The Commonwealth Office of Education was established in 1945, and in the early 1990s the Australian government instituted a national curriculum for elementary and secondary education that state governments were required to observe. As a consequence, the Australian states enjoy limited autonomy over education policy in their respective territories; the parameters of policy activity are crafted by officials in Canberra, who oversee a cohesive policy framework.

In the United States, under the Constitution, education falls under the purview of the states, yet the federal government has a strong record of influencing policies for American schools.[82] In the second half of the twentieth century, Washington began gathering strength in the education sector. The first major accomplishment in this regard was the Elementary and Secondary Education Act (ESEA) of 1965, which among other things committed the federal government to provide financial aid for schools and school districts with low-income families. In 1979, President Jimmy Carter signed into law the Department of Education Organization Act, which created the US Department of Education and tasked that body with monitoring the ESEA, compiling research and statistics, and generating policy prescriptions to influence the quality of American education. Washington's most recent infiltration into the education sector was the enactment in 2001 of the No Child Left Behind Act (NCLB), whose stated objective is to improve the quality of American education by ensuring that all students are given the opportunity to succeed. The policy imposes different forms of national programming designed to stimulate student achievement and to even out inconsistencies among the states. And today, the Obama administration is supporting the Common Core State Standards initiative. Despite Washington's increasing engagement, however, fundamental differences continue to demarcate the American educational landscape, and this has somewhat compromised the achievement of an integrated education framework for the country as a whole.[83]

Australia and the United States are but two illustrations of how the Canadian elementary and secondary education sector differs markedly from arrangements in other federations in terms of the central government's role in inculcating an overarching policy framework. Yet institutionalized substate autonomy in Canada does not immediately mean that provincial educational policies inevitably diverge or remain different. The Canadian provinces have markedly different politics, economies, and demographics, which public policy scholars implicate as critical factors that shape government programs and priorities.[84] Furthermore, multiple identities figure prominently in the dynamics of Canadian politics: federal institutions have preserved distinctive loyalties, and this has reinforced political orientations, policy priorities, and alternative patterns of values across the provinces.[85] Also, regional characteristics are often discernible, albeit with marked inconsistencies and unsystematic variations.[86] Due to these internal diversities, intergovernmental coordination in various policy areas is often difficult to achieve, because conflict, competition, and acrimony often characterize interactions, resulting in the emergence of sharp differences among the provinces in a number of policy fields.[87]

Arguably of most significance here is the fact that Canada is a multinational state, divided between the two official languages, English and French. One province, Quebec, maintains a majority francophone population with smaller minority anglophone communities; the remaining nine are majority anglophone, with minority francophone communities unevenly dispersed throughout the various territories. Corry made this point clear in 1978 when he described Canada as an "incorrigibly federal country ... Any constitution that gives parliament the power necessary to safeguard the interest of the whole will be open to the overriding preferences of Quebec on particular points."[88] How are these features of the social base expected to affect social policy and the education sector?

According to Béland and Lecours, nationalist policy makers can use their autonomy to develop distinctive policy packages in their efforts to execute a nation-building agenda.[89] For more than fifty years, Quebec has used its autonomy to opt out of various federal initiatives, and this has encouraged both formal and informal asymmetry in a variety of programs. Simultaneously, that province has implemented its own unique social programs, which sharply differentiate it from the rest of North America. For scholars like Jan Erk, the ethno-linguistic heterogeneity of Canadian society is reflected in the ways in which public policies function, with clear divisions between Quebec and the rest of Canada.[90] In his examination of the education field, Erk concluded that while the nine English-speaking provinces may collaborate, Quebec remains "an outlier" with regard to such initiatives.[91] What is the degree of Quebec's distinctiveness in education?

Variations appear at the margins of all the provincial systems. In structural terms, however, Quebec's system maintains an utterly unique form of secondary to post-secondary schooling for its students. Instead of finishing secondary school in grade twelve, which is the norm in the other Canadian provinces, students in Quebec finish high school in grade eleven and then enter a *Collège d'enseignement général et professionnel* (*Cégep*). The *Cégep* serves as a bridge between secondary and post-secondary education, offering pre-university and technical programs that provide increasingly specialized training to students and prepare them for particular career paths. This variation means that Quebec students who decide to pursue their university education outside the province must take an additional year of study or apply for advanced standing. In some senses, then, this policy variation could erode the consistency of the Canadian elementary and secondary education framework – a fact I will be attentive to in the coming chapters.

Canada's multinational polity, internal political and economic diversity, and its substate autonomy in the education sector all seem to suggest that Canadian elementary and secondary schooling could only be a great disaster. Surely, it is easy to think, provincial variations in strategies, programs, and practices must be accompanied by dramatic differences in how the respective systems are organized and configured, and this in turn must undermine the integrity and coherence of the sector as a whole. But it isn't so. Canadian education is therefore a crucial case when it comes to considering the need for direct central intervention, given that it seems the least likely policy sector to experience substate coordination and cooperation, or to witness the emergence of an effective policy framework that steers actors' choices in meaningful ways.

Methods of Inquiry

This book seeks to answer three empirical questions:

(1) What is the extent of interprovincial similarity in educational investments and achievements?
(2) What is the extent of interprovincial similarity in education policies?

(3) How can we account for the observed interprovincial similarities (and differences) in educational investments, achievements, and public policies?

Similarity is defined as an aspect or trait that resembles the characteristics of another; thus, it implicitly involves assessing and comparing two or more units. Taking a narrow and rigid definition, similarity could involve the complete absence of difference, thus setting a high threshold for empirical evidence. However, it seems unreasonable and unfruitful to set such a high standard, given that any complete absence of difference among the provinces would be difficult (if not impossible) to find. Therefore, building from the idea of resemblance, I use a broader interpretation of similarity and seek affinities, likenesses, parities, and commensurabilities among the educational investments, achievements, and substantive policies that would indicate a policy framework at work across the provinces.

To answer these questions, I engage in three types of comparisons: cross-national, cross-provincial, and cross-time. First, to see whether Canada is either underinvesting or underperforming in elementary and secondary education, I compare national averages in investments and achievements across the OECD community. Then, to measure the extent of similarity in investments and achievements, I take a snapshot of the current state of provincial elementary and secondary education systems and compare the extent of similarity in Canada with that of a selection of other OECD countries. This first line of cross-national comparison will enable us to see whether Canada's lack of central intervention has either compromised overall educational achievements or generated greater internal discrepancies relative to other countries that have more centralized systems.

Second, to determine the degree of substantive policy similarity, I break the education sector down into five dimensions – administration, finance, curriculum, assessment, and the teaching profession – and detail potential options and instruments that policy makers could deploy. I then compare the practices in each dimension of the education sector at work across the ten provincial systems relative to the universe of potential options. This will allow me to determine the degree of internal policy similarity currently exhibited across the provinces to see if we find evidence of an active policy framework in Canada.

Third, and finally, to understand how policy ideas have diffused across the provinces and to identify the factors or scope conditions that have encouraged (or discouraged) the adoption of similar policies, working historically with an inductive approach, I track the evolution of the ten provincial education systems. Unlike Herbert Spencer, for whom "one generation sufficed as a sample of eternity," this study thus follows in the spirit of Karl Polanyi, who described such an approach as "narrowly time-bound."[92] Concerned with causal analyses, historical analysis emphasizes the significance of processes over time while using contextualized and systematic comparisons.[93] This approach, moreover, allows researchers to identify and account for historical trajectories, build multiple time lines and social actors into the explanatory account, and explain how earlier outcomes shaped and influenced later results.[94] I also use process tracing, which "consists of analyzing a case into a sequence (or several concatenating sequences) of events and showing how those events are plausibly linked given the interests and situations faced by groups or individual actors."[95] The approach does not assume that all actions bring about their intended consequences, but rather that actions are "understandable in terms of the knowledge, intent, and circumstances that prevailed at the time decisions were made."[96] By tracking the iterative development, diffusion, and transmission of educational policies across the provinces, I will be able to uncover unique patterns of policy exchanges while bringing into sharper focus the connections among the policy climate, the processes of policy diffusion, and the subsequent adoption of ideas that led to the emergence of a pan-Canadian education policy framework.

Historical analysis and process tracing offer a number of advantages that are pertinent here. By taking history seriously, I can uncover deep and enduring patterns that have shaped Canadian education and influenced its evolution, and follow the footsteps of other institutionalists, like Tulia Falleti and Julia Lynch, who argue that "credible causal social scientific explanations can occur if and only if researchers are attentive to the interaction between causal mechanisms and the context in which they operate."[97] Process tracing, moreover, is a powerful tool for explaining deviant cases.[98] As Alexander L. George and Andrew Bennett argue, process tracing is an "indispensable tool ... not only because it generates numerous observations within a case, but because these observations must be linked in particular ways to constitute an explanation of the case."[99] Through process tracing it becomes possible to uncover evidence of the role that certain variables have systematically played in the evolution of Canadian education and distil the general elements to contribute to broader theory development.

I focus on context and processes using narrative techniques to create a model of action and theorize about the relations among the actors, institutions, and ideas that are a constituent part of this phenomenon.[100] No single causal mechanism or pathway single-handedly explains the processes of diffusion and policy convergence in the case of Canadian education. Indeed, this research takes seriously Sven Steinmo's recent admonition for political science: "In the desire to become a *predictive* science we look for linear relationships between independent variables even when we know that these variables are interdependent and non-linear, we invent equilibrium where none is to be found, and we assume things about human nature and motivation that no one really believes are true."[101] Understanding Canadian elementary and secondary education instead requires that we accept equifinality (the idea that different causal pathways can lead to the same outcome) and acknowledge the importance of institutional, ideational, and temporally rooted contexts. It is worth making concessions to parsimony to achieve both a more accurate explanation for our case at hand and a greater understanding of the conditions that underpin the emergence of policy frameworks in federations.

Conceding degrees of parsimony, however, does not mean that everything matters and that an inductive approach does not advance without a map. Rather, such inductive analysis "must be guided from the beginning by a framework of theoretical ideas. Without that, the analysis lacks orientation in the face of an endless multitude of possibly relevant facts."[102] So I will be building an analytical architecture that bridges the research terrains on policy diffusion and policy convergence while integrating components from the three traditions of institutionalism.

This architecture will enable me to divide the evolution of provincial education systems into four periods: the foundation and consolidation of education (1840–1945); the universalization of education (1945–67); the individualization of education (1967–82); and the standardization of education (1982–2008). When parcelling Canadian education into four periods, I will adhere to Richard Simeon's cautionary statement that "[any] division into distinct time periods is inherently arbitrary. There are few sharp breaks and discontinuities and the edges are often blurred."[103] In this book, periods have been identified on the basis of two criteria informed by my analytical architecture: first, in each period there were notable changes in the connectivity among the provinces; and second, each period can be distinguished by transformations in the prevailing ideas and educational paradigms, meaning that the policy climate itself changed over time.

Having broken the past into temporal chunks, I will use each period as a separate case, comparing one to the other, to tease out the relative significance of the alternative diffusion processes and the factors that conditioned the emergence of an institutionalized and coherent policy framework. Furthermore, to increase the number of observations, I will capitalize on the opportunity to consider the events in all ten provincial systems; this will allow me not only to understand the instances in which certain ideas became policy, but also to consider cases when policies did not develop.[104] My aim is to isolate the factors that explain these differences and, in so doing, offer a theoretically satisfying account of the gradual emergence of the policy framework.

The data used for this study include documents as well as interviews with key informants in the education sector. The primary sources for chronicling the historical development of elementary and secondary education include the following: Hansard records of the provincial legislative houses; reports of committees, commissions, and task forces struck to examine educational issues; statistical and annual reports issued by relevant ministries, agencies, and boards (e.g., Statistics Canada, provincial departments of education, and the Council of Ministers of Education Canada [CMEC]); non-government education stakeholders' reports (e.g., the Canadian Education Association and the Canadian Teachers' Federation); archival materials; government press releases, statements, and speeches; and bills, acts, and regulations in the education sector. These primary sources have been bolstered by numerous secondary assessments, including an array of scholarly books and articles on the history of Canadian education, as well as items from the popular press.

When dealing with the contemporary period of provincial educational development, I have sought out key informants. Over the course of this study, I have conducted seventy semi-structured, open-ended interviews to gain insight into the motivations underlying certain policy developments, understand the factors that helped or hindered interprovincial policy activity, and bridge any gaps that became visible in the documents. The respondents have included former ministers of education, active and retired ministry officials, stakeholder representatives (teachers, superintendents, principals, trustees, union representatives, and members of various interest groups), and individuals from intergovernmental organizations – specifically, the CMEC and the

Atlantic Provinces Education Foundation (APEF). Respondents were not systematically selected to gain a representative sample from all the provinces, as the key data source here is the primary documents. All interviews were granted on the condition that no expressed views would be individually attributed, to protect the anonymity of the participants.

Looking Forward

The opening chapters of this book lay the foundations for this inquiry by assessing the degree of provincial similarity in education in a number of comparative contexts. Chapter 1 assesses the current degree of parity in provincial investments in education as well as in scholastic achievement and finds an unexpected degree of similarity among the provinces, considering the lack of central intervention; this chapter also compares Canada with a number of other countries. Chapter 2 turns our attention to substantive policies for elementary and secondary education and determines the current state of interprovincial similarity in policy outputs, thus establishing the central focus for the remainder of the book. The education sector is broken down into five dimensions that serve to summarize the major policy debates that flow throughout the field. This discussion is a testimony to the fact that decision makers face myriad options such that radically different education sectors can emerge based on the choices made.

Drawing from a series of pertinent research traditions, chapter 3 lays out the processes, pathways, and conditions that are thought to enable the establishment of policy frameworks. This serves to carve out an analytical architecture that will guide the subsequent comparative historical investigation of Canadian educational development. This chapter begins with a discussion of interdependence and connectivity, the conceptual anchors of the argument. Alternative processes of policy diffusion and the conditions and pathways for policy convergence are then outlined so that we can appreciate the factors and mechanisms that influence the likelihood of substate policy similarities. Features of the policy ideas themselves are included in the mix. The chapter ends with an account of how choices in one area of a policy sector influence and reverberate in others, thereby opening windows for some alternatives to take hold while closing the door on others.

Chapters 4 to 7 are the empirical heart of this book. They track the evolution of provincial education policies in order to assess general policy trends, the penetration of policy ideas, and the impact that changes in the policy climate had on the causal processes of diffusion and the likelihood of policy convergence. These chapters have a similar, parallel structure: each opens with the key features of the policy climate that prevailed at the time and explores the key policy developments that then unfolded. The objective is to connect the characteristics of the policy climate – comprised of structural and ideational features shaped by international and domestic factors – with the processes of policy diffusion and with the subsequent installation of comparable policies across the provinces that contributed to the emergence of an integrated policy framework.

The concluding chapter summarizes the analysis of Canadian elementary and secondary education, clarifying the theoretical significance of understanding how overarching policy frameworks can emerge in federations without coercion or competition. While it is true that the education sector is highly idiosyncratic, this study allows us to develop a set of testable propositions that can be applied to future research. A richer appreciation of the importance of interdependence and connective links carries considerable implications for our understanding of Canadian federalism and of the dynamics of policy making in other systems of multilevel governance around the world.

1 Defying the Odds I: Investments and Achievements in Canadian Elementary and Secondary Education

To reconcile the tension between federalism and the welfare state, scholars and practitioners often implicate the central (or national) government as the necessary actor that is capable of achieving substantive inter-regional similarities in social policy.[1] In the words of Roy Romanow, a former premier of Saskatchewan, Linda Silas, president of the Canadian Federation of Nurses Unions, and Steven Lewis, a top Canadian health care analyst: "Only leadership from Ottawa can guarantee a common set of programs and standards and ensure that program enhancements are available to all Canadians."[2] Endowed with legitimate authority to mandate common standards, central governments are seen as the critical agent to create and maintain the conditions for equal social citizenship. Through such instruments as the regulatory and spending powers, the central state can uphold the logic of social citizenship to ensure that all citizens, regardless of residence, receive comparable levels of programming and benefits.[3] The central government can impart strong incentives and supports encouraging the constituent governments to adopt common policies, allocate comparable fiscal resources, and make available similar levels of benefits to standardize the provision of social programs across the country. Furthermore, the central government could use a variety of instruments to directly intervene in areas beyond its formal jurisdiction and ensure that all substate governments deploy the same programs.[4] For Canadians, one powerful lever Ottawa has at its disposal to accomplish such objectives is the federal spending power where in exchange for federal

Previously published in *Publius* 40(4) (2010): 646–71 – some adjustments have been made.

funds the provinces agree to comply with certain conditions stipulated by federal decision makers.

However, this propensity to look towards the central government raises this question: Is a national authority a necessary condition for similarity in investments and achievements in a federal state? To answer this question, this chapter considers the current state of investments and achievements in Canadian elementary and secondary education. The findings presented here are both unexpected and interesting. While Canada seems to invest slightly less in education than other advanced industrial nations, its educational attainments are strong, with high marks on international tests and elevated completion rates in secondary and tertiary education. Without a central authority, moreover, the Canadian provinces support their respective elementary and secondary systems with similar levels of investment. Canadian students, moreover, achieve high scores on measures of interprovincial equality in educational outcomes where school location is not an important determinant of educational performance. This suggests that the fragmentation of responsibilities ushered in through the federal bargain does not necessarily translate into ineffective or dissimilar policy investments and achievements. Moreover, these findings demonstrate that direct central intervention is not a necessary condition for interregional similarity in a critical area of social policy.

This chapter advances in four parts. To guide the empirical inquiry, I set the context by distilling two propositions from the federalism literature regarding the expected impact of shared-rule and self-rule for education in Canada. Parts Two and Three compare Canada's educational investments to those of other OECD countries and examine the extent of interprovincial similarity in education spending compared to a selection of other countries; this is followed by an assessment of the relative educational achievements of the Canadian provinces compared both cross-nationally and internally. The data reveal that despite expectations of lower investments and uneven achievements, the Canadian provinces exhibit striking similarities and Canada as a country performs remarkably well. Accounting for these puzzling results is the final step of this chapter. I argue that we need to synthesize three contextual factors – specifically, societal pressures, the federal fiscal architecture (which highlights the fact that the central government can play an important yet indirect role in bringing about substate policy similarity), and the configuration of public schooling programs. Together, these allow us to understand how the potential for substate differences can be overcome without the direct intervention of the central government.

Before proceeding, an important caveat needs to be made about research design. Ideally, provincial-level data from Canada would be compared systematically with other substate-level data from other countries. These comparisons would permit a comprehensive demonstration of whether or not Canada demonstrates elevated inter-regional dissimilarities compared to its more centralized counterparts. Unfortunately, data limitations have restricted the potential universe of cases and undermined any attempt at systematic comparison.[5] Despite notable advances made by the OECD and the UN, obtaining clearly comparable data on educational investments and achievements at the national level is a challenge. Gathering consistent data at the regional level is further compromised by the fact that every country adheres to its own methods of data collection and publication. The United States, for example, does not provide a representative sample at the state level for PISA testing, preferring to rely on its internal assessment programs to assess inter-regional (in)equality. Therefore, the comparison of internal results within Canada with those of other countries is relatively unstructured here. These unstructured comparisons nevertheless supply useful benchmarks for assessing the degree of internal interprovincial similarities in education investments and achievements in Canada.

Setting the Theoretical Context

Scanning the federalism literature, there are numerous debates regarding the impact of shared-rule and self-rule on investments and achievements in social policy.[6] However, as Richard Simeon writes, "if there is any consensus in the literature on the policy consequences of federalism it is this: that the size of government, and the commitment to social spending is lower in federal countries than in non-federal countries."[7] Researchers tend to agree that social spending has lagged in federal countries and often continues to be depressed.[8] Some macro-quantitative assessments have demonstrated that federations delayed introducing numerous components of the welfare state and chronically underfund initiatives once they are launched.[9] David Cameron, for example, determined that federalism was the key explanatory factor to account for variations in welfare spending.[10] More recently, Duane Swank has concluded that the combination of federalism and bicameralism has an undeniably negative impact on state investments in social policy.[11] It appears that the division of powers creates structural constraints that can act as a breaking mechanism for state expenditures, translating into lower policy investments overall.

Systematic underinvestment in social policy does not necessarily translate into embedded dissimilarities within a federation. At the risk of sounding trite, if all constituent governments underinvest equally in a policy sector, no portion of the population will receive uneven treatment. The problem is that resources are not evenly distributed across a country.[12] Some substates that have superior resources at their disposal may choose to invest more than others and provide a greater range of policies than their neighbours. Alternatively, economically weaker jurisdictions may be forced to tax their citizens at significantly higher rates in order to match the provisions offered in the other regions. "The critical issue," according to Keith Banting, "is whether social benefits are available to all citizens on equal terms."[13] A recent study conducted by Mark Carl Rom on elementary and secondary education in the United States illustrates this conundrum. Rom determined that the wealthier states were increasing their investments in a race to the top, while the poorer states were becoming increasingly miserly in a race to the bottom.[14] The citizens of economically weaker states thus receive different treatment from their counterparts in economically stronger states. Such outcomes suggest that the logic of diversity can supersede the goal of social citizenship, potentially compromising country-wide cohesion.[15]

Turning to achievements, the underlying concern of critics of federalism is that uneven investments will lead to systematic dissimilarities in policy outcomes, thus compromising the logic of social citizenship and undermining social cohesion. If certain substate governments are unable or unwilling to provide effective programs, those populations may suffer from, among other things, greater health problems, lower educational achievement, and poorer economic performance.[16] Furthermore, internal disparities may depress the overall results recorded by the country as a whole. It is therefore important to consider not only levels of investment in social programs but also the subsequent achievements or outcomes.

To reconcile the tension between federalism and the welfare state, scholars and practitioners often turn to the power of the central state.[17] Such intervention can take the form of ratifying policy standards that set either minimal provisions for programs or funding levels that all constituent governments are required to maintain. More intrusively, the central government can allocate targeted funds through conditional grants to support certain priorities in pertinent policy fields. Finally, the central government can introduce administrative oversight by installing a national department permanently staffed by bureaucrats to manage a policy field. Put together, these components could fashion what Banting refers to as a "policy framework that applies to the country as a whole."[18]

Given that the provinces maintain complete control over elementary and secondary education, and that the federal government has never intervened directly in the sector, it is possible to distil two bundles of propositions from the federalism literature to guide this investigation. First, based on the decentralization of the policy sector and the extensive autonomy afforded the provincial governments, Canada will underinvest in elementary and secondary education and there will be greater substate variation in investments than in other OECD countries. Second, given the institutional fragmentation of Canadian education, Canada will underperform in educational outcomes and there will be greater unevenness in educational achievements among the Canadian provinces compared to substates in other OECD countries.

Investments in Canadian Education

Two sets of indicators are used to measure the level of investment in Canadian education and situate it in a comparative context. The first set focuses on spending: average annual expenditures per pupil and educational spending as a proportion of GDP. Data on national level per pupil spending and as a proportion of GDP are taken from the OECD. Per pupil spending, however, is heavily influenced by contextual conditions, including the presence of right-wing parties, internal population demographics, the power of teachers' unions to press for higher salaries, transportation costs to bring students to schools, and other general overhead costs.[19] To reinforce the measure of spending, I also examine educational expenditures as a proportion of GDP. This allows me to assess the relative importance of education spending next to the overall fiscal capacity of the state. The second set of indicators addresses a different measure of inputs: student–teacher ratios. Borrowing from Mark Carl Rom and James Garand, this indicator assumes that the smaller the class size, the more generous the education policy.[20] OECD and Statistics Canada data are used for student–teacher ratios.

To measure the extent of substate parity in Canadian education, I look at the differences in investment levels among the provincial governments. The data on spending and student–teacher ratios are therefore broken down to see whether or not significant variations appear

Table 1.1 Annual expenditures on educational institutions, per student for all services, selected countries and as a percentage of GDP

	Pre-Primary	Primary	Secondary	Total public expenditure as a percentage of GDP
	(1)	(2)	(3)	(4)
Australia	M	5,226	7,408	4.11
Austria	6,064	6,978	8,740	3.83
Belgium	4,488	5,949	7,419	4.10
Canada[1,2]	X(3)	X(3)	6,317	3.55
Finland	3,582	4,684	6,516	3.98
France	4,615	4,805	8,419	4.21
Germany	4,838	4,599	7,133	3.54
Italy	5,743	6,916	7,453	3.65
Japan	3,316	5,590	6,411	2.97
New Zealand	4,147	4,614	5,458	4.92
UK	7,112	5,818	7,249	4.58
United States	7,755	8,305	9,590	4.20
Average	5,166[3]	5,713[3]	7,343[3]	3.90[4]

1. Public institutions only
2. Year of reference, 2002
3. Average from only selected countries, author's calculation
4. OECD average is for all countries, not just those selected
M = missing value
Source: OECD, Education at a Glance, 2006. Table X2.4, p. 433, Table B6.1, p. 252.

among the provinces. As noted earlier, data limitations have restricted the potential for a systematic assessment. Moreover, spending is reported in domestic dollar values, which further weakens the validity of the comparisons. The data nevertheless provide a valuable benchmark for determining whether greater internal variations appear in the Canadian case than in other polities with national departments of education. Here I compare substate variations in per pupil spending in Canada, Germany, the United States, and England.[21]

Does Canada underinvest in education relative to other OECD countries? The picture is a bit mixed. The data in Table 1.1 signal that per pupil spending is lower in Canada, which seems to confirm the consensus that institutional fragmentation can depress social spending in a federation. Of the twelve countries sampled, only New Zealand falls below Canada. However, other federations record higher per pupil spending, indicating that federalism does not necessarily lead to less investment in social programs. This suggests that federalism's effect on social policy spending is less clear-cut than is often presumed.[22]

Looking at spending as a proportion of GDP, Canada falls slightly below the OECD average, with only Germany and Japan investing less than Canada. The impact of federalism and decentralization on educational spending as a percentage of GDP is therefore inconsistent. These findings call into question the consensus that federalism – specifically, institutional fragmentation – leads to underinvestment in social programs. Institutional decentralization, on its own, thus cannot be implicated as the key explanatory factor.[23] Turning to our alternative measure of investments, at 16.3, Canada's student–teacher ratios are aligned with OECD averages (see Table 1.2). Canadian class sizes are therefore comparable to international averages. Based on the aforementioned assumption that class size can be used as a proxy for generosity, in contrast to our expectations, it suggests that Canada is no more or less generous in this measure of education policy than other, more centralized education systems in the world.

Are there significant interprovincial variations in the levels of educational investments? According to the data in Table 1.3, provincial governments invest at even rates, both in terms of spending per pupil and as a percentage of GDP. In 2001, for example, per pupil spending ranged from a high of $8,432 in Manitoba to a low of $6,239 in Prince Edward Island.[24] Student–teacher ratios are also reasonably aligned, with limited variations appearing across the provinces.

The extent of substate consistency in educational investments can be better appreciated by looking at substate comparability in per pupil spending in other countries. Data from England, Germany, and the United States provide a rough touchstone to ascertain whether the internal variations are comparatively high in Canada (Table 1.4). Relative to these other cases, the internal standard deviation as a percentage of the mean across the provinces is only slightly higher than regional variations in England, below that of Germany, and significantly less than in the United States. Zeroing in on the United States, in 2005, state per pupil spending ranged from a high of $13,740 in New Hampshire to a low of $5,574 in Utah.[25] What do these figures tell us? Despite the

Table 1.2 Ratio of students to teaching staff in schools, 2004

	Elementary	Secondary
	(1)	(2)
Australia	16.4	12.3
Austria	15.1	10.7
Belgium	12.9	9.6
Canada[1]	16.3	16.3
Czech Republic	17.9	13.1
Finland	16.3	13.1
France	19.4	12.1
Germany	18.8	15.1
Greece	11.3	8.3
Hungary	10.7	11.2
Ireland	18.3	14.3
Italy	10.7	11.0
Japan	19.6	14.1
Korea	29.1	17.9
Mexico	28.5	30.3
Netherlands	15.9	15.8
New Zealand	16.7	14.7
Norway	11.9	10.0
Portugal	11.1	8.4
Slovak Republic	18.9	14.0
Spain	14.3	10.8
Sweden	12.1	12.9
Switzerland	14.3	11.2
Turkey	26.5	16.9
United Kingdom	21.1	14.4
United States	15.0	15.5
OECD Average	16.9	13.3
EU19 Average	15.3	12.0

1. Canadian data combines both elementary and secondary student-teacher ratios together and they cannot be disaggregated.
Sources: Education at a Glance, OECD Indicators 2004, Table D2.2, p. 371; Statistics Canada, *Education Indicators in Canada,* 2003, Table C2.2, p. 310.

Table 1.3 Canadian and provincial investments in education, 1999–2000[1]

	Pre-elementary, elementary, secondary [2]	Expenditures as a percentage of GDP	Student-teacher ratio
CANADA	7,758	6.6	16.3
Newfoundland	6,503	8.5	14.1
PEI	6,239	8.2	16.8
Nova Scotia	7,072	8.3	15.9
New Brunswick	7,239	8.3	16.7
Quebec	7,333	7.4	15.0
Ontario	8,130	6.0	16.3
Manitoba	8,432	8.3	14.7
Saskatchewan	7,293	7.8	16.9
Alberta	7,401	5.4	16.9
British Columbia	7,905	6.9	16.9

1. In 2001 constant dollars
2. Public and private expenditures on education per student (based on full-time equivalents)
Sources: Statistics Canada, Report of the Pan-Canadian Education Indicators Program, 2003. Table B1.4, Table B1.6, Table C3.1.

institutional decentralization from the central to the substate level, internal disparities in educational spending are no greater in Canada than in other cases and are in fact less than in both Germany and the United States.

To summarize, Canadian provinces spend less per pupil and less as a percentage of GDP than other OECD countries, but student–teacher ratios are on par with international averages. When looking within Canada, the provinces match one another's educational investments. Canadian variation is on par with unitary England and is considerably less than its federal counterparts, Germany and the United States, even though both are considered to be more centralized federations than Canada.[27] It therefore seems that the absence of central educational standards has not undermined the Canadian provinces' abilities to achieve similarities in educational investments.

Table 1.4 Substate variations in per pupil spending, selected countries, standard deviation as a percentage of the mean[26]

	England	Canada	Germany	United States
Standard deviation as a % of the mean	8.55	8.85	11.77	22.99

Note: All figures were taken in domestic monetary values as reported by the individual cases. Because the spending is measured in national currency, the standard deviations are not comparable without some kind of standardization. The easiest way to accomplish this is to take the standard deviation as a percentage of the mean. In other words, the standard deviation of per pupil spending across regions in each case is standardized to a 0–100 scale, and is then comparable. Calculations were done by the author.

Achievements in Canadian Education

To assess educational achievements, I start with results from three rounds of the Program for International Student Assessment (PISA),[28] which give some indication of how Canada performs as a whole compared to other countries. These tests, however, are not without some controversy: some education experts question whether it is possible (or even appropriate) to assess the knowledge of students in different countries.[29] Therefore, in addition to the test scores, I also examine high school and tertiary completion rates to compare educational achievements in different countries. This measure assumes that countries with higher completion rates have stronger educational attainments overall. Tertiary completion is included because if secondary education is poor, tertiary completion rates are likely to be compromised. Finally, the OECD is now tracking the percentage of reading scores below the PISA proficiency level. I am including this measure based on the assumption that higher numbers of perilously low achievement would signal a country-wide failure of the schooling system.

Canadian students have been consistently near the top of the scale across the three rounds of PISA tests (Table 1.5). In the 2006 round of PISA, for example, only two countries (Finland and Hong Kong) received higher scores on the science assessment.[30] As national averages, Canadian educational outcomes are therefore quite high.

High school graduation rates are also comparably higher in Canada, with Canada ranked fourth among OECD countries.[31] In the 25–34 age

Table 1.5 Top ten performing countries in the Program for International Student Assessment, 2000–2006

2000	2003	2006
(Reading)	(Mathematics)	(Science)
Finland	Hong Kong–China	Finland
Canada	Finland	Hong Kong–China
New Zealand	Korea	Canada
Australia	Netherlands	Chinese Taipei
Ireland	Liechtenstein	Estonia
Korea	Japan	Japan
United Kingdom	Canada	New Zealand
Japan	Belgium	Australia
Sweden	Macao–China	Netherlands
Austria	Switzerland	Korea

Source: Measuring Up: The Performance of Canada's Youth in Reading, Mathematics, and Science, OECD PISA Study – First Results for Canadians Aged 15, Highlights.

bracket, 91 per cent of Canadian students have completed upper secondary education compared to the OECD average of 77 per cent. And at the tertiary level, in 2004, Canada was ranked first among OECD countries, with 45 per cent of the population aged 25 to 64 holding some form of higher education degree, compared to the OECD average of 25 per cent.[32] When we look only at 25 to 34 year olds, the completion rate increases to 53 per cent compared to the OECD average of 31 per cent. Finally, according to the 2009 PISA study, at 10.3 per cent, Canada recorded one of the lowest percentages of students with reading scores below level 2, far below the OECD average of 18.8 per cent, and was beaten only by Finland (8.1 per cent) and Korea (5.8 per cent).[33]

Have these positive national results been evenly distributed across the country? Looking at secondary graduation, some variations appear in high school completion rates (Table 1.6). At 66 per cent, Alberta's graduation rate is significantly lower than the national average of 78 per cent. Students in Atlantic Canada and Quebec, with the exception of Nova Scotia, generally complete high school at higher rates than the national average. What accounts for this discrepancy? Research confirms that when an economy is booming (as it has been in Alberta), students

Table 1.6 High school graduation rates and PISA results, by province, 2000–2006

	Graduation Rates (2000)	PISA 2000 Ranking[1]	PISA 2003 Ranking[1]	PISA 2006 Ranking[1]
CANADA	78	534 (2)	532 (7)	534 (3)
Newfoundland	82	517 (8)	517 (13)	526 (9)
PEI	84	517 (8)	500 (21)	509 (20)
Nova Scotia	77	521 (8)	515 (14)	520 (12)
New Brunswick	86	501 (15)	512 (16)	506 (22)
Quebec	85	536 (2)	537 (5)	531 (7)
Ontario	78	533 (3)	530 (8)	537 (3)
Manitoba	77	529 (3)	528 (9)	523 (10)
Saskatchewan	79	529 (3)	516 (13)	517 (14)
Alberta	66	550 (1)	549 (2)	550 (2)
British Columbia	75	538 (2)	538 (4)	539 (3)

• PISA 2000 – 31 countries; PISA 2003 – 41 countries; PISA 2006 – 57 countries.
1. Ranking is according to position on the international level, not within Canada
Sources: Measuring Up: The Performance of Canada's Youth in Reading, Mathematics, and Science, OECD PISA Study – First Results for Canadians Aged 15, Complete Reports, 2000, 2003, 2006.

tend to prematurely end their studies to enter the workforce, whereas when the economy is depressed (as in Atlantic Canada), students stay in the school system and delay their entry into the workforce. Provincial graduation rates simply replicate these well-documented patterns and do not necessarily reflect the quality of education provided by the different jurisdictions.[34]

Turning to the PISA results across the country, differences in assessment outcomes appear among the Canadian provinces. In all three rounds of the assessments, Alberta consistently received the highest results while New Brunswick and Prince Edward Island lagged behind. Despite the variations, all of the Canadian provinces nevertheless exceeded the OECD average of 500 points. The data thus indicate positive educational outcomes across all 10 jurisdictions.

Contrasting Canada's PISA results with those from other countries that release substate data (with the United States as a notable exception) reveals a considerable degree of internal parity in Canadian provincial

Table 1.7 Substate variation in the results of the Program for International Student Assessment, 2006, selected countries

Country	National score	Overall rank	Standard deviation
Australia	527	5	19.7
Belgium	510	13	16.5
Canada	534	2	13.7
Germany	516	8	13.8
Italy	475	26	35.3
Spain	488	23	11.7
UK	515	9	7.9

Source: J. Wallner, "Beyond National Standards: Reconciling the Tension between Federalism and the Welfare State," Publius: The Journal of Federalism (Fall 2010).

scores. Canada's internal variation is higher than in the United Kingdom, slightly above Spain's, similar to Germany's, lower than Belgium's and Australia's, and significantly lower than Italy's (Table 1.7). Moreover, unlike Canada, many of these countries have regions that fall below the OECD's average score. Two regions in Germany, three regions in Spain, and seven regions in Italy received scores below 500. Finally, while the United Kingsdom's internal variation is relatively low, its overall score is below that of Canada. These findings demonstrate that Canada's internal variations are no greater than – and are in fact less than – the internal variations recorded in other countries that maintain a formal national framework in education.

Finally, the OECD has developed a measure of internal educational equality and ranks countries according to the impact that locational variables have on educational outcomes, referred to as "between-school variation." According to this metric, between-school variance in Canada is around one-tenth the OECD average. This signifies that students' performance is largely unrelated to the location of the schools in which they are enrolled. According to OECD data, in countries such as Austria, Belgium, Germany, and Italy the proportion of between-school variance is one-and-a-half times that of the OECD average.[35] Moreover, in Belgium and Germany, socio-economic backgrounds have a major impact on assessment outcomes. These inequalities appear despite the fact that, in all of these other cases, the national governments maintain central departments of education capable of issuing directives that the substate governments must follow. To quote from the 2006 PISA report: "Parents in [Canada] can be less concerned about school choice in order to enhance their children's performance, and can be confident of high and consistent performance standards across schools in the entire education system."[36] Put together, it is clear that Canada's results in interprovincial similarity in educational achievement exceed those of other, more centralized education systems.

A brief recap seems in order. At the national level, Canada records high marks on international assessments and maintains an elevated high school and tertiary completion rate relative to other OECD and non-OECD countries. Looking within Canada, some variations in provincial achievement appear both in graduation rates and assessment results. However, according to OECD data, the importance of socioeconomic variables as determinants of educational outcomes is highly limited in Canada, and between-school variation is minimal. Taken together, these results suggest that central standards are not a necessary condition for realizing of high interjurisdictional similarity in education achievements.

Building an Explanation

Decentralization and institutional fragmentation have neither compromised Canada's overall performance nor undermined the achievement of substate similarity in educational investments and achievements. What factors have allowed the provinces to defy the odds and fashion a *de facto* pan-Canadian system of education, measured in terms of investments and achievements, in the absence of central standards? There is no single causal factor that can be implicated here. Instead, to develop an explanation, I turn to the power of three contextual factors: societal pressures, fiscal federalism, and the configuration of the policy sector.

Societal Pressures

According to Clem Brooks and Jeff Manza, a "defining feature of democratic polities is the likelihood of some degree of public influence over the shape and direction of policymaking."[37] Citizens tend to have common expectations when it comes to the shape and scope of government programs regardless of their place of residence. From a society-centred perspective, then, the explanation for interjurisdictional similarities in the social policies of federated states begins with the people. Citizens place comparable demands on their regional governments.[38] Public preferences thus act as an incentive for substate governments to consider the choices of other regional governments, and this increases the potential for substate similarity in levels of investment and the achievements recorded without the engagement of the central government.

Scholars of policy communities also implicate stakeholders as crucial stimulators of policy choices.[39] Particular groups of stakeholders tend to maintain relatively homogeneous interests by virtue of the fact that they experience similar effects from decisions that are made in the policy sector. Teachers, for example, have similar interests with regard to salaries, benefits, and professional working conditions, regardless of where they live. Furthermore, stakeholders also frequently form associations that transcend political boundaries and carry ideas on policy activities across the various jurisdictions. The result is that stakeholders simultaneously enhance the exchange of policy ideas among the substate governments and exert pressure for comparable policies from the authoritative actors in each jurisdiction.

For many students of federalism, these assertions may seem counterintuitive. Federalism is justified as a means to permit constituent governments to tailor policies to local needs and interests, thus preserving substate policy diversity.[40] However, as Keith Banting maintains, "regional political autonomy is driven less by different policy preferences than by the politics of ethno-linguistic diversity and distinctive conceptions of political community and identity."[41] Federal publics may desire the preservation of substate policy autonomy to reflect internal ethnolinguistic heterogeneity, but this does not mean that their substantive policy preferences will vary greatly, or that substate differences in investments and achievements will be the norm.[42]

This pattern is clearly apparent in the case of Canadian education. Citizens from coast to coast consistently demand and expect high-quality education programming from their respective provincial governments. A recent study of public opinion conducted by the Canadian Education Association found that Canadians have "remarkably similar views across the country, especially in the areas of teaching, learning, and overall satisfaction with teachers and the school system."[43] During provincial elections, moreover, education is always a main item and often appears at the top of voters' priority lists. When surveyed, with the notable exception of Quebecers, provincial residents often request federal intervention in the policy field. This puts additional pressure on the provincial governments to provide quality programs in order to maintain their jurisdiction.[44] One former Director-General of the CMEC put it this way: "When I say I work for the CMEC, people get confused and ask 'Don't we have a federal minister for that?' Which is why when we do polls on jurisdictional issues, Canadians couldn't care less. All they want is quality education."[45] All of these dispositions pressure the provinces to provide programs of a comparably high quality.

This analysis helps us begin to understand how degrees of substate similarity can be achieved despite institutional fragmentation. Societal pressures, however, do not allow us to account for the observed differences in the extent of substate similarity in investments that appear between Canada and some of the other countries discussed here. Moreover, public preferences do not help us account for the differences in the achievements recorded by the cases. To rest only on societal factors would be to imply that Canadian citizens are somehow less willing to accept discrepancies in education policies than citizens from regions in other countries. Given that this is highly unlikely, I turn to a second contextual factor: the architecture of fiscal federalism.

Fiscal Federalism

Federalism is viewed as a means to enhance policy responsiveness by allocating powers to substate governments that are closer to the people. However, policy responsiveness is only possible if the governments have the capacity to use the powers at their disposal. As Richard Simeon and Christina Murray point out, legislative and administrative jurisdiction is meaningless without the fiscal resources to sustain policy action.[46] But fiscal resources are never evenly distributed within a state. Therefore, many researchers emphasize the critical importance of the central state as an agent of economic redistribution to ensure that regional governments have somewhat comparable levels of fiscal capacity to act in the areas of their jurisdiction.[47]

To correct substate imbalances, or horizontal disparities, central governments develop schemes of financial transfers that vary from country to country; this is commonly referred to as fiscal federalism.[48] These variations in turn affect the extent of internal discrepancies that materialize within a particular federation. Differences between the architecture of fiscal federalism in the United States and Canada are instructive.[49] The United States relies on a model of conditional grants where 100 per cent of federal transfers have conditions attached to them.[50] Prioritizing accountability, Washington earmarks all of its funds for specific programs to influence how states allocate the monies. Moreover, the lion's share of revenue-raising powers rests in federal hands, thus restricting the autonomy of the states from national interference.[51] Changes in the arrangements between the national and state governments have led such scholars as Timothy Conlan to describe American federalism as being in an era of coercive or "cooptive" relations, with Washington exerting considerable influence over a variety of policy areas, including education.[52]

Canada, in contrast, has developed a transfer system that scholars regard at most as semi-conditional, or more commonly as unconditional.[53] Observers have also noted a secular decline in standards set by Ottawa cutting across numerous policy areas dating back through the 1980s.[54] Canadian provinces also retain greater independent taxation powers than their US counterparts, further strengthening their autonomy from Ottawa.[55] Finally, since the late 1950s, Ottawa has maintained a broad equalization program to adjust for the different revenue-raising capacities of the respective provinces in an effort to level the playing field and help the provinces discharge their constitutional responsibilities at reasonably comparable rates of taxation.[56]

US fiscal federalism is highly centralized, with strong levers afforded to Washington to impose policy prescriptions and limit the autonomy of state governments. The Canadian fiscal architecture, by contrast, is highly decentralized in nature and provides extensive financial independence to the provincial governments. So why has this contributed to similarity in Canadian education while permitting divergence in educational investments in the United States?

With its less restrictive conditionality, Canadian fiscal architecture increases the capacity of the provincial governments to spend on programs and initiatives of their choosing. Furthermore, equalization helps ameliorate fiscal disparities among the provinces and ensures that they are able to provide comparable programs and services irrespective of variations in economic strength. Since equalization is entirely unconditional, jurisdictions can allocate the funds where they are deemed necessary. Under the US model, extensive conditionality obligates the states to spend in areas dictated by Washington. Since they cannot cut funds from federally sponsored programs, when faced with economic downturns state governments are forced to trim from areas where the federal government does not spend. The result is, as argued by Rom, an exacerbation of divergent educational spending patterns among the American states while the Canadian provinces are able to maintain their investments in education at comparable levels.[57]

Zeroing in on fiscal federalism thus provides a powerful means to account for variations in substate education investments that have appeared, particularly between Canada and the United States. However, while this economic architecture helps us understand why investments may or may not vary across substate governments, they cannot clearly account for the presence or absence of internal variations in educational achievements. Results from the Canadian case suggest that a direct link between high investments and high performance cannot be made, particularly since Canada records high achievements with less spending than some other countries. To understand why outcomes vary, we need to consider a third contextual variable – the configuration of the sector itself.

The Configuration of the Sector

I have demonstrated that the division of powers and fragmentation of a policy sector does not necessarily translate into entrenched discrepancies among the substates. This does not mean, however, that institutions are irrelevant. While one aspect of institutional design has not mattered in the way initially anticipated, it does not mean that the norms and rules of the game are not an important factor in accounting for the puzzling results.

There are particular insights that can be gained from the sociological strand of institutionalism. Sociological institutionalists start from the premise that institutions should be seen as "culturally-specific practices akin to the myths and ceremonies devised by many societies and assimilated into organizations."[58] Where others see institutions as a means to achieve efficient decision making and rationalize human interactions by structuring and constraining behaviour,[59] for sociologists, institutions take on a different meaning as they emphasize the "social and cognitive features"[60] of organizations. Institutions do not simply maximize the abilities of agents to achieve pre-existing preferences; rather, they maintain a mutually constitutive dynamic that shapes the preferences and behaviour of individual actors. In the words of Peter Hall and Rosemary Taylor, "institutions influence behaviour by providing the cognitive scripts, categories and models that are indispensable for action, not least because without them the world and the behaviour of others cannot be interpreted."[61] This strand of institutionalism allows us to consider how the norms and principles that underpin the policies and practices at work in Canadian education influence its performance and how the organization of relations among governments may shape the dynamics in intergovernmental relations, which are a crucial mechanism in federations for developing policy frameworks.

The norms and practices embedded in public schooling have implications for educational performance. Internationally, there is a clear commitment to the goal of universal elementary education for all, and this has generated a global convergence on the rate of educational achievements to the end of childhood.[62] This consensus, however, breaks down as we advance through the teenage years. While all countries are committed to providing some form of secondary education for adolescents, the organization of these programs varies considerably, with significant implications for students' achievements overall.[63]

Some education systems are highly stratified, with students slotted at an early age into general, vocational, and academic streams that prepare them for particular career paths. Due to this specialization, once a student has been allocated to a stream, transferring between streams can be extremely complicated if not virtually impossible. Other education systems operate according to different a different logic. Rather than prioritizing subject specialization, an alternative model delays any form of streaming for as long as possible and leaves multiple escape hatches in place in case a student wishes to change his or her options after starting down a particular path. Known as comprehensive or composite schooling, the system privileges inclusiveness and flexibility over subject specialization and targeted labour market training.[64] How do these differences in the respective models of education help us understand why Canada's performance is relatively even across the provinces?

Many continental European systems personify the former model of schooling. They are highly stratified and elitist; students are streamed at an early age (prior to adolescence) with little opportunity to change pathways once they find themselves in a particular stream. Recent reports have implicated the structure of education programs as a key factor accounting for the persistent between-school variations in educational achievements uncovered in the PISA test results. According to research by scholars such as Ludger Wöessmann, the consequence of the rigid streaming practices is that pre-existing socio-economic conditions are often replicated, and children end up in the same occupations as their parents.[65]

Canadian education, by contrast, embodies the principles of comprehensive schooling. Across of all the provinces, secondary education is underpinned by a commitment to extend flexibility to students; it affords them considerable time to determine where their strengths and skills lie before sending them down a particular path.[66] Often criticized in the popular press for watering down the quality of education and reducing workforce preparation,[67] comprehensive schooling nevertheless allows students the opportunity to reconsider their options and thus potentially increase their likelihood of successfully completing the initial stages of education.

Moving to the intergovernmental arena, we can also consider how the arrangements of a policy sector may affect relations among the substate governments themselves. Although it is admittedly impossible to conclusively prove here, it is feasible to speculate that the absence of coercive authority in Canadian education may have facilitated intergovernmental cooperation and information sharing. Acrimonious relations and jealous turf guarding by both orders of government often characterize federal–provincial intergovernmental organizations in areas such as health and the environment.[68] Unencumbered by the threat of federal incursions in the education sector, the provinces may be freer to interact with one another without the potential of unilateral action or edicts from Ottawa. Instead of being socialized into hierarchical roles and positions of dominance or subservience, as may be the case in other areas where the federal government is directly involved, the provinces maintain relations on a relatively equal plane. To be sure, larger provinces could try to overwhelm the interests of the smaller ones and attempt to compel certain activities, but the CMEC preserves the axiom of provincial autonomy through the conventions of voluntary participation and consensus decision making. Workable relations among the various jurisdictions may in turn facilitate the realization of interprovincial similarities in educational investments and achievements, and thus help account for the counter-intuitive findings presented here.

Conclusion

Conventional wisdom asserts that national standards, supported by a central authority, are a necessary ingredient to reconcile the tensions between federalism and the welfare state. The necessity of such standards, however, has been rarely tested and often presumed. This chapter has demonstrated that direct involvement by a central government is not a necessary condition for the achievement of substate similarity in a policy sector. The Canadian provinces have managed to fashion a *de facto* pan-Canadian system of elementary and secondary education, measured according to investments and achievements, without Ottawa's direct intervention. Societal pressures, the architecture of fiscal federalism, and the practices at work in the policy sector were the three contextual factors that help us explain how the provinces have managed to defy the odds.

That central standards are not a necessary condition for substate similarity is a particularly important finding for multinational federations. In any political system (federal or other), the drive to ratify overarching standards requires the expenditure of significant political capital, as compromises need to made among the various state and non-state players that are involved in a particular arena. In multinational federations, these processes are further exacerbated by questions of identity politics. Frequently, attempts to implement standards and practices degenerate into intense debates on thorny issues of national unity and the legitimacy of one government to speak on behalf of all. These debates moreover, in addition to their divisive force, can sidetrack policy makers' attention from the substantive problems of the day. In fact, we do not need to choose between either substate autonomy and disparities or central standards and similarity. Rather, the Canadian case demonstrates that substate autonomy can be both protected and deployed while still enabling the establishment of a successful policy system that produces relatively even results for citizens across the country as a whole.

For some, the marginalization of the central government in the education sector may be disquieting. However, far from marginalization, this research draws attention to the crucial indirect role played by the federal government. Fiscal federalism is a critical factor that has fostered similarity in educational investments across the provincial systems. What is more, as I have argued, the relatively unrestricted equalization program operated by Ottawa has successfully elevated the fiscal capacity of economically weaker provinces to invest in education at levels comparable to those with greater fiscal resources, if the public demands it. Without this vital indirect influence from the federal government, it is highly unlikely that substate similarity in education would have been achieved across Canada. Federal decision makers should tread cautiously before reducing Ottawa's redistributive capacities in the Canadian state.

Looking beyond Canada, the implications of the findings in this chapter suggest that when deciding upon arrangements of fiscal federalism, other federal and non-federal countries should consider the potential benefits afforded by relatively unconditional grants bolstered by a consistent equalization program. To be sure, there is an important trade-off. Specifically, the Canadian system privileges flexibility over the priority of accountability that is ingrained in the American fiscal architecture. Decision makers must therefore weigh the alternatives and determine an effective balance between the different priorities.

This research also suggests that norms and principles embedded in a policy sector can have an important impact on policy outcomes. The Canadian commitment to destratification in secondary education seems to have helped avoid cementing significant between-school variations in educational achievements, thus contributing to similarly strong results across the provinces. Moreover, the absence of the federal government as a coercive force in the policy sector may have helped sidestep some of the conflict-ridden and hierarchical patterns that have characterized intergovernmental relations in other fields. In education, the provinces meet and interact as equals, and this socializes them into alternative roles that can further constructive interactions among them.

But these findings generate a second set of compelling questions. Do these results in investments and achievements also indicate a high degree of interprovincial similarity in the content of education policies? If there is a high degree of substantive similarity among the provinces, how was this achieved without a coercive authority mandating common standards in the field? How, for example, did the interprovincial consensus to destratify secondary school emerge? It is to these questions that I now turn.

2 Defying the Odds II: Provincial Education Policies

When determining whether the provinces have fashioned a policy framework and installed similar policies, the immediate question is: Relative to what? The answer is straightforward. Barring some important variations, next to the universe of potential policy options, the ten provinces have adopted a relatively consistent approach to elementary and secondary schooling. The following pages serve three purposes.

The opening section maps out the five dimensions of the education sector to detail the options that policy makers, politicians, and stakeholders can choose. This description reveals that the configuration of elementary and secondary education is rife with possibilities and that choices among the respective policy instruments and their settings have dramatically different implications for the overall shape and character of the schooling system. Through this discussion, we begin to see how policy choices in each dimension can act as a grillwork of gears where decisions in one domain reverberate in others, opening or closing doors for particular options and enhancing or diminishing the feasibility of particular ideas that may be desired in the future.

The subsequent section provides a contemporary snapshot of the policies at work across the ten provincial education systems. The evidence indicates that notwithstanding the expectation that major differences will demarcate the provincial systems, the elementary and secondary systems across the ten jurisdictions are remarkably similar.

The chapter concludes by briefly considering the explanations that might account for the emergence of this policy framework. Specifically, I reflect on the prospective explanatory power of the globalization thesis, the influence of internationalization, and the role of ideas, as plausible interpretations of these puzzling results. I argue that while each of these models offers useful starting points, none on its own provides a sufficient explanation for the emergence of the *de facto* policy framework in Canadian education. All of this sets the stage for chapter 3, which constructs an alternative analytical architecture.

The Five Dimensions of Education

To appreciate the universe of options and instruments available to decision makers, I have broken the elementary and secondary education sector into five components: educational administration, education finance, curriculum, evaluation, and the teaching profession. These five domains constitute the substantive heart of the education arena; each contains a wealth of alternatives from which decision makers can choose.

Educational Administration

Educational administration refers to the policies that set down the organizational structures and managerial parameters of the sector, from the central authority that oversees the system down to the management of local schools. Decisions regarding the configuration of educational administration involve debates that hinge on the relationship between state and society. State control over education is an irrefutable attribute of the modern nation-state; but this public control was not achieved without dispute. Religious orders, which until the late 1800s had been providing education for those willing to pay, were reluctant to cede authority over schooling to the central state. Local community leaders, moreover, often took issue with the infiltration of a central authority into their educational affairs: "With only a few exceptions public elementary and secondary schools have been established historically as local institutions."[1] Local authorities strongly contested the proposed weakening of their authority by the central state. Advocates and planners of public education needed to find ways to mollify these various opponents in order to secure state control over the education enterprise; this included creating or maintaining different units of educational administration, determining the degree of centralization or decentralization of authority, deciding whether room should be given for collective identities to be represented, and finalizing the role of partisan politics in public schooling.

Four main units or levels with varying degrees of scope and power tend to be involved in educational administration, creating nested layers of management and governance. First, there can be total central-ization in the hands of the state, with all decision-making authority at the national level, so that policy changes by any unit within the system (such as a school) cannot be undertaken without the approval of these central authorities. A second option allocates some responsibilities to substate bodies – such as provinces or states – in conjunction with the central state. Below the substate level, regional educational authorities typically known as school boards or local districts can provide a third administrative layer that acts as a bridge between individual schools and the central authority. Finally, individual schools can act as admin-istrative units directly delivering education.

Casting a glance around the globe, we quickly realize that policy ac-tors can choose among – and even bypass – any of these four levels when designing the administrative architecture for an education sector. With its historically hierarchical decision making, France is the crown-ing example of an essentially centralized education system. Austra-lia, for its part, has witnessed the gradual withering away of multiple administrative layers, with the state governments eliminating local school boards so that authority now divided between Canberra and the states.[2] In New Zealand in 1989, based on the prescriptions in the reports *Administering for Excellence* and *Tomorrow's Schools*, the central government "reduced the staff of the central Ministry of Education, abolished the regional level of administration entirely, and shifted the responsibility for budget allocation, staff employment, and educational decision-making to individual schools."[3] All of this radically decentral-ized authority over public schooling to the local level.

Educational administration can also be combined with other political entities. For example, in the Czech Republic and the United States, edu-cation is either entirely or occasionally under the purview of municipal and regional governments rather than isolated units. In such systems, it is municipal leaders rather than stand-alone administrators who over-see the direction of public education. Regarding the United States, it is worth noting that the approaches to administrative management vary considerably among the state education systems and that intra-state dif-ferences begin at the peak of the governance structure. Still more diver-sity is found among the state boards of education, which vary greatly in terms of the degree of influence enjoyed by the electorate directly and by the governor.[4] In thirty-three states, for example, the board of edu-cation is appointed directly by the governor; in eight other states, the boards are elected. Some states combine gubernatorial appointments with direct election; in a few others, either the state legislature appoints the board or the board is appointed by multiple authorities. As a result, there are major differences in educational administration across the United States. Clearly, policy actors can choose among a multitude of options when devising the administrative architecture for overseeing a public schooling system, and policy variations can appear within a specific federation itself.

One primary point of interest in educational administration is the degree of centralization or decentralization in the sector. This is a function of the responsibilities allocated to the different administrative layers. Applying a framework initially devised by Michael Atkinson and William Coleman (later refined with Grace Skogstad) to measure the relative strength of the state in various arenas in the education sector, we can assess these characteristics to ascertain the extent of autonomy and capacity enjoyed by the different levels of educational administration relative to one another.[5] Autonomy focuses on the degree to which school boards and individual school administrators are able to act independently from central overseers in terms of finances, curriculum design, assessments, and hiring practices. If boards or schools gain too much autonomy from central administrators, the education system may become overly fragmented, thus compromising cohesion with the system. Conversely, if the autonomy of boards or schools is heavily circumscribed and curtailed, the sector may become overly rigid, hindering the capacity of local educators to tailor programs to fit local demands.

Capacity refers to the extent to which actors are able to carry out their assigned roles and responsibilities without assistance from the other units. It calls for us to assess how well pertinent players can "draw on sufficient institutional resources both to design policies that will realize its policy objectives and to implement these policies."[6] For example, in systems with local boards, if a board is too small, it may be unable to provide for the educational needs of its community, for it is likely to "lack the resources needed to provide the specialized teaching, broader curricula, and resources of support services."[7] Conversely, if a board is too large, the system may become unmanageable, rendering meaningless the idea of local representation. Decision makers must weigh these factors when determining the appropriate size of intermediary units of educational administration.

Flowing alongside these largely technical considerations are other, more normative and ideational debates related to the representation of subgroups within a particular polity and to the "institutional separation of education politics, policy, and administration."[8] According to Ronald Manzer, liberal and socialist theories hold that citizens elect their representatives, who then represent the will of the majority while protecting the rights of minorities.[9] For adherents to these theories, no special representation should be given to collective identities in educational administration. In marked contrast, under the principles of conservative theory, public authorities – including those for education – can be partitioned "on the basis of communal group membership, such as language or religion."[10] Under the terms of this debate and the relative salience and influence that each perspective – liberal, socialist, or conservative – may carry within a particular polity, education systems may thus vary in terms of whether internal communal groups – such as minority linguistic communities – are granted specific authority over the governance of education through such measures as separate school boards and guaranteed representation in specific administrative units.

The second component of this debate centres on the role of partisan politics in education. According to some, education policy must be devised for the sake of the common good, "which requires the effective insulation of policy formulation from the pressures of particularistic and partisan political interests."[11] Others contest this position, arguing that "the public interest has no meaning apart from the preferences of individual members of the political community."[12] According to this view, education policy must emerge from open democratic contests waged by political parties that are embedded in the political institutions that legitimately govern the polity.

The implications of these debates are obvious when we focus squarely on the organization and execution of central educational administration. Manzer developed a cogent typology to describe the four configurations of central authority that have appeared at various times in Anglo-American democracies: civic trusteeship, religious trusteeship, collective ministerial responsibility, and individual ministerial responsibility.[13] The first model involves strong central control in the hands of a secular civic board headed by a provincial superintendent. Adhering to the conservative paradigm, the second model preserves the influence of organized religion by entrusting responsibility to councils run by ecclesiastical officials. The latter two models embrace a liberal theory of parliamentary government by apportioning the responsibility for education to elected leaders. With collective ministerial responsibility, the entire political executive (or cabinet) is in command, while under the terms of individual responsibility, a single member of cabinet is appointed to act as the political head of the sector. Each arrangement offers alternative means to lead elementary and secondary education, with important implications for how the sector as a whole is organized and managed.

Finance

Education finance involves "the acquisition, allocation, and management of funds to support formal educational institutions and programs."[14] Four types of fiscal arrangements have been used across national and substate education systems, each of which has meaningful implications for the degree of centralization and the extent of public authority over schooling. First, under *laissez-faire* economic liberalism, public decision makers can choose not to financially support education, leaving it to individuals and families to pay for schooling delivered by private organizations.[15] Adherents to this philosophy, such as Herbert Spencer, regard any state-led intervention in schooling as a pursuit of "restrictive legislation."[16] Minimal public subsidies can be made available for impoverished families, but businesses or charitable organizations provide the instruction of their choosing and charge tuition to cover expenses. This position is grounded on the principle of limiting government intervention and maximizing the autonomy of the individual and the free market. Under this regime, the state exercises little influence over schooling, leaving educational decisions in the hands of parents and other societal interests (including the private operators of the respective schools), which are free to express their educational preferences and to break away from the confines of political conformity.

A second option sees the central state allocating some taxation powers to local authorities and requiring them to use the revenues thereby generated to supply the funds for a centrally regulated schooling system. Under this model, local authorities are directly responsible for finance and administration and must generate sufficient monies to finance the full school program. However, by mandating the basic requirements that local authorities need to comply with in return for the devolved taxation powers, the central state is able to establish a minimal education program that all schools within the system must provide. The state can use this authority to establish attendance laws, regulate the length of the school year, and perhaps set down minimal curricular requirements or salary schedules for teachers. The authority and capacity of the central state to impose mandates and compel certain activities is nevertheless curbed by the fiscal autonomy exercised by local decision makers, who can use their taxation powers to endow educational programs of their own concoction. What is more, major variations in local capacity are likely to emerge depending on the relative fiscal health of the individual communities. Boards in wealthy areas will reap considerable rewards, while schools in poorer regions are likely to suffer due to economic shortfalls that translate into marked inequalities within the schooling system itself.

Addressing some of the deficiencies of the second model, the third merges central with local financing. The taxation powers that are most readily and efficiently administered at the local level – typically, property taxation powers – are assigned to local school boards. As with the previous model, the boards use these resources to provide basic funding to the schools in their districts. Additional revenues are raised and supplied by the central state and are allocated through grants that supplement local contributions. In effect, this third option erects a cost-sharing framework, one that recognizes that the local tax base may be insufficient to guarantee the necessary resources to support all educational endeavours. As they smooth out fiscal disparities, central authorities can use targeted grants to give local boards incentives to expand certain desired programs. By retaining a greater share of the fiscal responsibility for education, the central state is also able to exercise greater influence through the enacting of more detailed regulations and policy prescriptions, which districts must fulfil in order to qualify for the annual grants.

Finally, the fourth arrangement calls for the central authority to fully fund the entire education sector; this is known as full-state funding. However the responsibilities among various units of educational administration are allocated, the central state is required to provide all the funds to cover the costs of the schooling system. Local boards may continue to help deliver education programs, but they are under the complete fiscal purview of the central authority; they have no local autonomy. Under such a system, the central authority exercises the greatest possible influence over the substance and direction of the sector; through the exercise of financial control, centralization is maximized.

One consequence of the global rise of education has been the gradual elimination of the first model as a viable option for financing elementary and secondary education. The remaining three are still regularly deployed across a variety of countries. More interesting in the context of this study, however, is evidence of substate variation in certain federations.[17] In many American states, for example, local boards have the power to levy taxes, which means they are fiscally independent from other levels of government. Some states, however, have entrusted the funding of schools to other administrative units, such as municipal or county governments. Boards in these jurisdictions are regarded as fiscally dependent. And these arrangements in turn can vary within the individual states themselves. Of the 285 districts in Maine, for example, 86 enjoy fiscal independence; the remaining 199 are fiscally dependent. The key message here is that in federations, decision makers have the authority and ability to institute financial policies that differentiate education systems from one another.

Clearly, the financial and administrative dimensions of the education sector are linked. This was touched on earlier, but I will articulate more thoroughly now. The four financial models vary considerably in terms of the degree of centralization or decentralization of autonomy afforded to the respective components of the schooling system. Under the first model, local autonomy is at its apex – indeed, as is the free market – with the central state fiscally absent from the sector. The private sector's influence over schooling is maximized; individual providers, families, and local interests retain total control over their educational destinies. The devolution of taxing powers to local boards prescribed by the second model introduces the idea that the central state can impose basic minimum standards that local administrators are required to fulfil, and this installs a modicum of standardization on the system as a whole. The reasoning here is straightforward: the achievement of a somewhat uniform program that is universally available throughout a territory compensates for the central state's sacrifice of the taxation base.

In the final two models, the distribution of authority tips decisively in favour of the central state. Shared-cost programs introduce the idea of conditional grants tied to individualized programs targeting specific goals set by the central state. The receipt of money thus depends on the satisfactory implementation of policies mandated by the central government; this in turn necessitates regular supervision by these higher authorities. Finally, under the full-funding model, the central state enjoys the ability to set the broad budget and to allocate funds to educational programs as it sees fit. This is not to deny the influence of other actors engaged in the education sector; even under full funding, the central authority must take care not to alienate either its electorate or its education partners.[18] Nevertheless, by creating a monopoly over educational finance, the central state concentrates significant power over schooling in its own hands.

Curriculum

Curriculum is the set of courses or content given in the schools. It establishes the educational requirements that authorities require students to meet during their time in the public education system. In the words of Joseph Katz, curriculum is "a body of thought and activity intended to develop in children those skills and abilities deemed necessary for growth to youth and adulthood."[19] Curriculum choices involve addressing the following issues: the educational philosophy that underpins schooling, the crafting and execution of the programs themselves, and determining who actually has the responsibility and authority for developing the curriculum.

Debates and disagreements arise regarding the appropriate groupings of students in schools, the number of subjects to be taught, and the amount of hours to be devoted to various courses throughout the day. Underlying these functional questions are various educational paradigms about learning that inform choices about curriculum organization and design. The traditional approach to education posits that students possess certain inherent abilities and limitations that can be identified early on. Policy actors focus on determining the resources that should be available to students, depending on their abilities, with clear specifications and requirements (or inputs) for teaching and learning. Courses are separated into particular silos, specific hours are allocated to each subject, mandatory textbooks are assigned, and teachers are prescribed specific instructional activities.[20] For example, in the early twentieth century, England's Board of Education issued the following statement on curriculum in England:[21]

> The courses should provide for instruction in the English Language and Literature, at least one Language other than English, Geography, History, Mathematics, Science and Drawing, with due provision for Manual Work and Physical Exercises, and in a girls' school for Housewifery. Not less than 4 ½ hours per week must be allotted to English, Geography and History; not less than 3 ½ hours to the Languages where one is taken or less than 6 hours where two are taken; and not less than 7 ½ hours to Science and Mathematics, of which at least 3 must be for Science.[21]

Formal education is regarded as a preparation for university, and the emphasis is on core courses that set the foundations for the broader range of academic disciplines. For students who lack the inherent ability to continue to university, the course offerings under the traditional approach made available in secondary school tend to be quite limited.

By the turn of the twentieth century, a new pedagogical philosophy had emerged known as New Education, under the rubric of "progressive" ideas. Its proponents based their efforts on the recognition that, as Alexander McKay of Nova Scotia put it, "in schools where only the three Rs are taught the childmind starves."[22] This philosophy called for a break from rigid courses of study and for a more flexible curriculum that recognized that each individual child had unique needs and potential.

The term "progressive" has come to encompass a broad range of ideas about education. At various times throughout the twentieth and into the twenty-first century, "a progressive educator was someone associated with the industrial education movement, the scientific movement in education, the mental-testing movement, the child-centered school movement, the mental hygiene movement, or the life adjustment movement."[23] The most recent iteration (and arguably reinterpretation) is known as objectives education. Instead of focusing on the inputs required for students and teachers, proponents of objectives education draw attention to the goals or desired ends of education and the needs and interests of the individual student. Formally referred to as outcomes-based education (OBE), adherents of this model specify targets to be pursued and are preoccupied with determining the ends of a particular course or program.[24] It is then up to education professionals as the program deliverers to determine how these outcomes would be best achieved.

Embedded in these pedagogical philosophies and educational paradigms is a debate about the organization and purpose of secondary education. These debates became particularly prominent in the twentieth century as the goal of expanding educational opportunities for all citizens took firm hold. Dovetailing with the competing perceptions of individual abilities and the appropriate scope of public schooling, a number of positions have emerged with regard to the ways in which schooling should advance beyond grade eight. For traditionalists, high schools are generally for university preparation; for adherents to various streams of the progressive movement, mandatory secondary school is a chance to expose students to technical and vocational training as well as university preparation.

There are three general models for secondary school: partite, bilateral, and comprehensive.[25] In the partite system, separate buildings house each major type of secondary program – vocational and general – and students are streamed into these at the conclusion of their elementary studies; this streaming is often determined by external exams. Vocational schools prepare students for careers in fields such as agriculture, industry, commerce, and the domestic arts. General secondary schools provide advanced education that prepares students bound for university. One practical concern with this model is that a school district must have a fairly large population in order for physically separate schools to make sense. In a more pragmatic variation, bilateral schools house academic and vocational programs in the same building while simultaneously adhering to the streaming principle. Both the partite and bilateral systems call for highly specialized programs for particular career paths; as a consequence, once a student starts on a given pathway, transferring to an alternative program becomes difficult.

In the third system, known as comprehensive schooling, students are extended the opportunity to draw from a variety of courses and to switch between different programs or tracks. Instead of being streamed by external exams at the end of elementary school, students – usually in conjunction with their parents and teachers – choose the program best suited to their needs and interests. Course offerings expand dramatically as more and more students are expected to complete the high school program. Curriculum in this system thus includes academic, commercial, industrial, and general courses in a variety of disciplines and trades. Program specialization is weakest in composite schools, but students have the opportunity to move laterally between the tracks should they wish to change the direction of their schooling.

Decision makers must also choose between prescribing an overarching curriculum and allowing jurisdictions to develop their own programs. In some federal systems – like Australia – common national standards have been established that provide a basic foundation for the general curriculum such that every Australian is exposed to the same type of programming for the duration of elementary and secondary schooling.[26] In other federations, such as Canada and Switzerland, substate jurisdictions are able to set down their own curricula, free from direct federal interference. The central authority must also decide the extent to which it will permit local autonomy and foster the participation of stakeholder groups in curriculum development. In the United States, prior to the Obama administration, there were no regional or national curriculum initiatives and significant control over curriculum development remained in the hands of local boards, some of which even contracted out the responsibility for curriculum development to private firms.[27] In other countries, such as Germany, local authorities have some power to develop limited courses but are generally responsible for implementing the curriculum set by higher authorities.[28]

There are two issues at the core of this debate. First, there is the tension between the desire for content tailored to local needs and the importance of maintaining uniform standards so that students from different regions are not disproportionately treated. For example, if one region introduces certain course content earlier than the others, students moving into that region will be at a disadvantage. Second, decentralizing curriculum development may enhance the potential for creativity and innovation as one board can test a new program without risking the system as a whole. However, to return to Atkinson, Coleman, and Skogstad's framework on administrative capacity, if local boards lack the necessary resources and capacity for effective curriculum development, such as dedicated curriculum specialists and publishers willing to supply alternative textbooks, the quality of the curriculum may be compromised and innovations less likely to occur. Decision makers must therefore determine which curricular arrangement is best suited to their surroundings. This further reinforces the interconnectedness of policy choices in each of the dimensions of the education sector.

Evaluation

The fourth dimension of education policy can be divided into two components: tests (or examinations) and assessments. Tests have been a permanent feature of schooling since the establishment of grades and formal curriculum. Assessments have materialized more recently and have become a prominent feature of most education systems worldwide; they are deployed to evaluate the efficacy of the curriculum and to hold educational professionals to account.

It is hardly contentious to say that tests are part of everyday life. We take tests for driving, undergo them for diagnostic purposes, and even answer skill-testing questions to claim lottery prizes. In the context of public education systems, a test is defined as a formal attempt to gauge the distance between a student's knowledge and some identified learning outcome.[29] Tests that have been designed by individual teachers for particular classes are further distinguished from *standardized tests*. According to Ross Traub:

> Generically, an achievement test is designed to assess the knowledge and understanding a student has acquired of a school subject. A standardized achievement test is further defined by its being given and scored in the same way, whenever and wherever it is used. Standardization means that the scores of all students tested can be fairly compared, one against the other.[30]

Standardized tests thus act as a form of system-wide quality assurance to determine whether individual students are meeting certain benchmarks across a particular education system.

Lorna Earl defines assessments as programs that "provide policy makers with information about student achievement for reporting to the public ... done periodically to provide an index of educational health."[31] Tests end at the individual; assessments involve regularized data collection to allow decision makers to compare cohorts across space and time. The key rests in the orderly collection and consistent collation of the results to permit systematic comparisons.[32]

Besides measuring academic achievements, assessments perform two supplementary tasks. First, they provide information on the comparative performance of schools, within and potentially across jurisdictional boundaries depending on the configuration of the assessment regime. Second, in a formative sense, large-scale assessments can be used to improve pedagogy and curriculum by providing diagnostic information and identifying systemic failures in the schooling system; this is valuable information that decision makers can use when determining a future course of action. "They work like x-rays," explains Earl. "An x-ray does not cure cancer, it helps to locate it and determine its extent."[33] To continue the metaphor, it is then up to the medical professionals to decide what the best response will be to ameliorate or eliminate the unhealthy condition.

Setting aside the differences between them, tests and assessments can have somewhat similar consequences arising from the implications of the results. These consequences vary in terms of severity. Low-stakes tests and assessments have little if any direct consequences attached to the particular results. Moderate stakes occur when test or assessment results are made public and authorities make comparisons to gauge the relative performance of schools and districts. Finally, high stakes occur when serious consequences are attached to results that can target every level of the education hierarchy – students, teachers, classrooms, schools, districts, substate jurisdictions, and the country as a whole. When graduation requirements hinge on positive results on mandatory exams, for example, the stakes are high for individual students. If funding is contingent on successful results in school-wide assessments, the stakes are high for individual schools. When creating testing or assessment regimes, decision makers must therefore determine the stakes that will be attached to the results.

The arguments against standardized tests and assessments are well documented; they face similar batteries of critics. M.L. Smith and C. Rottenberg suggest there are six negative consequences of testing, including reduced ordinary instruction time, neglect of material not covered in the tests, and the imposition of "cruel and unusual punishment" on the students.[34] Going beyond this critique, the Canadian Teachers' Federation (CTF) observes that standardized tests are often restricted to multiple choice items, which limits the scope of what can be tested and disadvantages those who may not be adept in that form of testing. Furthermore, according to the CTF, instead of increasing accountability, standardized tests "merely shift it from teachers and school authorities to anonymous government officials or corporate bureaucrats who cannot be confronted or held accountable if tests are poorly constructed, administered, or marked."[35] Decision makers must factor in these critiques from both the epistemic community and stakeholder associations when determining their own positions on standardized tests and assessments and the potential inclusion of these policy instruments in their respective education sectors.

Teaching Profession

The final dimension of the education sector is the teaching profession – the area that pertains to the instructors employed by the public sector. It sets down the qualifications that individuals must obtain and the rules and regulations they must adhere to in order to work in the arena. The teaching profession can be subdivided into two components: teacher education and teacher certification.[36]

Teacher education includes a vast array of items such as pre-service (or initial) teacher education, in-service training, supplemental courses, and other professional development activities. Here I focus on initial teacher education. This refers to the formative training a potential teacher receives prior to entering the classroom. Programs are generally broken down into three sections: academic disciplines or subject content; pedagogy, including teaching methods and education theory; and practice teaching.

The principal debate in teacher education centres on the appropriate locus for pre-service instruction.[37] The traditional option developed in Europe for teacher education is known as the "normal school." These institutions fall under the strict control of central authorities, which dictate both the curriculum and the structure of the training program, employing experienced teachers to transmit their knowledge to the new candidates. These institutions provide practical training and emphasize a close connection between experienced practitioners and candidates. Curricular subjects are treated as sovereign disciplines, with particular weight placed on practical skills such as lesson plans, classroom organization, and behaviour management.

Although they exhibited a number of strengths, normal schools were never known for encouraging personal growth in teachers or enabling self-reflection or self-critique. Therefore, education experts began to seek an alternative and turned to universities under the assumption that these independent institutes for higher education could provide a number of valuable benefits.[38] First, university-led teacher education could elevate teachers' subject knowledge and boost the overall status of the profession. Second, universities offered the chance for prospective teachers to develop critical thinking skills, which might help attract stronger candidates to the profession. There were, however, trade-offs accompanying this policy innovation. Allocating the responsibility for initial teacher education to universities would fragment authority by diminishing the influence of government officials over teacher preparation programs. Deans of Education would become active policy players in the sector and would be able to influence the direction of teacher education in partnership with the central authority. Despite this trade-off, university-led teacher education has taken a prominent place in many education systems worldwide, including Canada's.

University-led teacher education programs tend to be organized in two ways. Consecutive programs occur after a candidate has completed an undergraduate bachelor's degree in a particular discipline. Concurrent programs occur as a prospective candidate is completing a bachelor's degree. There is no scholarly, professional, or popular consensus on which type of program is most effective.[39] Recipients of consecutive degrees are often criticized for not having enough classroom experience before entering the job market and for lacking a sophisticated appreciation for pedagogy, given their condensed exposure to teaching philosophies. Concurrent programs offer a greater emphasis on practicum and pedagogies but are criticized for limiting the candidate's knowledge of broader subject areas and affording insufficient attention to the personal growth of the individual before he or she enters the teaching profession. In the context of decentralized education sectors, particularly in federations, differences in teacher education programs can reduce the interjurisdictional mobility of those involved in the profession. If one jurisdiction prefers a particular type of program, this could make it more difficult for teachers who have been trained in the alternative system to gain certification and employment if they move across provincial borders.

Teacher certification refers to the regulations surrounding the formal licensing of instructors by an authoritative body to confirm employment eligibility. The key issue at play here is who should determine and control the process. Local authorities, for example, could set down formal standards required to gain positions in particular schools. In this system, parents, community leaders, and school administrators establish the qualifications that any teacher needs to meet for employment. Alternatively, central administrators – at the national or the substate level – could streamline control over certification, thus centralizing the credentialing process. The former option privileges local control, potentially at the expense of interjurisdictional uniformity, while the latter favours harmonization at the expense of local influence. Both alternatives thus introduce the idea of general oversight of the teaching profession but fall in marked contrast to the supervisory regimes at work in other professions.

Unlike medicine, law, and engineering, the teaching profession often lacks independent bodies capable of ensuring credentials. Instead, certification comes under the purview of people outside the field; according to Frank McKinnon, this relegates the teaching profession to a "kind of low-drawer civil service, trained, licensed, hired, inspected and directed by the state."[40] This may not be the most appropriate system for the profession, and in recent years, a emerging option has seen some central authorities, inspired by associations in other professions, empowering independent associations to oversee the teaching profession. One implication of this policy development is the further fragmentation of authority in this particular dimension of the education sector. Such professional associations become yet another authoritative player – not unlike university faculties of education – with a formal stake in the policy process.

Summary

To recap, in each of the five dimensions of education policy, decision makers and other members of the community are faced with myriad options, each of which has markedly different implications for the overall direction and character of the sector. There are clear links among the five dimensions, with choices in one area reverberating in others. A central theme that emerges across all the components is the tension between centralization and decentralization in the policy field: options in each dimension can propel certain developments and embed particular logics in each individual education sector, leading to particular configurations. Education officials must reconcile the tensions between local and stakeholder engagement and attempt to fashion a coherent and cohesive education sector that can function efficiently and effectively. Given the policy autonomy, individual capacity, and salient socio-political differences among the ten Canadian provinces, it seems logical to anticipate that significant policy variation should be apparent in the elementary and secondary education sector. The evidence, however, paints a remarkably different picture.

A Contemporary Snapshot of Education in Canada

Education Administration

A current snapshot of Canadian educational administration captures an image of extensive policy similarity stretching across the provinces. Each of the provinces employs an administrative model that revolves around strong central authority vested in the hands of a Minister of Education who heads a department devoted almost exclusively to educational affairs.[41] Historical differences that once demarcated the central administrative systems of the provinces have been peeled away; there has been a convergence on the model of individual ministerial responsibility.

Beyond this individual ministerial responsibility, the provinces in turn parcel out administrative powers to local school boards (or divisions), which are comprised of elected (or appointed) trustees advised

Table 2.1 Educational administration in Canada, 2008

Central Level
Ministry of Education
• headed by a minister appointed by the premier
• assisted by a deputy minister and assistant deputy ministers
• responsible for managing the direction of the sector
Intermediate Level
School Boards
• headed by locally elected and/or provincially appointed trustees
• advised by a provincially approved superintendent
• responsible for implementing the decisions of the ministry and administering the delivery of public schooling
Local Level
Schools
• committees made up of parents, teachers, community members, and (sometimes) students
• responsible for advising the principal on educational matters that pertain to the school

by provincially appointed superintendents. Since the 1980s, all provinces have incrementally expanded the role of local schools by creating individual school councils consisting of parents, teachers, staff, community representatives, and in some cases students.[42] The responsibilities allocated to local councils are generally consistent across the country. Here, we can use Alberta as an example. In that province, local councils advise the principal on educational matters, consult with the principal on achieving educational standards set by the minister, develop a process for school-based decision making for local practices, and establish formal lines of communication between the school and the local community.[43] Despite this tacit nod towards decentralization, however, the bulk of authority remains firmly in the hands of the provincial ministers. This common three-tiered framework is displayed in Table 2.1.

In the 1990s, all of the provinces reduced the number of school boards, justifying this action as a means to improve performance and efficiency.

Nevertheless, it is important to acknowledge that the schemes for implementing this varied among the provinces.[44] Ontario, for example, took a top-down approach, forcibly amalgamating school boards with little input from the front-line employees. In a marked contrast, Alberta allowed the boards to determine their own arrangements but imposed a tight one-year timeline to make the necessary changes. Manitoba and Saskatchewan pursued yet another strategy, first allowing boards to voluntarily establish shared arrangements on an extended timeline. After giving the boards a few years to consider their options and craft tentative agreements, the ministers of education in both provinces enacted legislation that compelled any reluctant boards to consolidate.[45] Differences in implementation strategies may therefore signal subtle variations in the internal educational regimes of the provinces – variations that should not be ignored, given that they may affect the degree to which provinces adopt similar policies and the extent to which an effective policy framework will persist, besides helping us to anticipate the future directions – or likely partners – in educational initiatives to come.

Regarding the representation of communal groups, for much of Canada's history, the issue of language of instruction and control over educational governance for linguistic minorities was one of violent debate in many of the provinces.[46] In July 1912, for example, to stem the rising tide of French Canadians in the province, Ontario's Ministry of Education introduced Regulation 17 to restrict the use of French as a language of instruction beyond the first two years of schooling.[47] School boards were required to hire teachers certified in Ontario and fully fluent in English, and school boards that operated bilingual schools were to require their French-Canadian teachers to obtain Ontario certificates and learn English. Teachers who refused were no longer eligible to teach in provincially funded schools.[48] The Franco-Ontarian community mobilized, creating a small system of private French-language Catholic schools in various parts of the province. Regulation 17 was repealed in 1927, but not until 1968 were French-language schools recognized under the provincial Education Act. The result of all this was considerable inequities between the francophone and anglophone systems. Similar patterns developed in other provinces; some jurisdictions imposed English as the sole language of instruction, with no administrative authority extended to minority-language communities within their borders.[49] During the 1980s and 1990s, however, the representation for official-language minority populations in educational administration was expanded across the country; all of the provinces created French- or English-language school boards where the population warranted it, in order to conform to provisions that had come into effect under Section 23 of the Charter of Rights and Freedoms.[50]

But despite this recent policy uniformity in educational administration for official linguistic minorities, the authority allocated to religious orders in educational administration continues to vary among the provinces. In half the provinces, educational administration and public schooling have both been under secular control since the turn of the twentieth century. In Newfoundland, Quebec, Ontario, Saskatchewan, and Alberta, however, religious minorities gained control over educational administration, and these rights were protected under the terms of the Constitution Act, 1867. During the 1990s, Newfoundland and Quebec secured constitutional amendments to secularize education in their respective jurisdictions, and in this way converged with the five provinces whose education systems were already secularized. In Ontario, Saskatchewan, and Alberta, however, Catholic administrators continue to operate separate school boards. It remains to be seen whether these three provinces will seek similar constitutional amendments to end the tradition of minority religious representation in local educational administration. However, because these Catholic schools fall under the purview of the provincial Ministries of Education, they are subject to the same rules and regulations as their secular counterparts (see below).

Finance

The primary sources of education finance are general provincial taxes (particularly on income), supplemented by local property taxes. Eight provinces – British Columbia, Alberta, Ontario, Quebec, New Brunswick, Nova Scotia, Prince Edward Island, and Newfoundland – have embraced full state funding, albeit with some small differences. New Brunswick, for example, does not have local taxation for educational purposes. Boards in Quebec can impose a limited property tax – up to 5 per cent of the local rate – to finance certain expenditures that deviate from the provincial program. The provinces also vary in terms of how full funding is distributed. In Alberta, education funds are apportioned in a series of envelopes and school boards can transfer monies between them, while in British Columbia, boards are not permitted to move funds from their original envelopes. Despite these marginal differences, the general trend has been towards extensive fiscal centralization, and this has curbed both the autonomy and the capacity of local school boards across the provinces.[51]

The two exceptions to this trend toward extensive fiscal centralization are Saskatchewan and Manitoba. These two prairie provinces have largely kept the shared cost model, with local districts empowered to set and collect their own property taxes largely free from interference by the central state. Equalization grants are paid out by the provinces to guarantee that all communities enjoy relatively equal funding levels, regardless of differences in economic wealth. Also, categorical grants are allocated to support specific programs such as transportation, special education, and French immersion.

Until recently, both Saskatchewan and Manitoba had resisted the national trend towards full state funding. During the 2007 Manitoba election, however, the New Democratic Party promised to increase provincial funding for education and to elevate government support up to 80 per cent of the recognized costs for education; they kept their promise after the election, so that a *de facto* form of full provincial funding was achieved through stealth.[52] And, in 2009, the newly elected Saskatchewan Party (formerly the Conservative Party) led by Premier Brad Wall announced its intention to transform Saskatchewan's education finance regime and introduce full state funding in the province. It seems, then, that financial change is on the horizon and that within a few years the policies for education finance will be uniform across the country.

Curriculum

Reversing certain trends that pervaded the 1960s, the 1980s and 1990s saw all of the provinces recentralizing curriculum development and diminishing the role of local boards in curriculum design. In recent years, centralization has even appeared regionally, with some provincial governments undertaking ambitious collective curriculum initiatives. The western provinces ratified the Western Canadian Protocol for Collaboration in Basic Education in 1993, which resulted in the identification and adoption of common learning outcomes across the signatory jurisdictions. Each province, however, continues to use its own curriculum independent from the others in the group. The Atlantic provinces also initiated a program to facilitate common curriculum development across a variety of subject areas. Exceeding the efforts of the western provinces, Atlantic Canada has harmonized its curriculum guides, which means that all four provinces are using the same materials. Some collaboration has even appeared at the pan-Canadian level; in 1993, the CMEC approved the Victoria Declaration. Under its terms, the ministers agreed to a statement of shared beliefs. To summarize them: education is a lifelong learning process; the future of Canadian society depends on educated citizens; and all citizens should have a "fair and equitable opportunity in whatever educational and training endeavours they may pursue."[53]

Furthermore, all of the provinces have adopted an outcomes-based philosophy for their curriculum. Instead of adhering to the tenets of traditional education, the Ministries of Education mandate the learning outcomes they expect students to have achieved by the conclusion of a specific program. Saskatchewan's grade one English Language Arts curriculum, for example, breaks down the learning objectives into six components: listening, speaking, reading, writing, viewing, and representing.[54] Students in Ontario are required to accomplish similar outcomes, with the additional component of media literacy.[55] Consequently, while the broad philosophical approach to curriculum is consistent across the country, the provinces continue to experiment within this ideational framework to tailor programs according to internally defined priorities.

Looking at the structure and organization of secondary education, nine of the ten provinces use the composite model of high school. The exception to this model is found in Quebec. In lieu of a complete composite system, Quebec has fashioned a hybrid approach that integrates aspects of the composite and partite systems. High school in the province ends in grade eleven, at which time students attend a *Collège d'enseignement général et professionnel* (*Cégep*), which acts as a provincially run bridge between secondary and post-secondary education. Most *Cégeps* offer pre-university and technical programs that provide specialized training to students and prepare them for particular career paths. This arrangement in Quebec, which has the most idiosyncratic and distinctive schooling program in Canada, has recently inspired certain provinces, such as British Columbia, to invest greater time and energy in transition programs between secondary and post-secondary schooling.

Evaluation

Examination and assessment policies across the provinces show a high degree of similarity (see Appendices 2 and 3). Since the mid-1980s, all of the provinces except Prince Edward Island have reintroduced high school graduation exams; and all of them, now including Prince Edward Island, have implemented universal assessment programs to monitor the quality of public schooling in their jurisdictions. Through the CMEC, moreover, the provinces have established a pan-Canadian assessment program to gauge the performance of Canadian students in each province and to compare outcomes across the country. Finally, moving beyond the domestic arena, all of the provinces participate in a variety of international assessment protocols, including the OECD's Program for International Student Assessment (PISA).

Differences nevertheless appear among the provinces with regard to this dimension of education policy. To start, the respective provincial arrangements vary in terms of the publication of the results of standardized assessments; as a consequence, the implications of the assessments are different. In some jurisdictions, to eliminate the potential for inter-board comparisons, only provincial-level data are released. Some provinces, however, release the district results to the public, and a few even release the results from individual schools. Parents can use this information when selecting a school for their children, and this places schools in competition with one another on the basis of achievements on provincial tests. The provinces that have pursued this option have markedly increased the stakes of assessments, potentially reflecting alternative configurations of the internal education regimes in operation across the country.

Variations also emerge in terms of how standardized tests affect students' grades. In BC, 40 per cent of students' final marks in grades ten, eleven, and twelve are derived from results on provincial exams. In Alberta, 50 per cent of a student's final mark in grade twelve comes from provincial exams, and results from provincial assessments in grades three, six, and nine contribute to a portion of the final grades. For Manitoba students, 30 per cent of their final grade comes from provincial tests, while in Ontario, neither provincial exams nor assessments influence individual grades. Once again, while all the provinces operate a version of a common program, the stakes are clearly different from coast to coast.

Teaching Profession

For some time, universities have been providing all teacher education in Canada and all elementary and secondary teachers employed in the public system have been required to hold a university degree in order to gain certification. Beneath these broad-brush similarities, however, lie distinctive features that distinguish the provinces. These differences begin with the training that universities offer to potential candidates for the profession.

Universities do not deploy a uniform model of initial teacher education (see Appendix 4 for details). Prospective teachers in Canada can choose between two types of pre-service programs. They can pursue teacher education after completing a Bachelor of Arts or Science through a one- or two-year post-degree (also known as a consecutive program). Alternatively, they can apply for a concurrent Bachelor of Education program that folds teacher education into a four-year degree. In some provinces, universities offer both types of programs, allowing students to select the option most suited to their individual needs. In Quebec, however, all teacher education is conducted in the four-year concurrent program, which makes it more difficult for individuals to enter the profession as a second career when compared to the other jurisdictions.

Anecdotal reports from provincial education officials suggest that variations in teacher preparation programs can act as barriers to interprovincial teacher mobility.[56] In most provinces, the consecutive program takes two years to complete; in Ontario, only one year. Some members of the education community believe that Ontario teachers who have taken the consecutive degree are not sufficiently prepared for the classroom. "Some educators," in the words of one source, "raise concerns about the quality of Ontario teachers who have been trained in a consecutive program. While it may suit the Ontario system, it is not clear how those teachers will fit in the rest of the country."[57] The implication being that this perception hinders the transfer of teachers from Ontario to other parts of the country.

Although they occupy a prominent space in the policy community that surrounds this dimension, until recently Canadian deans of education resisted entering the fray and refused to offer a position on the overarching goals of initial teacher education. In May 2006, however, the Association of Canadian Deans of Education (ACDE) issued a general statement on the common objectives of teacher preparation programs. While declaring that the "agreement respects Canada's tradition of provincially-bound education initiatives,"[58] the signatories nevertheless recognize a set of normative principles for establishing common ground among the Faculties of Education, and this may eventually increase the similarities in the provision of initial teacher education in Canada.

Table 2.2 Summary of interprovincial similarities and differences in teacher education and certification, 2008

Location of initial teacher education	Sequencing of program	Duration of program	Certification authority	Certification regime
Independent universities in all ten provinces develop and operate separate initial teacher education programs	Concurrent or consecutive as decided by the individual university	Four to six years ON – candidates in consecutive programs receive only one year of teacher education as opposed to the minimum of two years in other provinces	Eight provinces – the Minister of Education ON – Ontario College of Teachers BC – BC College of Teachers*	Nine provinces – specialized certifications according to grade levels or specific training (e.g., Special Education) AB – K–12 inclusive

* Disbanded in 2012 and authority for certification transferred back to the Ministry of Education.

Likewise, certification regimes continue to vary among the provinces as registrars maintain alternative definitions of and scope conditions for professional accreditation. In Alberta, for example, teachers are certified from K–12 inclusive, with no specified grade range applied. In other words, teachers can be placed in any classroom once they have been certified. In Saskatchewan, certificates are divided between "Professional A" and "Professional B," with the holders restricted to certain areas of specialization. Ontario teachers can obtain four different types of certificates, organized according to the studies in teaching methodology that candidates have successfully completed: Primary (K–3), Junior (4–6), Intermediate (7–10), and Senior (11–12). Further designations are given to teachers who complete additional qualification programs, such as special education, to extend the areas in which they are licensed to teach. These variations in certification regimes make it more difficult for teachers to move among the provinces. These similarities and differences in teacher education and certification are summarized in Table 2.2.

In most of the provinces, each ministry is responsible for teacher certification. In 1987, British Columbia broke away from this conventional practice and established the BC College of Teachers (BCCT), a self-regulatory body with a mandate to set professional standards for educators, assess applicants to the profession, and issue certificates. Ten years later, Ontario followed suit and created the Ontario College of Teachers (OCT). It remains to be seen whether this new policy idea will take hold in other provinces. Regardless, the creation of these institutions has altered the policy context of certification in these two provinces.[59] Specifically, authority has been delegated to external bodies that enjoy autonomy from the provincial governments, fragmenting the policy process in this particular dimension, which may subsequently affect the sector as a whole.

Summary

Retreating from the detailed "weeds" of the education sector, this snapshot of the provincial education systems reveals a number of important and interesting traits. Under the auspices of the respective ministries of education, each province has established fairly centralized systems of administration and finance to manage public schooling. Clearly, there is a functioning framework operating in the sector. It remains to be seen whether this was achieved intentionally or accidently, but we would be hard pressed to deny that striking policy similarities have been realized in elementary and secondary education. Across much of the education sector, provincial policies demonstrate more affinity than differentiation relative to the universe of options that are available, and the ten jurisdictions have more in common than one would expect, given the potential for substantive variation. The provinces are free to design and maintain their own elementary and secondary education policies, yet save for a few disparities, substate commonalities unquestionably outweigh any divergences. In both the configuration of authority and the substate conformity of policies, the Canadian provinces have installed remarkably coherent systems without any direct intervention from the federal government.

Explaining the *de facto* "Pan-Canadian" Policy Framework

How can we explain the emergence of this policy framework? Since students of federalism have tended to focus on policy sectors where the central government intervened to fashion regulations, encourage standards, and advocate preferences, much of this research underestimates the ways in which the substate actors themselves can work together. Analysts of education policy, moreover, have tended to track the developments in specific dimensions of the sector, studying administration, finance, curriculum, assessment, and the teaching profession in isolated silos, rather than considering the interactive effects of choices across the various dimensions and how those choices may affect the sector's overall shape and character. We therefore need to look elsewhere to develop a framework that is capable of explaining and understanding these puzzling results in Canadian education. I begin with globalization and internationalization before considering the potential role of ideas.

Globalization and Internationalization

Given the ubiquity of elementary and secondary education around the world, perhaps there is an easy answer for how a pan-Canadian policy framework came to be installed: the provinces have established a *de facto* system of education due to the influence of global standards. Put most starkly, hyper-globalizationists predict the end of national economies and the waning of independent states as the primary loci of political identity.[60] In their view, as a result of cultural homogenization and capital mobility, differentiated national (and, by logical extension, provincial) schooling systems are no longer able to carry out their function of promoting a distinctive culture and identity; nor can they generate human capital tailored to local labour market conditions. Somewhat less radically, according to sociologist John Meyer and others, it appears that a Western political culture has diffused around the world, homogenizing key institutions and policy-making apparatuses.[61] According to these scholars, these effects are apparent now that mass schooling has become a worldwide institution, "both as a normative principle and as an organizational reality."[62] National – and provincial – education systems are thus increasingly converging on global norms, which include a world culture that produces a single broad model of schooling available worldwide. According to the globalization thesis, then, the striking policy similarities among the Canadian provinces are easily explained.

Three problems mar this explanation. Andy Green, for one, has argued that "these futuristic scenarios are somewhat overdrawn and unconvincing."[63] While some withering of national autonomy has appeared in certain policy areas, many states have reinforced their influence over education and maintained distinctive policy pathways. Our contemporary snapshot of education also indicates that substate similarities are stronger in Canada than in other countries, including the United States – a signal that the influence of global norms at the substate level is varied at best. The prioritization of international and external pressures by globalizationists thus marginalizes the significance of domestic factors, which must be identified and assessed in order to appreciate the dynamics of policy making, for these domestic factors mediate the influence and penetration of global forces.[64] The final challenge besetting the globalization thesis is that broad norms and world cultures are not necessarily operationalized or transformed into the same instruments. As John Campbell contends, "world culture is rife with deep internal contradictions."[65] Among other things, this means that "world culture" is neither homogeneous nor uniform, and that to the extent it may exist, different aspects of the world culture can be prioritized by particular sets of actors or the same aspect of a world culture can be differentially interpreted. Today, evidence of these internal contradictions is readily apparent: national education systems demonstrate marked variability even though most countries (especially those in the industrialized world) have committed themselves to the goal of universal education. Finnish education, for example, is markedly different from the schooling available in South Korea, yet both countries perform exceptionally well on international tests and both are completely committed to providing high-quality education to all their citizens.[66] How, then, did the provinces manage to all interpret the assorted components of the world culture on education so consistently? Globalization, on its own, does not seem to provide a sufficient explanation.

A second potential explanation for provincial similarity can be uncovered in the literature on internationalization. Steven Bernstein and Benjamin Cashore define internationalization as situations where domestic policies face "increased scrutiny, participation, or influence from transnational actors and international institutions, and the rules and norms they embody."[67] Pushing the concept further, for Grace Skogstad internationalization refers to two developments: "The first is international regulatory governance via the heightened importance of newly empowered international institutions that exercise rule-making and rule-adjudication authority. The second is transnational political activity via cross-national linkages and networks of not only state/bureaucratic actors but also actors representing civil society."[68] This concept of internationalization has been used to account for transformations in a variety of policy areas, including agriculture, criminal justice, food safety, monetary policy, and environmental regulations.[69] How might this concept shed light on the evolution of the provincial education systems?

Looking at the elementary and secondary education sector, there is scant evidence of the first attribute of internationalization. In sharp contrast to other sectors, such as food safety regulation and international criminal justice, international organizations have not been empowered to exercise rule-making or rule-adjudication authority of the sort that would transfer policy legitimization beyond the domestic realm. A comparable regime may perhaps be coming into view on the horizon as the tertiary sector begins to witness the emergence of such supranational authority, encouraged by the pressures for credential recognition in response to growing patterns of international migration,[70] but so far, such a regime has yet to emerge that could authoritatively influence elementary and secondary education. Consequently, this first form of internationalization has not materialized in elementary and secondary education, which suggests that it cannot lie at the root of interprovincial similarity.

Yet there is no doubt that some aspects of internationalization have arrived in education, as evidenced by the growing cross-national linkages of state and non-state actors in the policy community and by the rise of active transnational actors. On 16 November 1945, the Constitution of UNESCO was signed, coming into force the following year after being ratified by twenty countries, including Canada. Today, UNESCO's overarching objectives include attaining quality education for all, including lifelong learning; promoting sustainable development; and building inclusive knowledge societies. UNESCO activities on the education file were reinforced in 1961 with the founding of the OECD, of which Canada is a member. Of particular significance here is that it is the provinces that officially represent Canada in the OECD, not the federal government. The OECD has become a powerful force, especially among industrialized countries, and this has encouraged, among other things, the prioritization of lifelong learning, as well as the installation of outcomes-based curriculum practices and universal assessment programs. All of this has contributed to the spread of global norms in educational practices as well as to new cognitive ideas on which to base policy making.

These organizations have intensified the cross-national linkages and networks of state and non-state actors in domestic education policy communities. According to Mitchell Orenstein, transnational actors have considerable influence as "proposal actors" with "the power to formulate legitimate and well-elaborated policy proposals"; this can drive the diffusion and implementation of particular policy packages around the world.[71] Investigating the trend of pension privatization, Orenstein argues that the influence of these actors arrives across a series of phases of the policy process and that the power of these interventions is "determined by the ideas, resources, and decision-making processes of transnational actors themselves and that these organizational factors change over time."[72] Building from Wade Jacoby's work,[73] moreover, transnational actors can organize and coordinate campaigns, build coalitions with domestic actors, and seek to influence policy making by inspiring particular ideas, subsidizing certain policy options, or partnering directly to encourage the implementation of preferred practices. Could transnational actors be the driving force of the Canadian educational policy framework?

Looking at the transnational community in education, while the OECD carries considerable weight and has coordinated a number of campaigns and initiatives, these developments are largely a recent phenomenon that coalesced in the early 1990s. If the influence of transnational actors is at the root of provincial similarity, the historical record should reflect this by indicating a marked increase in provincial comparability in the past two decades, a hypothesis that will be tested in later chapters. Unfortunately for the explanatory power of transnational actors, where Orenstein uncovered a dedicated and highly organized campaign for pension privatization orchestrated by leading international organizations, including the World Bank and USAID, education is not marked by a comparable complement of organizations that enjoy the capacity to exert such marked influence on domestic affairs. Finally, similar to a weakness of the globalization thesis, comparable substate similarity has not unfolded in other federations, including that of the United States, even though that country has been just as exposed to the influence of transnational actors. Consequently, the potential effectiveness or applicability of this model to the puzzle of Canadian education is somewhat diminished.

Neither the globalization thesis nor the internationalization model can on its own account for the emergence of the Canadian education policy framework. This does not, however, render them completely inapplicable to this study. As will be explored in the next chapter, these two approaches offer possible keys for opening explanatory doors. Specifically, globalization draws our attention to the idea of interdependence, while the literature on internationalization emphasizes the importance of a domestic policy community. These two concepts, when synthesized effectively with features of the domestic arena, may provide a useful foundation for a compelling analytical architecture to understand the development and installation of policy frameworks in federations.

Ideas

A growing number of political scientists and public policy scholars have turned their attention to the importance of ideas in policy making. Ideas, declares Jal Mehta, "are central to questions about agenda-setting ... diffusion, policy choice, the conceptual categories that underlie politics, path dependency and path-shaping chance, institutional stability, institutional change ... and political coalition building."[74] This body of research has identified how different types of ideas shape policy-making processes, acknowledging that ideas come in many packages, including programs, public sentiments, and paradigms, each of which has its own forms of influence.[75] Programs are the narrowest conceptualizations of ideas; they offer specific solutions or options that people can choose from when resolving a given problem. As defined by John Campbell, public sentiments are "normative background assumptions that ... [limit] the range of programs that decision-making elites are likely perceive as acceptable and legitimate ... Public opinion, values, norms, identities ... are what I have in mind here."[76] Finally, residing in the background of policy debates, paradigms – referred to by some as "mental models"[77] – are formulations of cause-and-effect relations among particular phenomena that set out what people are likely to see as worthwhile and legitimate and thus help conceptualize both the nature of a problem and the goals that actors are seeking to achieve through policy.[78] What types of effects are ideas supposed to have?

Building from Max Weber's early metaphor, Judith Goldstein contends that especially in times of uncertainty, ideas serve as "switches" or "roadmaps" to channel and syphon off certain policy choices as they provide policy makers with particular strategies.[79] Ideas, assert Daniel Béland and Robert Cox, allow people to make sense of the world: "These ideas guide our actions and shape our interactions with others."[80] And, according to Alan Jacobs, "we have evidence that conceptual frameworks, once adopted by decision makers, can shape their goals, their causal beliefs, and their preferences among alternatives."[81] Pushing ideas to the forefront of theories of institutional change, Mark Blyth writes that they have a series of pertinent effects: they reduce uncertainty in times of crisis; they render collective action and coalition forming more achievable; during struggles, they can be used by actors as weapons to promote or suppress certain options; and they make institutional stability possible.[82] Finally, in an effort to connect ideas with actions, John Campbell and Ove Pedersen have advanced the concept of "knowledge regimes." By these, they mean "sets of actors, organizations, and institutions that produce and disseminate policy ideas that affect how policy-making and production regimes are organized and operate in the first place."[83] For ideational scholars, then, the key is to uncover the ideational frameworks, public sentiments, paradigms, and knowledge regimes – in the case at hand, this refers to the ideas that permeate Canada's education sector and encourage provinces to adopt comparable policies.

A number of scholars have examined the influence of ideological traditions in educational policy making and how policy paradigms have emerged in the field so as to blanket policy activity. "From its foundation in the middle of the nineteenth century," Ronald Manzer tells us, "the political principles of public education in Canada have been dominated by liberal conceptions of the purpose of public education, liberal understandings of the proper criteria of political evaluation, and liberal principles of state organization and public policy."[84] These broad philosophical currents set a common ideational environment within which provincial decision makers operate. Moving into the narrower realm of specific educational practices, Scott Davies and others have tracked the evolution of education paradigms, detailing the transformation from the traditional approach centred on the 3 R's to the accession of the progressive education movement, which has offered markedly different prescriptions designed to improve both student opportunities and outcomes.[85] Common philosophies and shared educational paradigms could underpin the emergence of a *de facto* educational framework in Canada.

Ideas thus seem to provide a firm launch pad from which to develop an explanation. Institutions craft a political opportunity structure; ideas help us understand the goals actors may have and the issues they see as important.[86] But to fully appreciate the effect of ideas, we need to move beyond simply asserting that ideas matter and specify *how* ideas produce certain effects and *which* mechanisms encourage the dissemination of policy ideas. Furthermore – and this harks back to the problems that beset the globalization thesis – seeing ideas as homogeneous and monolithic entities does not allow us to account for the policy variations that persist in Canada and for the significant variations that characterize other national policy systems. Ideas must be translated into action to have effects, but this translation occurs neither automatically nor uniformly: "the enactment of a social rule is never perfect and ... there always is a gap between the ideal pattern of a rule and the real pattern of life under it."[87] We should therefore take the opportunity to explore why certain provinces adopted particular policies at a given time while others eschewed similar strategies, despite being situated within the same ideational climate. To accomplish this, we need to construct an analytical architecture that builds bridges across existing theoretical terrains and that integrates aspects from the three traditions of institutionalism.

3 Theorizing Policy Frameworks in Federations

How are policy frameworks created in federal systems? This chapter crafts an analytical architecture to help us analyse the dynamics of policy making in federations and guide the comparative historical analysis that unfolds in later chapters. My emphasis lies in understanding the processes and mechanisms that carry ideas across various polities while identifying the conditions and pathways that lead different polities to adopt comparable policies. To accomplish this goal, I bridge two research terrains – policy diffusion and policy convergence – linking them together with insights drawn from the three traditions of institutionalism to consider the ways in which these processes, mechanisms, and pathways shape the dynamics of policy making and the emergence of policy frameworks in federations.

Federalism scholars have often deployed the concept of diffusion with considerable success.[1] Jack Walker set the stage for diffusion research when he sought to understand the factors that influenced the speed at which policy innovations spread among the American states.[2] Using his work as a springboard, scholars have considered the relative significance of such factors as geographic proximity, shared attributes among states (e.g., ideological or resource similarities), and the perceived success of particular policies as catalysts for policy diffusion, emphasizing the incentives of intergovernmental competition as a key mechanism for policy exchanges.[3] Other researchers have focused on the role the central government plays in the spread of practices across a federal state through instruments such as mandates and conditional grants, highlighting the importance of coercion as a key to policy framework formulation in federations.[4]

While extremely fruitful, much of the work by federal scholars has tended to downplay alternative mechanisms for policy diffusion, such as learning, emulation, and cooperation. The problem with relying solely on the concept of diffusion, moreover, is that we lack the tools to account for the actual processes of adoption, implementation, and potential adaptations by receiving jurisdictions leading to (or hindering) the creation of a shared policy framework. This is where the work on policy convergence, most often deployed to explain the growing similarities of countries, can help us understand why provinces may (or may not) choose to adopt the same policies and the ways in which these policies may be adjusted through implementation.

Interestingly, although they share many substantive research interests, public policy scholars and institutionalists have often worked in isolation from each other in what Daniel Wincott recently characterized as a "strange case of mutual neglect."[5] My analytical architecture is crafted specifically to better integrate institutionalism directly with the insights of public policy scholars. The three traditions of institutionalism provide useful threads with which to weave these two research terrains together to understand the nature and dynamics of policy framework formulation in federations.

The chapter opens with a discussion of interdependence and connectivity, two anchors of this analytical architecture that together constitute the structural components of the policy climate and are combined with the ideational aspects that prevail at particular moments in time. The second section endeavours to connect the features and characteristics of the policy climate with the various processes of diffusion. The third section applies this initial architecture to the case of Canadian education, estimating the probability that certain processes of policy diffusion either have occurred or are occurring. The final section incorporates the work on policy convergence to allow us to identify the pathways and conditions that may lead different polities to adopt comparable policies, leading to the emergence of an active policy framework that oversees a specific sector.

Diffusion, Interdependence, and Connectivity

In biology, diffusion refers to the passive movement of particles across a concentration gradient from an area of high concentration to an area of low concentration. A practical example seems in order. When a person enters a room wearing cologne, he creates an area of high concentration around himself. Because the cologne molecules are in constant motion, they begin to disperse, diffusing through the air, thus moving the cologne – and its accompanying odour – into areas of lower concentration. At times, this process can be facilitated by certain identifiable factors referred to as carrier molecules. This is active transport or facilitated diffusion, and it requires the assistance of an agent to secure the passage of molecules across a given membrane into an alternative space.

Drawing inspiration from this physical process, public policy scholars have applied the concept of diffusion to the social world, defining it as the mediated spread of policies, practices, or programs across and within political systems. For Everett Rogers, who wrote what has become the seminal text in diffusion studies, diffusion occurs when "an innovation is communicated through certain channels over time among the members of a social system."[6] It is, therefore, a process that occurs within a particular context or climate, and diffusion scholars base their work on the assumption that the actions and decisions of one political entity can be shaped and influenced by others. "Policy choices," declare Beth Simmons, Frank Dobbin, and Geoffrey Garrett, "are interdependent ... Governments adopt new policies not in isolation but in response to what their counterparts in other countries are doing."[7] The first step in understanding diffusion thus involves specifying with further clarity what we mean by interdependence and identifying the various actors that are involved as together they form crucial components of the policy climate within which decisions are made.

Interdependence refers to "contexts in which the outcomes of interest (i.e. dependent variables) in some units of analysis (i.e. countries) directly affect outcomes in others."[8] This kind situation can emerge from two paths. Policy externalities, also known as spillover effects, invariably affect neighbouring jurisdictions because they disregard the physically intangible barriers that ostensibly divide political communities.[9] However strong the regulations or contingency plans one polity may have, political borders cannot contain environmental disasters like oil spills or nuclear fallout. This can be referred to as the path of unintentional or unavoidable interdependence. Interdependence can also develop in situations where one actor cannot accomplish his or her goals without coordinating or cooperating with another.[10] Finding themselves in this kind of situation, actors may decide to pool their resources and willingly cede degrees of autonomy in pursuit of common goals, thus advancing down a path of intentional interdependence.

The effects of interdependence on policy making are considerable. According to Ernst B. Haas, interdependence means "that there is no fixed hierarchy of preference orderings for single actors or among actors."[11] Instead, actors can reorder their preferences and reconsider policy options in light of decisions made elsewhere by other actors, organizations, or governments. Appreciating interdependence requires researchers to look elsewhere than exclusively at the formal organs of the state and consider the influence of other non-state actors.[12] Governments rarely enjoy a monopoly on policy making and must often mobilize the support of other non-state players. Diffusion, as David Strang and John Meyer observe, "requires support from other kinds of actors as well: state authorities, large corporate actors, grassroots activists."[13] As a result, government actors not only make decisions in light of what other governments are doing, but also are influenced by the machinations and campaigns of non-state players, who contribute to the policy climate that persists at a particular point in time.

Much of this work on interdependence has emerged from the field of international relations, with scholars endeavouring to explain such things as the rise of regimes, the emergence of international institutions, the influence of transnational and non-state actors, and cooperation in world politics.[14] How can these insights into interdependence and the need to disaggregate the state be applied in a domestic context? Here, the scholarship on policy communities and policy networks sheds considerable light.

Using the concept of policy communities, we can investigate the structural and power relations between state and non-state actors to understand how the interactions among the various players engaged in a policy sector influence policy development. The term policy community suggests "a commonly understood belief system, code of conduct, and established pattern of behaviour"[15] shared by a group of actors. More directly, a policy community refers to "the set of actors, public and private, that coalesces around an issue area and shares a common interest in shaping its development."[16] What is more, Paul Sabatier argues that communities can form coalitions "who share a set of normative and causal beliefs and who often act in concert."[17] Identifying the state and non-state actors that together constitute the policy community thus ensures that researchers can locate the ones that are delineating policy problems, lobbying on behalf of particular solutions, and formulating the substance of policies themselves. These are the agents of policy diffusion, and they can be individuals such as bureaucrats and politicians, as well as networks, organizations, government departments and agencies, task forces, commissions of inquiry, political parties, media outlets, and regional and transnational organizations. "These actors," writes Diane Stone, "legitimate the character of public discourse, and endorse the adoption of new programs."[18] As John Kingdon demonstrates, it is through their support and entrepreneurialism that particular policies enter a new arena and arise on a specific agenda.[19] Furthermore, in federations, policy communities can play a key role in disseminating policy ideas among the constituent units by bringing officials and experts from different regions together, thus providing them with the opportunity to discuss alternative priorities and strategies.[20]

While the policy world may seem chaotic, it is far from unstructured. From David Marsh and Martin Smith we know that policy networks define the roles actors play and prescribe the issues that can be discussed and that they have distinctive sets of rules; all of this fashions a particular set of structural parameters within which decisions are made.[21] These networks are sets of formal institutional and informal links between governmental and other actors and are structured by shared (yet negotiated) beliefs about and interests in policy making and implementation.[22] Networks can vary according to the density of the interactions, the institutionalization of desired goals, and the articulation of appropriate formal and informal rules of conduct that shape actors' behaviour. The configuration of the policy network and the players that constitute the policy community must therefore be assessed to appreciate the climate of interdependence that characterizes a policy arena.

However, as Grace Skogstad astutely notes, using these concepts of policy communities and policy networks runs the risk of envisioning the policy world as "static, capturing a patterned relationship at a point in time."[23] Furthermore, those who deploy these concepts have been criticized for downplaying the significance of broader macro-political, economic, and ideological structures within which the networks are situated.[24] Two correctives can be offered to address these shortcomings. First, following Colin Hay and David Richards, networks should be seen as sites of strategic action comprised of two-way interactions between network structures and political actors whereby modes of governance can influence behaviours that in turn recursively (re)constitute the network.[25] This approach places greater emphasis on the dynamic nature of policy networks/communities. It sees networks not only as structures but also as agents; at the same time, it leaves room for the agency of the actors themselves. Second, networks are situated in a wider climate, and while they can mediate the effects of this climate, changes in the broader environment can influence the resources, material interests, and other ideas of actors within a network.[26] By keeping these two correctives at the forefront of this architecture, the dialectical interpretation allows us to see how policy development and the formulation of frameworks reflect the interactions of structures and agents that together produce public policies.

Interdependence, however, is only one type of relationship among actors and/or polities within a particular policy climate. To fully appreciate diffusion, we must also recognize that actors and polities can be connected as well. The idea of connectivity taps the reciprocal links that can form among actors and/or polities; in contrast to interdependence, connectivity does not necessarily mean that the decisions of one directly or immediately affect the outcomes for others. Connectivity instead acknowledges that actors and communities are part of a shared system, with the result that certain types of bonds akin to interstitial tissues emerge, acting as transmission lines or conduits. This has two primary effects. First, information that is exchanged along these lines may shape and influence the preferences of policy actors, potentially inspiring (but not necessitating) a reordering of preferences or a reconsideration of a particular strategy. Second, the nature and intensity of the connections themselves and any changes to them impacts both the mechanisms of diffusion and the types of interactions that occur among the actors embedded in the system. These effects will be detailed below, but for the moment we must answer a simple question: How do interdependence and connectivity emerge in federal systems?

It is hardly contentious to say that interdependence and connectivity among the political units of a federation can take a number of forms. All federations involve independent political communities pooling their resources to collectively increase their capacity on a particular issue or in a broader field. The Fathers of Confederation, for example, used fear of an American military incursion to promote the union of the colonies of British North America.[27] This logic resonates below the level of the central state down into individual sectors and specific policy initiatives. Substate governments may decide to collaborate formally in pursuit of common goals or shared policy objectives, bring together policy experts, ratify collective agreements, establish joint programs, or harmonize policies to enhance performance and achieve greater efficiency. In this way, collective action reinforces the interdependence among the participating jurisdictions, for if one jurisdiction withdraws from the initiative, the activities of the others are likely to be compromised. This is particularly significant when we consider the first major form of interdependence in federations: legal interdependence.

All federations establish legal interdependence through the constitutional bargain. Under the terms of a formal agreement, which is overseen by an independent arbitrator such as the courts, the political communities in a federation are bonded together by common rights and obligations to which all jurisdictions must adhere. Changes to this agreement, moreover, can alter the legal bonds among the respective parties and the obligations that each is expected to fulfil; this then translates into new mandates and requirements that install specific incentives or inducements for policy activity. The entrenchment of the Charter of Rights and Freedoms in 1982, for example, ushered in a new era of policy making by codifying the principle of individual and collective rights available across the country while introducing new mandates that the provinces were now legally required to fulfil.[28]

A common feature of all federations is the creation of an economic union among the constituent members; this involves reducing trade barriers and guaranteeing labour mobility among the various territories.[29] Moreover, because resources are never evenly distributed across a country, governments often devise means to redistribute wealth among the different jurisdictions. This is a component of the fiscal architecture of a federation, and at times it includes strategies to shift financial resources to economically weaker regions to help ensure that all citizens are able to receive the benefits of adequate policies and to access comparable programs regardless of where they live.[30] Economic growth or decline in one jurisdiction may therefore impact the economic capacity of the other jurisdictions. Canadian events in 2009 are illustrative. After generations of acting as an engine of Canada's economic growth, Ontario became what is colloquially known as a "have-not" province and now receives redistributive payments from Ottawa. Moreover, changes to the redistributive regime can increase or decrease the substate governments' abilities to support the policy fields that fall under their purview. Therefore, together with the economic union, the structure of fiscal federalism is a crucial aspect of economic interdependence, one that shapes and mediates policy dynamics in federations. Thus, in addition to the resource-pooling that occurs in all federations, we can operationalize two broad forms of interdependence among the constituent units in federations: legal and economic. Together, these forms of interdependence constitute certain aspects of the policy climate within which the various state and non-state policy players in a particular domain are situated.

Two nodes of connectivity are germane to this analytical architecture: organizational and cultural. Organizational connectivity recognizes that state and non-state actors can create different types of organizations ranging from the informal and ad hoc to the formal and permanent. United by common interests in a particular policy sector, state and non-state actors can fashion formal networks that transcend the internal territorial borders of the respective jurisdictions to communicate ideas among the constituent members of a federation. Conferences, publications, and regular interactions among the various members of a policy system can all contribute actively to policy diffusion: "such forums serve as more than opportunities for communication, however; they are designed specifically to promote the homogenization of their members around models of progressive policy."[31] We can therefore expect participation in such forums to increase the likelihood of policy diffusion and policy similarity; conversely, isolation from these forums reduces the opportunity for diffusion and the likelihood of policy similarity. State officials can also create dedicated intergovernmental organizations to facilitate cooperative agreements and shared initiatives among themselves. These organizations can reduce transaction costs by providing institutionalized rules and long-standing "memory banks" to reduce the complexities that accompany intergovernmental interactions.[32] These organizations, it must be said, may not result in formal interdependence. If, for example, the organization is grounded upon voluntary participation and flexible decision-making rules, full interdependence will not materialize. Nevertheless, each type of organization serves to reinforce the conduits for diffusion among the members of a federal system.

The second node of connectivity is cultural. For some, the deployment of cultural factors in this analytical architecture may be a cause for disappointment. "It's reached the point," writes Anthony Appiah, "that when you hear the word 'culture,' you reach for your dictionary."[33] Keeping his admonishment in mind, we can start unpacking the concept by reaching back to Gabriel Almond and G. Bingham Powell, Jr, who defined culture as "the pattern of individual attitudes and orientations toward politics among the members of a political system."[34] It embodies, as Alan Patten further proposes, "what people share when they have shared subjection to a common formative context."[35] Culture thus includes shared beliefs and values that are socially enacted; these then configure a framework of shared meanings that explicitly acknowledge the intersubjective nature of the human condition, a nature that is made apparent through the social construction of knowledge and the construction of social reality.[36] Integrating culture into this architecture allows me to further the sustained dialogue across the three traditions of institutionalism and to integrate the material and ideational elements that together contribute to policy making.

To appreciate culture's impact, Almond and Powell contended that "the kinds of orientations which exist in a population will have a significant influence on the ways in which the political system works" and are "likely to support certain general political goals and procedures and to reject others."[37] Advancing this observation and elevating it to an intersubjective plane, Beth Simmons and Zachary Elkins point out that "the voluminous literature on diffusion and social influence has found that entities that share similar cultural attributes tend to adopt the same practices."[38] What is more, culture has the potential to trigger a self-reinforcing dynamic. "Social systems can get 'locked in' to certain patterns by the logic of shared knowledge, adding a source of social inertia or glue that would not exist in a system without culture."[39] In other words, culture can privilege certain ideas, increase diffusion within certain groups, and act as a mechanism for path dependence.

In federations, while some national culture might be identifiable, the notion of a uniform and coherent fabric is highly unlikely if not impossible.[40] Indeed, Clifford Geertz dismissed the notion of a coherent national culture when he ridiculed that it conjures up an image of a "seamless superorganic unit within whose collective embrace the individual simply disappears into a cloud of mystic harmony."[41] Instead, particular members of a federation may share stronger linguistic, social, historical, or religious links that help fashion self-identified peer groups within the broader body politic. As these ties strengthen, the connective bonds between the pertinent groups are likely strengthened as well, which in turn influences the exchange and penetration of policy ideas.[42] In contrast, where internal cultural ties are weaker, policy actors may selectively disregard the choices and ideas that emerge from beyond their own group. The cultural bonds among respective units can thus provide shortcuts that filter the diffusion and reception of new ideas into a specific jurisdiction. Put together, as Strang and Meyer argue, "cultural linkages, and particularly those informed by compelling models of behaviour, should accelerate the pace of diffusion within the populations they describe."[43]

The nature of interdependence and the bonds of connectivity at work among the constituent members of a federation constitute a crucial component of the policy climate, for they establish the structural parameters within which policy exchanges occur. In addition to these interstitial tissues among the substate jurisdictions, the policy climate includes ideas. Using the literature on ideas discussed in chapter 2, certain public sentiments, paradigms, and programs tend to be salient at a particular point in time and to resonate across a policy climate. Actors are influenced by these ideational trends and mould proposals around them to help legitimize the policies in their own particular context. For example, in his assessment of Canada's and Germany's citizenship and immigration policies, Triadafilos Triadafilopoulos argues that changing normative contexts encouraged incremental changes as policy makers sought "to reconcile the unfamiliar demands of a new normative order with the deeply engrained, path dependent logic of established policy paradigms."[44] As actors mould proposals, this may in turn reshape the ideas themselves, meaning that there is an interactive dynamic at play in this component of the policy climate. Furthermore, ideas come in two interrelated forms. On the one hand, ideas are cognitive constructs that inform our logical understanding of a particular phenomenon, thus providing "the recipes, guidelines and maps for political action and serv[ing] to justify policies and programs by speaking to their interest-based logic and necessity."[45] On the other hand, ideas are also normative constructs made up of attitudes, identities, and values, which together form the backdrop of debates by sketching out the parameters for what actions are to be regarded as legitimate and acceptable.[46] A prominent and familiar example of an ideational trend will help clarify the significance of ideas as a key component of the policy climate – that of neoliberalism.

As a package of ideas about the most appropriate and effective relationship between the state and the market, neoliberalism took hold in the last two decades of the twentieth century, replacing the Keynesian consensus that had been forged during the postwar period.[47] To account for declining revenues and slowing economic growth, neoliberals implicate government deficits and social spending as key impediments to economic development. Among its many prescriptions, neoliberalism calls for greater reliance on market forces rather than state intervention to govern economic activity. It emphasizes the benefits of private investments, market deregulation, state decentralization, and reduced state intervention; these hallmarks of neoliberalism have been advanced by conservative governments around the world.[48] This example reveals the ways in which ideas can shape and condition the content of policy proposals and the articulation of particular goals and objectives that a given polity is considering.[49] Moreover, as advocates and entrepreneurs, actors can deploy ideas that leverage ideational trends, using them as a bulwark to advance preferred options as they attempt to shape policies in particular ways. Jane Jenson, for example, in her assessment of change in citizenship regimes, argues that all countries were pressed to make adjustments "with neoliberal political forces operating both within and from outside the country ... [and] there was a move away from the policies and practices of the three decades after 1945."[50] Alternatively, if new ideas threaten an existing institutional order, actors can mobilize to resist their implementation, as was the case during the 1980s and 1990s with unions, which were threatened by the recommendations of the neoliberal model.[51] Finally, neoliberalism rests on an image that individuals, not groups, are the "building blocks of economy and politics and advocate unmediated relations between individualism and the state."[52] Neoliberalism thus has both cognitive components (the "recipes" or "analytical maps" for action) and normative ones (the values that form the backdrop for debate), and these can become institutionalized through iterative processes influencing the policy-making process. Consequently, to fully appreciate the tenor of the policy climate, we must identify the broader public sentiments, paradigms, and programmatic ideas that prevail at a particular point in time and determine the degree to which the dominant ideas have coalesced into a clear agenda, for this will have an impact on their potential influence on a particular policy sector.[53]

While helpful in terms of describing the structural and ideational components of the policy climate, the precise relationship between the prevailing climate and the subsequent mechanisms of policy diffusion are less clear and have been largely unexplored in this literature. David Strang and John Meyer argue that existing accounts tend to "underspecify the variety of effects that may be induced by interaction and interdependence ... We need, at minimum, to formulate the wider conditions under which expanded social relationships lead to rapid diffusion. In doing so, we call attention to a class of quite distinct factors that act to increase and redirect the flow of social material."[54] My second step in building this analytical architecture thus involves identifying the alternative processes and mechanisms that are thought to encourage the movement of policy ideas across concentration gradients, or in scientific parlance, identifying the carrier molecules of facilitated diffusion and systematically connecting them with the active characteristics of the policy climate.

Mechanisms of Policy Diffusion

Diffusion is thought to advance through four primary mechanisms: coercion, competition, learning, and emulation.[55] Coercive diffusion occurs when powerful actors intentionally influence weaker actors to adopt their preferred policy, either through direct action or mediated through an organizational structure. Diffusion through competition takes place when states (or other political communities) vying for investments or other types of market shares systematically match the policy choices of another player to ensure that they remain attractive to potential investors. Learning, defined as a change of beliefs or the development of new beliefs, skills, or procedures as a result of experience and the identification of best practices, can also generate policy diffusion.[56] The final channel of diffusion is emulation, which is grounded on the conviction that while actors should determine best practices they cannot accurately determine whether one option is conclusively better than another. When making decisions, moreover, actors have a tendency to turn to others in a self-identified peer group who are perceived as legitimate to help inform their choices. Emulation thus offers shortcuts to reduce the costs of information gathering and sidestep the task of acquiring complex technical knowledge that another individual (or community) already has.

Saying that actors and polities are interdependent and connected does not help us understand why they look to one another when making decisions and what may encourage, privilege, or generate certain types of diffusion mechanisms over others. The incentives and conditions that underpin these alternative processes must be specified, and we can start with coercion. Coercion has the most obvious causal force. A strong actor intentionally imposes its preferred option on others, through either direct or indirect measures that often rest on material implications. Direct coercion includes such things as physical force or sanctions, while indirect coercion includes monopolization of information and experts or ostracism.[57] The coercive enforcer is thus the primary causal factor. The forces of competitive diffusion are slightly less tangible than the clear epicentre of the dominant actor in coercive diffusion. Theories of competition (the preferred approach of many federal scholars)[58] start from the premise that equilibrium can be achieved among the members of a pertinent group. However, one member of the group can destabilize that equilibrium if it introduces a change that is more appealing for potential investors, triggering a chain reaction that causes others to follow the leader. The incentive thus turns critically on how the change affects the receipt of a particular market share. Both of these mechanisms tend to flourish in environments comprised of vertical networks that link unequal agents in relations of hierarchy and dependence where a powerful or stronger agent can compel certain preferred activities or lead a policy agenda.

Causal forces in learning are empirically more difficult to pin down. In his seminal work on social policy, Hugh Heclo wrote: "Governments not only 'power'...; they also puzzle. Policy-making is a form of collective puzzlement on society's behalf; it entails both deciding and knowing."[59] Heclo's work on British and Swedish social policy led him to conclude that specific policies have not emerged exclusively from material conditions, interests, or particular power brokers. Rather, political interactions of individuals generate processes of social learning that produce changed patterns of collective action. Learning is based on the assumption that actors treat the decisions of others as experiments whose outcomes provide useful information. Because information is costly – which highlights the potential material aspects of learning – decision makers have an incentive to gather knowledge from other communities and draw from their experiences when weighing prospective choices.[60] Many learning theorists thus draw upon a largely rational model of decision making, where actors have access to considerable information and weigh their options according to ranked preferences in an effort to maximize the realization of particular goals informed by the logics of instrumentality and consequences.[61] Since Herbert Simon, scholars have increasingly recognized that actors are bound by certain restraints as they lack complete information or unlimited time and are restricted by routines "based on interpretations of the past more than anticipations of the future."[62] Boundaries on rationality mean that diffusion through learning is more likely to occur among actors who share a common set of beliefs based on internally defined criteria for evaluation, common projects, and shared normative commitments.[63] This bounded interpretation of policy learning nevertheless remains rooted in the premise that individuals make choices based on their perceptions of the consequences they face in the pursuit of largely material interests.

Beyond the internal motor of learning where actors are motivated to seek examples and evidence from others, researchers also implicate epistemic communities and knowledge regimes as crucial to diffusion. An epistemic community is defined as a network of knowledge-based experts or organizations with an authoritative claim to policy-relevant knowledge.[64] Knowledge regimes, moreover, are comprised of the actors, organizations, and institutions that produce and distribute knowledge; they include scholarly research units, advocacy research units, party research units, and state research units.[65] Policy actors who draw from a common epistemic community or knowledge regime are thus exposed to similar lessons and evidence; engagement in these communities or regimes thus subsequently propels the diffusion of ideas across jurisdictional boundaries.[66] These communities of experts are nested in turn within wider groups of policy communities or "all actors or potential actors with a direct or indirect interest in a policy area or function who share a common 'policy focus,' and who, with varying degrees of influence shape policy outcomes over the long run."[67] Where members of an epistemic community are presumed to remain somewhat objective and personally disinterested in the particular outcomes of the policy sector, as noted earlier, a policy community refers to the full spectrum of groups, including those that may have a particular stake in the sector. A tangible example will help clarify this distinction. In education, members of the epistemic community include academic researchers at universities or independent task forces, such as Royal Commissions, created to study the system on the government's behalf, while the policy community includes teachers' federations, trustee associations, and parental groups. Both types of groups can fashion horizontal networks that transcend political borders and potentially amplify interprovincial learning through ideational exchanges.

Emulation involves the "social construction of appropriate behaviour, where actors model their conduct on the examples provided by others."[68] The evidence that can be brought to bear on emulation is the least tangible of all the diffusion processes. According to Michael Howlett, emulation "is more difficult to trace, since there generally is neither a record of conquest nor a formal treaty … and its origins are more difficult to understand since there is not necessarily any conscious recognition by governments or other policy actors."[69] Indeed, choices that emerge from emulation are often "based on fads, revered exemplars, or abstract theories, rather than solid evidence."[70] Some causal forces can nevertheless be distilled.

Simmons and Elkins suggest that the decisions of one government produce externalities that take an ideational form influencing the decisions of other governments and operating through the "more subjective pressures of prevailing global norms."[71] When a consensus emerges on a particular subject, such as human rights or environmental protection, there are reputational payoffs for making certain choices. "Governments," Kurt Weyland observes, "dread the stigma of backwardness and therefore eagerly adopt policy innovations, regardless of functional needs."[72] This means that governments are often sensitive to the number or proportion of countries that have adopted a particular stance. Captured in the idea of "thresholds" or "tipping points," these effects tend to be amplified within self-identified peer groups, with actors integrated in a common network or knowledge regime, including those who share language, history, religion, or a general psychological proximity. As a consequence, actors will tend to emulate others in their own peer group and downplay the examples of outsiders, which may generate unique patterns of policy diffusion that can be tracked over time.

Presenting learning and emulation as distinct processes nevertheless raises a number of pertinent questions. How do we know empirically when the process is emulation as opposed to learning? When actors or organizations emulate the actions of others, have they not also learned from those others? What distinguishes a "fad" from "solid evidence"? Simply put – when one emulates, does one not also learn, to some degree; and when one learns, does one not also emulate? The roots of the strict demarcation between learning and emulation seem to lie in debates between rationalists and constructivists and the distinction between objective and subjective knowledge. Students of rational choice have already acknowledged that actors use heuristics and other shortcuts when making decisions, thus blurring the line between learning and emulation.[73] Moreover, from James March and Johan Olsen, we know that actors are motivated by both the logic of consequences and the logic of appropriateness, which signals that actions are driven by more than estimations of strictly material consequences.[74] Those working with an ideational approach also implicate both cognitive and normative ideas as crucial aspects that shape policy making. Finally, a growing number of researchers dedicated to bridging the gulf that has traditionally separated these approaches argue that we must combine the influences of material incentives and ethereal ideas as shapers of policy behaviour.[75] Building upon this work, it therefore seems more productive to view learning and emulation as points on a continuum, instead of retaining the strict demarcation that may compromise empirical study.[76]

At this point, a particular myopia in the diffusion literature needs to be addressed. Students of diffusion tend to view intergovernmental organizations as a platform for coercion, as a producer and advocate of specific policy prescriptions and paradigms, or as a passive venue for ideational exchanges enabling diffusion through emulation or learning.[77] Inspired by the work of Elinor Ostrom, I would like to offer an alternative interpretation of the potential impact of these organizations that generates an additional channel of diffusion. Intergovernmental organizations can encourage diffusion through cooperation.

Ostrom set out to unravel the ways in which people can resolve problems of common pool resources and challenged the efficacy of the three most influential models of collective action, namely, the tragedy of the commons, prisoner's dilemma, and the logic of collective action.[78] While differing in many ways, these three models nevertheless offer a common recommendation for resolving problems of common pool resources: an external Leviathan to manage supply, to maintain credible commitments, and to oversee reliable monitoring process. Her work, however, focused on unpacking the strategies deployed in specific communities to resolve these problems of collective action through self-governing institutions rather than by resorting to a Leviathan identifying a set of design principles that appear in successful management institutions. These design principles include clearly defined boundaries, congruence between rules and local conditions, collective decision-making arrangements as opposed to hierarchy or veto rules, collective monitoring arrangements, and a right for all participants to organize free from external authorities.[79] Intergovernmental organizations in federations have the potential to achieve many of Ostrom's design principles and to help substate actors resolve problems of collective action to build policy frameworks.

Motivated by a desire to coordinate group activities, substate actors can establish intergovernmental organizations to create a venue with formal rules of decision making to reduce transaction costs and possibly provide a strong framework for constituent members to cooperate.[80] When supported by an active secretariat, an intergovernmental organization can facilitate collective action, policy harmonization, and the ratification of comprehensive agreements, thereby intensifying the interdependence among the constituent groups. Whereas diffusion through the other channels generally adheres to a linear chain of leader–follower–laggard, cooperation involves constant exchanges and interactive effects as actors work together to fortify common goals, cultivate common strategies, and ratify collective agreements, thereby creating new contours in policy systems. For those engaged in the process, moreover, the interaction may generate policy learning in areas beyond the particular initiative. However, in this instance, learning is a by-product rather than the result of deliberate action. This suggests that diffusion processes are not always easily isolated and that more than one process can be at work at any given time.

To recap, diffusion occurs through the interactions among state and non-state actors situated in particular contexts. These actors, moreover, are not isolated from one another. Instead they are located within a climate of interdependence and connectivity comprised of both structural and ideational components. Moreover, the characteristics of the policy climate influence the processes of diffusion. Hierarchical relations among pertinent actors are likely to privilege coercion and competition; horizontal relations greased by cultural affinities and an interconnected policy community are likely to privilege learning; formal organizations can foster cooperation. With these conceptualizations of interdependence and connectivity, combined with the refinement and specification of the causal processes of diffusion, we can now begin to consider the plausibility and potential of each of these processes in the context of Canadian education and start making connections to the active policy climate. The intention here is to develop some initial propositions to guide the subsequent historical analysis of the evolution of Canadian education policy. It begins with coercion.

Considering Diffusion in Canadian Education

Given the institutionalized configuration of the education sector, it is unlikely that coercion has played a large role in the movement of educational policies across the provinces. In fields where the federal government is an active player (health, for example) coercive mechanisms are more readily apparent. The autonomy enjoyed by the ten provincial governments over elementary and secondary education, however, precludes the mechanism of a powerful actor intentionally influencing weaker ones towards a preferred policy option. There is scant evidence, moreover, of larger provinces attempting to unilaterally impose their will on the smaller provinces to propel education in a certain direction.

Furthermore, unlike organizations such as the World Bank, the International Monetary Fund, and the OECD, intergovernmental organizations like the CMEC and the Council of Atlantic Ministers of Education and Training (CAMET) neither develop nor promote specific policy packages for provincial policy makers, instead leaving that to the representatives themselves. The characteristics of both the sector and the organizations that operate within it thus reduce the likelihood that coercion is the primary causal process of interprovincial policy diffusion.

Despite the limited potential for coercion, it would be rash to disregard it entirely here. The federal government maintains its spending power, which is a powerful lever to deploy to encourage certain policy activities. We must therefore be attentive to any instance when the federal government intervened with its spending power as a potential occasion of coercion, where particular mandates were installed that the provinces were in effect required to follow. Later in this book, in the empirical chapters, two questions will need to be answered: How frequently did the federal government use its spending power? And how effective were its efforts?

Students of federalism often implicate competition as the key driver of intergovernmental policy dynamics. According to this analysis, the mobility of both individuals and capital induces interjurisdictional competition in various policy fields, including taxes, environmental policy, and welfare standards. Michael S. Greve writes that "the citizens' ability to vote with their feet and to take their talents and assets elsewhere will discipline government in the same way in which consumer choice, in nonmonopolistic markets, disciplines producers."[81] Competition has been extensively examined in areas of regulatory and redistributive policy; how will it influence choices in a sector that is largely developmental?

Competition may drive jurisdictions to increase or decrease their investments in the education sector so that they remain competitive with their neighbours. Competitive pressures may also stimulate increases or decreases in the standards for teacher certification, a regulatory component of the sector. The spread of curriculum and assessment policies may also be driven by competition, given that a challenging program and high results on universal assessments could signal to investors the presence of a well-educated workforce and in this way contribute to capital investments.

The salience of competition nevertheless turns on three conditions. First, diffusion through competition presumes that citizens (as investors) pay close attention to education policies and are willing to move between provinces when changes are made. Second, it assumes that citizens move between provinces at a considerable rate, or at least enough to encourage governments to change their policies for fear that out-migration will irreparably reduce the province's population. Finally, competition suggests that citizens are themselves intimately aware of and understand the policy differences among the provinces, so much so that they are willing to relocate in pursuit of better education systems, thus forcing their home government to respond to ensure their continued residency. But, as Kathryn Harrison writes, "the credibility of the threat that an actor will relocate in response to provincial policy differences will depend on both the costs and the benefits of relocation to that actor."[82] Given that the prominent actors in question for education are families and not firms, the high level of mobility necessary to engender effective competition is rendered less likely "given the resource constraints and familial and social ties."[83] Consequently, these conditions may somewhat mute the direct impact of competition in education.

The competitive model theorizes that provincial decision makers are constantly racing one another for individuals, goods, or investments in zero sum games. By contrast, models of learning portray decision makers, policy experts, stakeholders, and citizens as information seekers.[84] In Canadian education, when one province introduces a policy, others may gradually consider it and decide to implement a similar program, making certain adjustments to tailor the strategy to local needs and conditions. Various formal and informal networks in the policy community, including those among education professionals, government officials, and elected politicians, can facilitate the movement of information across provincial borders as policy actors draw lessons from one another. This implies that engagement in such networks increases policy learning. And because learning can be interactive, actors from the innovating jurisdiction may use new information from the followers to further evaluate the workability of the strategy in their own jurisdiction. Therefore, jurisdictions that follow a leader are not simply free riders poaching ideas from their counterparts; rather, they may contribute to the collective knowledge of the attributes and benefits of a given policy, cascading its benefits through the individual systems.

Nevertheless, this kind of cross-pollination of ideas may not always appear evenly among the ten provinces. Observers of Canada have long emphasized the importance of regionalism, with certain provinces aligning together and others more hesitant to collaborate.[85] The Atlantic provinces, for example, are often regarded as a self-identified internal peer group within the federation because they share certain historical and cultural affinities that have tightened their bonds. This in turn may increase the extent of interprovincial learning and emulation among the provinces in this group. Quebec, alternatively, may emphasize its differences from the other provinces and resist certain types of collaboration, particularly in curriculum, which by nature is culturally sensitive. Consequently, variations in the cultural bonds among the provinces may generate distinctive patterns of policy learning, with certain provinces drawing more lessons from within particular groups than from across the country as a whole.

The final channel of diffusion is cooperation, which is most likely orchestrated under the auspices of formal intergovernmental organizations. Likely outcomes of diffusion through cooperation include formal harmonization of procedures or policies among the participating actors, pooling of resources to enhance limited capacities, and the establishment of shared programs in a policy sector. Curricula could be harmonized to elevate efficiency and standardization of course materials, interprovincial assessments could be created to provide comparable data regarding student achievement across the provinces, and teachers' certification requirements could be standardized to ensure common qualifications and ensure the mobility of labour among the jurisdictions. Furthermore, we can expect some form of intergovernmental organization providing an institutional memory and easing transaction costs to be a precondition for cooperation. The CMEC and the CAMET may prove to be pivotal in the realization of this diffusion process.

The diffusion literature combined with my own reflections on the implications of intergovernmental organizations reveals a series of channels or processes that have the potential to propel interprovincial policy exchanges in the active climate of interdependence and connectivity. While coercion and competition tend to be the dominant channels in the prevailing research on policy making in federations, I have suggested that learning is the most likely process at work across the spectrum of policies in the Canadian education sector, supplemented by cooperation when formal intergovernmental organizations are established. At this point, however, it remains unclear how diffusion can lead to interprovincial policy similarity. Every diffusion process has the potential to generate increased similarities and differences, for actors can choose between following the options of others and taking an alternative path.[86] Thus, the final task for completing this analytical architecture is to identify the pathways and conditions that increase the probability of substate policy similarity and the realization of policy frameworks. This brings us to the literature on policy convergence.

Pathways and Conditions for Convergence

Understanding convergence, or the "tendency of societies to grow more and more alike,"[87] involves examining the similarities in goals, policy content, instruments, outcomes, and styles, both within and among political communities. While the definition of convergence seems straightforward, its causes remain opaque.[88] Despite "enormous research efforts, it is generally acknowledged that we still have a limited understanding of the causes and conditions of policy convergence."[89] In fact, many of the causes of convergence overlap with those implicated in policy diffusion, and what are regarded as distinct processes in one literature are sometimes conflated in another. Therefore, instead of settling on a specific set of causal factors that consistently lead to convergence – which is akin to tilting at windmills – we need to accept the realities of equifinality and multicolinearity to account for policy convergence across political systems. This means reducing the emphasis on parsimony in explanations and recognizing that similar policies can arise from different combinations of factors influenced by the specific contexts in which they occur. Moreover, it encourages the development of a probabilistic model where we can relax standards to include causes that are "usually" or "almost always" necessary or sufficient.[90] Put together, this lends itself to identifying certain pathways and conditions that are more or less conducive for policy convergence. The paragraphs that follow present three pathways for convergence and outline a series of conditions, initially quite broad before narrowing, with the focus on the attributes of policies themselves that are likely to either help or hinder the achievement of interprovincial similarity.

In their work on cross-national policy developments in Canada and the United States, Keith Banting, George Hoberg, and Richard Simeon have identified three pathways to policy convergence, which can also be applied within a federal country.[91] First, interprovincial convergence can result from parallel factors that are internal to the particular political communities without reference to the relations that may exist among them. Jurisdictions that face similar problems (i.e., a population boom, an aging society, or pollution) and that experience similar public pressures may end up adopting similar solutions without any external influence either directly through interdependence or more indirectly from other forms of connections. Second, building upon theories of diffusion, Banting, Hoberg, and Simeon recognize that convergence arises from learning: "in this context, governments continually learn from one another, and the policies of two countries can converge if one country adopts the policies of another because it finds the program and experience of that country attractive."[92] The third and final pathway is a result of interdependence among political communities. If, for example, identified goals are unattainable in the absence of coordinated action, the policies that emerge are likely to exhibit interjurisdictional convergence as those communities seek to achieve both individual and collective benefits.

These three pathways to convergence are filtered through the existing conditions or specific contexts of the individual jurisdictions. Institutional features, characteristics of the policy networks, the internal ideational context, and the prevailing educational regime are all conditions that shape the likelihood of interprovincial policy convergence.

The most significant insight from new institutionalism is the recognition that the macro-political institutions of a jurisdiction provide certain opportunities and constraints for policy actors. In his analysis of economic policy making in Britain and France, Peter Hall, for example, contends that

> the view from the Elysée is not the same as the view from Whitehall. The range of customary policy instruments at hand and the kind of societal resistance to be expected in the face of a given policy vary according to organizational differences that affect the perceived costs and benefits of policy in many issue areas.[93]

The institutional context shapes the policy process by establishing the rules and norms for policy formulation, development, implementation, and assessment. John Campbell and Ove Pedersen have also implicated political institutions as a key variable that shapes policy-making regimes for a society.[94] Parliamentary systems, like those of the Canadian provinces, are said to afford considerable autonomy to the political executive, who are often supported by an extensive, permanent, and highly professional service.[95] Similarities in the macro-political institutions among different communities, moreover, will likely generate similar policy processes as they adhere to a comparable logic of policy formulation. As a result, interjurisdictional macro-institutional comparability can install strong incentives to put in place common practices and strategies that fit within the prevailing institutional configuration, thus encouraging convergence and the emergence of a policy framework in a federation.

The literature on policy communities also suggests that networks shape the prevailing relations between public and private actors in various systems, thus influencing the degree of state strength in a given policy sector. Recognizing this fact, Michael Atkinson and William Coleman made the cogent observation that "the matter of state strength cannot be settled by an appeal to constitutional norms, the embeddedness of the party system, recruitment practices or the degree of state centralization."[96] Rather, we need to determine the degree to which decision-making power is concentrated in the hands of a relatively small number of officials and the degree to which these officials are able to act autonomously from other actors in the community. Applying this insight to federations, we could anticipate that substate policy similarity may be easier when provincial governing officials enjoy greater autonomy from the policy community, as the scope of authoritative actors is limited and fewer players are involved in the collaborations.

Looking within the jurisdictions themselves, diffusing ideas also encounter internal normative and cultural characteristics within each province. Ideational features are likely to influence the goals that decision makers intend to pursue and the content of the policy itself. Furthermore, actors from different jurisdictions who share ideational proclivities, such as cultural characteristics and value sets, may be more willing to look within their particular subgroup when developing new strategies. Alternatively, interjurisdictional variations in "collectively shared expectations"[97] may generate policy heterogeneities, thus increasing differences among the jurisdictions and potentially stymieing the emergence of a policy framework as elected and appointed officials tailor programs to fit with particular characteristics of their respective populations. Finally, decision makers may decide to deploy alternative implementation strategies, depending on the cultural dispositions and traditions of their populations. Policies, and the processes by which they unfold, are thus influenced by contingent internal ideational characteristics of the various jurisdictions. The result is that the probability of policy convergence is mediated by the internal ideational contexts of each of the pertinent political communities.

Finally, the specific educational regime that is operating within the province also influences the likelihood of policy convergence and the gradual formulation of a potential policy framework. Ronald Manzer defines an educational regime as including "the establishment of institutions and procedures for educational governance, allocation of public authority, and style of public decision making as well as the design and implementation of educational programs."[98] Regimes are said to establish actor expectations in a given issue area over an extended period of time. More than temporary arrangements, regimes embody some sense of general obligation that compels certain behaviours, establishes the mechanisms by which policy-relevant ideas are generated, and involves "implicit and explicit principles, norms, rules, and decision-making procedures around which actors' expectations converge."[99] In this way, the configuration of the educational regime establishes certain parameters for action that influence behaviour. Stability, however, must not be conflated with immutability. Changes in rules and decision-making practices can alter the dynamics within regimes, while changes in principles and norms can propel a change in the regime itself. Those who benefit from the current configuration of the regime, moreover, are constantly working to maintain their position and its formation. Those whose interests and aspirations either are not being met or are being compromised by the regime are constantly jockeying for change. Therefore, the active educational regime shapes but does not determine possibilities for policy convergence.

Now that we have fleshed out the macro- and meso-level conditions for convergence, the question remains as to why some policies are taken up by jurisdictions while others are left to languish. For Kingdon, the answer lies in the entrepreneurs who attach solutions to identified problems, overcome constraints within the policy system, and take advantage of "politically propitious events," which include changes in governments, focusing events, and shifts in public opinion.[100] But while managing to get items on the active policy agenda, entrepreneurs often fail to successfully implement their preferred strategy. Characteristics of the proposed policies themselves, the interactions of proposed policies with both the internal context of the jurisdiction and the broader policy climate, and the machinations of the actors also affect subsequent outcomes and the potential for policy convergence. Here, Peter Hall's concept of viability can be used to understand why some policy prescriptions gain more currency than others.[101] According to Hall, the viability of a proposed policy – and concomitantly the likelihood of its subsequent adoption – turn on (a) the alignment between the idea and the problems of the day, (b) its fit with historical and administrative experiences, and (c) the support that is given by relevant authorities to the proposed policy.

The "problem viability" of policies refers to the apparent capacity of a proposed policy to rectify a pertinent set of concerns. In education, a policy proposal must resonate with the problems of the day in a particular jurisdiction. Moreover, Hall argues that ideas must also be "theoretically appealing," meaning that they correspond in some way to existing doctrines. Beyond corresponding, to gain a modicum of acceptability, policy proposals must be minimally coherent with the existing policy regime. In the education sector, professional research communities in universities and other education associations in the policy community develop and evaluate new ideas. If the strategies are determined to be substantively sound, the members of the policy community may promote the proposal as a plausible option, thus increasing its appeal for decision makers.

"Administrative viability" signals that new policies are more likely to be implemented if they fit with the prevailing administrative traditions, policy legacies, and educational regime of the jurisdiction in question. In education, the relative powers of a department of education, the school boards, and the teachers' associations affect the structural capacity to implement particular policy proposals. Previous policies, moreover, "constitute important rules of the game, influencing the allocation of economic and political resources, modifying the costs and benefits associated with alternative political strategies, and consequently altering ensuing political development."[102] It is here, as Neil Bradford notes, that the potential for "organizational politics to frustrate" policy change is apparent and that "the need for political leadership to channel administrative resources or direct the formation of new capacities" typically arises.[103] This leads to the third component of viability: political appeal.

If an idea gains the support of the relevant policy community or receives positive endorsements from the broader public, it increases the likelihood that politicians will accept the idea. Vivian Schmidt argues, moreover, that when presenting proposals to the public, policy entrepreneurs try to structure and frame the discourse in ways that resonate with the political culture of their target population.[104] A coalition of support can form around a particular proposal, and as more and more individuals and groups support the idea, a bandwagon effect may develop, causing the idea to finally catch on.[105] Actors can subsequently intensify their promotion of a preferred idea to garner the necessary currency to guarantee the successful implementation of a particular policy, acting as entrepreneurs encouraging the diffusion of particular innovations.[106]

One final component completes this analytical architecture. Both Paul Pierson and Jacob Hacker have argued that the timing and sequencing of policy choices carry considerable weight in the configuration, evolution, and adaptation of a policy sector.[107] Reflecting on the supposedly universal process of urbanization, Charles Tilly writes: "How cities grow and gain importance in any particular setting depends significantly on earlier urban experience in the same setting ... What has happened in the past shapes what happens now."[108] Pierson nevertheless cautions us when he says that timing and sequencing do not imply determinism: "It certainly seems plausible that issues of sequencing may be significant without implying that a particular path is necessarily 'locked in.'"[109] Furthermore, in his recent work on welfare state retrenchment in the United States, Hacker contends that, contrary to the common narrative that little change has occurred in America's welfare state, major adjustments have taken place through "a set of decentralized and semiautonomous processes of alteration *within* existing policy bounds."[110] Consequently, Hacker speaks directly to contemporary debates about the nature of institutional change whereby incremental adjustments can produce revolutionary change, and he alludes to the potential cumulative effects that seemingly disparate policy choices can have on an arena as a whole.[111] These insights have been fruitfully applied to sectors as a whole; I argue, however, that to accurately explore policy sectors and the dynamics of policy making in federations, researchers must be willing to deconstruct a sector and systematically identify the various components that, when put together, constitute the whole area under investigation.

Deconstructing a sector allows us to appreciate how choices in one dimension can reverberate across the others, creating occasions for the installation of particular instruments while closing doors on others. Certain instruments and options selected in one dimension of a sector interact with other dimensions, over time acting like a grillwork of gears, installing a certain logic that can come to characterize the sector as a whole. In the previous chapter I broke the education sector down into five dimensions, outlining the various debates and programs that decision makers and members of the policy community consider as they endeavour to build their schooling systems. Among the potential effects, instrument choices in various dimensions of the education sector influence the degree of centralization of authority in the hands of state actors; they also condition the degree of state autonomy and capacity over a particular sector. Both are concomitantly anticipated to influence the plausibility and likelihood of inter-state activity.[112] Breaking down a policy sector into its individual components thus allows us to gain traction over complicated fields while simultaneously allowing us to better appreciate interjurisdictional similarities and differences in programs and strategies.[113]

Putting It All Together: A Model of Action for Policy Frameworks in Federations

By combining insights from theories of diffusion and convergence and weaving them together with the threads of institutionalism, we can develop a model of action to explain how and why seemingly independent provinces can overcome the problems associated with collaboration and collective action and develop a coherent policy framework. Anchored by the ideas of interdependence and connectivity, situations of mutual dependence and interstitial tissues fashion pathways through which policy ideas are exchanged among jurisdictions. When combined with the prevailing ideational trends, these structural links create a policy climate within which policy exchanges occur. Certain types of pathways, moreover, are anticipated to privilege particular processes of diffusion. Although coercion and competition tend to dominate accounts in the federalism literature, I have argued that learning and cooperation could be the crucial drivers in the case under investigation here.

Policy diffusion nevertheless does not necessarily lead to interprovincial policy convergence. Instead, three pathways – parallel problems, intentional exchanges, and interdependence – can lead to convergent results. These pathways are mediated by the internal contexts of each jurisdiction, within which certain scope conditions influence the probability that interprovincial similarity will arise. The wider institutional and cultural context influences the potential adoption of ideas from other jurisdictions, and the greater the similarities, the more likely that comparable practices will be adopted. Also, the internal configuration of the educational regime at work in each of the provinces sets down certain parameters by establishing expectations and legitimate behaviours in the policy field. The character of the regime thus influences whether a policy idea from another jurisdiction will be accepted and successfully implemented in another.

These scope conditions help us establish the structural probability that an idea from one jurisdiction will be adopted and successfully implemented in another. We have also seen that characteristics of the ideas themselves affect the prospects for interjurisdictional convergence. From Peter Hall, we know that ideas must demonstrate problem, administrative, and political viability to be seriously considered by actors engaged in the pertinent sector. If an idea from another province meets these conditions, the likelihood that it will be adopted will increase. Finally, policy choices across the different dimensions of a sector itself can engender a certain logic, furthering or hindering the achievement of an overarching policy framework in a federation.

The next four chapters trace the historical evolution of the provincial elementary and secondary education systems in order to examine how changes in the policy climate influenced the processes of policy diffusion and how relations among the provinces interacting with the internal contexts within each jurisdiction affected the probability of policy convergence and the subsequent emergence of a meaningful education policy framework. The story begins in 1840, when the colonial governments of the territories of British North America made their first forays into the education arena.

4 Founding and Consolidating Provincial Schooling (1840–1945)

The rich possess ample means to realize any theory they may chuse to adopt in the education of their children, regardless of the costs; but it is not so with him whose Subsistence is derived from industry. Attention to this as a primary object, ignorance, and incapacity, often prevent his having proper views on the important subject of education, and when he has, slender resources as often prevent their being reduced to practice; yet, among this class of men, are found many who are not only useful members, but ornaments of society: and from the labours of these it is, that the public derive the conveniences, and many of the comforts of life: but while they are toiling for the production of those comforts, their children are left destitute of a suitable education. Therefore, it has long been acknowledged, that education, as it respects those who are unprovided with it, ought to become a national concern.

Joseph Lancaster, 1803

From the 1840s to 1945, the period during which public schooling was founded and consolidated in Canada, provincial officials, experts, and stakeholders looked around for models and examples of viable practices with which to build their respective education systems. While departing from markedly different starting points, by the middle of the twentieth century, seven of the nine provinces had converged on a common model of central administration; all had adopted a similar means to finance the sector; the majority were using comparable curricula at the elementary level; and all the provinces were using the same model of teacher training. There was a lack of formal structures and robust institutionalized mechanisms to facilitate the process, yet intermittent and irregular learning enabled policy diffusion across the provinces. Faced with common problems, and situated in comparable policy climate, many of the provinces converged on similar sets of policies. This fashioned the early skeleton of what would gradually evolve into the Canadian education policy framework.

Despite these notable steps towards the establishment of a policy framework, in 1945, two important differences nevertheless remained in place that undermined comparability across the country and compromised the achievement of an equal system of education for Canadian citizens from coast to coast. Regarding the organization and management of the sector, certain provinces and Newfoundland continued to deploy alternative models of central administration; at the same time, the spread and institutionalization of secondary education was sporadic at best. Understanding the roots of these differences will further our appreciation of the dynamics of policy making in federations, for they signal that institutional and cultural factors within each province can have significant effects on the implementation of policy ideas that come from beyond provincial borders. As such, these discrepancies will help us unravel the aspects and attributes that impede the penetration of common goals or instruments and the factors that contribute to the clustering of similarities; we will also be able to start appreciating the ways in which the internal policy context of each province interacts with the wider policy climate, thus shaping policy activity.

Before we delve into the narrative, a clarification is necessary. Throughout this period, only nine of the eventual ten provinces were formal members of the Canadian federation, for Newfoundland joined only in 1949. However, even though Newfoundland remained outside the formal structures of interdependence and connectivity that bonded the provinces together, the colony had early on begun sending out tendrils to the Canadian education policy communities. Furthermore, policy choices made by colonial governors during this period established important legacies that would shape what later became the provincial elementary and secondary education system. For these reasons, the history of Newfoundland's educational development is included in this chapter.

The Policy Climate

Before the 1800s, education was largely seen as a privilege of the aristocracy and as a bastion of religious orders. Over the course of that century, however, a revolution occurred and the idea of mass public education began to take root across northern Europe and its colonial offshoots.[1] A common set of ideas emerged that were driven by three goals. The first of these was the achievement of basic literacy for all citizens, regardless of religious background or residency in a particular territory. A growing number of educational advocates believed that to accomplish this objective, the state needed to take control of scholastic institutions and extend educational opportunities to the entire polity, thereby ensuring that everyone obtained a basic grasp of reading, writing, and arithmetic. The second objective centred on mitigating the influence of religious authorities in general schooling. An expanding number of political leaders saw the value of public education as a tool to further social cohesion, foster a collective identity, and encourage economic growth, thereby consolidating the state's authority. Third and finally, as expounded in the writings of intellectual leaders such as Alfred Marshall,[2] education was increasingly recognized as a crucial instrument for ameliorating economic disparities among the classes. While initially embryonic, these three goals provided the ideational foundation for the prolific expansion of mass education throughout the nineteenth and twentieth centuries.

In 1867, four colonies became permanently connected under the British North America Act (later renamed the Constitution Act, 1867). This act solidified two core ideas. First, citizens of the signatory colonies would be able to move freely throughout the new federated state; and second, the agreeing parties would fashion an economic union in order to collectively secure social and technological advancements that would be otherwise unattainable. The act thus created the conditions for legal and economic interdependence, binding the constituent units together through certain powers and responsibilities. Originally involving Ontario, Quebec, Nova Scotia, and New Brunswick, over the next decades the scope of the Constitution Act, 1867, gradually expanded to include the vast majority of the territory north of the 49th parallel.

Sections 92 and 93 of the Constitution Act, 1867, allocated the responsibility for education to the provinces – an arrangement not unanimously desired by the Fathers of Confederation. In fact, during the negotiations that preceded the agreement of 1867, early listings of federal powers included the authority to enforce uniformity in education.[3] In the final version of the text, however, control of education was given exclusively to the provincial legislatures, subject to certain restrictions. Constitutional guarantees were extended to religious minorities (Protestant and Roman Catholic) that had already been operating public schools in certain colonies and could be institutionalized in new provinces should those governments chose to do so. Specifically, Section 93(1) reads: "Nothing in any such Law shall prejudicially affect Right or Privilege with respect to Denominational Schools which any Class of Persons have by Law in the Province at the Union." Ottawa thus became the sentinel to protect denominational control in the new Canadian state, and this stipulation established a lasting policy legacy for educational administration in some provincial systems – namely, a parallel administrative structure to govern separate denominational schools. Records from the day indicate that this stipulation in Section 93 was an indispensible condition to secure the agreement of the original signatories to Confederation. As one of the Fathers of Confederation, Sir Charles Tupper, declared to the federal Parliament in 1896:

> I say with knowledge that but for the consent to the proposal of Mr. Galt, who represented especially the Protestants of Quebec, and but for the assent of that conference to the proposal of Mr. Galt, that in the Confederation Act should be embodied a clause which would protect the rights of minorities, whether Catholics or Protestants, in this country, there would have been no Confederation.[4]

In addition, certain classes of people were excluded from the provincial jurisdiction: Ottawa was entrusted with providing education for Aboriginal Peoples who lived on reserves and for children of military personnel who lived on bases.

The conceding of education to the provinces stemmed from a series of institutional and cultural realities that were at work across British North America. First and foremost, institutions providing embryonic forms of elementary schooling pre-dated Confederation; the nascent education systems of the colonies were in a chrysalis stage. Statutes authorizing grammar schools in districts and counties had by then been enacted in Upper Canada (1807), Nova Scotia (1811), New Brunswick (1816), and Prince Edward Island (1825). In 1824, under the Fabrique School Act, Lower Canada had authorized each parish corporation to devote one-quarter of its budget to the founding and maintenance of schools. The individual colonies involved in the Confederation negotiations already had their own schooling arrangements and did not wish to have a common system unilaterally imposed from above by decision makers based in the new country's capital. Any leader who wished to centralize education in federal hands thus faced stiff opposition from entrenched (and empowered) interests. Throughout the negotiations, moreover, political elites well remembered the disastrous attempt to create a common education system in a united Canada (what had previously been Upper and Lower Canada – or in contemporary parlance, Ontario and Quebec) between 1840 and 1866.[5] And, perhaps most importantly, many around the negotiating table understood full well that education has a powerful cultural component. Provincial control over education was thus of special importance not only in French-speaking and Catholic Quebec but for other colonial representatives as well. For these three reasons, the Fathers of Confederation ultimately decided to place education under provincial control, subject to the aforementioned stipulations.

The provinces had been placed firmly in charge of the educational welfare of their respective populations. This, however, did not prevent Ottawa from trying to influence the educational policy choices of certain provinces. As Canada expanded westward, the national Parliament attempted to play a meaningful role in some of the early decisions about public education in what would later become Manitoba, Saskatchewan, and Alberta. Among other things, Section 93 of the Constitution Act, which stipulated that the "educational rights and privileges of religious minorities, enjoyed 'by law' prior to Confederation or granted by the province after the date of union, would be protected from invasion by any acts of the provincial legislature,"[6] provoked a bitter controversy in the new provinces of western Canada. This differentiated the policy climate for decision makers in those regions from that of their counterparts in the rest of Canada.

After Confederation, the top priority for political leaders was the creation of a pan-Canadian economy. Spearheaded by federal Prime Ministers John A. Macdonald and Wilfrid Laurier, federal policies to achieve this end included national tariffs, railway construction, and the encouragement of immigration to populate the western territories and consolidate Canadian sovereignty from coast to coast.[7] Industrialization furthered the demand for educated citizens, and provincial officials needed to find ways to satisfy the growing needs of their respective populations. The wheat boom at the turn of the nineteenth century, moreover, brought new waves of settlers to the West: "Sons and daughters of the Maritimes and Central Canada migrated to the plains and built up the West, thus forging innumerable links between the older Canada and the new."[8] Internal migration and the development of the country's infrastructure strengthened the economic and social connections among the provinces. This enabled Canada to enjoy considerable economic growth in the early 1900s. Industrialization also heightened the demand for a better-educated citizenry, and as a consequence, schooling was a consistently high item on provincial policy agendas.

Prosperity, however, was not unending: in the 1930s, a global economic collapse and a massive drought shook the country. The economic calamity of the Great Depression quickly replaced the prosperity of the early twentieth century. The rapid economic downturn revealed specific weaknesses in the Canadian federation: the vulnerability of the provincial fiscal systems, and the federal government's reluctance to relieve provinces in financial straits or compensate them for regional disparities.[9] Economic austerity did much to slow the expansion of provincial schooling systems, and in the years to come this would lead to some important differences, particularly in the area of secondary schooling.

In 1891, education professionals from a number of the provinces convened in Montreal to launch a new initiative. Over the course of the proceedings, the group issued the following declaration:

> In the opinion of the representatives from the difference provinces of the Dominion present, it is desirable that an association for the teachers of the Dominion of Canada should be formed and called the Educational Association of the Dominion of Canada.[10]

This declaration set the stage for Canada's first interprovincial organization for education. Stated the first chairman of the DEA:

> The circumstances of our union as one country have rendered it impossible for the Dominion Government or Legislature to take cognizance to any extent of the matter of education. That affair has been left in our Federal constitution to the wisdom of the different Provinces; but as we all know it will not do to educate the people of Canada as sectionalists or provincialists, the necessity for a general plan of education has made itself felt. If our people are to grow up as members of one common country with a sentiment for Canada common to all, it becomes imperatively necessary that there should be a union of educators, a Dominion association irrespective of race, province, origin, creed or language, in the interest of that unity of our people which alone can be secured by the training of our children not as sectionalists but as Canadians, and beyond this as integral parts of the great empire to which we belong.[11]

Sir William Dawson's comments succinctly captured the motives behind the DEA's creation: to help those who were crafting provincial
education policy develop a coherent system of public education from
coast to coast. Under the terms of the DEA's constitution, any person
with an interest in the work of education was eligible for membership, meaning that the organization included all members of the policy
community: principals, teachers and school trustees, officials working
within the government, and politicians themselves.[12] As a consequence,
state and non-state actors were equally embedded in the management
and operations of the association, with all representatives of the policy
community enjoying access to the agenda, integrated within a shared
organizational framework; this suggests that state actors did not have
clear independence from societal groups as they formulated and pursued policy objectives.

The DEA provided the first arena for government officials of the provinces and non-state policy actors to exchange ideas about the pressing
issues they faced as they developed their budding education systems.
Many members of the policy community felt that for Canadian education to flourish, the federal government needed to be involved. One of
these people was Dr J.M. Harper, a Protestant high school inspector
from Quebec. During his address to the DEA in 1898, Harper urged
Ottawa to establish a national Department of Education modelled after
the US Bureau of Education, responsible for such things as improving
and coordinating the various schooling systems, collecting documents
on education, preparing annual reports and gathering statistics, disseminating new educational innovations from other countries to the
provincial governments, and publishing addresses and conference proceedings.[13] Other members of the DEA agreed with Harper's position
and throughout the early 1900s used the association as a platform to
encourage Ottawa to create a national Department of Education.

This position, however, was far from unanimous, and the fallout
from the DEA's requests for federal intervention was particularly dramatic in some quarters of the policy community. The response from
Harper's francophone colleagues in Quebec was especially succinct:
"the establishment of a federal department is neither constitutional nor
desirable," argued Boucher de la Bruère, Chief Superintendent of the
province's Catholic Committee. Once it became clear that the DEA was
going to advance such a proposal, francophone representatives from
Quebec completely withdrew from the DEA, refusing to support any
initiative involving the federal government on the grounds that such

activity would infringe on their constitutionally guaranteed autonomy in the field. As a result, the francophone sector of the province isolated itself from the activities of the country's other education systems. Fortunately, this separation was only temporary. In 1918, the DEA saw the return of the French-Catholic representatives when it was reconstituted as the Canadian Education Association (CEA) and any and all proposals for a federal Department of Education were permanently dropped.

Throughout this opening period, the activities of the CEA were haphazard at best. According to Freeman K. Stewart, a long-time director of the CEA, the association's capacity was hindered by three factors.[14] First, the CEA lacked a clear focus due to the multitude of interests that were welcomed as members. Second, despite the inclusive membership criteria, representation from all the provinces was rarely obtained because cross-country travel presented a considerable obstacle for many would-be participants. Third, and perhaps most importantly, the CEA lacked a permanent secretariat; this exacerbated the two other problems Stewart identified. Without a permanent staff, the association's capacity to systematically gather and disseminate information evenly and consistently across the country was markedly restricted.

To ameliorate these shortcomings, at the CEA's convention in 1934, representatives from across the country agreed to create a committee to systematically identify the educational problems that were common across the provinces so as to better focus the organization's efforts. At the same time, the CEA's executive decided to rotate future meetings to different areas of the country with a view to encouraging underrepresented regions to strengthen their engagement with the association. Furthermore, the CEA's influence began to extend beyond Canadian borders when, in 1938, Newfoundland asked to join the association even though it was still a British colony.[15] The reason for this request was straightforward: officials there knew that joining the CEA would increase Newfoundland's educational assets by providing access to new policy expertise as well as solid points of comparison with which to measure the colony's educational advancement. It would also, perhaps, further the cause for reform on the island. The other provinces willingly accepted this new member, and the constitution was amended to change the CEA into the Canada and Newfoundland Education Association (CNEA).[16]

In spite of all these advances and marked organizational progress, the CNEA never established a permanent secretariat to manage the association's affairs, and this weakened its capacity to regularly disseminate ideas across the provinces and coordinate policy activities. It seemed that the provinces lacked sufficient financial resources to invest in and support an intergovernmental bureaucracy. Furthermore, while its inclusive membership practice permitted the discussion of a wide array of educational issues, the CNEA's omnibus configuration afforded scant opportunity for particular interests to press specific agendas. As a consequence, by the beginning of the twentieth century, province-wide associations for teachers and trustees were beginning to crop up.[17]

Starting within their own provinces and then branching out to form interprovincial associations, teachers and school trustees founded organizations to articulate their interests, exchange ideas, and stimulate discussions of educational methods and practices. In July 1920, representatives of various provincial teachers' federations held the inaugural meeting of the Canadian Teachers' Federation (CTF).[18] Three years later, trustees from Ontario, Manitoba, Saskatchewan, and British Columbia founded the Canadian School Boards Association (CSBA). These groups further linked the provincial education policy communities by sponsoring conferences, conducting research, and comparing the various provincial systems.

Along with increased legal and economic interdependence and organizational connectivity, evidence of cultural ties began appearing among the provinces. Interprovincial migration, such as the aforementioned flows to the Prairies during the wheat boom, saw groups of people socialized in one setting carry their ideas about and expectations for educational programs to other parts of the country. This did not signal the emergence of a pan-Canadian identity, however. In Quebec, cultural connectivity was bifurcated, with English-speaking Quebecers looking to the other provinces while French-speaking Quebecers focused on their own denominational system. At the same time, the three Maritime provinces were exhibiting deeper cultural ties as a regional group. This development was neatly encapsulated by New Brunswick's Chief Superintendent of Education at the opening session of the DEA:

> These three Provinces facing the Atlantic Ocean are in one sense which cannot apply to any other group of Provinces of the Dominion. Geographically, historically, traditionally, in sentiment we are very intimately connected, and though we have our little rivalries, and taunt each other occasionally as to the relative merits of our respective towns – of the amount of fog or ice in the Bay of Fundy or in Chebucto's famous harbour

– yet after all, these are only little family jars, which show our kinship to the race and help to intensify the family attachment.[19]

Provincial interdependence and connectivity thus underwent a remarkable metamorphosis between 1840 and 1945 through the development of a federal union that was political, legal, and increasingly social. With the exception of Newfoundland, which had long resisted the overtures of Canadian politicians to join Confederation – even going so far as to lyrically warn, "come near at your peril, Canadian Wolf"[20] – the independent colonies and separate territories had become formally connected under the terms of the Constitution Act, 1867. Political leaders and education stakeholders created organizations to raise the profile of educational issues and advance the cause of public schooling within their respective borders. Interprovincial organizations were eventually created to connect the nascent policy community, a development driven by emerging ideas of national political identity and by the members' desire to learn from one another; in this way, the first education network was fashioned. Finally, while cultural bonds increased among the jurisdictions through interprovincial migration, distinctive identities and regional particularities remained. As these bonds developed, policy leaders became committed to the idea of universal public education for all. The impulse to establish a form of public schooling that reached all citizens served as a common goal that all the members of the policy community made efforts to achieve. In this way, the policy climate of British North America transformed itself from a weakly linked chain of autonomous colonial governments into a fledgling multilayered network stretching from coast to coast. It was within this changed policy climate that developments in provincial educational policy occurred.

Establishing Central Educational Administration

Throughout the colonies of British North America, one-room schools had been meeting settlers' basic educational needs since the 1700s. Run primarily by religious orders and occasionally managed by local community leaders, these rudimentary institutions pioneered the Canadian educational enterprise. By the 1840s, colonial officials had begun to see the importance of education and a small group of political elites had started advocating for public control over schools. The political leaders of the day could have chosen to end the practice of local control and centralize all authority in the state's hands.[21] However, officials in British North America preferred to conserve the tradition of local administration, for three reasons.

First, maintaining some form of local control was less politically contentious than eliminating it unilaterally. Local leaders enjoyed the trust of their communities and would have resisted any attempts by remote officials to centralize educational administration. Furthermore, assertions of public control were highly divisive, due in no small part to the composition of the Canadian population. Historian George Weir wrote in 1934: "When it is remembered that the population of Canada is, in the main, composed of two racial groups, corresponding roughly to the two great branches of the Christian faith, one can readily understand why racial and religious considerations should have been important factors in determining the fundamental School Law (Section 93, British North America Act)."[22] Weir then observed that the debate in Canada over the nature of instruction and whether it should be imparted through secular or religious organizations "proved to be a subject of unremitting and ... acrimonious discussion."[23] Preserving the tradition of local school boards helped somewhat to dampen the debate by deflecting exclusive attention away from central provincial administrators.

Second, local boards bring government closer to the people, further entrenching democracy while simultaneously divvying up administrative burdens. This allows some degree of flexibility and decentralization in the system. The idea is that smaller communities can influence the direction of their schools through locally elected trustees, thus helping ensure that education policies respond to local needs and conditions. And in functional terms, local boards release the central government from tasks such as hiring teachers, purchasing textbooks, erecting buildings, and collecting local revenues for school operations. All of these things, at the time, were viewed primarily as matters of local control.[24]

Third and finally, the colonies were sparsely populated, and communications within colonies were poor. This rendered the complete centralization of educational administration a practical impossibility. For political, administrative, and practical reasons, all of the colonies thus converged on the common practice of maintaining local school boards to administer public education. Local boards were aligned to conditions within the colonies and were sufficiently viable that political leaders allowed them to continue.

Setting aside this interprovincial convergence with regard to local administration, the provinces differed greatly in terms of how they organized their central authority over education. Here, four models jockeyed for dominance during the foundation and consolidation of education in Canada: civic trusteeship, religious trusteeship, collective ministerial responsibility, and individual ministerial responsibility.[25] A comparative analysis of the development of these four models reveals competing pressures for convergence and divergence. As this chapter endeavours to demonstrate, the logic embedded in the common macro-political structure at work in each of the provinces – specifically, parliamentary government – exerted a powerful incentive for policy convergence on a particular model of central educational administration, namely, individual ministerial responsibility. However, variations in the internal characteristics at work within each jurisdiction generated countervailing pressures that influenced the patterns and timing of the accession of ministerial responsibility and the extent to which policy similarities emerged. The story starts in Ontario and the creation of civic trusteeship.

Few figures in Canadian educational history stand taller than Egerton Ryerson. Believing that educated citizens were the "best security of a good government and constitutional liberty" and that ignorant individuals were destined to become "the slaves of despots and the dupes of demagogues," Ryerson wished to fashion an education system "established by Acts of our Provincial Legislature ... in which the different bodies of the clergy will not interfere – a system which will bring the blessing of education to every family."[26] Motivated by the conviction that the achievement of a good society rested upon civil and religious liberty for all its members, Ryerson wrested control over education from the churches and placed it in the hands of a secular council in Upper Canada known first as the General Board and later as the Council for Public Instruction.

The General Board had the authority to draw up schedules of instruction, establish qualifications for teachers, and designate textbooks and curricula.[27] Local school boards, comprised of elected trustees, were responsible in turn for the day-to-day operations of the individual schools. These trustees could hire teachers who met provincial qualifications and select texts from the provincially sanctioned list, and they were to ensure that their schools were governed according to provincial regulations. To maintain a connection between the local boards and the central administration, the General Board appointed superintendents to oversee the actions of the elected trustees. These superintendents served as the "crucial supervisory link between the central authority and the local trustees."[28]

Upper Canada's Act for the Establishment and Maintenance of Common Schools (1843) put in place secular civic governance led by the Council for Public Instruction, non-denominational common schools, and separate schools for denominational minorities – in this case, Roman Catholics. At first blush, this last seemed to contradict Ryerson's own views:

> Sectarianism is not morality … To teach a child the dogma and spirit of a sect, before he is taught the essential principles of religion and morality is to invert the pyramid, – to reserve the order of nature, – to feed with the bones of controversy instead of with the nourishing milk of truth and charity.[29]

Yet as Chief Superintendent, Ryerson supported the right of Catholics to operate a parallel school system, and he defeated a number of government-led efforts to abolish or undermine the separate school system.[30] However, these denominational schools still fell squarely under the purview of the Council of Public Instruction; thus, they were subject to the same rules and regulations as the common schools, including those relating to curriculum protocols, teacher training, and funding requirements.

Ryerson's model of civic trusteeship set the example for the rapidly developing systems in most of western Canada. As one school inspector wrote: "In seeking the origins of our patterns of school administration in Canada, we must turn first to the Province of Ontario. This province, originally known as Upper Canada, has been a laboratory for the development of the Canadian government, both local and national."[31] Furthermore, because the territorial administrators for the Northwest Territories imported Ryerson's model, separate schools managed by Roman Catholic authorities gained constitutional protection in what would become Alberta and Saskatchewan. The result was the entrenchment across the prairie provinces of a particular policy legacy: religious education subsumed beneath a secular system. Not all provinces, however, followed the route of civic trusteeship.

Flowing against the tide of secularism, Newfoundland instituted a system of religious trusteeship and conferred the responsibility for education to ecclesiastical leaders. This policy was driven by pragmatism. For much of Newfoundland's history, the British government had regarded the island not as a colony but as a summer fishing ground. As a consequence, Newfoundland was not offered the aid or attention that the other mainland colonies enjoyed.[32] The settlers' educational needs thus were met solely by religious orders, with little intervention from secular leaders or government officials. The result was that the island colonists broadly accepted denominational control as legitimate. The Education Act of 1843 partitioned trusteeship in the colony of Newfoundland among a number of Christian faiths.[33]

Quebec, too, rejected civic administration, creating a dual confessional system to administer education. According to Groulx: "Respect for confessionalism and liberty, keeping politics out of education, this is what characterizes educational legislation in French Canada since Confederation."[34] The political salience of religious authority in Quebec was in part a reflection of the cultural battle between francophones and anglophones in the province. Ecclesiastical leaders from the Catholic Church asserted themselves as the protectors of French culture and appropriated control of educational affairs for that portion of the population; meanwhile, the minority anglophones entrusted their educational interests in the Protestant Church while hoping to follow in Ryerson's footsteps and establish civic leadership.[35]

In 1869, the Council of Public Instruction took control of schooling in Quebec and partitioned it along denominational lines. The result was a "dual hierarchy headed by a common superintendent, with separate Roman Catholic and Protestant secretaries who were responsible respectively to the Roman Catholic and Protestant committees of the Council of Public Instruction."[36] The accession of religious control marked a victory for the religious and linguistic forces that wished to preserve the isolation between the English Protestant and the French Catholic populations. By the end of the nineteenth century, public education was run by two boards, "functioning side by side but rarely touching, each governed by its own administrative apparatus and distinct philosophy, and each serving different clientele."[37]

Manitoba also followed the path of religious trusteeship for central educational administration; but there, in contrast to developments in Newfoundland and Quebec, external forces in the form of the national Parliament played a role in the initial adoption of this arrangement, and the results were substantially different. When the federal government officially recognized Manitoba in 1870 as separate from the Northwest

Territories, its demographic characteristics were similar to those in Quebec. The province was linguistically and religiously divided between French Catholics and English Protestants, with the Red River serving as a border between the two communities. The federal government had a significant stake in Manitoba politics and sought to influence its early policy choices.[38] Spurred on by Ottawa, in 1871 the Manitoba government passed the Act to Establish a System of Public Education in Manitoba, modelled specifically on Quebec's system rather than Ontario's. But in Quebec there was a long-established consensus on religious trusteeship; the situation in Manitoba was more dynamic, and this generated considerable conflict, culminating in a pitched and protracted battle known as the Manitoba Schools Crisis, which divided the province's population along religious and linguistic lines.

The 1871 legislation created twenty-four school districts, half of them considered Protestant and half Roman Catholic. Interprovincial migration patterns and federal immigration policy in the 1870s, however, had a dramatic impact on Manitoba politics (see Appendix 5). A large Ontario-born population entered Manitoba determined to "develop institutions consistent with those they were familiar with"[39] and began pressuring the provincial government to change the existing schooling system. The new migrants also included Jews, Mennonites, and Icelanders, who also upset the prevailing demographic balance between francophones and anglophones and Catholics and Protestants in the province.[40] The numbers from the decennial census of 1891 speak for themselves. Of the total population of 108,017, only 7,555 were born in Quebec while 46,630 were born in Ontario; Roman Catholics totalled only 20,571, less than one-fifth of the population.[41] By 1890, there were 629 districts under the Protestant sector of the Board of Education and only 90 under the authority of Roman Catholic ecclesiastical leaders. This numerical imbalance reflected the massive transformation in the Manitoba population.

Linguistic and religious polarization was ignited by key events in the 1880s. The Métis Rebellion in 1884 and the execution of Louis Riel in 1885 – with his subsequent honourable burial in the Cathedral at St Boniface – further accelerated administrative reforms in the province.[42] As one writer of the day described it, "rancour ... had been aroused in this dispute by the stirring up of religious animosities by the Orange Lodges and certain Protestant speakers throughout the Dominion," who argued that the "Roman Catholic schools were almost completely under control of the Church," which were only fostering "French ideas and aspirations ... to the almost entire exclusion of those that are British. The student of English was rare in the French schools."[43] Another wrote: "The clerical papers, after their usual fashion, denounce the P.P.A.'s the Orangemen, and the Ontario people generally, and make it appear that dove-like peace would reign throughout the land but for their ferocious bigotry"; he described the movement to secularize education as "supported by all the Satanic elements."[44]

Finally, educational outcomes from the time were indicating that the quality of education in Roman Catholic schools lagged substantially behind that of schools in the Protestant system. Provincial politicians grew aware of the growing inequalities between the Catholic and Protestant systems: "the teachers being to a great extent priests and sisters, whose qualifications were unknown outside, while the inspectorate consisted of priests alone. The inefficiency of the system is shown by giving instances of the absurdity of papers set in examinations for teachers' certificates, and by the illiteracy of the French Half-breeds."[45] Clifford Sifton, an Ontario-raised official in the government of Manitoba Premier Thomas Greenway, contended that teacher training in Catholic districts was substandard, noting that illiteracy rates soared among that portion of the population.[46] Under Sifton's leadership, the Greenway government began dismantling religious trusteeship. To quote the premier:

> In 1870 a certain way of life was thrust upon us, when we were still in embryo, not at our behest but to suit the political convenience of Ottawa. Under the Canadian constitution, education is the business of the Province. So let it be. Dual schools and dual language we find a nuisance, and we will have none of them.[47]

In 1890, the Manitoba legislature passed two new statutes to establish a system of free schools and institute a regime of educational governance closer to that of Ontario than of Quebec. Schools would be non-sectarian, and by regulation, only those schools conforming to provincial standards would receive public funding. In other words, if Roman Catholic authorities chose to continue providing religious education in schools, they would be deprived of public funding, while still being taxed to support the non-sectarian system.

Education historian Charles Sissons has written that the new act was "like the scorpion." The "sting was in the tail," in that the last section read, "In cases where ... Catholic school districts have been established ... such Catholic school districts shall ... cease to exist."[48] The new legislation quickly became the subject of prolonged litigation, with protracted battles both between different segments of the Manitoba population and between the Manitoba government and the federal Parliament. The French-Canadian minority in Manitoba challenged the act of 1890 in the courts on the grounds that it prejudicially affected the status of their denominational schools. The courts, however, ruled that the imposition of additional financial burdens did not constitute an infringement on the educational rights of the group, and the secularist desires of the Manitoba government ended up winning the day.[49]

How can the history of religious trusteeship in Newfoundland, Quebec, and Manitoba be explained? And what insights can be drawn from that history? First, while Newfoundland and Quebec pursued the same policy, there is no evidence that decision makers in those jurisdictions were inspired by or informed about the other's actions; this suggests that each decided independently to pursue the strategy of religious trusteeship. This in turn empirically supports the argument that parallel problem solving can lead to convergent outcomes. The early history of education governance in Manitoba also generates an important finding. Initially, the federal government attempted to drive the configuration of public schooling in the province. Perhaps it might have succeeded except for the massive transformation in the province's demographics – ironically, a transformation generated in part by federal immigration policies whose intent was to encourage new settlers to move to the province. This transformation, combined with the politics of language and the glaring failures of the Catholic system, motivated decision makers to break the shackles placed on them by Ottawa and pursue their own educational destiny. Coercion, it seemed, could not install a lasting legacy; Ottawa's option failed to prove itself viable in the changing province, whose leaders decided to learn other lessons and follow Ontario's lead.

As civic and religious trusteeship advanced in some areas of Canada, the Maritime colonies took a different path. The colonies on the Atlantic coast were among the oldest in North America and the sites of the earliest evidence of government action in education in the New World. Like political leaders in Ontario, elites in these colonies favoured secular control of education. But in contrast to Ryerson and his followers, the policy actors in this region decided to adopt a political rather than a civic model of educational administration. Nova Scotia provides a useful illustration of the arrangements in the Maritimes and the factors that led to its configuration.

Political officials in Nova Scotia, the first colony to achieve responsible government in 1848 "not by rebellion or revolt, but through evolution,"[50] viewed British institutions positively and wished to preserve their influence. In 1864, the government created the Council of Public Instruction with the premier as president and the Executive Council as members. In doing so, Nova Scotia became the first jurisdiction in North America to adopt a system of collective ministerial responsibility for educational administration. The two other Maritime colonies followed soon after, thus institutionalizing this administrative system in eastern Canada.

Maritime officials found certain features of collective responsibility appealing. Because all of the Executive Council as a collective oversaw education, the model shielded any one particular individual from powerful denominational forces that wished to challenge public control of schooling.[51] Maritime officials also realized that, given that the Executive Council was already compelled to meet, it was more economical to entrust the responsibility to them instead of calling upon a second civic group to dedicate their time to the sector. The New Brunswick Attorney-General articulated this precise argument when, after reviewing the systems of educational administration in Nova Scotia and England, he observed that if a Board of Education were a civic body made up of individuals from across the province, members would need compensation for their travel throughout the year, which would unnecessarily drive up the cost of education.[52] Finally, proponents of collective ministerial decision making argued that the committee system would help control the costs of education and limit the potentially unpredictable and rapid increases that could result if a single individual were responsible for education.[53]

Until the end of the nineteenth century, provincial educational policy across Canada was developed under the administrative arrangements of civic trusteeship, religious trusteeship, or collective ministerial responsibility. Soon after, however, a new model emerged that most provincial leaders would eventually accept. Once again, it was Ontario's – and Ryerson's – actions that instigated change.

Notwithstanding the advances made through civic trusteeship, this model of central educational administration had some crucial shortcomings. Under Ryerson's regime, the Chief Superintendent could circumvent elected officials by applying his regulatory powers. Indeed, during the 1860s, Ryerson used these powers to pass a series of unpopular education policies.[54] His actions generated resentment among his supporters and heightened mistrust among his opponents. Making note of the superintendent's autocratic powers, Premier Oliver Mowat sought to reduce that position's autonomy in order to ensure that all decisions flowed through the cabinet and the legislature.[55]

Civic trusteeship also conflicted with the rules of parliamentary democracy. Under the rules of procedure, only a cabinet minister is allowed to answer questions directly on the floor of the legislature.[56] Bureaucrats are shielded from public scrutiny in order to preserve the principle of administrative autonomy. The Chief Superintendent was therefore unable to answer questions or respond to critics in the public forum. Ryerson himself admitted that this lack of accountability was a serious weakness of the post and that the only possible remedy was to create the position of Minister of Education.[57] Ryerson's retirement in 1876 opened a convenient window of opportunity for the Mowat government to abolish the Chief Superintendent position and create the post of Minister of Education, who would be directly responsible to the legislature.[58]

By the turn of the twentieth century, all of the provinces west of Ontario had established the post of Minister of Education. Thus, there was a convergence on the model of individual responsibility. In contrast to the pattern of rapid transformation in Ontario, however, when moving away from civic or religious trusteeship the western provinces opted to shift incrementally towards individual ministerial responsibility by way of collective ministerial responsibility. The logic of this choice was straightforward. Just as it had in the Maritime provinces, the collective model offered useful protection from the heated opposition of entrenched civic and religious interests (especially in Manitoba). Nevertheless, the legacy of collective responsibility was short-lived west of the Red River. Political leaders were heavily influenced by Ontario's choices and subsequently adopted individual ministerial responsibility as the preferred mode of central educational administration.[59]

East of the Ottawa River, the accession of individual ministerial responsibility was delayed. Prince Edward Island and New Brunswick only gradually abandoned their preferred system of collective ministerial responsibility in the 1930s and 1940s, leaving Nova Scotia as the sole adherent to this British tradition. Also, Newfoundland and Quebec maintained their systems of religious trusteeship. Much is revealed by an analysis of these important variations. How can we unpack the politics of administrative change, and what insights can thereby be distilled?

While viable in the context of parliamentary government, the model of collective ministerial responsibility suffered from a particular deficiency that limited educational expansion. Under the administrative arrangement, the sector lacked a clear advocate at the cabinet table, and since decisions were reached through consensus, proposals were often watered down to satisfy the interests of all those involved. The result was that education spending systematically lagged in the Maritime provinces, regardless of economic growth overall, and it was difficult to encourage progressive change.[60] Occasionally, provincial superintendents attempted to take a greater leadership role and encourage innovation; these efforts, however, were often slapped down by the Executive Council, as New Brunswick Superintendent Marshall d'Avery discovered when he found himself dismissed "because of his progressive and enthusiastic advocacy of public schools and replaced by the brother of Charles Fisher, the new government leader."[61] This model of central educational administration thus dampened the internal capacity of these provinces to pursue innovative policies and foster growth in the sector.

As the public grew more vocal in its demands for quality education, the effectiveness of collective ministerial responsibility decayed. Indeed, this problem was a key catalyst for change, as demonstrated by New Brunswick's *Annual Report*: "The most forward step taken [for the province] was the appointing of a Minister of education in the person of Honourable A.P. Patterson ... Under his efficient administration and competent leadership, progress will be made."[62] And when reporting on the policy change, the Dominion Bureau of Statistics signalled its approval: "Educational interests will thus have a special representative in government the way that they have in most of the other provinces."[63] So, while New Brunswick and Prince Edward Island lagged behind the provinces west of the Ottawa River, they nevertheless eventually followed the path blazed by Ontario because a system that provided for an individual Minister of Education was determined to be the best practice for educational administration. What were the conditions in the three remaining holdouts?

In Newfoundland in the 1920s, there were faint indicators of a willingness to change when the colonial administration attempted to create a Department of Education. Unfortunately, by this point, the churches had deeply embedded themselves in the system, and they succeeded in resisting this attempt to establish public control of the sector. The department was abolished in 1927 and replaced by a Bureau of Education similar to Quebec's Council of Public Instruction. With some adjustments, this model fit well with the province's prevailing religious traditions. Meanwhile, in Nova Scotia and Quebec, the different models of educational administration showed no signs of weakening. Indeed, administrative reforms in those two provinces would not gain prominence on the policy agenda until later, when internal conditions in those two jurisdictions became more conducive to policy change.

Financing Education – Who Should Pay and How?

Early in Canadian history, the costs of education were borne primarily by parents. This was sometimes offset by small government subsidies to deprived families or by piecemeal grants to individual schools. Teachers levied fees on students and were allowed to increase rates if attendance dropped. Poor families often covered their fees through goods, such as rum or shoes, or services, such as hauling hay for teachers. The effects of these fiscal policies "were vicious."[64] The provision of schooling was highly unstable because schools would periodically close throughout the year due to insufficient funds. Teachers were typically impoverished, as they often accepted goods for which they had no need. Conditions for teachers in rural areas were particularly grim, which made it difficult for local officials to attract and retain viable candidates.

Lacking financial levers, the provincial governments could exert little influence over educational affairs. Any effort to mandate common policies and uniform standards without providing some regular financial support challenged the accepted notions of legitimacy:

> No legislature could pursue this fiscal policy [of non-regular or irregular support] with respect to schools and at the same time require all children to attend schools, prescribe teachers' qualifications and class size, and make the many other mandatory provisions which make up the typical provincial schools acts and regulations.[65]

If elected and appointed officials wanted to regulate education, so the reasoning went, the state would have to provide stable financial backing.

As the goal of free and common elementary education gained currency throughout the 1800s, provincial officials and education leaders needed to find a means to stabilize funding for the schools.[66] During the

1840s, recommendations were made in the three Maritime assemblies for general tax assessments to ensure that all families, regardless of economic standing, could send their children to school. That same decade, in 1841, Judge Charles Mondelet of Quebec wrote a number of letters to the government requesting permanent government aid for education and that local taxation for public schools be introduced. Also, school trustees in Toronto pressed for public funds on the grounds that free universal education would benefit the city by "withdrawing from idleness and dissipation a large number of children who now loiter about the streets or frequent the haunts of vice, creating the most painful emotions in every well regulated mind."[67]

Policy actors debated the merits of alternative fiscal frameworks, and the terms of this discourse were neatly captured in the Ontario legislature.[68] In the 1830s, William Buell, Jr, of Brockville placed a proposal before the legislature that would have financed local school administration through central grants. He hoped to create a system of full state funding that would centralize the responsibility for education financing and provide all local boards with equal access to comparable levels of funds. Mahlon Burwell of London, however, opposed Buell's proposal on the grounds that it would increase the influence of the central government and reduce local control. Burwell called for a system of local taxes, similar to the one he had observed in New York. Under this configuration, local boards would have the right to set and collect property taxes to finance and administer the education system, which would be regulated by the central government. Local tax assessment would encourage parents to send their children to school as well as stabilize school finance.

Burwell's argument eventually won the day, and all the provinces converged on the second model of education finance. This interprovincial convergence can be attributed to the viability of the policy idea in the policy contexts within each province. By establishing a stable and relatively consistent source of revenues, local taxation offered a practical solution to the problem of irregular funding for public schools. Moreover, as Burwell had argued, universal property taxes would encourage parents to send their children to school, given that they were being forced to contribute regardless of attendance. Local property taxes were therefore seen as an effective and viable means to achieve universal elementary education. Politically, this model was palatable to provincial legislators because it put the often unpleasant responsibility for setting tax rates in the hands of local politicians. Finally, because all the provinces had preserved the tradition of local school boards with elected trustees, the necessary administrative apparatus to operate the model was already in place.

In addition to ensuring congruence between the local taxation model and prevailing problems, politics, and administrative conditions, the system suited the existing cultural traditions of the provincial populations – traditions that were reflected in the Putman Weir Report on BC's schools in 1925:

> In the opinion of the Survey, such a system of centralized [financial] control and administration – for administration and control cannot logically be separated – would be more Prussian than British in its essential characteristics. The enervating effect on our future democracy through the weakening of its powers of local self-government in school matters, with the consequent loss of local initiative and interest in the schools would more than counterbalance any real or imaginary gains from such a dangerous experiment ... The history of education in England, which is more pertinent to British Columbia's case than is that of education in Prussia, affords an answer to the question of financial administration and local control.[69]

Thus, this model of education finance was universally implemented from coast to coast as provincial decision makers, oriented by a common goal – namely, establishing basic education for their respective populations – and situated in similar circumstances whereby education was being administered by local school boards, converged on the system of local taxation.

Given the rapid expansion of public schooling, provincial decision makers realized that local revenues were likely insufficient to cover the full costs of education. As expenditures ballooned, it became apparent that fiscal inequalities within the provinces between urban and rural districts that had varying tax bases were hindering educational advancements. All of the provinces thus decided to supplement local revenues with central grants in an effort to rectify this problem. British Columbia started the practice in 1933 when it introduced a weighted population grant. Based on the recommendations of the Putnam–Weir Commission, the model distributed provincial aid in proportion to a population measure, such as number of pupils, classrooms, or teachers, adjusted according to local resources benchmarked to local property value.

Over the subsequent decade, other provinces introduced similar programs to offset the costs of education. According to a report from the CNEA, practically "all provinces are moving in the direction of larger provincial grants, with a correspondingly lower proportion of educational costs to be carried locally by taxes on real estate."[70] Provincial decision makers were interacting with one another through the embryonic policy network managed by the CNEA. In this way, responding to similar problems and having constructed a similar model of education finance from the outset, all of this buttressed by information exchanges facilitated through the policy community, the provinces uniformly adopted the shared-cost arrangement for education finance.

It is nevertheless important to recognize that while convergence occurred in the content of education finance policy throughout this period, it did not translate into subnational convergence in the levels of investment offered by each of the provinces (see Appendix 6). Significant variations in educational expenditures continued to distinguish the provinces from one another. In 1900, per pupil spending ranged from a low of $7.00 per child in Quebec to a high of $31.00 in British Columbia. By 1945, the gap in educational expenditures had widened: Prince Edward Island spent $37.00 per student while British Columbia topped the scale at $107.00 per student. These variations in educational investments contributed to substantial differences in provincial capacities to expand their educational programs; they were a particular impediment to the spread of secondary schooling (see below).

Fashioning Curriculum

Provincial policies for elementary school curriculum converged early on. Because most of the provinces had claimed a strong role in administration and had regularized funding for the education systems, central officials were able to influence the course content required in public schools. Furthermore, all demonstrated a commitment to the traditional orientation of education, structuring the universal curriculum around the goal of ensuring that students learned the "3 R's" – reading, writing, and arithmetic. By 1910, all of the provinces except Quebec and Newfoundland had adopted an eight-grade elementary system with children organized into homogeneous groups.[71] In his review of Canadian education at the end of the First World War, Peter Sandiford remarked that "the courses of study [in elementary schools] throughout any province is remarkably uniform. The department of education takes pride in making it so."[72] Visitors from the United States and the United Kingdom were similarly astonished at the influence of central authorities over curriculum content. Indeed, in the United States, centralized curriculum at the state level was virtually inconceivable as local authorities retained complete control over course standards and offerings.[73] How did such a rapid convergence emerge among eight provinces, concomitantly contributing to the establishment of a policy framework across those jurisdictions, while two provinces took different routes?

Three factors encouraged these results. First, regarding the variations between Quebec and Newfoundland and the rest of the provinces, there were ideational differences between civic and religious leaders regarding the purpose and goals of elementary education: the former supported mass literacy for all, while the latter continued to promote a more elitist conceptualization of schooling. Catholic ecclesiastical leaders were particularly oriented towards preserving the elitist understanding of education, favouring boys over girls and well as the sons of privileged families who could access prestigious employment opportunities after successfully completing high school.[74] Quebec and Newfoundland demonstrated greater curricular differentiation from the other provinces in part because religious leaders controlled the administration of the sector.

Second, in the provinces that accepted the idea of mass education, the necessary administrative structures had been erected to oversee the expansion of public schooling and decision makers had tied funding to local adoption of mandatory courses of study. Here we begin to see how policy choices in one dimension of education reverberated in others, resulting in a particular logic. Individual schools or districts that attempted to diverge from the prescribed curriculum were deemed ineligible for public funds either by provincially appointed superintendents or by representatives from the Departments of Education. Because provincial decision makers had installed a shared model of education finance, they had the necessary levers to compel local boards to adhere to centrally preferred curricula.

Furthermore, provincial officials targeted textbooks as a key instrument to ensure uniformity and standardization. "The variety of textbooks in the Schools, and the objectionable character of many of them, is a subject of serious and general complaints," Ryerson declared.[75] He therefore recommended that the province regulate the textbooks that could be used in schools. Once again, Ontario's influence was keenly felt from coast to coast. Since the costs of publishing alternative text-books were prohibitive, the other provinces tended to use the books that Ontario had authorized.[76] This cost-saving strategy contributed to substate policy convergence.

The third factor was the Dominion Educational Association, which would later become the CNEA. From its inception, a primary goal of the association had been to educate children "not as sectionalists but as Canadians."[77] At all of its national meetings, significant time was allocated to informational exchanges on curriculum, and this exposed provincial educational elites to the programs and practices of their counterparts in other jurisdictions.[78] Because the French-speaking sector in Quebec had withdrawn from the association for much of the period and Newfoundland did not engage with it until the 1930s, education officials in those jurisdictions were excluded from these informational exchanges. This analysis thus supports the argument that both interconnections among jurisdictions and internal characteristics within each jurisdiction affect the diffusion and establishment of policy frameworks.

Interprovincial similarity beyond the elementary level did not unfold so straightforwardly. In Canada's early years, secondary schooling had been reserved for students bound for university. The onset of industrialization, however, created a demand for better-educated workers. In addition, ideas about equality began to change during this period, and education experts began calling for the expansion of advanced schooling opportunities beyond the political and social elites.[79] As a consequence, provinces started experimenting with forms of secondary schooling. Much is revealed from the differences that emerged.

In concert with businesses, education reformers in a number of provinces sought to develop a partite system in which vocational schools would be institutionally and physically separate from academic high schools. The Ontario government spearheaded this movement in 1897 by ratifying the Ontario Technical Education Act, which supported existing secondary schools and encouraged local boards to expand their provision of vocational schooling. This initiative was a key topic at the DEA's meeting the following year, where W.J. Robertson presented the delegates with a detailed progress report.[80] Within a few years, initiatives emulating Ontario's example started to spring up in other provinces. By 1904, for example, with the BC government's support, the Vancouver Board of Education had introduced a commercial program in the Vancouver High School. Then in 1911, the Ontario government passed the Industrial Education Act to expand vocational training to villages and towns; this would become the model for similar legislation in Manitoba, Saskatchewan, and Alberta.[81]

Two structural barriers impeded the proliferation of partite schools from coast to coast. The first was fiscal: many provinces lacked the economic capacity to finance the expansion of secondary education. After reviewing the findings of the Royal Commission on Industrial Training and Technical Education, established by Ottawa in 1913, which included an exhaustive survey of systems in the United Kingdom and continental Europe as well as an audit of existing provincial efforts, the federal government in 1919 attempted to remedy this fiscal impediment by passing the Technical Education Act.[82] Under its terms, Ottawa offered to share up to 50 per cent of the provincial costs for vocational schools by providing grants totalling more than $10 million over a ten-year period; this was the first time ever that the federal government had used its spending power to intervene in provincial education policy. By 1929, however, Ontario was the only province that had used its entire allotment.

The second barrier was the size and capacity of local jurisdictions. Separate partite schools were feasible in large urban centres but completely untenable in most Canadian communities.[83] To make partite schools more viable, some provinces attempted to consolidate school boards to create larger districts that could sustain separate vocational schools. Local trustees and citizens vociferously opposed these proposals on the grounds that consolidation would dilute local power and influence. Furthermore, parents raised concerns about the practicality of transporting students over long distances to attend regional schools, given that country roads were scarce and winters long and harsh. Provincial decision makers failed to mollify these concerns, with the result that successful local board amalgamations were few and far between. So partite schools remained beyond the reach of many Canadian communities.[84] Funding and feasibility problems within each of the provinces thus prevented the effective transplanting of Ontario's innovation from coast to coast; this suggests that those jurisdictions lacked the conditions necessary to expand secondary schooling. Policy divergence in secondary schooling thus arose from differences in the internal conditions of the receiving jurisdictions.

Before leaving this dimension of education policy, it is important to address the state of secondary education in Quebec. In that province, secondary education diverged internally, with markedly different pathways demarcating the Protestant and Catholic systems.[85] Influenced by developments in the rest of Canada because it had remained active and engaged in the DEA, and having a greater tax base at its disposal, the Protestant sector began experimenting with partite and bilateral schools, in this way pulling secondary education towards the public system. Making this easier was that anglophone Quebecers tended to be concentrated geographically. Anglophone Quebecers thus benefited from educational improvements similar to those recorded in the rest of Canada. The Catholic sector, by contrast, was dominated by the clergy, which resisted any proposal to expand secondary schooling beyond the academic stream. Few efforts were made to provide vocational training to francophones, and, as a consequence, the growth of secondary schooling for that community lagged. Secondary instruction remained almost entirely under a system of classical colleges operated by the clergy and oriented exclusively towards the creation of a French-speaking elite. This arrangement "offered little opportunity for the exchange of ideas or for cooperation between two entirely distinct cultural communities."[86] In fact, between 1908 and 1960, the Council of Public Instruction was virtually inactive; the two committees developed and implemented their own programs of study without consulting each other.

This policy divergence translated into significant internal variations in the educational attainments of the anglophone and francophone populations of the province. Up until the middle of the twentieth century, Quebec was reported to have the lowest school attendance among the Canadian provinces; these provincial figures, however, masked a significant internal disparity. A federal study on pupil retention found that Catholic Quebec had the highest dropout rate in Canada and Protestant Quebec the lowest. For every 100 pupils who started the second grade in all provinces, 90 reached grade eight in Protestant Quebec, 90 in BC, 87 in Ontario, 66 in Newfoundland, and just 48 in Catholic Quebec.[87] As the population of Quebec began to industrialize and urbanize in the 1930s, these disparities between the anglophone and francophone sectors would become the focus for major reforms. These changes, though, would not arrive until the 1960s.

Teaching the Teachers and Developing Professional Standards

If there was a unity of feeling, then the same stuff that makes a good teacher in Prince Edward Island is what we want in Ontario; and if we could here by some means ascertain what would be a suitable common standard for all and work up to that standard, then the citizens of Canada would be citizens indeed.

George W. Ross, Ontario's Minister of Education, 1892

Under Egerton Ryerson, Ontario was an early leader in teacher education. In 1847, the province established the Toronto Normal School, the first of its kind in British North America.[88] New Brunswick opened its first teacher training School in Fredericton in 1848, and Nova Scotia followed soon after in 1854. Two years later, Prince Edward Island established its own teacher training program, and in 1857, the Council for Public Instruction in Quebec created two separate normal schools, one for Catholics and the other for Protestants.[89] The speed and consistency in the dissemination of the normal school model among the eastern colonies was a testament to the influence of European traditions in teacher education among the founding provinces.[90]

According to education historian F. Henry Johnson, Ryerson's model of normal schools "set the pattern for elementary teacher-training across western Canada for almost a century."[91] As had been the case with the diffusion of administrative practices, individuals arriving from Ontario were instrumental in bringing the normal school system to the new provinces. In BC, for example, the first Superintendent of Education, John Jessop, had been an early graduate of the Toronto Normal School. As such, Jessop had been inculcated with Ryerson's ideas on teacher education; acting as a classic policy entrepreneur,[92] he had brought them with him to the Pacific coast.[93] By the early twentieth century, the four Western provinces had set up a few normal schools to train teachers.[94]

At this point, we find strong evidence of interprovincial uniformity in the structure and delivery of teacher training. Convergence was achieved through policy learning based on eastern Canada's (and particularly Ryerson's) early lead. While the efforts of individual entrepreneurs were significant, ideas on teacher training were also exchanged among provincial education officials and stakeholders through various conferences organized by the DEA. At the first DEA conference, for example, a key item up for discussion was teacher training, and in 1919, Edmonton hosted the Conference on Teacher Education, which focused on explaining the features and benefits of the normal school system. These conferences bolstered the efforts of individuals who had arrived from Ontario and been appointed to key administrative positions in the new western provinces. Faced with the common problem of developing a strong teaching force, educators in the new jurisdictions looked for inspiration from the provinces with established programs, thus propelling the subnational convergence in teacher training.

Nevertheless, limited resources delayed the establishment of normal schools in the new provinces. To meet their growing need for teachers, provincial officials in the West recruited them not only from the eastern provinces and Great Britain (traditional sources of educators in Canada) but also from the United States.[95] After the western provinces had established their own high schools, governments began using them as temporary training grounds in the hope of reducing their dependence on imported teachers. In his report on public schools in 1874, Jessop wrote that high schools would "do good service as Training Institutes for teachers, till such time as the number of our school districts would warrant the establishment of a Provincial Normal School"[96] in British Columbia. His dream was realized in 1901 when the Vancouver Normal School was opened.

Developments in teacher certification followed a somewhat similar trajectory but with markedly different results. In the eastern provinces, teacher certification initially fell to local school boards, which led to highly incoherent and inconsistent regimes in Ontario, Quebec, New Brunswick, Nova Scotia, and Prince Edward Island. Recognizing this problem, Ryerson implemented mandatory standards for certification in Ontario. Superintendents could issue temporary licences when teachers were in short supply, but permanent certificates were only granted after the completion of a designated training period provided by a provincial normal school. Ryerson's certification model spread quickly across the country as provincial leaders centralized their authority over education. Once again, the DEA played a meaningful role in the dissemination of this practice, highlighting the centralization of teacher certification as a key policy priority for governments to address.[97] In fact, the DEA had been advocating a pan-Canadian standard for teacher certification since 1898 on the grounds that it would bolster the status of the profession.[98]

But centralization at the provincial level and the efforts of the DEA failed to translate into a uniform regime of teacher certification across the provinces. The explanation for persistent variation turns on three factors. First, as noted above, when faced with teacher shortages decision makers often lowered certification standards or offered temporary certificates to unqualified individuals to ensure that schools continued operating. Second, in all provinces, teachers' certificates were divided between elementary and secondary instructors and organized into different classes.[99] This panoply of certification practices was reproduced in each province and was further complicated by the fact that alternative terms were used for comparable positions. Finally, provincial officials were concerned that normal schools in other provinces were not necessarily up to the same standards. Consequently, they resisted recognizing the qualifications of external teachers without reaffirming their knowledge of teaching. These conflicting pressures resulted in a patchwork of certification standards that made harmonization and interprovincial coordination difficult.

Consistent with the patterns that emerged in curriculum, teacher education and certification policies did not follow the same trajectories in Quebec and Newfoundland. Not until 1939 were Quebec teachers required to hold some form of education diploma, and clergy were exempted from this regulation. The few normal schools that had been operating in the province played only a minor role in preparing teachers. Similar conditions were reported in Newfoundland. There being no central Department of Education, the examination and certification of teachers was left to individual boards, and no mention was ever made of training Roman Catholic teachers. The professional advancement of teachers in both provinces thus lagged behind the rest of Canada, exacerbating the disparities in this component of the education sector.

Building the Theoretical Links

Provincial interdependence and connectivity underwent a dramatic transformation during this period. Confederation and its associated political and economic union, as well as internal migration, forged stronger links among the provinces. In the absence of mass communications, policy ideas were literally carried by individuals physically migrating from one province to another. Concomitantly, to bolster opportunities for educational exchanges, educational leaders set up organizations within each province dedicated to the interests of public schooling. These organizations began establishing the infrastructure needed to connect the various provincial policy communities, thus exposing their members to one another's ideas and priorities. The tendrils of the initial policy network were thus established, and relationships between state and non-state actors in the policy communities began to emerge across the provinces. How did these transformations in the policy climate influence the processes of diffusion and the emergence of a policy framework?

By 1945, a number of interesting and meaningful similarities had appeared among the provinces. At the beginning of the period, four models of central administration competed for dominance; by the end, seven of the nine provinces had introduced individual ministerial responsibility to oversee education. The common macro-institutional logic of parliamentary government generated a strong incentive for the provinces to move towards this model of central administration as they drew lessons from one another, enabled through interprovincial migration, comparative studies, and the tendrils of the education policy network. In finance, building upon the legacy of local school boards, all of the provinces encouraged community control by allocating property taxes to the boards; simultaneously, however, recognizing the need to supplement these revenues with provincial funds, they developed shared-cost arrangements to support the expansion of elementary and secondary schooling. What is more, the unanimous consensus over universal elementary schooling set the stage for uniformity in the structure and design of elementary curriculum. These ideationally rooted motivations were further reinforced by a practical challenge: textbooks were both expensive and difficult to produce. It therefore made sense for the provinces to use the same books as a cost-saving measure. Finally, in teacher education, there was marked convergence as the normal school model that originated in eastern Canada was gradually institutionalized in the West.

But the emergence of an all-encompassing policy framework was neither uniform nor complete, and the nuances in provincial policy activity have crucial implications for our understanding of the dynamics of policy making in federations. Because the Maritime provinces had implemented collective ministerial responsibility from the outset, the institutional imperative to switch to individual ministerial responsibility was far weaker there; this accounts for its delayed ascension in Prince Edward Island and New Brunswick. Also, because of material and ideational factors, there was no move to reconfigure educational administration in Quebec and Newfoundland. The other provinces pursued civic trusteeship, which was far more amenable to public control; by contrast, the religious influence dominated in Quebec and Newfoundland, and this embedded alternative norms and practices deep in their education systems. While elementary curriculum was relatively consistent, secondary education displayed considerable variability as disparities in the respective fiscal capacities of the provincial governments and local school boards impeded the advancement of secondary schooling. Many of these differences, however, would be somewhat mitigated as the drive to universalize education up through the secondary level took hold in the coming years and as certain critical changes occurred in the overarching policy climate.

5 Universalizing Provincial Schooling (1945–1967)

The right to education is a genuine social right of citizenship, because the aim of education during childhood is to shape the future adult. Fundamentally it should be regarded, not as the right of the child to go to school, but as the right of the adult citizen to have been educated.

T.H. Marshall

We repeat, at the peril of all Canada, because in these days of mobility of population, the problems created by sub-standard services in one province will inevitably spill over into the other provinces of Canada. As a nation we must assure our youth equality of educational assistance which recognizes the dignity of each Canadian citizen.

Robert Stanfield, Premier of Nova Scotia
Federal–Provincial Conference, 1963

In the aftermath of the Second World War, governments around the world turned their attention to the social fabric of the state. There was a collective sense that the atrocities of the war could not be repeated and a general appetite for increasingly egalitarian forms of state intervention. British social researcher Richard Titmuss eloquently captured this attitudinal transformation:

The mood of the people changed, and in sympathetic response, values changed as well. If dangers were to be shared, then resources should also be shared ... Dramatic events on the home front served to reinforce the war-warmed impulse of people for a more generous society.[1]

Political leaders and policy actors thus began focusing on the creation of a universal safety net to protect all citizens and on cultivating public social programs to enhance the overall quality of life within the state.[2]

Public education became a cornerstone of state-directed endeavours, and there was dramatic growth in schooling systems worldwide. Falling in line with this global trend, educational expenditures in Canada jumped to almost 30 per cent of provincial spending; nearly 25 per cent of provincial populations were in school. Decision makers, stakeholders, and the public all committed themselves to the idea of universal education in the name of social betterment, functional necessity, and economic growth. Structural factors also played a role in the prioritization of public schooling on the public agenda. The postwar baby boom rapidly increased the number of children requiring education, and technological advances continued to fuel demands for highly skilled workers capable of adapting to changing conditions. Added to which, scholars within and beyond Canada's borders were building the links and recognizing the connections between a well-educated workforce and the economy, all the while encouraging governments to invest in what would later be called "human capital."[3]

During this period, the ideas of progressive educationists started to take hold, causing an ideational rift between the traditionalists, who prioritized the "3 R's," rote learning, and memorization, and those who advocated this new educational ethos. Progressivists championed schools as a means to foster future developments and pushed to extend the duration of formal schooling beyond eight years.[4] Inspired by these emerging policy ideas, many components of the policy community demanded a reconfiguration away from the traditional model, instead preferring to see that "each child is exceptional; each poses an educational problem which is, in fact, unique."[5] But in contrast to the consensus that emerged around mass elementary education in the early nineteenth century and the appropriate means to achieve it, the progressive education paradigm did not immediately coalesce around clear policy directives with sufficient political support to establish a common path across all ten jurisdictions.

The bulk of the policy activity between 1945 and 1967 fell into three dimensions of the education sector: administration, curriculum, and initial teacher education. By the end of this period, nine of the ten provinces had a Minister of Education, as the interprovincial learning that had commenced during the foundation and consolidation of elementary and secondary schooling continued. Motivated by similar problems and exposed to similar research, moreover, all of the provinces reduced the number of local school boards. The strategies for consolidating districts nevertheless varied considerably, signalling the institutionalization of different education regimes within the provinces. Finally, all of the provinces attempted to increase the opportunities for secondary education in their respective jurisdictions. Put together, these changes marked major advances towards the achievement of a *de facto* policy framework for elementary and secondary education in Canada.

Despite the convergence in some areas, up through Canada's centennial year, important differences persisted, impeding the consolidation of a clear policy framework in elementary and secondary education. One province, Newfoundland, maintained the tradition of religious trusteeship in central administration. Shared practices in secondary education remained elusive; there was no clear ideational consensus regarding the most effective way to organize high schools, and conditions in the individual provinces did not favour the uniform expansion of secondary schooling. Among other things, this meant that Canadian students from coast to coast were not receiving a comparable education. What is more, the policies for initial teacher education diverged dramatically as the western provinces allowed universities to take control while those east of the Manitoba border continued to maintain normal schools. As a result, teachers were not receiving similar forms of preparation before entering the classroom. Put together, while great strides had been made in the formulation of an active policy framework, the differences that continued to exist meant that Canadians from coast to coast still did not have access to comparable systems of education regardless of their place of residence.

The Policy Climate

The policy climate saw a number of subtle yet significant changes that shaped both the processes of diffusion and the further refinement of the nascent policy framework. Some of the developments had the potential to increase opportunities for interprovincial learning; others initiated countervailing pressures that opened up opportunities for policy divergence and diminished the potential for learning and collaboration. Included in the former category were the formalization of aspects of internationalization, the entrenchment of economic interdependence, the strengthening of intergovernmental organizations, and the institutionalization of other non-state members of the policy community fashioning the initial components of a knowledge regime. Included in the latter category were the absence of clear policy solutions to achieve certain goals, increased friction between Ottawa and the provinces, and the rise of Quebec nationalism, both of which had the potential to disrupt relations among the provinces.

From the violence of the Second World War emerged an international willingness to form organizations dedicated to rebuilding the devastated societies and to facilitating inter-state collaboration around a series of seemingly global aspirations. In 1946, twenty countries, including Canada, ratified an agreement that saw the creation of UNESCO, which was dedicated to helping European countries re-establish their education systems. In 1949, a number of European countries formed the Organisation for European Economic Co-operation (OEEC) to administer the European Recovery Program, colloquially known as the Marshall Plan. In September 1961, the OEEC was superseded by the Organisation for Economic Co-operation and Development (OECD); by then, this body had expanded to include Canada among its members. The OECD's objectives were to create a permanent communications network among the member and non-member states, to strengthen the tradition of cooperation among them, to promote sustainable economic growth, and to identify and disseminate best practices in a variety of policy fields, including education.[6]

As a member of the OECD, Canada was now formally connected to this emerging global network, and this broadened the scope of the domestic education epistemic community. The internationalization of education thus became a formal reality in the postwar era. What is more, because Canada did not have a national Department of Education, the provinces secured an agreement with the federal government to represent Canada internationally.[7] As a consequence, by the end of this period, provincial policy actors' exposure to the international education network had ballooned. But the effects of this exposure would only become apparent in the coming decades.

A reorientation of educational ideas also took root in the postwar period as policy entrepreneurs encouraged decision makers to expand educational opportunities and to remove the persistent barriers separating the classes. In the words of R.H. Tawney: "The intrusion into educational organization of the vulgarities of the class system is an irrelevance as mischievous in effect as it is odious in conception."[8] Building on the works of Rousseau, Frobel, Pestalozzi, Dewey, and Kilpatrick, these entrepreneurs – both within Canada and abroad – called for differentiated curricula as well as for more expansive programming that would include technical and vocational training at the secondary level. The basic prescription offered by these reformers was universal secondary education for all; however, this new goal was not uncontroversial. In the past, there had been unanimity on mass elementary education; this time, in contrast, a consensus on a uniform model for secondary education did not appear, for the traditional partite and bilateral models conflicted with the emerging idea of composite schooling inspired by the progressive ethos. (This will be discussed at length below.) Consequently, there was greater uncertainty in terms of the preferred policy solutions for realizing this new goal of secondary schooling for all.

Moving into the domestic realm, after the Second World War the federal government initiated a number of changes that affected the fiscal interdependence of the provinces. Somewhat contradictory dynamics emerged: some policy choices afforded greater autonomy to the provinces, encouraging decentralization; others inculcated more centralizing tendencies as Ottawa sought to gain more influence in provincial activities in the broader social policy arena. Centripetal and centrifugal forces were thus simultaneously at work across the country.

On the one hand, the federal government revolutionized the system of fiscal federalism in the postwar period, thus reinforcing the economic interdependence of the provinces while paradoxically enhancing the independent fiscal capacities of some jurisdictions. Equalization had been practised informally since Confederation; but in 1957, Ottawa introduced the first formal equalization program. Informed by the recommendations of the Rowell–Sirois Commission, which had been established by Prime Minister W.L. Mackenzie King in August 1937, equalization served as a means to redistribute wealth among the provinces. Its goal was to bring provinces with lower fiscal capacities up to a national average to ensure that they could provide comparable social programs at reasonably comparable rates of taxation. Furthermore, the equalization grants were unconditional, which meant that the provinces could allocate the funds at their own discretion and deploy them wherever they deemed it necessary, free from federal interference. The authors of Rowell–Sirois had explicitly rejected the idea that the federal government should involve itself directly in setting educational standards:

> Our financial proposals aim at placing every province in a position to discharge its responsibilities for education (on a scale that is within the means of the people of Canada) if it chooses to do so. Once this position

is established it seems to us best that education, like every other form of welfare service in a democratic community, should have to fight for its life, and that a generous provision for the education of the children of the nation should depend, not on any arbitrary constitutional provision, but on the persistent conviction of the mass of the people that they must be ready to deny themselves some of the good things of life in order to deal fairly by their children.[9]

The effects on education were felt immediately: variations in per pupil spending across the provinces began to diminish, and the legacy of Ottawa's indirect role in establishing an education policy framework commenced (Appendix 4).

On the other hand, injecting a centralizing dynamic into Canadian intergovernmental relations, Ottawa moved to direct its excess revenues to support a range of social programs that fell under provincial competencies, thus introducing a hierarchical alignment in a variety of policy fields. The federal government used coercive instruments to encourage the spread of certain policies and pave the way for a Canadian welfare state with comparable benefits for citizens from coast to coast regardless of province of residence. By the 1960s, a large number of federally supported cost-sharing programs based on conditional grants had been created to induce the provinces to initiate social assistance programs, strengthen vocational training, expand post-secondary schooling, and offer hospital and medical insurance plans, along with a host of other social programs.

These programs saw the federal government offer the provinces financial assistance through its spending power, enabling them to spend "50-cent dollars" tied to provincial expenditures. While some intergovernmental bargaining occurred, "ultimately the federal spending on these programs was usually the result of independent federal decisions."[10] These major adjustments to the fiscal architecture of the Canadian federation ushered in through the onset of conditional grants shook up relations between Ottawa and the provinces, with a number of provinces voicing concerns about Ottawa's largely unilateral deployment of its spending power. At Dominion–Provincial Conferences in the 1960s, for example, Premier Douglas of Saskatchewan "complained of excessive rigidities" and Premiers Frost of Ontario and Manning of Alberta "raised the fundamental question of whether it was proper for the federal government to skew provincial priorities through, in the words of the former, 'appetite whetting' grants.'"[11] But no province demonstrated greater opposition than Quebec.

In 1956, the Union Nationale government led by Premier Maurice Duplessis directly challenged the federal spending power, taking aim at Ottawa's initiative to give grants directly to post-secondary institutions. The Quebec premier informed the colleges and universities that they could not accept funds and demanded fiscal compensation from the federal government in the form of tax points. That same year, the premier appointed the Royal Commission of Inquiry on Constitutional Problems (the Tremblay Commission) to study the tax-sharing agreements between different orders of government and other constitutional issues. In its final report the Commission declared:

> Since Confederation, the sentiments of Quebecers, and French-Canadians in general, have not changed: exclusive provincial jurisdiction over education is one of the most important federal compromises. It should be jealously guarded and it should remain as comprehensive as possible.[12]

In 1958, Paul Sauvé, who succeeded Duplessis as Quebec premier, reached a deal with Prime Minister John Diefenbaker that excluded Quebec from the federal government's conditional grant program in education but with compensation, thus ensuring that the fiscal transfers from Ottawa to the provinces remained equal. This introduced a new Canadian policy legacy of asymmetry, with Quebec being able to opt out of federal–provincial programs with financial compensation. This would augment Quebec's capacity to pursue distinctive policy pathways, thus cementing a dualist compact in the Canadian federal state.[13]

While the rise of Quebec nationalism was dramatic, reconstituting social and cultural dynamics in the Canadian federation, this period also saw Newfoundland undergo a remarkable metamorphosis. After more than eighty years of resisting solicitations from North America, in 1949, Newfoundlanders voted narrowly in favour of entering Confederation with the rest of Canada. Union with Canada increased the general standard of living on the island through a massive influx of federal funds in the form of both conditional grants and equalization. As an official member of the Dominion, moreover, Newfoundland became a full participant in the CEA's activities and was now fully integrated into the Canadian education policy community. The influence of this transformation on the education sector would become more apparent in the coming decades: the impact of changes in the context, the mechanisms for diffusion, and the potential for convergence would be felt in Newfoundland throughout the 1960s. The key implication here, however, is that Confederation did not instantly transform the Newfoundland education system; the substantive effects of Confederation would lag for a number years.

The year 1945 marked a watershed in the organizational links among the provinces in educational affairs. That year, the CEA established its first permanent secretariat, based in Toronto and financed through a collective agreement among all the provinces.[14] A new constitution for the organization preserved the broad membership base while placing control over the CEA firmly in the hands of the provincial Departments of Education through the Deputy Ministers of Education. Representatives from the provincial departments managed to secure the change on the grounds that in exchange for their increased fiscal support, the provincial governments would be able to exert greater influence over the association's affairs and actions.

The deputy ministers quickly flexed their newfound authority, setting in motion a series of initiatives that were unequivocally aligned with provincial priorities. The new directives for the CEA included spearheading a major interprovincial research agenda and nurturing relations with other associations to expand and integrate the Canadian educational policy network. Among its many initiatives, the association completed the first complete survey of educational developments in the nine provinces and Newfoundland.[15] This study, the first of its kind, offered a pan-Canadian evaluation of the major challenges confronting each of the provinces, highlighting, among other things, the developing crisis in teacher supply, new plans for teacher training, the issue of financial reform, and the need to improve secondary education. Then in the 1950s, working with the CTF and l'Association canadienne des Educateurs de langue française, the CEA established the National Advisory Committee on Educational Research (NACER) to conduct studies on topics that had interprovincial implications that touched on the challenges revealed by the CEA and many other groups.[16] The CEA's new secretariat published and widely distributed these studies and subsequent conference papers and proceedings, thus helping disseminate policy-relevant research and information across provincial borders.[17] All of these initiatives reshaped the educational landscape and solidified opportunities for interprovincial learning.

The number of pan-Canadian conferences on education increased due to the strengthened links within the interprovincial policy network. In addition to the annual conventions held by the CEA, the CTF, and the CSBA, the Ministers of Education and the CTF established a national committee to develop a program for future pan-Canadian conferences. This culminated in three educational conferences, held in 1958, 1960, and 1962, that "left no doubts that education is of prime importance and that Canadians in all walks of life are keenly interested in the quality of education."[18] Attending these conferences were professional educators, deputy ministers, and representatives of provincial councils on education, along with such diverse groups as the Canadian Broadcasting Corporation, the Canadian Labour Congress, the Humanities Research Council of Canada, the Catholic Women's League, the Canadian Jewish Congress, and the Canadian Association for Adult Education.[19] These various initiatives and activities augmented interprovincial information exchanges on topics ranging from initial teacher education to education finance, curriculum, and administration. Clearly, the associational links in the education policy community were becoming stronger and denser throughout the postwar period, thus expanding opportunities for the provinces to draw lessons from one another in elementary and secondary education.

Not all relations within the education policy community remained amicable, however. As the CEA reached out to the CTF through NACER, its internal relations with professional educators were in decline. In a letter to the Secretary-General of the CEA, dated October 23, 1948, the CTF president stated:

> We understand that while there are matters of common interest on which we may act jointly, each organization has its own field of special interest ... We feel that it is necessary to reiterate our stand that the Canadian Teachers' Federation does not subscribe to the principle that the CEA coordinates and speaks for all educational interests in Canada.[20]

It seems that although the CEA remained an omnibus organization, the changes ushered in by the new constitution marked a turning point. The CEA was increasingly under political control, and the positions it took did not always align with the interests of teachers and other education professionals in the community. This led to a rift among the members of the association and set into motion an increasing separation between state and non-state actors in the sector.

In the meantime, research on education was not conducted solely at the pan-Canadian level. Concurrent with the inquiries spearheaded by the wider education policy community, many provinces launched their own Royal Commissions to assess education within their respective provinces: the Cameron Commission (1944) in BC; the Hope Commission (1950) in Ontario; the Cameron Commission (1959) in Alberta; the MacFarlane Commission (1959) in Manitoba; the Chant Commission (1960) in BC; and the Parent Commission (1963–6) in Quebec.[21] All of these investigations acknowledged that policy leadership in the education sector needed to come from the provincial ministers and deputy ministers; that secondary education needed to expand dramatically across the country; and that the quality of teaching required improvement. Each commission, moreover, embraced the ideas of progressive educationists, and this reinforced calls to transform the educational enterprise in line with the emerging paradigm. Of final significance here, each commission systematically examined policies and practices operating in the other provinces, either through official site visits or though written submissions from the respective provincial departments. These Royal Commissions thus served as opportunities for the provinces to exchange ideas and learn from one another's successes and failures.[22]

Central Educational Administration: And Then There Was One ...

As this period opened, three provinces continued to deploy alternative models for central educational administration: Nova Scotia, Quebec, and Newfoundland. Between 1945 and 1967, two of the three converged with the other provinces, adopting the model of individual ministerial responsibility, leaving Newfoundland the sole outlier. Nova Scotia was the first to change how it administered education.

Collective ministerial responsibility enjoyed its longest tenure in Nova Scotia largely because conditions there made that model highly viable. Collective responsibility resonated with the province's political culture and was consistent with the macro-institutional rules, norms, and principles of parliamentary government. Moreover, the philosophy of small government inculcated by Premier George Henry Murray during his time in office (1896 to 1923) was congruent with the idea of limiting the number of ministers and preserving the status quo of collective ministerial responsibility in the province. Given the synergy between the internal context and the original policy choice, the administrative change in favour of individual ministerial responsibility in Nova Scotia is interesting. What motivated decision makers in the province to break from the legacy of collective responsibility and follow the trends at work in the rest of Canada? Or – in the theoretical parlance of this study – what factors led Nova Scotia to abandon path dependency in favour of a path-breaking option? Much of the answer lies in the lessons that Nova Scotia could draw from its neighbouring provinces.

During the 1930s, Nova Scotia's regional peers, New Brunswick and Prince Edward Island, abandoned the system of collective responsibility in favour of individual ministerial responsibility. Leaders in Nova Scotia observed how these administrative adjustments increased government effectiveness, and in 1949, the government appointed its first Minister of Education.[23] A broad consensus regarding which actors should manage the education sector had emerged, and other regional leaders served as exemplars for the Government of Nova Scotia. Substate policy convergence was thus achieved through the pathway of similar problems, with policy actors drawing lessons from neighbouring jurisdictions as they made decisions within comparable macro-institutional structures.

Policy change in Nova Scotia was driven largely by the lessons the province drew from its regional peers. By contrast, administrative reform in Quebec was propelled largely by internal factors and a dissonance between historical arrangements and contemporary realities. At the time when elementary and secondary education in Quebec was being founded and consolidated, social and economic factors contributed to the triumph of religious trusteeship in education. Anglophone Quebecers sensed that their interests would best be served by the confessional structure of education, for it would allow them to operate independently from their francophone counterparts and to follow the path blazed by Egerton Ryerson in Ontario. In the meantime, French Quebecers feared that political and/or secular control of public education would ultimately lead to assimilation with the rest of Canada.[24] The Catholic Church had cast itself as a defender of French Quebec, thus solidifying its position of authority in the psyche of that portion of the population. And as a conservative institution, the Catholic Church had rebuffed many educational innovations, particularly in secondary and post-secondary schooling.[25]

The result of this bifurcated religious trusteeship was growing educational inequality between anglophones and francophones in the province, with evidence of lagging educational outcomes in a number of areas. The province was investing well below the national average in its public schools – less than 10 per cent of its budget.[26] Qualified teachers were in short supply, and the pupil–teacher ratio was higher in the province.[27] Compulsory attendance laws lagged, and Quebec came last among the provinces in rates of pupil retention. Even after compulsory attendance became the law in 1943, the Duplessis government refused to apply sanctions for non-compliance so that by 1958, Quebec had the lowest school attendance rate in Canada.[28]

For many years, French Quebecers had also resisted the trend towards urbanization and industrialization even while their anglophone counterparts embraced it, as did the rest of English Canada. Limited urbanization and industrialization in Quebec further delayed the economic imperative to expand educational opportunities for francophones, and this allowed the denominational system to maintain its legitimacy. These seemingly entrenched features of the province nevertheless began to lose their potency; Quebec's bifurcated and confessional schooling system began to erode once it lost its viability as an effective and appropriate policy option.

Changing demographics in Quebec provided the necessary space for the idea of political control over elementary and secondary education to gain traction. Increased urbanization and immigration from continental Europe was altering Quebec's traditional population profile, which was historically rural and bifurcated between English Protestants and French Catholics. By the late 1930s, more than 60 per cent of Quebecers were urban dwellers; by 1960, this figure had surpassed 75 per cent.[29] Moreover, the influx of English-speaking Catholics and Jews had disrupted the static binary linguistic and religious divisions that had once characterized the population, and the existing model of central educational administration was incapable of responding to this new pluralism. Finally, under the papal leadership of John XXIII, new views of education were germinating within the Catholic Church itself that sparked debates among provincial leaders about the need to reform the Quebec system and facilitate greater educational achievements and equality for the province's students. Quebec society was undergoing a remarkable transformation; led by Georges-Émile Lapalme, the Quebec Liberal Party became the most prominent political voice challenging the existing order. It attracted countless public intellectuals, promoting what would become known as the "Quiet Revolution."[30]

Quebec's educational turning point came in 1960 when the newly elected Liberal government took steps to end religious control of education and to secularize its administration. On 21 March 1961, an Order in Council established a Royal Commission of Inquiry on Education (hereafter the Parent Commission). The preamble to the inquiry included this statement: "Education at all levels is beset by many problems and it is therefore expedient to have a thorough and impartial study of the state of education in the Province."[31] Highlighting the structural challenges posed by the Industrial Revolution, immigration and population growth, economic expansion, and technical innovations, in its final report, the Parent Commission declared that the province needed a better-educated labour force with broader training and more advanced technical and vocational preparation.[32] The commissioners targeted the glaring disparities between Quebec's francophone and anglophone populations as requiring immediate attention, declaring that radical change was necessary. According to the commissioners, two main "defects" prevented the government from exercising its functions effectively: the fragmentation of the school system and the division of government authority over education among several ministries.[33]

In seeking a remedy, the Parent Commission examined the administrative arrangements employed in a series of other domestic and international jurisdictions. It first considered the idea of a Crown corporation, similar to the system used in the State of New York. This model was ultimately rejected, however, on the grounds that it was unsuitable in parliamentary government:

> Such a form of organization, in short, does not suit the political institutions of our democracy, which differ greatly from those of the State of New York. The rank of the Commissioner of Education in that state is the same as that of the other departmental secretaries, none of whom are elected. The Commissioner may himself defend the budget and educational legislation before the Assembly, whereas our system of government does not permit the Superintendent to do this. It seems preferable, under these circumstances to preserve the Department of Education within the framework of the provincial administration rather than to set it up as an independent agency.[34]

The macro-institutional logic of parliamentary government, shared by all Canadian provinces, thus seemed to encourage Quebec officials to draw lessons from the administrative practices of the other provinces instead of borrowing them from beyond Canada's borders. It would mean creating a provincially controlled Department of Education headed by a minister who would be individually responsible to cabinet. Individual ministerial responsibility was administratively viable;

in addition, this model would be able to address the pertinent problems of the day while resonating with the contemporary political atmosphere. So the province implemented that model.

Yet there was one administrative anomaly in Quebec. Sensitive to the potential backlash that this revolution could trigger, the commission suggested that an advisory council be established to maintain some representation for the religious orders in the education sector. Seeing the wisdom of this, the Quebec government created the *Conseil supérieur de l'éducation* (CSE), comprised of a Catholic Committee and a Protestant Committee, to advise the minister on education-related issues. The *Conseil* ensured the continuity of the confessional system without impeding the establishment of political control of the sector. The result was policy convergence with the other provinces, albeit while preserving some past traditions in order to ensure that the new policy remained consistent with the internal educational regime and policy context that characterized Quebec. This subtle adaptation helped mollify opposition to the secularization of administrative practices in the province. As a consequence, by 1967 Newfoundland was the sole outlier in Canada in terms of how it administered education. Soon, however, this anomaly would be remedied (see chapter 6).

Consolidating Local School Boards

When schooling was limited to the fundamentals of "reading, writing, and arithmetic," small districts with one-room schools could provide for the educational needs of Canadians. As education broadened to include the goal of providing instruction at the secondary level to all students, the size of local districts was found to be seriously hindering the expansion of schooling opportunities. With its larger population and increased urbanization, Ontario had been better able to capitalize on the funding opportunities provided by Ottawa through the Technical Education Act (1919) to enlarge secondary programs. However, even in that province, decision makers recognized that despite the advances, they needed to consolidate smaller rural districts in order to improve schooling opportunities:

> It is realized that in Ontario the present system of rural school administration is neither economically sound nor in any sense efficient. Larger units of administration ... are being formed, and immediately better results are forthcoming from both the economic and the educational point of view.[35]

The problem, as articulated in Ontario, was amplified in the smaller and less urbanized provinces, where tiny school boards were incapable of expanding programming beyond the elementary level. Yet throughout the first half of the twentieth century, these tiny boards were able to block efforts by provincial officials to amalgamate districts. Local trustees often mobilized against government-led campaigns to merge boards.

Over the opposition of local trustees, education professionals in the policy community aligned themselves with provincial decision makers in support of district consolidation. Teachers' federations saw larger administrative units as a means to improve their job security and working conditions.[36] Small boards often lacked the necessary revenues to cover salaries and subjected teachers to random layoffs. Trustees in smaller districts often had problems raising revenues to pay teachers. During the 1930s and 1940s, for example, the minimum teachers' salary was officially set at $840, but the salaries offered by local trustees often fell significantly below that minimum.[37] Larger units, it was reasoned, could more easily generate the revenues needed to cover salaries and thereby guarantee teachers regular employment. The organizations also supported larger units as a means to systematize new regimes for promoting teachers and for professional development; this, they hoped, would enhance the professional status of teachers and attract stronger candidates to the field. Using their internal and pan-Canadian associational networks and so acting as carrier molecules, teachers' organizations pressed provincial decision makers to institute major reforms; this expedited interprovincial learning and helped disseminate policy ideas across provincial boundaries. The increased integration of the policy community through the policy network that had emerged as a result of changes in the broader policy climate thus occasioned greater opportunities for informational exchanges.

It is interesting that even though individual local trustees often opposed amalgamations, the Canadian School Trustees' Association formally endorsed them, arguing that the education sector and public schooling would reap five principal benefits: assessment and tax rates would be more equalized across the school boards; the number of one-room schools would be reduced; regional high schools could be established; opportunities would be equalized for rural and urban children; and improvements in health, physical education, and libraries would be realized.[38] The CSTA's commitment moved proposals for district consolidations higher up the policy agenda, for it suggested that – to quote John Kingdon – amalgamations were an "idea whose time had come."[39]

Despite this elite and expert support across the policy community and the seemingly winning conditions across the country, consolidation proved to be an onerous task. First, transporting students across sparsely settled landscapes to a common centre was a major logistical challenge that many provinces could not afford.[40] Also, local populations often opposed amalgamation, fearing that they would lose influence over education in their communities and that property taxes would rise to cover expanding educational programs.[41] Some provincial politicians were thus reluctant to oppose the wishes of their local electorates. To contend with this opposition, provincial governments pursued three different implementation strategies: hierarchical unilateralism; presumed local consent; and local voluntarism. The cases of BC, Saskatchewan, and Manitoba are instructive. The experiences of these three provinces reveal how internal features of a provincial policy context both influence and reinforce the characteristics of particular educational regimes, locking in certain normative and cultural proclivities and thereby installing lasting legacies of policy development.

In 1925, the *Report of the Survey of the School System*, submitted by J.H. Putnam and G.M. Weir to the BC government, recommended that "the consolidation of assisted schools be carried out wherever it seems educationally or financially desirable."[42] At the time, provincial legislation allowed districts to consolidate voluntarily, but no board had ever opted to do so. Nine years later, the BC government decided to unilaterally abolish the boundaries of sixty-three impoverished rural districts in the Peace River Block, setting up a single administrative unit; however, it left the rest of the districts alone. In 1944, the Cameron Commission recommended that the province be divided into seventy-four larger districts, adding that this should occur without local approval to expedite the process.[43]

In 1944, based on the recommendations of the Committee on School Administration, the Saskatchewan legislature passed the Larger School Units Act, which among other things stated the following: consolidations were to be carried out gradually, with the government incrementally determining which districts would be grouped together; and local ratepayers would have the opportunity to petition for a vote on amalgamation. If petitions were not forthcoming, the government could presume local consent and proceed with the consolidation.[44] In the 1950s, to further democratic participation, Saskatchewan's CCF government amended the legislation so that a plebiscite would be required before any additional units were established.[45]

In Manitoba, a special select committee of the legislature was appointed in 1944 to examine the state of schooling in the province. That committee called for the establishment of larger school areas modelled on those in Alberta and Saskatchewan; it also recommended that "an educational campaign be initiated to inform the public and to gain public approval and support for the re-organization of educational administration."[46] The expert panel thus encouraged the Manitoba government to engage the public directly in the reform process. On the heels of this recommendation, the legislature passed an act that created two experimental district areas, subject to the approval of local ratepayers, and set in motion an information campaign to explain the plan to Manitobans in the hope that the information would help the public see the wisdom of the proposed strategy.

Clearly, all three provinces pursued the same policy but in contrasting ways. As it turned out, the outcomes also varied dramatically. Adopting the Cameron Commission's recommendation, the BC legislature unilaterally reduced the number of school boards from 653 to 89, transforming educational administration almost overnight. BC's unilateral imposition subsequently achieved impressive results but at the cost of democratic participation. Under Saskatchewan's scheme, forty-six large districts had been formed by 1949, and the government received few petitions opposing later consolidations. Even after the province mandated plebiscites, ratepayers in the province consistently voted in favour of the larger units, confirming that the public had accepted the agenda and its implementation.[47]

In Manitoba, the strategy of local voluntarism had less fruitful results, and as a result, later administrations were compelled to pursue stronger – less democratic – tactics. By 1950, only one experimental school area – the Dauphin–Ochre River Area – had been established in the province and no further consolidations had occurred. Dissatisfied with this result, the legislature appointed a Royal Commission in 1958 (the MacFarlane Commission) to study and report on all aspects of education in the province. The members of the MacFarlane Commission immediately began comparing conditions in Manitoba with those in other provinces (a common approach for such bodies). It became apparent that progress was being made, particularly in neighbouring Saskatchewan, whose tactics were worth emulating. The MacFarlane Commission recommended the unilateral establishment of larger administrative units to oversee secondary education in Manitoba, believing the elementary education could continue under more localized control.[48]

After campaigning on the issue, the newly elected Conservative government led by Duff Roblin quickly passed an amendment to the Public Schools Act that gave the Manitoba government the authority to establish school divisions subject to local approval via plebiscite. After a series of campaigns to rally public support, the vote of local residents took place in February 1959. Thirty-two new consolidated districts were approved, with only four rejecting the plan. The benefits of this strategic adjustment did not go unnoticed by the education policy community. The CEA, for one, affirmed:

> What are the influences that play upon education that education change is so slow in coming about? And they are slow in Manitoba where initiative is left to the people. The only really successful venture in the field of larger units was the campaign to organize the one hundred consolidations which was done by aggressive departmental leadership.[49]

The interprovincial drive to consolidate districts confirms two aspects of the analytical architecture developed in chapter 3. First, regarding the dissemination of information and the gradual crafting of a policy framework, when faced with common problems, provincial decision makers and other policy actors looked to one another for information that shaped subsequent courses of action. Here, Manitoba's initial failures served as a valuable lesson to other provinces that had delayed pursuing consolidations.[50] To quote Ontario's Hope Commission: "The fact that no other area has since been formed [in Manitoba] suggests that the voluntary formation of larger units … is impracticable."[51] The Hope Commission then went further, attesting that

> this successful experiment on a large scale [in BC] convinced educators across Canada of the possibilities of the larger unit as a solution for the educational problems developed by social changes and aggravated by the Depression. It resulted in legislation in Alberta, New Brunswick, Nova Scotia, Saskatchewan, Manitoba, and Ontario to enable the establishment of larger units of administration.[52]

In this vein, information from the other provinces had spurred the Roblin government to abandon voluntary strategies in favour of government-led amalgamations. Provincial studies from the period thus contributed to Manitoba's learning process, serving as an interactive mechanism; evidence from different jurisdictions was used to inform internal decision making and policy choices in a province that had attempted to do something and failed.

Second, it is also clear that even when adopting the same policy, provinces can implement it in very different ways that reflect internal concerns and priorities. This confirms the importance of internal educational regimes as factors auguring against complete interprovincial uniformity. Differences in implementation strategies, moreover, established certain expectations among stakeholders and the public alike regarding the ways in which the provincial government would be allowed to approach particular problems influencing the configuration of the internal educational regime. For BC residents, a pattern of hierarchical authority was set, resulting in a legacy of strong government intervention; for the people of Saskatchewan and Manitoba, the respective governments had entrenched a procedure of public engagement, thus establishing an alternative tone in the policy process that would continue to resonate in policy initiatives even beyond the dimension of educational administration.

Universalizing Secondary Education

Since the early decades of the twentieth century, provincial governments had been trying to expand educational opportunities and widen the scope of secondary schooling. These efforts had garnered little success. Prior to district consolidations, secondary schools were hard to operate outside of urban centres; this meant that before 1945, most Canadians still did not have access to programs beyond grade eight. Where greater opportunities did exist, moreover, they came through the offerings provided by the partite and bilateral models of secondary schooling. These models of secondary schooling, however, tended to reinforce rather than mitigate class divisions, in contradiction to the new educational ideas that had been gathering force in the years after the Second World War.

Inherent deficiencies in both the partite and bilateral models of secondary schooling caused them to fail the tests of efficiency, effectiveness, and legitimacy.[53] Partite schools failed the efficiency test because they were impossible to operate outside large urban environments; they failed the effectiveness test because academic schools remained in higher demand and vocational schools were stigmatized; and, finally, they failed the legitimacy test because partite schools reinforced and reproduced class divisions, an outcome that was no longer congruent with the ideological climate of the day. While passing the efficiency test because they were possible in rural areas, bilateral schools similarly failed the tests of efficiency and legitimacy because they reinforced class divisions and emphasized academic studies. In 1944, observing that "the academic and vocational secondary schools have failed to retain their students,"[54] the CEA endorsed a new system for secondary schooling and outlined the idea of composite education.

Described as an adaptation "in part to community and individual needs, but essentially a common secondary school for all the people,"[55] composite schools were viewed as a means to break down barriers between the streams of educational programs such that

> youth may secure both a general education (including the opportunity to explore their interests and capacities through a variety of experiences) and specialized education suited to their abilities and introductory to their vocational goals and aspirations.[56]

Over the next decades, the composite model gained support and endorsements from powerful components the Canadian education policy community, becoming a preferred policy option among education experts from coast to coast.[57]

Galvanized by the CEA's recommendations, Saskatchewan's CCF government worked to institute the composite system. The CCF's ideological tendencies were such that progressive educationalists felt at home in the party. The government soon set in motion a series of reforms designed to expand educational opportunities for the citizenry. The Department of Education reported that by 1949, composite schools had been established in most of the province's districts and were serving a significant portion of the population.[58] Following Saskatchewan's lead, by the early 1950s Alberta was operating ten composite schools that were educating 25 per cent of the province's secondary students; BC was also encouraging the spread of composite schools throughout its districts. Observers from both provinces were nevertheless dismayed with the progress. "The program of the high schools has been largely confined to 'general' or pre-university studies," noted Alberta's Cameron Commission;[59] the Department of Education had failed to disrupt the partite and bilateral policy legacy. In the meantime, BC's Chant Commission determined that outside Vancouver, most high schools were offering only academic high school programs; it concluded that the attempt to diffuse composite schooling had failed.[60] Partite and bilateral schooling thus remained in operation concurrently with some limited composite schools in both Alberta and BC.

Results were similarly mixed in eastern Canada. Because partite and bilateral schools were firmly entrenched in Ontario – some programs dated back to 1900, when millionaire Sir William MacDonald decided to support secondary schooling – adjusting the policy pathway to align with the principles of composite schooling proved to be a challenge. Unlike the CCF government in Saskatchewan, moreover, Ontario's political leaders were biased in favour of traditional scholastic programs. Throughout the 1950s, Ontario's Minister of Education, W.J. Dunlop, gave high priority to academic programs and allowed technical programs to languish.[61] Moving eastwards, under the Protestant authority, anglophones in Quebec had seen some advances in composite schooling, but secondary schools in the Catholic sector remained committed to an elite academic curriculum thanks in large part to the traditional schooling paradigm endorsed by the Catholic Church. In Nova Scotia, the Vocational Education Act of 1953 had locked the partite system in place. Finally, running against national trends, secondary education in Newfoundland and Prince Edward Island remained exclusively academic in the main public system. Vocational and technical training programs in those two provinces were offered in provincially run trade schools, which charged tuition and were segregated from the public education system.[62]

The central government in Ottawa contributed to these interprovincial policy irregularities and impeded the spread of composite schooling when it passed the Technical and Vocational Training Assistance Act (TVTA) in 1960. To encourage the expansion of technical and vocational education across the country, the TVTA offered federal funds for the provinces to build new schools, on the condition that at least half the space in those schools be devoted to those subjects. As a result of the TVTA, 622 new schools were built across the country; yet again, the federal government was attempting to coerce the provinces to follow a particular policy trajectory in education. Reflecting on the federal government's action, Harold S. Baker – an education professor at the University of Alberta – stated that

what the [TVTA] grants have done is to provide special support for one kind of programme (or one group of programmes) and so to accelerate the differentiation of high school programs generally. And they have probably helped eliminate – at least for the time being – an earlier concept of the comprehensive (or composite) school in which it was thought that there could be a kind of interdisciplinary enrichment (as between academic and non-academic programmes) and even a good deal of common study for all students.[63]

In Ontario, the Progressive Conservative government of Premier John Robarts quickly agreed to the terms of the TVTA. Just as quickly, the province's Minister of Education revamped the curriculum to allow for the streaming of students into technical and vocational programs. Because the Ontario government was operating under significant time constraints imposed by Ottawa, Robarts authored the reorganization program without consulting the province's education stakeholders: "The plan had merely been announced to them."[64] Between 1961 and 1966, more than $805 million of federal funds were transferred to Ontario, resulting in the construction of 335 new schools and additions to 83 existing schools that were already dedicated to technical and vocational training.[65] Similar deals between the federal and provincial governments – including Quebec, which was now accepting federal funds for education – resulted in the building of hundreds of new schools across the country. But the sudden influx of funds translated into programs being "hastily conceived and prematurely announced" so that "those who had to live with the plan had nothing to do with its conceptions."[66] The intent of the TVTA had been to increase flexibility in secondary education; the result was the introduction of rigid streaming systems that reinforced rather than mitigated class divisions in the provinces.

Consequently, despite the best efforts of education experts working within the policy community, who had been diligently promoting the composite model, throughout the 1960s the provision of secondary education across the provinces continued to be characterized by panoply of practices. Coercion in the form of federal incentives to encourage vocational training was no doubt part of the story, but only part of it. It would be foolhardy to ignore the degree to which the bilateral and partite systems were locked into the respective educational regimes of the respective provincial policy systems, and that circumstance propelled a self-reinforcing logic that stymied the efforts of dedicated entrepreneurs to adjust the trajectory in favour of progressive education. Many policy officials had entrenched predilections, and this led them to fortify the existing partite and bilateral programs, which in turn hindered the uniform implementation of this new policy idea across the provincial jurisdictions. In its review of Canadian secondary education, the Committee on Educational Research declared:

> Across Canada there is uniformity in neither the lower nor the upper limits of composite schools. The contributors to the survey pointed out that these differences were deeply rooted in their traditions or in the former solutions to previous problems within each of the provinces.[67]

Clearly, decisions made when Canadian education was being founded and consolidated continued to resonate in the contemporary actions of political and policy authorities, many of whom worked against the wishes of key entrepreneurs of composite schooling, who would be able to realize their goals only in the 1970s, when they succeeded in disrupting the prevailing monopoly in favour of policy change.

Teacher Education: A Regionally-Based Policy Innovation

Between 1840 and 1945, the accepted form of teacher training was the normal school. This interprovincial consensus on initial teacher education changed dramatically in the years following the Second World War. Teachers' federations, superintendents, and the CEA had been voicing concerns about the quality of the teaching profession and were seeking ways to enhance the prevailing programs.[68] In the past, limits in the teacher supply had hindered the expansion of public schooling, and officials were now turning their attention to the available programs and the need to attract stronger and better candidates to the profession. According to a CSTA report, in 1952–3 there were approximately 5,150 instructors in Canadian classrooms without any professional training and almost 4,000 more whose education and training were below the prescribed minimum in their province.[69] Poorly trained teachers compromised the capacity for public education to expand beyond the elementary level because education professionals required more specialized training to instruct the senior schooling levels.[70] Individual teachers' federations thus became actively engaged in the issue of teacher education and lobbied in favour of reforming existing practices. The CEA similarly weighed in, releasing a report titled "An SOS from the Schools" that decried the quality of teacher preparation in Canada.[71] These conditions, reports, and opinions all elevated the issue of initial teacher education on provincial policy agendas. This time a series of developments in Alberta would set the stage for more than a generation of policy reform across the country.

South of the Canadian border, new ideas on initial teacher education had been germinating. Specifically, across the United States, universities had started offering programs to train potential teachers, creating bachelor's degrees in education. Stimulated by these emerging American educational ideas, in 1928, Dr H.M. Tory founded the School of Education at the University of Alberta, which offered a four-year program for initial teacher education. Under the leadership of Dean Ezra LaZerte, the school was transformed into an official Faculty of Education in 1942. Supported by the Alberta Teachers' Association (ATA), the new Faculty of Education at the University of Alberta offered a three-year program that led to a B.Ed. and a teaching certificate, the first of its kind in Canada.

Despite the university's initiative and the active support of key stakeholders, political acceptance of the new ideas was not immediately forthcoming. Specifically, the Alberta government's concerns over labour supply and uncertain costs, and its desire to maintain control over the structure and delivery of initial teacher education, impeded the program's transfer to universities in the province.[72] Under the normal school system, training took only four months, with the Minister of Education exercising complete control over the program's structure and delivery. If the government transferred this control to universities, program requirements would likely be expanded and the entry of candidates into the workforce would be subsequently delayed. Moreover, the costs of teacher education provided by a university would inevitably rise, increasing the financial burden for potential candidates. Political leaders feared this would discourage individuals from entering the profession and thereby exacerbate the shortage of teachers that was already dogging Alberta public schooling.

Reform would have languished had it not been for a window of opportunity that opened in 1935 in the form of a provincial election. That year, a change in government created the possibility for major modifications as William Aberhart became premier. Aberhart, a former educator, had first-hand experience of the trials that faced poorly trained teachers, and he agreed it was necessary to reform the existing normal schools program.[73] To that end, he appointed himself Minister of Education and then appointed Dr Fred McNally, a long-time supporter of university-led teacher education, as his deputy minister to promote the policy idea within the bureaucracy and to ensure that it gained the necessary currency within the provincial department.[74]

Political and professional interests were now firmly aligned behind the policy idea, and on 22 February 1945 the Government of Alberta issued the following statement:

> An agreement has been entered into with the University of Alberta, whereby its Faculty of Education will, henceforth, carry on the entire programme of teacher training, subject to control of policy by the Minister of Education. In this way students will receive full credit for the time so spent towards a university degree.[75]

A metamorphosis in teacher education followed as the active staffs of the normal schools were transferred into this new university system. "Staff members," writes Bernard Keeler, "found themselves wearing the new dignity of academic rank and responding to the title of professor instead of looking over their shoulders to see who was being addressed."[76] The transformation thus advanced relatively painlessly as existing instructors were assured employment under the new configuration of initial teacher education.

After Alberta changed its policy, the four western provinces held a conference devoted to teacher education. There, the delegates decided to establish a forum for regular exchanges among the region's elites in the education sector.[77] At the same time, interprovincial migration carried top officials across borders to take up positions in the region's various Ministries of Education and university faculties.[78] Perhaps inspired by the University of Alberta, universities in BC, Saskatchewan, and Manitoba had already initiated programs for teacher education and were willing to enter into cooperative agreements with their respective governments. Members of the policy community in the western provinces, as late adopters of the normal school model, appeared to be quite receptive to the potential benefits of this policy change. As a result, the four jurisdictions west of Ontario converged on the arrangement and universities took over this dimension of the education sector.[79] The evidence demonstrates, then, that western Canada provided a receptive environment for the policy idea, expediting convergence across this regional group.

East of the Manitoba border there was a completely different response to the idea of university-led teacher education. Provincial officials in eastern Canada seemed generally content with the normal school model, and no policy entrepreneurs demonstrated any strong interest in creating new programs.[80] The problem simply was not salient at the time, despite the CTF's best efforts to convince the regions' policy makers otherwise. What is more, unlike their western counter-parts, eastern policy actors tended to be quite critical of American education scholars, going to great lengths to minimize their influence in Canadian education by actively rejecting textbooks and enforcing British Dominion citizenship on anyone wishing to teach in the region.[81] This warding off of American ideas can be traced back to none other than Egerton Ryerson. Historical documents reveal that Ryerson and his peers openly lambasted the ideas of American educationists. Ryerson himself once charged that "the American writers present their works to the public as original, except acknowledging in the preface, that several useful thoughts have been suggested by such and such, or by some German Authors."[82] Furthermore, major education reports in the region, such as the Hope Commission's report, were obviously ambivalent towards the idea of transferring teacher education to universities: "We are unable to concur in the view that the training of teachers should be provided by the university."[83] Finally, university administrators were extremely reluctant to embrace the idea; they rejected the notion of teacher training as an academic discipline, and of teaching as a profession worthy of the prestige of university education.[84] According to Michael Fullan and F. Michael Connelly, university administrators in provinces such as Ontario prolonged the anti-American ethos that had been inculcated in Ryerson's era, in the belief that university-led teacher training was too "American" or "Western" and therefore unsuitable for their provinces.[85] When a university did initiate some programs, the offerings were piecemeal at best; they were exclusively for secondary teachers and were coordinated with neither government programs nor the existing certification regimes. The idea of university-led teacher education thus did not take hold in eastern Canada.

These developments in teacher education lend credence to the argument that the diffusion of policy ideas is mediated by regional cultural connectivity, internal policy contexts, and the educational regimes of the individual provinces. Provincial decision makers from coast to coast were exposed to similar criticisms about the quality of existing teacher preparation programs and faced comparable problems with teacher supply.[86] Moreover, provincial decision makers were aware of the American innovation of university-led teacher education, due in no small part to reports and conferences held by organizations like the CTF.[87] Conditions in western Canada, however, were more conducive to the new policy idea. The western provinces had been accepting American-educated teachers, who once they arrived began acting as entrepreneurs, bringing to the debates their experiences with university-led programs. Furthermore, prior to Confederation there had been no universities west of Ontario; those that eventually emerged in the region were heavily influenced by the American state university model and quickly developed short-cycle programs in applied fields such as agriculture.[88] This meant that western universities had a long tradition of vocationally oriented learning and were markedly less traditional than their counterparts in eastern Canada. University administrators allowed the idea of initial teacher education to percolate from below, and they did not shun the notion of providing it. They were also open to initiating programs that aligned with government regulations. Finally, policy entrepreneurs within the provincial Ministries of Education supplied the necessary support to make the idea viable for political decision makers. The result was that by 1967, all of the provinces west of Ontario had formally transferred responsibility for initial teacher education to universities, while those to the east maintained the normal school tradition. This signalled a major policy divergence between the two sides of the country.

Building the Theoretical Links

Over more than twenty years, the Canadian education sector witnessed a number of marked transformations in the policy climate. Interprovincial associations grew in strength and developed more permanent lines of communication across provincial borders. Conventions and conferences were held with greater regularity, and the CEA emerged as a key instrument for ideational exchanges linking the formerly disparate provincial education policy communities. It is fair to say that the Canadian education policy network matured considerably from the embryo that had been the DEA. Increasingly, the dissemination of ideas was orchestrated and regularized through these channels as opportunities for learning were formalized through various organizations including the CEA, the CTA, the CSBA, and the NACER. Formalization did not, however, foreshadow the installation of hierarchical relations in the policy network where certain organizations or provinces could impose sanctions on others. Mandatory curriculum standards, for example, never emerged, nor did binding provisions for teacher certification. This attribute of the Canadian policy network did not go unnoticed by those involved in education:

In these meetings there can be no intention of developing a single philosophy or series of procedures in education for all provinces alike. On the other hand, this rare opportunity to exchange ideas and experiences between educators from widely-separated parts of the country has been mutually helpful.[89]

Despite the increased density of the connections across the policy community generated by changes in the climate, evidence of corresponding policy convergence was mixed at best. The narrative of this period clearly demonstrates that diffusion through learning does not immediately translate into policy convergence and that convergence does not always appear for the same reasons. The postwar period saw two provinces break with the past in favour of path-shaping change: Nova Scotia and Quebec established individual ministerial responsibility. But these policy changes were driven by different factors. Nova Scotia seemed to be following regional trends that were at work across the Maritimes, whereas decision makers in Quebec were responding to dramatic societal changes within the province that had rendered the previous model of religious trusteeship obsolete.

Evidence from Quebec also confirms two suppositions of the analytical architecture. On the one hand, the common macro-institutional logic across the Canadian provinces proved to be a compelling driver of policy convergence as decision makers in Quebec – especially the members of the Parent Commission – were pushed into following the lead of the rest of the country. On the other hand, macro-institutional logic does not determine the full scope of policy choices; decision makers in that province installed individual ministerial responsibility, but with a twist in the form of the CSE, which reflected the province's unique historical traditions.

Meanwhile, the expansion and universalization of secondary school had arisen as a core goal within the individual provincial policy communities, across the country, and beyond Canada's borders. This demanded the creation of larger school districts – an initiative in administration that was also shared from coast to coast. The interplay between these two dimensions of the education sector – administration and curriculum – illuminates how choices in one area can reverberate in others, opening (or closing) opportunities to pursue particular options. The implementation of district consolidations nevertheless varied as the policy choices reflected and in turn reinforced alternative rules and norms in the respective educational regimes of the provinces. Furthermore, while the goal of expanding secondary schooling was now universal, the particular policy choices to achieve that objective were not: there was no ideational consensus across the policy community. Consequently, there was a noticeable patchwork of strategies in the provinces' efforts to provide secondary schooling for their respective citizenries. Finally, a clear policy divergence emerged in teacher education. Led by Alberta, the western provinces spearheaded a new model of initial teacher education in Canada; the provinces east of Manitoba shunned this innovation and maintained their past practices. It is in this dimension of education policy that we begin to see the importance of state and non-state actors that have a stake in decision making, in that the fragmentation of authority over teacher education diluted the policy monopoly formerly enjoyed by those provincial governments.

There were also a number of ideational tensions as adherents to the developing progressive paradigm sought to reconfigure mandatory schooling away from rote learning towards tailoring programs to meet the needs of individual learners. Such goals proved elusive as the need to universalize education claimed the attention of the policy community throughout the postwar period. Only with the rise of the Civil Rights movement and the social revolutions of the 1960s would a clear consensus on child-centred educational orthodoxy emerge.

6 Individualizing Provincial Schooling (1967–1982)

Choices should not irrevocably confine a child to one single sphere; it must be possible to correct an unwise choice, or to guide in a new direction a child whose aptitudes and tastes turn out to be other than was thought, or change with the passage of time, without forcing the child, if it is at all possible, to retrace his steps through one or several years of study.

The Parent Commission

Canada's centennial year, 1967, was a time of great optimism in Canada. By then the welfare state was largely in place and prosperity across the country was at an all-time high. This optimism, however, proved to be short-lived; in the words of Pierre Berton, 1967 was Canada's "last good year."[1] In the 1970s, skyrocketing oil prices and stagflation resulted in a major economic downturn that cast a long shadow over the landscape. Inflation and unemployment both rose, shaking foundational beliefs in the effectiveness of state action. Meanwhile, animosity and hostility appeared on the political horizon. The intergovernmental cooperation that had erected the Canadian welfare state deteriorated into conflict and acrimony as the two orders of government battled in public over programs and policies; a number of provinces were frustrated with the limits on their jurisdictional autonomy that had been wrangled by officials in Ottawa. By the mid-1970s, the very future of the Canadian federation was in serious jeopardy when Quebecers elected a party to office committed to independence. Within a few short years, Canadian optimism had given way to insecurity and anxiety as a result of the pounding of these remarkably stormy seas.

Public education similarly felt the onset of a tempest: a rising chorus of voices questioned the quality of the elementary and secondary schooling being provided by the state. Diane Ravitch, an American education expert, suggested that by the start of the 1970s,

the indictment of the school was overwhelming. In the eyes of critics, the school destroyed the souls of children, whether black or white, middle-class or poor. It coerced unwilling youths to sit through hours of stultifying classes, breaking their spirits before turning them out as either rebellious misfits or conforming cogs in the great industrial machine. It neglected the needs of individuals while slighting the history and culture of diverse minorities. It clung to a boring, irrelevant curriculum and to methods that obliterated whatever curiosity children brought with them. It drove away creative teachers and gave tenure to petty martinets.[2]

These perceptions reverberated across the 49th parallel.[3] Policy actors shifted their focus away from the objective of simply universalizing public education towards progressive ideals that viewed students as individuals. As they did so, they pioneered programs for an ever-expanding diversity of needs and interests. The child-centred paradigm took hold in virtually every corner of the policy community, propelling a series of developments in provincial schools that would transform curriculum and assessment practices from coast to coast. Efforts were made to decentralize decision making to the local level and to assign school boards greater responsibility for curriculum development. Teacher education programs in the eastern provinces were targeted for reform, and a new model for education finance appeared on the landscape. All of this led to tectonic shifts in the provincial schooling systems.

During this thirteen-year period, Newfoundland finally established individual ministerial responsibility; provinces in eastern Canada adopted the western practice of university-led education; and all ten provinces reconfigured their curricula in line with the pedagogy of child-centred learning and consolidated the composite model of secondary education. The result of all these adjustments was the achievement of a reasonably consistent policy framework in elementary and secondary education; Canadian students from coast to coast now had access to comparable programs provided by the individual provinces. The ten systems had coalesced around a commitment to universally accessible public education, available to children and teenagers between the ages of six and eighteen, under the authority of a secular Ministry of Education led by an elected minister, supported by public funds and staffed by publicly accredited teaching professionals.

Yet as these similarities materialized, some provinces diverged from the pack in a number of areas, confirming that policy frameworks neither necessitate complete uniformity nor prevent the use of alternative strategies or policy instruments. Quebec pioneered an alternative model for high school – a hybrid between the composite and partite systems. In the area of assessments, seven provinces terminated the practice of universal exams, but Saskatchewan, Quebec, and Newfoundland maintained some form of universal mandatory testing. And in education finance, a number of provinces in eastern Canada introduced full-state funding, while west of the Ottawa River, shared-cost arrangements were maintained. The explanation for these alternative patterns of convergence and divergence turns on the interactions between developments in the policy climate and the internal policy contexts of the ten jurisdictions.

The Policy Climate

The 1960s were a time of significant social, economic, and political upheaval that affected the public education enterprise. A powerful coalition formed within the education policy community in favour of child-centred schooling, the goals of which were to treat children as individuals and to approach education as a means to enhance ongoing personal growth. Officials and stakeholders committed themselves to the notion of tailoring education programs to the needs of students instead of making students conform to inflexible regimes.[4] Also targeted for reform was educational administration: the reform agenda included an attempt to relocate decision making by shifting authority away from the central ministries towards local school boards.[5] Elements of this discourse had been visible immediately following the Second World War and can be found in the pages of Quebec's Parent Commission and Newfoundland's Warren Commission; now, however, these ideas gained new credibility and came to dominate the knowledge regime. This was most evident in three provincial reports completed during the period under investigation here: the Worth Report (Alberta), the Hall–Dennis Report (Ontario), and the Graham Report (Nova Scotia). Other components of the policy community reinforced the call for child-centred schooling. Teachers' federations, for example, favoured decentralizing curriculum to local schools because it would help teachers improve their professional standing and strengthen their capacity to directly influence the materials that students would be learning. Trustees, for their part, recognized that decentralization would afford them greater control over the destiny of their respective boards and increase their influence over local governance. Putting all of this together, there clearly was a shared sense of fundamental direction, with key policy priorities held in common among the various state and non-state components of the provincial education policy communities.

As this ideational consensus in the knowledge regime of the education arena emerged, serious rifts appeared on the Canadian political stage. Between 1967 and 1982, relations between the federal and provincial governments became increasingly strained as the somewhat amicable intergovernmental relations that had led to the establishment the welfare state broke down. Indications of disharmony grew as provincial "docility with respect to taxation agreements and shared cost programmes began to evaporate."[6] Building on the foundation that had been established by Maurice Duplessis, and further buoyed by the unfolding Quiet Revolution, Quebec led the charge against national interventions. According to David Cameron and Richard Simeon, the Quiet Revolution "unleashed a progressive nationalism that transformed Quebec and challenged traditional assumptions about Canadian federalism."[7] This drama, as Alan Cairns described it, proved both passionate and volatile and was punctuated with sporadic violence "when a terrorist group kidnapped a diplomat, murdered a Quebec cabinet minister, and the War Measures Act was proclaimed."[8] These events helped generate an upsurge in the sovereigntist movement until independence rose to the forefront of the political agenda with the election of the Parti Québécois in 1976. The PQ presented a new model, "sovereignty-association," which called for the establishment of a binational framework, one in which an independent Quebec would maintain certain ties with Canada. Prime Minister Pierre Trudeau, for his part, articulated an alternative model of federalism in opposition to "what he considered an atavistic and retrograde Quebec nationalism."[9] The future of the province, according to Trudeau, lay with a bilingual and bicultural united Canada helmed by a strong central government. Pitched battles between Trudeau and Quebec Premier René Lévesque thus took centre stage, and constitutional questions came to dominate the Canadian political discourse.

But Quebec was not alone in its opposition to federal encroachments. Other provinces "were also chafing under the growing influence of the federal government."[10] By the 1970s, the larger provinces were challenging Ottawa's dominance and actively working against major federal initiatives. Meanwhile, regionally based conflicts flared when federal ideas about energy policy aligned the energy-rich provinces against central Canada, culminating in the fierce battle over the National Energy Program, whose intent was to insulate eastern Canada from rising oil prices at the expense of western Canadian oil producers. Dynamics in the intergovernmental arena thus turned to conflict rather than compromise as tensions grew between the two orders of government.

The federal government made a series of adjustments to its system of fiscal federalism, some of which targeted education specifically. This had major implications for the provinces. On 24 October 1966, Prime Minister Lester B. Pearson announced an end to shared-cost programs in technical and vocational training. Instead of turning funds over to the provinces to support vocational training, Ottawa would be delivering programs itself by purchasing spaces directly from provincial institutions or the private sector. "By this federal initiative, the longest standing conditional grant relationship in the history of Canadian federalism was abruptly discarded."[11] Almost overnight, the federal government had abandoned the secondary school arena, leaving the provinces completely autonomous in the field. Then, in the 1970s, determined to further reverse provincial clout, which had been building through the support of "50-cent dollars," the federal government introduced Established Programs Financing (EPF) to detach shared-cost programs in health and post-secondary education from actual provincial spending. Both policy shifts were motivated by Ottawa's desire to gain more public recognition for federal activities and to regain control of its own spending. The funding formula was now less oriented towards provincial programming needs in favour of addressing the worsening federal fiscal position. Many provinces thus faced sizeable budgetary shortfalls, which reinforced resentment towards Ottawa.

But did this vertical hostility that pervaded federal–provincial relations impede horizontal collaboration among the provinces? In fact, cooperation among them increased, and there was a new enthusiasm for formal province-to-province interactions. An organizational revolution began in 1967 with the establishment of the Council of Ministers of Education, Canada (CMEC). The CMEC was the culmination of nearly a decade of efforts by provincial politicians and education officials, spurred by two factors: fear of unilateral federal intervention in the sector, and a desire to improve coordinative leadership in education.

The federal government signalled that it was considering an intervention in the education sector. At the close of the 1950s, the British Commonwealth was organizing the First Commonwealth Education Conference. Instead of consulting with the provinces through the CEA, which had been the standard practice to date, the Secretary of State for External Affairs and the Prime Minister unilaterally developed Canada's program for the conference. This did not augur well for relations with the provinces, which demanded an explanation. Federal officials claimed they did not know whom to contact on the education portfolio, as provincial leadership was unclear. Provincial officials moved quickly to inform federal leaders of a new protocol:

> The Minister's reply served to confirm rather than allay our concern that the competent education authorities had been completely overlooked in the preparation for a Conference in which they should have been particularly involved ... There has now been established a Standing Committee of the Ministers responsible for education and I suggested that if the External Aid Office had matters of important policy on the Commonwealth Program to discuss with the Ministers of Education, I would be glad to ask the Chairman of the new Committee of Ministers to arrange for a place on the agenda.[12]

The same provincial officials recognized that they needed to strengthen their own leadership in the field, given that other members of the policy community had harsh words about the state of Canadian education. The president of the CTF, for example, launched a highly public campaign demanding that the federal government establish national standards in schools across Canada. The Federation claimed that while "Canadians pay lip service to the goddess of equality ... the inequalities in our schools are swelling into a national scandal."[13] According to the CTF, it was vitally important to address provincial disparities, and for this to happen, the federal government needed to create mandatory standards applicable to all the provinces.

The CTF's campaign was bolstered by a growing sense that the provincial public schooling systems were failing to prepare students adequately for the new knowledge economy. Meanwhile, the Bladen Commission, initiated by the Canadian Universities Foundation, recommended the appointment of a federal Minister of Education to improve interprovincial comparability of programs and ensure that schools were meeting the demands of the new labour market.[14] A *Globe and Mail* editorial succinctly captured this sentiment, which found traction at the time:

> A small but growing number of professional educators and school trustees have come to deplore the fact that, because of Canada's system of government, it is generally assumed a Dominion Government department or office of education is unlikely ... In a world where the yardstick of a nation's strength is the number of its intellectual elite – the percentage of professional and skilled persons in its population – the idea has gradually grown in Canada that the time has come for educational leadership from Ottawa.[15]

Hence the expediency of creating a separate body where the Ministers of Education would be able to build their capacity to coordinate their activities. This started with the creation of a separate standing committee under the auspices of the CEA. Following its inaugural meeting, Freeman K. Stewart, the Director General of the CEA, indicated his own aspirations for the committee: "I am hopeful that this new Standing Committee of Ministers will be able to give us more of a sense of direction in Canadian education than we have previously been able to have."[16] This committee would later act as the formal springboard for the organizational evolution that culminated in the CMEC.

Throughout the 1960s, expanding enrolments, increased spending, innovations in vocational training, and intensifying international activities in the education portfolio all motivated the ministers to formalize their relations beyond the subcommittee of the CEA. The heterogeneity of the CEA membership had exposed the ministers directly to the competing interests of various education stakeholders while restricting the ability of political officials to focus on interprovincial initiatives. The ministers thus opted to establish a separate intergovernmental organization to strengthen their capacity to coordinate independently. This also finally resolved the issue of international representation, for the Ministers of Education secured a deal with the Department of External Affairs to permanently appoint the head of CMEC as the official spokesperson for Canadian education on the international stage, including in bodies such as the OECD.

The timing of the CMEC's creation was significant for a number of reasons. First, a shared sense of national identity had spilled over from the Centennial celebrations in 1967. Caught up in the nationalist senti-ment, provincial leaders wanted to show a cohesive front in key policy sectors. What is more, the education sector had garnered considerable attention both domestically and abroad as studies connected economic development and productivity to educational attainments.[17] Human capital theory, advanced by scholars such as Gary S. Becker,[18] had cap-tured the minds of political leaders and education experts. As a result, the ministers of education wanted to establish a "clearer identity"[19] for the education sector. Moreover, as Donald Smiley cogently argued, the late 1960s and early 1970s saw "a vast amount of effort expended in Ottawa and the provinces in pursuit of the rationalization and coordi-nation of governmental operations on a jurisdiction-wide basis."[20] Ex-ecutive federalism, or ongoing intergovernmental negotiations, became the preferred arrangement for structuring political relations among the different governments. As captured in Richard Simeon's seminal book *Federal–Provincial Diplomacy*,[21] these dynamics were akin to those in international relations and played out not only vertically between the federal and provincial governments but also horizontally among the provinces. The provincial ministers thus chose to establish a separate intergovernmental organization to enhance their capacity to coordinate in elementary and secondary education in Canada.

The impetus for one of the first important projects tackled by the CMEC came from the international arena. In the 1970s, the OECD conducted a series of reviews of the education policies of its member states. National governments were asked to compile information and data on the various programs, policies, and financial arrangements for education in their respective states, and the OECD deployed teams of independent reviewers to assess and evaluate the state of educa-tion in its member countries. In the absence of a national Department of Education, the CMEC was tapped as the legitimate authority to gather the material for Canada, and this helped fortify the organiza-tion's role in the Canadian education policy network. The result of this initiative was the most comprehensive evaluation of Canadian education to date, and one that provided the provinces with unprec-edented access to information on the activities of the other jurisdic-tions.[22] In their final report, quoted on the opening page of this book, the independent reviewers made a damning indictment of Canadian education. If the provincial ministers of education needed any further excuse to nurture the CMEC, they found it in the evaluation of the OECD's examiners.[23]

Regional connectivity also changed in the early 1970s when New Brunswick, Nova Scotia, and Prince Edward Island created the Council of Maritime Premiers (CMP). Building on the conclusions of the *Report on Maritime Union* (the Deutsch Report), the CMP established a legal framework to coordinate the activities of the Maritime provinces, harmonize provincial programs and policies, and ratify common positions on matters involving all parties. The impact of this change in regional connectivity on education was not immediate; it did, however, lead to a major conference on education in Atlantic Canada, held in 1978. That conference considered the common problems facing schools in the region. It also heralded a new era in Atlantic Canada, one that would coalesce in the 1990s. For the moment, however, the years 1967 to 1982 are our focus. We begin on the easternmost point in North America – the province of Newfoundland.

Central Educational Administration – Complete Convergence

While the other nine provinces were moving towards public, secular control over education, Newfoundland's system had remained firmly under the thumb of religious leaders. Politicians had sometimes tried to wrest control from the clerics, but their efforts had failed to bring about transformative change. In the early 1900s, a time when British and Canadian businesses were investing in Newfoundland's natural resources, the Education Act of 1903 authorized the Governor in Council to establish amalgamated schools that would bundle the denominations together, thereby secularizing the institutions. Only nine such schools, however, were operating by the end of the 1920s.[24] In 1935, the Commission government announced its intention to abolish the denominational superintendents that represented seven different Christian sects. Religious leaders sprang into action and campaigned vigorously against the proposal. Galvanizing the support of the public, which had long seen the religious institutions as the sole providers of public programs, the clerics forced the Commission government to withdraw the plan. Unwilling to completely concede the idea of secular influence in education, the Commission government forged a compromise of sorts, creating a bifurcated Council of Education in which leadership was split between an elected minister (representing Newfoundland in the CEA) and denominational superintendents (representing each of the major sects in the province). Despite this effort, the lion's share of authority remained with the denominational superintendents, who easily worked around the hapless political minister. According to the Council's rules of operation, moreover, all policy-related decisions required unanimous approval; as a consequence, the religious superintendents engaged in complex negotiations among themselves, with generally unsatisfactory results. In the words of one official from the Council of Education, "after the compromises between Superintendents the resultant decision is often nebulous and vague."[25]

After entering Confederation in 1950, Premier Joey Smallwood – who had committed himself to addressing the dearth of viable public programs available to Newfoundlanders – used federal transfers to help create new social programs and built roads to connect outport communities. The improved transportation infrastructure made regional high schools feasible, and Family Allowance payments were linked to school attendance to encourage steady participation. This strategy of conditional provincial payments was designed to improve school participation rates that had long lagged behind the rest of Canada.[26] Per pupil spending rose from $64.00 to $98.00 between 1950 and 1955, and attendance rose from 76.4 per cent in 1947–8 to 92.4 per cent in 1964–5. Clearly, the federal government could play an important indirect role in the expansion of social programs. However, the traditional means of administering education remained firmly in place, and denominational leaders lost none of their authority.

In 1964, the Newfoundland government convened a Royal Commission to assess the province's schools. In the course of its detailed research, the Warren Commission determined that, although there had been some improvements, Newfoundland schools still remained markedly behind those in the rest of Canada. What is more, the commissioners placed the blame for this firmly on fractured and fragmented administrative practices:

> The Department of Education as it now operates is a divisive force in our educational system. We believe that all officials of the Department should be fully committed to all the children of the Province, irrespective of their religious beliefs.[27]

After reviewing the arrangements in the other provinces, the Warren Commission recommended that the Department of Education be reorganized along functional lines and that the Council of Education be reduced to an advisory role, mirroring the strategy advocated by the Parent Commission in Quebec. Premier Smallwood took decisive action, passing the Department of Education Act (1968), which ended "the reign of the czars of Newfoundland education, the denominational superintendents."[28] The legislation established individual ministerial responsibility backed by a stronger, functionally organized Department of Education.

With the passage of the 1968 act in Newfoundland, interprovincial uniformity in central educational administration was achieved. A number of important insights can be distilled from Newfoundland's convergence that speak back to the analytical architecture developed in chapter 3. First, changes in the former colony's connections to the rest of Canada had a significant impact on Newfoundland's society and its education sector. Union with Canada increased the province's financial resources and further strengthened its engagement with the Canadian education policy community. However, new information and increased financial resources continued to run up against an internal education regime that – as the Warren Commission argued – hindered educational advancement. This confirms how the internal context affects how new information is received by a particular jurisdiction, which leads to the second insight that emerges from this policy history.

The transformation in Newfoundland exemplified the second pathway to convergence. Increased connections across the policy communities intensified the exchange of ideas between the former British colony and the other provinces. Results from the rest of Canada were now the benchmark against which Newfoundland measured its educational advances, and the results were troubling. Faced with these challenges in an institutional setting comparable to those of the other Canadian provinces (in this case, administering a policy sector in a parliamentary system), policy actors – such as the members of the Warren Commission – looked to the other jurisdictions for inspiration. The commission, moreover, took careful note of the tactics used by Quebec policy makers when they wrested control over education from the confessional boards. Having found a workable option that was demonstrably successful, decision makers implemented a policy change that completed the interprovincial convergence in educational administration, with similar administrative structures overseeing the systems from coast to coast.

The Rise of Composite Secondary Schooling

In the 1950s, a consensus had formed among Canadian educators in favour of composite secondary education. Education experts, the CEA, and various other associations promoted this policy idea and encouraged its adoption across the provinces. In spite of these enterprising efforts, activities in secondary education remained haphazard at best; the legacy of streaming students into specialized programs proved difficult to dismantle. Also, the federal government's Technical and Vocational Training Assistance Act (TVTA) sought to fortify the bilateral option, thus contradicting the recommendations of education experts and the CEA. Between 1967 and 1982, however, the bilateral model lost its resilience and the composite model became the preferred choice for secondary schooling. This policy transformation and the accompanying path-shaping choice was provoked by two factors. First, because new schools had been built earlier in the 1960s with federal funds, the implementation of the composite system did not place undue strain on provincial coffers, for the necessary infrastructure was already in place. Second, the growing coalition of support around child-centred education created a hospitable ideational climate for the ascension of the composite model across the ten provincial systems. Both these forces are discussed in further detail below.

Through the TVTA, the federal government had hoped to expand bilateral schools and multiply the provision of vocational training in provincially run high schools. Despite Ottawa's intentions, the TVTA proved to be an inadequate device for encouraging the provinces down a particular pathway. Because it lacked long-term oversight mechanisms, once federal funds were turned over, the provincial Departments of Education could rewrite secondary school regulations as they saw fit. Schools built with federal funds, ostensibly for the purpose of vocational training, were simply reorganized by the ministries according to the principles of composite schooling once the viability of the strategy had been accepted. The TVTA thus failed to coercively influence provincial policy choices; decision makers instead followed the option advocated and disseminated through the epistemic and broader policy community.

Although the federal government had failed to install its preferred policy option, its indirect role in expanding and institutionalizing composite schooling must be acknowledged. Simply put, the federal funds used to support the construction of schools ensured that the physical buildings necessary to house the programs were already in place. Although this is difficult to determine conclusively, given the fiscal problems that had earlier beset the provinces when they tried to expand secondary schooling, we can surmise that without federal funds, this critical infrastructure might not have been erected.

Also, there was strong synergy between composite schooling and the goals of child-centred educationalists, which had gained "considerable ideological hegemony over elementary and secondary educational policy making."[29] Child-centred education focused on enabling individuals to achieve personal "self-fulfillment ... [and] the cultivation and enrichment of all human beings."[30] Experts declared that citizens needed to be "more than mere clients of the educational system. They must share in determining it."[31] With its emphasis on individual choice and flexibility, the composite model offered a viable alternative for child-centred advocates intent on reconfiguring the system. Provincial policy makers therefore moved to diversify secondary school course offerings and to eliminate (or dramatically reduce) aspects of streaming in secondary schools.[32]

Interprovincial convergence on secondary schooling was not, however, absolute. Quebec developed an alternative model. This policy divergence grew out of the historical legacy of the dual system and the efforts then under way to revolutionize the sector. Similar to the commissions in other provinces, the Parent Report recognized that Quebec needed to diversify its high school offerings:

> Obviously secondary education cannot be the same for everyone. All will participate but not all will start out with the same talents, the same preparation, the same interests, and the same needs. All will not persevere to the end, and all will not seek identical training. Some intend to pursue later studies that vary greatly from each other and require widely different preparation ... The diversification of secondary education is still a goal to be attained, and it will considerably change the organization of programmes and courses.[33]

But rather than simply adhering to the practices of the other Canadian provinces, the Parent Commission advised the government to create a unique system.

Contending that a student "is not yet ready to embark on specialized higher studies before reaching the age of eighteen or even nineteen,"[34] the commission drew inspiration from systems beyond Canadian borders. Impressed by the American junior college system, the English "sixth forms," and the findings of a French report produced by the *Groupe d'étude des Grandes Écoles*, the commissioners called for separate two-year post-secondary institutions that would provide pre-university general academic education and vocational training under the umbrella of the public education system.[35] In June 1967, the Quebec cabinet issued an Order in Council and a new regime for secondary and post-secondary studies appeared in the province. Instant institutions were created by amalgamating the existing classical colleges, normal schools, and institutes of technology. In this way, Quebec fashioned a revolutionary model that combined features of both the composite and partite systems, a model that has come to be known as the *Cégep*. Marked improvements were quickly realized: the number of fifteen-year-olds attending high school jumped from 75 per cent in 1961 to 97 per cent in 1977.[36]

The difference between the Quebec model and the one at work throughout the rest of Canada is straightforward. Students in most provinces attend the same secondary school until they graduate from grade twelve (or, in the past in some provinces, grade thirteen for those who plan to go to university). In Quebec, students graduate at the end of grade eleven and then attend an institute that prepares them either for university or for entry into a technical profession. The Quebec model thus combines the composite and partite systems.[37] And, unlike the four-year norm in the rest of Canada, the Government of Quebec expected its universities to reduce their undergraduate programs from four to three years.[38]

Quebec was able to transform its system in part because it was now willing to accept conditional grants and use federal funds for techni-cal and vocational manpower training programs. Soon after coming to power in 1960, the Liberal government led by Premier Jean Lesage an-nounced that it would be his administration's policy "to take the nec-essary steps to accept, on a temporary basis and without prejudice to its full sovereignty, all the conditional grants it is not now receiving which are made to the other provinces by the Federal Government."[39] The rapid influx of funds supported the new direction the province was trying to take; however, given that all of the provinces had received funds yet had not introduced similar hybrid arrangements, federal dol-lars alone do not explain this alternative model. Instead, circumstances within the province made it a suitable space for the creative strategy.

Because the first public high schools for French-speaking Quebecers only opened in 1956, private colleges had been providing the bulk of secondary education in the province.[40] Meanwhile, English-speaking Quebecers were being served by high schools operated by the Prot-estant school boards. The Parent Commission found a hodgepodge of strongly elitist institutions with limited opportunities for students as well as significant disparities between the two linguistic communities. Reformers knew they needed to create a regime that would expand access to post-secondary education, turn secondary education away from its focus on classical academics, and address the inequality between the Catholic and Protestant systems, all while maintaining the support of vested interests. To achieve these ends, the commission advocated capitalizing on the institutional diversity already at work in Quebec and transforming the patchwork of practices into an integrated schooling system:

> Hence, owing their existence to fortuitous needs and to population pressures, a considerable number of elements are available out of which to erect a system of diversified education. The sum total of these, for the moment made up of unrelated parts, needs to be rethought and rationally coordinated into a harmonious whole, intended to correspond to the aptitudes and talents of all children and to prepare each of them for life.[41]

The province had the physical infrastructure necessary to house the programs and the personnel to carry them out. Thus, the Parent Commission's proposed new model of secondary schooling was administratively viable in terms of existing conditions in Quebec. The commissioners and the Quebec government persuaded the province's education stakeholders to buy into the transformation, which made its implementation politically viable. Indeed, the innovative approach was endorsed by all the key members of the policy community, who acknowledged it as a viable solution to a serious problem in the province. The hybrid model was put in place, and the system that resulted continues to differentiate Quebec from the rest of Canada today.

Before leaving this dimension of the education sector, a final question needs to be addressed: Has the *Cégep* system impeded the emergence of a *de facto* policy framework in Canadian education? The simplest and most straightforward answer is no. First, looking within the province, *Cégeps* have had quite a positive impact on education in Quebec. According to a 2003 Statistics Canada study examining pathways to tertiary education, Quebec residents were 1.6 times less likely to delay post-secondary enrolment than respondents living in Ontario, and this had helped increase educational achievement. Also according to the StatsCan report, *Cégeps* can be given much of the credit for this: "The CEGEP system in Quebec facilitates a relatively easy transition from high school to post-secondary institution."[42] Second, thinking more broadly, the *Cégep* system does *not* make it harder for Quebecers to attend post-secondary institutions outside the province, nor does it prevent other Canadian students from gaining post-secondary degrees in Quebec. Clearly, then, the diversity exemplified by the *Cégep* system is tolerable and has not hindered the development of a pan-Canadian education framework. Indeed, this policy diversity proves the value of federalism as an institutional arrangement, for it enables multiple orders of government to pursue distinctive pathways and fashion unique policy systems, which can then be interwoven with those developed in the rest of the country.

Cancelling the Provincial Departmentals

Universal exams had been a standard component of provincial regulations since the inception of mass schooling. In most provinces, students needed to write exams to get into secondary school, and in every province, students were subjected to intense ministry-approved exams, colloquially known as "departmentals," the results of which determined whether a student would be accepted by a university. The prevalence of mandatory examinations reflected a propitious alignment between the policy instrument and the needs of the sector; education officials valued the practice as a tool for central control and quality assurance. Moreover, before teacher training improved, standardized exams were a means to ensure that students were learning mandatory course requirements regardless of where they lived. This was especially important, given that the Canadian population was both sparse and scattered. The Cameron Report summarized the value of mandatory exams thusly:

> Since they [provincial exams] are imposed from outside the school, they provide for both pupils and teachers a strong form of extrinsic motivation for better achievement of the type measured by written examinations. They provide also a powerful means of central control over the curriculum, ensuring province-wide emphasis upon those parts of the curriculum considered by the central authority to be the most important.[43]

In the 1950s, provincial commissions began debating the merits of standardized exams. Interestingly, while voicing a number of concerns, all of the ensuing reports came out in favour of continuing the departmentals.[44] Perhaps more incredibly, within ten years, this had reversed;

the hegemonic support for the instrument came unhinged and most provinces turned their backs on the practice. The reasons for this policy transformation were threefold. The first highlights the ways in which decisions in different dimensions of the education sector can open the way to particular policy options.

After the district consolidations of the 1950s, school boards were large enough to hire district-level specialists capable of evaluating schools and providing on-site guidance for teaching and learning.[45] This reduced the need for universal exams as a means of quality control. Teachers' training and certification standards were improving, and there was a secular upgrade of the profession (see Appendix 7). With their expanding skill sets, teachers were less supportive of standardized exams, seeing them as a restriction on their professional freedom. Unions and associations began lobbying provincial leaders to end the practice, a sign that important members of the policy community were withdrawing their support for this traditional policy instrument. All of this rendered the arguments in favour of mandatory assessments less compelling.

Larger boards and upgrades in the teaching profession also enabled a shift towards administrative and policy decentralization, which in the 1960s was a prominent objective of Canadian education officials. Ministries of Education loosened their control over a variety of areas of public schooling, including curriculum development and mandated assessments. In certain districts of Prince Edward Island, for example, the provincial government decided to assign control over instructional content, program design, and supervisory processes to qualified professionals.[46] This trend drew inspiration from the broader international movement to decentralize government control over education and introduce much-needed flexibility to the system.

The final piece of the puzzle locked into place following a series of provincial reports that questioned the continued validity of mandatory, centralized, high-stakes testing. In this marked reassessment of previous declarations, they were informed by the tenets of child-centred education.[47] On being told of "inflexible programs, outdated curricula, unrealistic regulations, regimented organization, and mistaken aims of education,"[48] the Provincial Committee on Aims and Objectives in the Schools of Ontario (the Hall–Dennis Report) called for public schooling to be reinvigorated and recommended the institutionalization of ungraded classrooms in the province. The same report went on to argue that ungraded classrooms would be "disappointing if year-end examinations and competitive report cards were not abolished at the same time."[49] Ontario decided to retain graded classrooms, but following the report's recommendations, it did end the practice of universal exams in 1968, setting off a domino effect across the country.

Almost immediately after Ontario announced its decision, British Columbia indicated that it would no longer conduct provincial exams. Manitoba and Prince Edward Island changed their regimes in 1970; Nova Scotia and Alberta abolished exams in 1972. Deviating slightly from this general trajectory, Saskatchewan maintained a limited standardized examination program for students from small rural schools whose teachers lacked provincial accreditation. It seemed that while the Saskatchewan government endorsed the child-centred philosophy, material conditions in the province made it a practical impossibility to put a complete end to standardized exams. The other outliers were Quebec and Newfoundland. Even though provincial reports had endorsed the child-centred paradigm, both provinces maintained the practice of standardized exams. Were the two provinces rejecting the tenets of child-centred education? Or were the actors unaware of the developments in the rest of Canada? The short answer to both these questions is no, judging from the policy statements and reports in these two provinces. The Parent Commission endorsed the child-centred paradigm clearly and consistently throughout its volumes:

> We have outlined the pedagogical themes which have served as guidelines for this second section: the need for an activist pedagogy more completely centred on the child and the adolescent; the necessity for general training more available to all ... the desire for an education which will respect the intellect, the creative gifts, the spirit of inquiry; the development of a teaching less bookish, closer to direct observation, to social experience and to mass culture.[50]

Similar ideas were regularly articulated in the pages of the Warren Commission:

> The Commission believes that the narrow academic programme which may have served Newfoundland students reasonably well in the past is woefully inadequate and unsuitable today. Radical changes must be introduced in curriculum policies, allowing greater flexibility within individual schools and individual grades. Enriched and remedial programmes must be provided at the elementary and secondary level.[51]

Furthermore, decision makers and members of those two provinces' policy communities were well aware that policies in this regard were changing in the rest of Canada, for they were plugged into the national network through various organizations, including the CMEC. The explanation for policy divergence thus lies elsewhere.

It seems that, much as with Saskatchewan's pragmatic choice, the decisions made in Quebec and Newfoundland were driven by internal features of their respective education regimes. The longevity of denominational control in both jurisdictions had seriously delayed teacher professionalization, the expansion of secondary schooling, and curricular reform.[52] With regard to Newfoundland, the Warren Commission put it bluntly:

> The abolition of external examinations has been recommended by a number of Royal Commissions in Canada. It is the view of this Commission, however, that this Province is far from the point where such a recommendation can be seriously considered. The level of teacher qualifications in this Province, the proliferation of small school systems and small schools, the meagre resources of local boards of education, the dearth of highly qualified administrators, supervisory personnel, department heads and subject consultants at the local level, and the general inadequacy of staffing regulations must surely indicate that the majority of schools and school systems are not prepared to receive this measure of professional responsibility and indeed would be reluctant to accept it.[53]

Finally, where the governments of other provinces had long enjoyed substantial control over the content of curriculum and the supervision of schools, the state had only recently gained supremacy over education in Quebec and Newfoundland. Given these conditions, the idea of ending provincial exams lacked the necessary internal viability to gain acceptance, and the two provinces did not follow the general trend that was sweeping the rest of Canada.

University-Led Teacher Education Moves to the East

The relative youth of normal schools in western Canada and the willingness of universities there to experiment in teacher education created a hospitable climate for incubating and fostering a new approach to teacher training. In eastern Canada, however, the policy context was less conducive to the idea. It was only in the 1960s that provinces east of Manitoba started considering the notion, driven in large part by the growing perception that normal schools were providing insufficient training for teachers in the region and that teachers in western Canada were receiving better preparation through the universities. However, once the eastern provinces started considering the idea – thanks to competitive pressures – policy entrepreneurs encountered a number of hurdles. To see why, it is helpful to consider events in Ontario.

In March 1966, William Davis, the Minister of Education (and later premier) informed the legislature that the government intended to transfer responsibility for teacher education to the provincial universities. In this, he was following the recommendations of the MacLeod Report, which had examined the teacher education programs in western Canada and advocated a similar approach for Ontario.[54] Davis warned Ontarians that "sweeping changes in teacher education cannot be made overnight";[55] nonetheless, he was hopeful that within a few years, teacher training would be housed in the university system.

Negotiations between the province and the universities proved problematic. The latter were reluctant to provide teacher education, particularly for elementary teachers.[56] Faculty members and administrators did not perceive teacher training as a legitimate component of university education, for it was not a classical discipline, nor was it regarded as a genuine profession. Minister Davis was also adamant that normal school instructors should be guaranteed places in the new Faculties of Education, similar to arrangements made in Alberta. Represented by their faculty associations, university professors opposed this plan on the grounds that normal school instructors did not have the necessary credentials for academia.[57] The final impediment stemmed from university officials' apprehensions that university autonomy would be compromised if teacher preparation fell to them. Under the normal school system, the Ministry of Education controlled virtually every aspect of teacher training. The fear among administrators was that the minister would attempt to install a similar type of monopoly when transferring responsibilities to the universities.[58] The successful implementation (and subsequent convergence) of university-led teacher education to the east thus needed further encouragement.

That support first arrived in the form of Royal Commissions, as members of the epistemic community had started to alter their position. The Hall–Dennis Report, for one, stated that "the Committee is insistent that every teacher must have a longer and broader pre-service education, general and professional, at university and leading to a university degree."[59] The Graham Report in Nova Scotia similarly held that "the programme for teacher education and training should lead to a degree granted by the affiliated university. The programme should include university-level general education, intensive professional training, and a year of internship."[60] Government officials in the Ministries of Education were thus receiving cogent directives from influential members of the epistemic community to follow the lead of the western provinces.

Meanwhile, teachers east of the Manitoba border were throwing their support behind the policy idea. Since 1965, the CTF had been sponsoring an ongoing project in teacher education and certification; its conferences generated a series of publications.[61] Teachers believed that university education would elevate the standing of their occupation and further their goal of professional independence from provincial officials. University-led teacher education thus became linked to a more general drive to transfer the locus of decision making from the central departments down to school boards and particular schools; it was thought that university training would afford teachers greater legitimacy to claim professional status next to lawyers, surgeons, and engineers.

A consensus emerged throughout the policy community that the end of the normal school system was inevitable. The Committee on Teacher Education at the University of Prince Edward Island declared:

> Within a very brief time, all teacher education will take place in universities. Teaching at all levels will soon become a degree profession involving up to five years of university studies for basic certification. The traditional distinction in status between elementary and secondary schoolteachers is fast disappearing as qualifications and pay are equalized. There is a growing recognition that elementary education is the most crucial stage of the educational continuum and that it is sheer nonsense to put the least prepared teachers in the early grades. Teachers are actively seeking professional status by demanding improved standards, increased length of preparation, greater autonomy, a share in educational decision-making, and better pay. Teachers' organizations are seeking and gradually winning some control over the award of permanent teaching certificates. It is acknowledged that the achievement of a degree is only the first step in a continuous process of education and re-education. In-service education will be essential in the future for all teachers.[62]

Drawing from the experience of their western counterparts, and motivated in part by the desire to remain competitive, decision makers in eastern Canada decided to adopt the same policy innovation. Parallel pressures to enhance initial teacher education, the trends observed in other parts of the country, and the endorsements of key members of the epistemic and broader policy communities who were concerned that teachers in eastern Canada were falling behind those educated in western Canada provided the necessary lubricant to push decision makers into ending the practice of normal schools. PEI formalized the transfer in 1969; between 1969 and 1971, normal schools disappeared in Quebec; New Brunswick finalized its arrangements in 1973. In Ontario, despite Davis's early optimism, the transfer was not completed until 1978.

There is no question that the idea of university-led teacher education diffused from western Canada to the eastern provinces. This process was mobilized through the interactive effects of alterations in the broader policy climate and subtle adjustments within the policy contexts of the eastern education systems. Conferences sponsored by the CEA, the CTF, and the Canadian Conference on Education allowed decision makers and education stakeholders to debate the merits of the policy option openly and to learn from the examples set by others.[63] When teacher education reform appeared on the policy agenda, bureaucrats and politicians looked to the systems in other provinces and used them as benchmarks for their own activities. Almost every provincial Royal Commission or special report on the subject contained sections describing the models of university-led teacher education being used in other parts of Canada, and this provided the necessary encouragement to shake the legitimacy of the prevailing policy legacy in favour of path-shaping change.[64] Furthermore, these reports and commissions highlighted the differences in the quality of teacher preparation being offered by the universities relative to that in the normal schools. In this way, the provinces were virtual laboratories of policy experimentation, with policy diffusion taking place through active lesson drawing somewhat motivated by competitive pressures as decision makers in eastern Canada learned from the example set by Alberta and the other western provinces. The policies for initial teacher education converged across the country, restoring the uniformity that had once existed.

Before we move on to the final developments in education, it is important for us to pause and consider an important unintended consequence of this path-shaping change. Under the normal school regime, Ministries of Education had occupied the central position in the policy network, maintaining total control over this dimension of education policy. When teacher training was shifted to universities, this monopoly ended. The principle of university autonomy meant that these new Departments of Education could control the structure, design, and delivery of initial teacher training – subject to ministry accreditation. The impact of this would be felt in the coming years (although not immediately), with the effects bleeding beyond the dimension of teacher education and into teacher certification and credential recognition.

A New Model of Education Finance

Considering all of these policy developments in the sector, it should come as no surprise that elementary and secondary education had become one of the largest public expenditures in Canada. By the 1920s, spending for public schooling had outstripped government allocations for all other social programs, and teachers were the largest group of public employees in the country.[65] The Great Depression caused some reductions in spending, but in the 1950s it began to rise again, and in 1965, expenditure on public schools as a percentage of total spending reached its highest point since 1926, at 28.7 per cent (see Appendix 8).

Education finance was a frequent topic at all the national conventions, due in no small part to the changing policy climate, which was characterized by growing uncertainty and economic instability. In 1961, for example, the Canadian Conference on Education released a report titled *Financing Education in Canada*. Observing that provincial grants for education had swelled since 1945 relative to the costs covered by local property taxes, the report predicted that the overall costs of education would continue to rise "so long as public education is expected to widen its range of services, to raise the quality of its performance, and to serve a growing proportion of our population."[66] According to the research, the factors contributing to the rising costs included the following: expanding secondary education; changing student–teacher ratios; rising capital costs; improved educational resources; rising administrative costs; and a marked increase in teachers' salaries. Provincial decision makers were well aware of the growing problem of education finance and needed to develop a means to control seemingly unsustainable increases in schooling expenditures.

Individual components of the policy community also entered the fray.[67] In 1955, the CSTA released a report titled *School Finance in Canada*. Among other things, that report advocated equalization grants and uniform tax rates to finance basic programs in all the provinces.[68] The CTF similarly highlighted the fiscal imbalances facing the education sector: internal disparities within the provinces were translating into gross inequalities between school boards. In its own report, the CTF bluntly stated

the most important facts concerning the financing of education in Canada, namely, that support for education by each level of government is inversely related to the revenue available to it. The federal government, which has the largest and most broadly based taxation sources, spent only 4.0 per cent on education in 1962. The provincial governments, which have the second highest resources, spent 29.4 per cent of them on education. The municipal governments, with the smallest financial resources and the narrowest tax base, spent 35.3 per cent on education.[69]

Given the significance of teachers' salaries as a cost in the sector,[70] it was not unexpected that both the CSTA and the CTF raised the issue. The CTF sponsored a series of conferences specifically about education finance that shifted the topic still higher on the active policy agenda.

· Now, individual provincial associations were taking up the banner of fiscal reform. One of the most succinct discussions of education finance was put forward by the Alberta Teachers' Association in its report *Quality Education: What Price?*:

It is not difficult to understand why education today costs more than it did twenty-five years ago. Twenty-five years ago Alberta was primarily a rural province with a stable population. Most children had to settle for an elementary level of education and those who did go on to receive high school education had a narrow range of subjects from which to choose. The schools were often small and overcrowded and lacking in libraries, laboratories, gymnasia or other facilities now considered basic. Teachers, when their services were available, were often marginally qualified and received an average salary lower than the average wage or salary of the Alberta labour force as a whole. The picture today is radically different.[71]

Education associations thus propelled the spread of information on the state of education finance in each of the provinces to individuals and associations in the ten jurisdictions.[72]

In 1967, under a Liberal government, New Brunswick spearheaded a new way of thinking about education finance. Breaking with the traditional approach, which entailed local property taxes buttressed by provincial grants, the government moved to centralize all education funding, thus installing a path-shaping change in the province. Under the terms of Bill 22, the province reclaimed all taxation powers from local districts and drew funds for public schooling from general provincial revenues. Simultaneously, the province reduced the number of school boards from 422 to 33. The New Brunswick model was designed to accomplish two objectives: to mitigate internal disparities and to expand the delivery of secondary schooling.

New Brunswick's program was intended to ensure that all districts had comparable access to funds, yet substantial disparities persisted because of pernicious discrepancies in local revenue-raising capacities.[73] When introducing Bill 22 in the legislature, Minister of Education W. Wynn Meldrum had declared:

> To us, in this session, is given the privilege of removing some of the generations' old inequities which geography and economics have created and replacing them by an education system designed to fit our children for the challenges of the most vital and changing times in the history of mankind.[74]

Eradicating the financial inequalities between school boards was therefore a key objective of the provincial government.

Provincial leaders, especially in the Department of Education, were acutely aware of critical problems in the provision of secondary education in the province:

> In this technological age where minimum educational requirements are steadily rising and where individuals lack adequate training which will enable them to secure satisfactory employment a greater emphasis must be placed on the importance of making available to every child the highest possible amount of education. The day of the unskilled worker is fast disappearing.[75]

New Brunswick's minister and deputy minister both realized that many of the province's districts lacked the necessary revenues to operate high schools. Even after the previous round of district consolidations, many regions continued to face budgetary shortfalls. For these reasons, the project of elevating the quality of education and ensuring that its benefits were felt equally across the provinces faced a major barrier.[76] The ministry's educational elite thus supported fiscal centralization as a key instrument for expanding secondary education, recognizing the connections between these two dimensions of the education sector.

After Bill 22 was enacted, the fiscal disparities disappeared almost overnight in New Brunswick and the newly consolidated districts rapidly expanded their high school programs. Full provincial funding thus achieved the government's objective of equalizing districts in the province. Francophone communities in the province particularly benefited from the policy change, for they now enjoyed revenue levels comparable to those of Anglophone communities. In return for full funding, the New Brunswick government demanded close control over how those funds were spent; by this means, it was able to leverage its authority over other dimensions of the education sector. The province also assumed responsibility for collective bargaining and implemented a provincial property tax system that contributed to the province's overall revenues.[77] By the end of the 1960s, New Brunswick had established one of the most centralized education systems in North America; concomitantly, it reaped marked improvements in a number of key areas. Observing its success, other provinces in eastern Canada moved to institute full provincial funding. West of the Ottawa River, however, the model received a different reception. The explanation for this divergence lies in variations in economic health, the legitimacy of this sort of administrative and financial centralization, stakeholder activity within policy communities, and, to some extent, differences between provincial political cultures.

Full funding was more appealing in eastern Canada due in large part to the relative economic weakness of those provinces. General revenues in Atlantic Canada and Quebec lagged behind those of the other provinces; in 1967, provincial governments' per capita revenues, before intergovernmental transfers, as a percentage of the Canadian average, varied from 42.2 per cent in Newfoundland to 114.4 per cent in Ontario.[78] In the words of William J. McCordic: "It was in the poorer provinces such as New Brunswick, Prince Edward Island ... that the inadequacies of some local school boards to support an adequate school program first became apparent."[79] Provincial officials, recognizing the economic failings of impoverished local boards, had already increased central grants to local boards, and in New Brunswick and Prince Edward Island they were already paying teachers' salaries directly.[80] Centralized bargaining and spending practices were not a reality west of the Ottawa River. Consequently, the autonomy of local boards was already more circumscribed in eastern Canada than elsewhere in the country, making it easier for those provincial governments to reclaim the tax base.

Also, stakeholder associations in the western provinces actively campaigned against the policy idea, revealing divisions in the policy community on the issue. The BC Teachers' Federation (BCTF), for example, articulated two principles that informed its position on education finance: first, every child was entitled to an education; and second, every community should be able to offer programming beyond what the provincial government mandated. The federation continued:

> To achieve this freedom of action, fiscal independence, resulting in real management power and authority, has to exist at the school district level. The ability to tax and to expend monies must rest with the local citizens; otherwise, local autonomy is not possible.[81]

The BC School Trustees Association (BCSTA) echoed these sentiments, declaring that "local control by school boards is exercised in making decisions whether to go beyond the basic program, in determining the complete expenditure budget of the school district, and in deciding how the basic program is to be implemented."[82] Meanwhile, the Manitoba Teachers' Society (MTS) argued that "most authorities agree that the continuation of local autonomy is dependent primarily on some form of local discretion over expenditures."[83] Stakeholders' associations in western Canada thus favoured the continuation of shared-cost arrangements and local taxation rather than the installation of full provincial funding.

Finally, the political cultures of the western provinces were not amenable to the New Brunswick model. Events in Manitoba are instructive. Soon after New Brunswick implemented the change, the Manitoba government considered adopting full provincial funding. Consistent with its behaviour on district consolidations, it put the funding proposal to a province-wide plebiscite; the initiative failed to gain public approval. Manitobans opposed the extensive centralization that would inevitably result from full provincial funding. Unlike the educational elite in New Brunswick, Manitobans had not been persuaded that the benefits of centralization would outweigh the costs in terms of local autonomy and parental control.[84] Consequently, the previous uniformity in education finance no longer prevailed; the provinces west of the Ottawa River decided against following the early lead set by New Brunswick and other eastern provinces.

Building the Theoretical Links

The years between 1967 and 1982 saw subtle changes in structural aspects of the policy climate as well as considerable adjustments in its ideational components. Structurally, relations between the provinces and the federal government chilled, and this period witnessed the dramatic rise of Quebec nationalism; yet interprovincial interactions in the education sector remained extremely positive, and indeed were reinforced by the founding of the CMEC. Ideationally, provincial educationalists launched a revolution in public schooling. Progressive ideas, percolating since the 1920s, were finally anchored in certain dimensions of the education sector. Under the new paradigm, some traditional instruments, such as mandatory examinations, were largely eradicated, and some decision-making authority was transferred from the central ministries to local boards. The transfer of authority to the local level was possible thanks to the practice of consolidating boards that had swept the country. The goal of individualizing education programs had taken firm hold in the policy community, and this reverberated in the programmatic changes that developed in secondary schooling. These various policy changes across the respective provincial systems brought about and consolidated a reasonably integrated policy framework in Canadian education. What factors and processes enabled this remarkable achievement?

To start, the indirect role played by the federal government as financier must be acknowledged. It is unlikely that Newfoundland would have achieved such marked improvements without federal funds, or that universal secondary schooling would have been achieved from coast to coast. However, this indirect federal role does not detract from the central argument advanced here: that the provinces, on their own, fashioned the education policy framework. The provinces decisively rejected any conditions or stipulations the federal government attached to its funds – in the area of secondary schooling, for example, they chose to pursue their own preferred model centred on the tenets of composite schooling. Ottawa's attempts to coercively encourage its preferred policy options proved incapable of determining provincial policy trajectories.

Clearly, the broad ideational consensus that emerged across the policy community regarding progressive education resulted in remarkable consistency in the principle recommendations that flowed through the individual provincial systems. This ideational consensus helped pull all the provinces towards installing the composite model for high schools in their drive to improve educational access and opportunities for all Canadian students. That ideational consensus would have had scant effects had the provincial policy communities been fragmented or decoupled. Thanks to the efforts of both state and non-state actors in the education sector throughout earlier periods, the provincial communities had become quite integrated, with regular and frequent opportunities for information exchanges and policy learning. Consequently, the ideational consensus found the necessary transmission lines along which ideas could be carried and disseminated across the jurisdictional boundaries.

While it nurtured a policy framework, the broad ideational consensus and integrated policy community neither determined nor required complete uniformity. Regional innovations emerged – for example, in the area of education finance, when New Brunswick pioneered the model of full-state funding, which was later taken up by its eastern counterparts. Furthermore, not all provinces followed all of the recommendations based on the progressive paradigm. Internal attributes of the respective educational regimes mediated the installation of certain ideas; for example, Quebec and Newfoundland decided to retain mandatory exams, while the other provinces terminated that practice. Evidence from this period strengthens the argument that choices in one dimension of a particular sector can reverberate and ricochet in other dimensions, thus opening the door to certain options and rendering particular ideas more plausible. The establishment of full-state funding in New Brunswick, for example, allowed that province to expedite district consolidations while rapidly expanding secondary schooling. In fact, the achievement of the modestly integrated education framework was a culmination of previous decisions within each province interacting with the attributes and characteristics of the contemporary policy climate.

The reign of the child-centred paradigm, with its emphasis on individualization and equity, would prove to be short-lived, however. It would be replaced in the coming years by a new agenda focused on accountability and standardization. That agenda would be ushered in by wave of administrative reforms under the moniker of New Public Management. Now a different set of questions emerges: How robust would the Canadian education policy framework prove to be? Would the provinces adapt in comparable ways to this new administrative paradigm, or would marked variations emerge, winnowing the similarity and general consistency that had been achieved?

7 Standardizing Provincial Schooling (1982–2007)

In 1984, the Canadian Education Association commissioned a major opinion poll to gauge public sentiments towards elementary and secondary education. The survey found that only 10 per cent of Canadians were willing to give their schools an "A" grade. By 1990, this figure had dropped to 6 per cent and a sizeable 35 per cent of Canadians thought their schools were only worth about a "C" grade.[1] Prime Minister Brian Mulroney waded into the debate when he declared that public education was "shortchanging many Canadians and imposing a severe burden on our national competitiveness."[2] Business interests and expert panels voiced similar concerns about the quality of Canadian education; in 1988, the Canadian Business Task Force on Literacy pronounced that illiteracy cost Canada approximately $10 billion per year.[3] Reports also suggested that high school education was not preparing students for the challenge of university learning and that teachers had been artificially inflating grades unchecked by any real oversight.[4] None of this boded well for the provincial schooling systems.

Quality replaced the goals of equity and individualization as the motivating objective of policy reform. Politicians, education officials, and members of the public committed themselves to yet another "educational orthodoxy," this one geared towards improving the economy by tightening the connections among schools, employment, trade, and productivity.[5] Also central to the policy trajectory during these years was a government-wide reform agenda that had captured the minds of many decision makers from coast to coast. Public confidence in government was in a free fall, and there was a growing sense that citizens no longer trusted the institutions of the state.[6] The public service was increasingly criticized by citizens and elected politicians alike as an inefficient and ineffective tool for accomplishing collective goals; it became "fashionable to malign government and the people working for it."[7] The prescribed remedy for these administrative shortfalls emerged in the managerial paradigm of New Public Management (NPM), which called for performance-based measures, standardized reporting practices, and the expansion of non-standardized services, and for generally inculcating "entrepreneurial government."[8]

All of this translated into a tumultuous period for the education sector, one that saw the spread of centralized finance across the provinces, the rise of standardized assessments, the emergence of a new approach to curriculum, and an overall increase in the answerability of education professionals to political leaders. As the twin goals of standardization and improving the calibre of education uniformly took hold, Ministers of Education redoubled their efforts at collaboration both through the CMEC and in regionalized policy initiatives. Incredibly, while public education faced considerable scrutiny and critique, the integrity of the policy framework that had taken root in the previous period remained largely intact. This outcome is a testament to the robust integration of the provincial policy communities and the broad commitment shared from coast to coast to the general tenets of publicly delivered, universal education available to all Canadians regardless of their place of residence.

The Policy Climate

In August 1981, reacting to concerns that something was amiss in American education, the US Secretary of Education, T.H. Bell, commissioned a study to assess the quality of teaching and learning in American schools. The National Commission on Excellence in Education released its report, *A Nation at Risk*, which argued that America's "once unchallenged pre-eminence in commerce, industry, science, and technological innovation is being overtaken by competitors throughout the world."[9] This report attributed the decline to four general factors: the directionless content of public schooling (the "curricular smorgasbord"); low expectations and demands put on students; weak teacher preparation programs; and the generally unacceptable professional working life of instructors. To rectify these problems, the report called for the creation of a "New Basics" curriculum and the adoption of more rigorous and measurable standards for the nation's public schools. *A Nation at Risk* garnered significant international attention and became the cornerstone of calls for education reform across the Canadian provinces.

The OECD reinforced the contemporary reform agenda. The Directorate for Education and the Centre for Education Research and Innovation (CERI) redoubled their efforts to identify and disseminate best practices among the member states. The primary message in all this was that in order to foster human capital, countries needed to refocus their educational efforts and forge stronger links between education programs and the economy. These ideas were encapsulated in the OECD's *Education at a Glance* from 1993:

> Only a well-trained and highly adaptable labour force can provide the capacity to adjust to structural change and seize new employment opportunities created by technological progress. Achieving this will in many cases entail a re-examination, perhaps radical, of the economic treatment of human resources and education.[10]

As active participants in the OECD through the CMEC, the Canadian provinces were directly exposed to these critiques and policy trends in the international community. The rhetoric of effectiveness thus penetrated the domestic policy agenda, finding its way not only into individual Ministries of Education but also onto the CMEC's table.

In 2000, the Directorate for Education launched the Program for International Student Assessment (PISA). Arguing that international "surveys of educational achievement can be a valuable instrument for education policy analysis," the OECD designed this program to assess how well students near the end of compulsory education had acquired "some of the knowledge and skills essential for full participation in society."[11] To date, four rounds of the assessment have been completed in reading, mathematics, and science, and Canada's participation has been formidable. Orchestrated by the CMEC, each province provides a representative sample to ensure that a comprehensive and comparable image of the state of education is captured. In the latest round of the assessment, for example, approximately 23,000 fifteen-year-olds from 1,000 schools participated across the ten provinces.[12]

The sector-specific components of education reform were also carried by a wave of administrative reforms, labelled New Public Management, which targeted the broader public sector. NPM's conception of public accountability involved shifting the emphasis away from process accountability towards accountability for results:

> The idea of a shift in emphasis from policy making to management skills, from a stress on process to a stress on output, from orderly hierarchies to

an intendedly more competitive basis for providing public service, from fixed to variable pay and from a uniform and inclusive public service to a variant structure with more emphasis on contract provision.[13]

Some of the themes of NPM would resonate in the contemporary discourse of the education sector, for the new paradigm reinforced the notion that policy makers needed to improve the efficiency and accountability of the sector while increasing the flexibility and responsiveness of the public system. However, while certain elements of NPM, such as increasing accountability, carried weight in education, other potential aspects, including the intensification of public–private partnerships and the private provision of schooling, failed to gain a strong foothold across the various provincial education systems.[14] Consequently, despite the potential challenges presented by the NPM revolution, the pillars of the Canadian education policy framework remained safely intact.

Turning to the domestic arena, in 1982, a revolution occurred in Canadian interdependence: the Charter of Rights and Freedoms was ratified, and the Constitution was patriated. The Charter established a system of nationwide rights so that Canadians were now empowered to demand access to common programs set at relatively comparable standards across various policy areas.[15] Among the Charter's provisions were the unequivocal guarantee of mobility and a reinforcement of the common market. There was also a clause dedicated explicitly to the education sector. All of this ushered in some significant changes to the education sector, particularly in the areas of curriculum development and teacher certification (see below). For the moment, however, the implications of Section 23 – which guaranteed minority-language education – take centre stage.

Under Section 23, "where the numbers warranted," English or French linguistic minority populations were now guaranteed the right to educate their children in publicly funded schools. This provision was the product of a long campaign by provincial linguistic minority communities, which sought assurances of their right to manage their own schools.[16] The provision was subjected to intense critique by both "francophone organizations and the Commission of Official Languages pertaining to the recognition of collective rights and to the right of the linguistic communities to fully manage their own schools on the basis of that recognition."[17] According to its critics, Section 23 was overly vague and gave the courts too much power to interpret the phrase "where the numbers warranted." After the Charter was enacted, the expansion of minority-language facilities was neither automatic nor immediate, and many provinces struggled to find a way to comply with Section 23. Moreover, the implications ran even deeper than the opening of new schools. Chantal Hébert writes that "the article [s23] allowed much more: it included implicitly that minority communities could run their own school systems."[18] Section 23 thus drew attention not only to curriculum and course offerings but also to administrative practices in education more broadly, and this eventually forced reticent provinces to extend educational control to minority linguistic communities within their borders. Thanks in large part to the new constitutional provision, French-language school boards gradually became a permanent feature in all provincial systems.

This period also marked Canada's first foray into transnational governance and "complex sovereignty"[19] when, in 1989, the Canada–United States Free Trade Agreement came into effect. Free trade with the United States generated considerable debate in Canada, with the public almost evenly divided. The main concern was the impact it would have on Canadian earnings and employment. Within a year of its enactment, Canadians found themselves in negotiations with Mexico that culminated in the North American Free Trade Agreement (NAFTA). Canada was now part of an increasingly integrated market of 444 million people. As free trade advanced, the Canadian economy encountered a series of recessions, and fears grew in some corners of the population that the Canadian east–west union would be superseded by a strengthening north–south network that stretched down to Mexico.[20] Canadian economic integration thus became a key item on the agenda for policy makers across the country, one that would culminate in certain changes outlined in further detail below.

Economic relations between the federal and provincial governments once again witnessed contradictory trends. Ottawa unilaterally eroded targeted provincial transfers, even while the pan-Canadian commitment to interprovincial redistribution and common markets was considerably reinforced. In 1976, in its efforts to reduce its fiscal burden, the federal government delinked the value of its transfers from actual provincial spending. In 1990, it imposed a unilateral ceiling on payments made to the richest provinces through the Canada Assistance Plan (CAP); this move was known colloquially as the "cap on CAP." Ottawa's actions sparked a legal challenge led by British Columbia, which argued that the federal government could not change its fiscal transfers to the provinces without the approval of the affected parties. The Supreme Court disagreed, ruling that Ottawa had not acted illegally and was not obligated to gain the consent of the provinces in its fiscal affairs.[21] This decision confirmed that the provinces could not rely on consistent funds from the federal government to offset the costs of their social programs. This increased the fiscal uncertainty for the Canadian substate governments.

The impact of the cap on CAP was quickly overshadowed when the federal government declared in 1995 that the time had come "to complete the gradual evolution away from cost-sharing to block funding of programs in areas of provincial responsibility."[22] To that end, it introduced the Canada Health and Social Transfer (CHST), which federal officials couched as a way to free the provinces from unnecessary rules and entanglements with Ottawa. The CHST reduced conditionality; at the same time, however, it substantially cut federal transfers by what amounted to almost 5 per cent of total annual provincial spending.[23] Once again, Ottawa had pursued these changes with scant consultations; the provinces had few means to oppose this federal unilateralism and could only endure it.[24]

However, some of this destabilization in economic relations was counterbalanced by two developments. During the negotiations to patriate the Constitution, the governments of Canada had committed themselves to equality of regional economic opportunity, codifying the principle of equalization in Section 36 of the 1982 Constitution Act. Unlike other federal–provincial transfers, equalization payments were thus "spared the relentless cuts in either the growth rate or the actual cash of intergovernmental transfers after 1981."[25] As a result, the less affluent provinces were not forced to disproportionately reduce education spending compared to their wealthier counterparts; the fundamental similarities in the levels of educational investments were thereby maintained (Appendix 6). At the risk of crude speculation, it is likely that had the federal government imposed cuts to equalization, the provincial education policy framework would have been either eroded or somewhat compromised, for the economically weaker jurisdictions would have had no choice but to reduce their support for educational endeavours, thus compromising the quality of schooling for Canadians in the affected jurisdictions.[26]

In 1994, the federal and provincial governments also ratified the Agreement on Internal Trade (AIT), the seminal objective being for "parties to reduce and eliminate, to the extent possible, barriers to the free movement of persons, goods, services and investments within Canada, and to establish an open, efficient and stable domestic market."[27] The goal of securing a cohesive internal market had proven quite elusive in Canada; now, new provisions in the Charter guaranteeing mobility rights had revitalized this issue on the political policy agenda. The Charter had set down a legal framework, but work still needed to be done to integrate the Canadian common market, which was the goal of the AIT. The principle of parliamentary sovereignty, embedded in each of the provincial legislatures, meant that the agreement had no direct legal effect; nevertheless, the AIT inculcated a normative obligation among the governments of Canada to minimize barriers to interprovincial trade and mobility, and this concomitantly strengthened the economic union of the country.[28] Progress in many areas has been slow at best, as will be discussed below; that said, the AIT generated considerable efforts in the education sector to reform teacher certification so as to enable the movement of teachers across provincial borders.

By the 1980s, the CMEC had eclipsed the Canadian Education Association (which was now exclusively an educational think tank) as the preeminent intergovernmental organization in the education sector. The rise of the CMEC was accompanied by the emergence of regionalized initiatives. Assisted by the Canadian Intergovernmental Conference Secretariat (CICS), the western premiers began meeting more regularly; individual line departments, including education, followed suit. On the opposite side of the country, following a series of iterations, the four provinces of Atlantic Canada established the Council of Atlantic Ministers of Education and Training (CAMET), a permanent organization not unlike the CMEC, dedicated to achieving collaborative programs among the signatory provinces.

The Canadian provinces thus experienced a number of changes to their legal, economic, and organizational interdependence and connectivity, all the while influenced by a new educational orthodoxy and paradigm for public administration that called for standardization, cost-effectiveness, and accountability. This leaves only the cultural bonds of the policy climate to be considered. One connection took centre stage for much of this period: the relationship between Quebec and the rest of Canada. In 1976, the Parti Québécois was elected for the first time, with René Lévesque as premier. The PQ set out to attain political, economic, and social autonomy for the province from the rest of Canada, under the term sovereignty-association, and it committed itself to holding a referendum on the question. The federal government, helmed by the

Liberals under Pierre Trudeau, launched a counter-offensive, arguing that "Quebec had gained from its participation in Confederation ... Quebecers did exercise broader and effective power from Ottawa, and that a much brighter future lay in making French Canadians at home from sea to sea."[29] Keeping its campaign promise, the PQ held a referendum in 1980. When the results came in, 60 per cent of the population had rejected the question; thus, the PQ failed to gain a mandate to negotiate independence. In the aftermath, the federal government engaged in constitutional negotiations that culminated in patriation and the ratification of the Charter of Rights and Freedoms. Unfortunately, this constitutional renewal had been achieved with the consent of all the provinces except Quebec, which meant that the question of Quebec's place in Canada was far from resolved. In 1995, the PQ held a second referendum, and this time Quebec came within a whisker of separating when the result was 49.42 per cent in favour of secession. Remarkably, in spite of these caustic and tumultuous relations, Quebec's education system did not drift away from the practices in the rest of Canada; nor did the province exclude itself from interprovincial activity. This suggests that Quebec's relations with Ottawa may not impede its interactions with the other governments of the country.

With these features of the policy climate and the interstitial bonds of connectivity in mind, our task turns to explore subsequent developments in the respective educational systems. Are new ideas that diffuse into the respective provinces still mediated by the regimes actively working within each of the provinces? Did the organizational revolution achieved with the creation of the CMEC during the previous period open up new opportunities or processes of policy diffusion among the provinces? Do cultural bonds still influence policy diffusion, and do they affect policy convergence? How did the changes in legal interdependence among the provinces influence education policy making and practices? To begin answering these questions, we start by looking at education finance.

Education Finance

Education finance dominated the policy agenda of the 1980s and 1990s. Faced with declining revenues, rising costs, and shrinking birth rates, the provinces that had retained the shared-cost model of education finance began reconsidering that system. By the 1990s, eight of the ten provinces had implemented full-state funding, emulating the strategy pioneered by New Brunswick; Manitoba and Saskatchewan were the lone outliers. Did all the provinces introduce full-state funding in a similar way? And why did some provinces converge while others did not?

In 1974, Nova Scotia's *Report of the Royal Commission on Education, Public Service, and Provincial–Municipal Relations* (the Graham Report) found that there were "considerable and unacceptable variations in the level of education services from municipality to municipality."[30] This report echoed the sentiments of other provincial commissions when it stated that "education is a service of general concern to provincial society as a whole, and not merely to the particular community or region in which a student resides or attends school."[31] Education being a public good, it was vital for the government to ensure that high-quality education be made available to all Nova Scotians, regardless of their place of residence.

The 1981 report of the Royal Commission on Public Education Finance (the Walker Report) reinforced these conclusions and encouraged the government to consolidate districts, establish mandatory provincial levies, and create a detailed foundation program, endowed by the province, to support local revenues.[32] After the Walker Report was tabled, the Nova Scotia government began incrementally centralizing education finance in the province, and by 1990, it was providing more than 80 per cent of the necessary funds to support education, leaving less than 17 per cent to local ratepayers. However, given that the province had set up a uniform local tax rate, financial control was in fact fully in the hands of the central government. For reasons similar to those identified in New Brunswick, Nova Scotia had implemented a *de facto* system of full state funding through incremental means.

On the opposite side of the country, BC had introduced full provincial funding for comparable reasons, taking a similarly incremental approach. In the early 1980s, the province had experienced significant economic decline. In response to this, the BC government had introduced fiscal reforms to curb public spending; this included four changes in education finance.[33] First, the government shifted the non-residential property tax from the local to the provincial level. Second, it implemented a resource cost model (RCM), with the education program set by the province and costs determined by a survey of local market conditions.[34] Third, to control increases in teachers' salaries, it imposed a system for reviewing wage settlements in the public sector. Finally, it unilaterally suspended the right of school boards to levy taxes to raise local revenues above the level established by the province. On paper, like Nova Scotia, BC continued to apply a cost-sharing arrangement for education finance, in that the province covered 60 per cent of the costs, shared 35 per cent depending on local wealth, and required the local boards to independently cover the remaining 5 per cent. In practice, however, since the province determined all the rates and set the expenditure levels, the system was a form of full provincial funding. Local autonomy was thus circumscribed, and BC became the first province west of Quebec to adopt the model by stealth.

Over the next ten years, provincial financing arrangements remained stable. At the end of the 1980s, however, state and non-state actors were increasingly questioning the fiscal health of the provinces. Economists and politicians deemed ballooning deficits to be dampers on economic development,[35] and provincial Ministers of Finance needed to find ways to cut spending and limit the rising costs of social programs. Ministers of Education across the country were also aware of growing concerns among taxpayers regarding the effectiveness and accountability of the education system.[36] Debates about education finance therefore rose on the political agendas of Alberta, Ontario, Manitoba, and Saskatchewan.

Under Ralph Klein, the Alberta government embarked on a program to overhaul education finance. During the debates on the proposed legislation, the Minister of Education, Halvor Jonson, declared that

> the current system is inequitable both in terms of the tax burden borne by the residential and nonresidential property owners across the province and with respect to the moneys individual school boards are able to spend to provide provincially mandated education. Local expenditure mill rates vary from 3 mills to 18 mills with a resulting difference in expenditure per child ranging from $4,010 to $21,346.[37]

In his statement justifying the policy shift, the minister cited recommendations received through public consultations, following this with the demand that "changes in education and spending reductions must achieve efficiencies in the administration of the education system and minimize the effect on the student in the classroom."[38] He also argued that full state funding would be a viable system in Alberta, given that it was "a model of funding used by the majority of the provinces in Canada."[39] The Alberta government thus justified its policy changes in light of developments in the other provinces, invoking a form of lesson drawing to demonstrate the efficacy of the new policy idea as well as its legitimacy.

Policy actors in Ontario considered full state funding almost simultaneously. In 1994, the Bégin Commission stated that

> equity in education requires financial equity. Although the very complex issue of education funding in general was not a specific part of our mandate, we are convinced that our goal of providing an excellent education for all learners cannot become a reality unless the way education is funded in Ontario is changed radically.[40]

Because school boards collectively raised more than half their total revenues from property taxes, local jurisdictions were marked by sizeable disparities, compromising educational equity within the province. Noting the benefits reaped in the jurisdictions that had already implemented full state funding, the Bégin Commission concluded that education finance should be centralized in Ontario.

In 1997, the Conservative government decided to follow these recommendations and implement full-state funding. When presenting Bill 160 to the legislature, Minister of Education John Snobelen framed the initiative in the context of decisions made in other Canadian jurisdictions: "Ontario has not kept pace with the other provinces or countries. The *Globe and Mail* recently described Ontario as the caboose at the end of the education train."[41] Harkening to the logic of the Graham Report, the minister declared that "it makes sense to pay tax at the same rate for a common service that benefits us all." The bill passed, marking the end of the shared-cost legacy in the province virtually overnight.

Interprovincial convergence emerged as provincial policy makers found themselves facing similar problems and looked to one another for ways to solve them. By justifying choices in light of practices in other jurisdictions, the provinces that advanced change through revolutionary means were seeking to deflect sustained opposition from local boards in their respective jurisdictions. In addition, full provincial funding was a potent means to strengthen accountability in the education sector, for local boards would be under the full fiscal purview of central decision makers based in the respective Ministries of Education.

In two provinces, however, these arguments failed to dislodge the shared-cost model. Why did the prairie provinces balk at this policy idea? The answer to that question begins to reveal itself in a Saskatchewan government report from 1933:

By far the largest measure of school support comes from local taxation. This is as it should be. It is one of the essential features of our democratic order that our citizens should, in large measure, control the tax rate and the expenditure of money raised locally. So long as the present system of school districts is continued, local support should remain a fundamental principle of the financial administration of schools.[42]

Both provinces, then, had long been committed to local control, which was preserved through many iterations of policy reform. Whenever either province considered options that would reconfigure how authority in the education sector was allocated, potentially tipping the balance in favour of the central government, the issue was consistently put to a provincial plebiscite instead of being enacted through legislative fiat, which was the preferred approach in the other provinces. The principles of democratic populism and public consultation seem to resonate most strongly in central Canada, and this has translated into a distinctive educational regime in both jurisdictions.[43]

The implementation of full provincial funding also requires a willingness among political actors to confront resistance from both citizens and school boards. Some provinces, including Nova Scotia and BC, sidestepped the issue by advancing change incrementally. Others, such as Ontario and Alberta, imposed the system unilaterally from above, using the other provinces as exemplars in order to counteract opposition. In Manitoba and Saskatchewan, however, the centralization of education finance went squarely against the interests of the electorate, and this undermined its implementation.[44] The case of Manitoba is instructive.

In Manitoba, the Conservatives under Gary Filmon had been elected largely by voters in rural communities, who treasured their local autonomy.[45] The Filmon government was reluctant to upset its strongest supporters by extinguishing the power of local districts to levy taxes. In 1994, determined to reduce the provincial deficit, Filmon froze school funding for five years and eliminated six hundred teaching positions across the province – roughly 5 per cent of the teaching force.[46] Furthermore, school boards would have to raise property taxes to sustain their local programs. As a consequence, between 1994 and 1999, "local education property taxes in Manitoba rose overall by more than $90 million, nearly 30 percent, and the province's share of funding dropped from 66 percent in 1994 to 60 percent in 1999."[47]

In 2000, the NDP took office in Manitoba, having campaigned on a promise to restore the proportion of provincial funding to pre-Filmon budget levels.[48] The Manitoba Teachers' Society (MTS), having reversed its position since the late 1960s owing to lessons it had drawn from other provinces, now called for full state funding, but the new government did not publicly contemplate doing so.[49] Like the Filmon government, the new NDP government realized it would face resistance from rural voters. Also, officials in the Department of Education were concerned about the potential outcry from "those districts that would be the biggest losers."[50] Backlash from key districts and negative public opinion would undermine the NDP's chances of re-election. Setting aside these societal interests, the implementation of full state funding often requires either an increase in income or sales tax or cuts to education programming.[51] In the political and fiscal contexts of the day, neither option appealed to the new government.

This analysis of the politics of education finance in Manitoba can easily be applied to Saskatchewan. One government was left-wing, the other right-wing, but in each province, the government relied on the support of rural voters, and officials in the Department of Education were concerned about the potential outcry from those affected.[52] Similarly, officials in Alberta and Ontario faced political consequences, in the form of teachers' strikes and electoral backlash, from the unilateral implementation of full provincial funding.[53] One former Minister of Education from Saskatchewan would recall that as he watched the acrimony unfold in those other provinces, he advised his cabinet colleagues not to pursue the option: "We decided it simply wasn't the best option for our government to pursue. The citizens of Saskatchewan are committed to local control and we knew that reclaiming the power of local taxation wouldn't fly."[54]

Continued policy divergence reinforces a central contention of the analytical architecture advanced in this book: no policy encounters a clean slate in the receiving jurisdiction. Rather, legacies and the regimes at work within each province mediate the introduction of new ideas and influence the likelihood that they will be adopted. In eight provinces, full funding enjoyed the necessary congruence with existing conditions in the specific policy context; in Manitoba and Saskatchewan, by contrast, full state funding failed to resonate with the education regimes at hand. This is not to suggest that change is impossible; in fact, there are clear signs in both Saskatchewan and Manitoba that full-funding will be achieved in the coming years. Rather, this confirms that new ideas can encounter delays when they lack the necessary compatibility with the internal features of the regime at work in the specific policy sector.

Provincial Exams and Pan-Canadian Assessments

Public opinion surveys, commissioned reports, and expert panels of business interests were lining up during the 1980s and 1990s to decry the state of Canadian public education. Andrew Nikiforuk wrote that

> if the U.S. school system resembles a homeless beggar on the streets of New York, Canada's expensive counterpart defensively limps along in a state of humiliation and confusion. Our schools are far from what people expect them to be ... My anger, which admittedly drives this polemic, comes from my awareness as a father of two boys that some parents have totally abandoned the public school system while others have been shut out of it by administrators.[55]

Ministers of Education were aware of rising concerns among taxpayers regarding the effectiveness and accountability of the education system:

> Recent years have witnessed a strengthening in Canada and elsewhere, of a trend to translate traditional concerns about educational quality into concrete plans for evaluation. Such actions, generally considered under the heading of accountability, are frequently linked to taxpayer concerns about the cost-effectiveness of the school system, and to employer dissatisfaction with the skills, knowledge and attitudes of their graduates.[56]

The problem was somewhat ironic as it stemmed in part from the reform agenda that had prevailed under the progressive education paradigm. Because most provinces had eliminated standardized exams in the 1960s and 1970s, public officials had limited means to measure and determine the quality of the education they were providing students. So, bolstered by the broader rhetoric of performance-based measurement advocated by NPM, the notion of standardized exams began to penetrate the policy scene.

The Alberta government, one of Canada's stronger supporters of NPM, was the first to reinstate mandatory grade twelve exams, in 1984. In the 1990s, BC, Manitoba, Saskatchewan, and Nova Scotia followed suit. Ontario and New Brunswick established mandatory literacy exams for students in grades ten and nine respectively. With some variations, nine of the ten provinces converged on the general practice (Appendix 3). The lone exception was Prince Edward Island. According to sources in the province, parents and teachers did not endorse mandatory exams in secondary schools, seeing them as an ineffective use of resources, given the size of the population.[57]

Standardized tests arrived in tandem with debates on universal assessments. In the 1980s, Alberta, under Minister of Education David King, created one of the first provincial assessment programs:

> We created cohort tests that sampled groups of students from across the province to gather diagnostic information on the quality of education in Alberta. Results were not used for the purposes of individual grades but simply for ministry officials to see how different regions in the province were faring.[58]

With this policy development, Alberta led the Canadian assessment agenda and pioneered a new way of thinking that would have a lasting impact on provincial education.

The CMEC did much to drive the agenda on national assessments. In September 1989, more than a decade before the OECD launched the PISA, the council announced that it intended to develop the School Achievement Indicators Project (SAIP), which would generate annual reports on educational attainments across Canada, with representative samples drawn from every province and territory that would provide comparable data from coast to coast. In publicizing this initiative, the CMEC explained that

> calls for more stringent evaluation of both school programs and student achievement have drawn responses from the ministries and departments of education across Canada, and have led to consensus that the issue of quality in education needs to be addressed in a national context.[59]

The CMEC Secretariat thus embarked on the most demanding project in its history to gain the cooperation of all constituent governments and establish a formal pan-Canadian assessment program. Most of the provinces (including Quebec) quickly signalled their willingness to participate, and within a few years all of the provinces were fully engaged. Even though both Ontario and Saskatchewan initially resisted the idea, the program advanced uninhibited because initiatives shepherded by the CMEC do not require unanimous consent. It seemed that a pan-Canadian assessment was an "idea whose time had come."[60]

After the SAIP was created, proposals for universal assessments rose on the individual policy agendas of the respective provinces.

Proponents of them found strong support in a number of provincial commissions. The New Brunswick Commission on Excellence in Education, for example, argued:

> We believe that an effective evaluation and monitoring system is essential to a strong curriculum and to excellence in education ... Competing against high but reasonable provincial standards could help teachers and students alike to find a common cause so conspicuously absent at present from many classrooms.[61]

In Ontario, the Bégin Commission expressed similar sentiments: "We believe it's absolutely essential that the progress of all students be monitored systematically and thoroughly from the very beginning of their school careers, with an eye to constant improvement both of the individual and the program."[62] Seemingly inspired by NPM, Nova Scotia's Select Committee on Education linked universal assessments to teacher accountability: "The public expects teachers to teach and be accountable ... We should have provincial examinations at grade 6, 9, and 12. Parents should have a means of judging school results with a common measure."[63] Research from within the education epistemic community thus gave credence to the idea of universal assessments.

Nevertheless, assessments faced strong resistance from some quarters of the policy community.[64] Some questioned how accurate such programs could be and raised concerns about how the assessments would be structured. Others argued that the costs of standardized tests, in terms of both money and the psychological impact on individual students, outweighed the potential benefits. Teachers' associations, including the CTF, were stalwart opponents of large-scale assessment programs; they preferred to see student evaluations remain solely in the hands of classroom teachers. Clearly, divisions within the policy community threatened to generate contrasting results when provincial assessment programs were implemented. However, motivated by ideational considerations, by 2005, all of the provinces had instituted mandatory universal assessments, albeit with variations in terms of the stakes that were attached to them (see chapter 2).

One survey of education officials found a number of common factors supporting the decision to create provincial assessment programs: the fiscal climate, the need for Canada's education systems to be internationally competitive, the public demand for performance and accountability, the need to heighten student achievement, and the need to improve individual teacher accountability.[65] One former Minister of Education from Ontario put it in a nutshell: "Why did all the provinces create these programs? Because we were all responding to the same information that kids weren't doing well – and this was part of a wave of education reform that cut across partisan lines."[66] An education official from Quebec echoed this: "Assessments were part of wider international trends. We were all getting the same information about the quality of education in Canada and it was clear that we needed to do something about it."[67]

Beyond these ideational considerations, provincial officials saw the value of standardized assessments through their engagement in the CMEC's SAIP. They also gained valuable experience in the strategies and techniques necessary to design such programs without putting their individual systems at risk. This finding marks an interesting twist to the traditional interpretation of policy making in federations. Normally, federalism is valued because it allows substate governments to experiment without risking the collective state. Should these experiments succeed, the central government can intervene and universalize the strategy. In this situation, the collective pooling of resources to launch the pan-Canadian program afforded the provinces a novel opportunity to build up their respective capacities to create provincial assessment programs in the coming years.

In spite of its strengths, the pan-Canadian program could not provide sufficient data on the individual provinces. Policy actors realized that to gain this type of information, each province would need to establish its own program – a point made in the New Brunswick report *Schools for a New Century*: "It is the Commission's view that the SAIPs will be a valuable tool in taking a measure of the performance of New Brunswick schools compared to those in other provinces in the areas tested. They cannot, however, fill the need for universal assessment of New Brunswick students."[68] Officials in the various Ministries of Education could draw from the experiences they had gained when cooperating in the development of the SAIP and apply those lessons as they built their own internal assessment programs.

Exposure to the SAIP, and later to PISA, also helped allay or at least assuage the fears of professional educators regarding standardized assessments. The case of PEI is instructive. In contrast to the other provinces, PEI never reinstated mandatory tests, and teachers lobbied strongly against any proposal to create universal assessments. However, teachers could not prevent the government from participating in external assessment programs, such as SAIP and PISA. According to one official,

> it became evident that there was real value in this new type of province-wide assessment program. Assessments, in this form, became more acceptable in this province after the implementation of PISA and SAIP. We could see from our neighbouring provinces some real improvements in student achievement that were attributed to strong testing programs. We just needed time to build a culture of assessment in PEI among our teaching force.[69]

By taking the time to frame the policy in a manner consonant with the prevailing regime, the provincial government was able to install a universal assessment program in 2005, thus completing the pan-Canadian convergence on the policy option.

The evolution of assessment policy demonstrates the power of cooperation as a force of diffusion. Through pan-Canadian and international cooperation, made possible by the institutionalization of the intergovernmental organization, provincial decision makers gained valuable expertise that they could apply in their respective jurisdictions; and for key stakeholders, programs like SAIP further normalized the idea of universal assessments. The unanimous uptake of this policy trend was also a result of its synergy with the prevailing policy climate of the day. Universal assessments fit well with the new education goals, which emphasized quality, as well as with the NPM paradigm, which prioritized accountability and evidence-based policy. Officials needed a means to evaluate the system, and universal assessments proved to be a viable instrument for consistently evaluating all students. The assessments also furthered the cause of curricular reform, the third branch of the standardization agenda and the subject of the next section.

Outcomes-Based Education and Interprovincial Curriculum

In 1988, the OECD's Centre for Education Research and Innovation asked the CMEC to prepare a report on provincial elementary and secondary school curriculum. After surveying the provincial policies, the CMEC pronounced:

> Today in Canada, the predominant trends in curriculum reform are toward infusing school programming with a stronger sense of direction, and

concomitantly, subjecting its outcomes to a more rigorous and systematic assessment. These trends, which might be seen as representing two sides of the "back to basics" coin, embody a desire for greater coherence and substance in the curriculum, and for assurance that stated objectives are actually being met.[70]

Under the rubric of Outcomes-Based Education (OBE), all of the provinces adopted the new education paradigm, opting to readjust the child-centred philosophy that had dominated in the 1960s. Curriculum developers thus shifted their focus from determining inputs to specifying outcomes and learning expectations that children should achieve in each of the subject areas throughout the various stages of elementary and secondary schooling. This initiative gained further viability after mandatory assessments were implemented; these provided provincial officials with the necessary tools for determining whether learning outcomes were being achieved. In this way, decisions in the assessment dimension reverberated in the curriculum dimension, opening a window of opportunity for a particular policy instrument to take hold in the education sector.

As had been the case with universal assessments, the new curricular paradigm was congruent with the broader ideational climate of the day. In the 1960s, the decentralizing curriculum reforms had been driven by the goals of flexibility and individualization; now, in the 1990s, observers of Canadian education were increasingly questioning the virtues and merits of that policy choice. According to one poll, most Canadians believed that schools "were not preparing young people to meet the challenges of current economic realities."[71] Unwilling to return to the rigidities of the past but wanting to respond to the critics, proponents of OBE were offering decision makers a viable policy alternative. What is more, OBE's precepts conformed to the prescriptions of NPM, in that they called for a loosening of the "hold over inputs, opportunity and educational content" in favour of directing "attention to the specification of goals for education and the setting of performance standards for students, schools and education systems as a whole."[72]

The interprovincial consensus on the principles of OBE set the stage for three collaborative initiatives in curriculum development. Under the auspices of the Atlantic Provinces Education Foundation (APEF), in 1993, the four provinces of Atlantic Canada ratified a common statement on essential graduation learnings; this was followed by foundation documents across six curriculum areas, which led to the harmonization of curriculum across the jurisdictions by 2000.[73] At the same time, together with the territories, British Columbia, Alberta, Saskatchewan, and Manitoba signed the Western Canadian Protocol for Collaboration in Basic Education (WCP). The WCP resulted in the articulation of common learning outcomes in a wide array of subject areas; but, rather than harmonization similar to what had been achieved in Atlantic Canada, each signatory province would decide whether to use the outcomes when engaging in its curriculum renewal processes. Finally, in 1995, the CMEC adopted the Pan-Canadian Protocol for Collaboration on School Curriculum. This led to the formulation of common learning outcomes in science, released in 1997; there have been no further advancements in other areas, however. Two questions arise from these developments. First, what motivated the provinces to work together, both regionally and at the pan-Canadian level? And second, why did the efforts generate such widely varied results?

The drivers for these interprovincial collaborations were both underlying and proximate. First and foremost, provincial officials wanted to "maximize jurisdictional resources, teacher expertise, and stakeholder involvement"[74] in curriculum development. By combining the capacities of multiple jurisdictions, the provinces might increase the quality of their curricula and capitalize on their collective resources. As one Nova Scotia official observed: "There is a synergy between four curriculum experts from different provinces that are highly qualified and committed to their work; by bringing them together, at least in theory, we should end up with a higher quality product."[75] Furthermore, all of the provinces recognized that common learning outcomes among all jurisdictions would lighten the burden for students transferring between the provinces and reassure employers that all students had comparable training whatever their place of residence, thus facilitating interprovincial mobility.

Both of these concerns, however, had previously been raised without interprovincial cooperation emerging. How did these underlying factors gain new salience in the 1980s? Two changes in the overarching policy climate helped bring about this sustained interprovincial cooperation: legal and economic. The Charter of Rights and Freedoms was an immediate trigger for collaboration, as illustrated by events in Atlantic Canada. Section 23 presented a major challenge for that region's provinces; because of their size, they lacked the capacity to develop French-language programs. New Brunswick already had a bilingual public education system, so the other three provinces drew on its expertise when crafting their new curricula for francophone schooling. Having noted the benefits of resource sharing through that experience, education policy makers invested in curriculum collaboration beyond the confines of the francophone division. In this way, changes to the legal component of the policy climate that had direct implications for minority-language education and the expansion of administrative control to minority-language groups led indirectly to greater cooperation among the provinces across the broader curriculum.

The fiscal downturn of the early 1990s was the second catalyst. Policy actors viewed collective curriculum development as a potential cost-saving measure in that it would spread the costs across a greater number of jurisdictions. "It's becoming increasingly a direction for all governments to think about how to share to get more bang for their buck," said Roger Palmer, Assistant Deputy Minister of Education in Alberta. "We are all too poor to do things separately."[76] Similarly, PEI's Deputy Minister, Keith Wornell, noted that "the emphasis is on developing common curriculum in specific subject areas so as to improve quality within ever diminishing resources. Regional cooperation is very important to the development of curriculum for this province."[77] Clearly, the desire for economic efficiency in curriculum development encouraged interprovincial cooperation in elementary and secondary education.

Although their motivations and objectives were similar, the three initiatives generated starkly different results. The impact of the CMEC's pan-Canadian project has been limited at best. According to one official, "the Pan-Canadian framework on science, it has way too many outcomes because of the number of provinces believing what is important – so you still need to filter from what's there to shrink it to a doable size."[78] One official offered the following assessment of the CMEC's initiative: "Working through the CMEC is often an unwieldy process. Getting all of the governments to agree is a real challenge and the results are frequently watered-down."[79] When the CMEC announced that science would be the first area for collaboration, it justified the selection on the following grounds: "Ministers recognized that, as Canada moves into the twenty-first century, it is essential that all jurisdictions provide students with the necessary knowledge, skills, and attitudes for scientific literacy."[80] Beyond this principled justification, it may well be that science was a pragmatic choice for the Ministers of Education. Other areas, such as language arts or history, might easily have descended into a morass of interprovincial bickering spurred by ideological and cultural differences that would have prevented successful ratification. Given that there has been no headway in other areas, it seems likely that identifying common learning outcomes in other subjects is simply beyond the capacity of the pan-Canadian organization. The CMEC should probably recognize the limits of its capacity and dedicate its energies elsewhere.

Regional curriculum collaborations were much more successful than the pan-Canadian one shepherded by the CMEC. Yet contrasting results emerged here as well, with Atlantic Canada fully harmonizing while the western provinces maintain separate curricula to this day. The explanation for this turns on differences in material conditions, the organizational and cultural bonds of the regions, internal educational regimes, and the degree of interdependence of the individual provinces.

In Atlantic Canada, the APEF (which later became the CAMET) provided crucial support throughout the stages of harmonization; its permanent secretariat offered vital administrative assistance to provincial policy makers. As one respondent from Nova Scotia put it, "without the CAMET, the harmonized curriculum would never have been achieved."[81] Such organizational supports were not a reality in western Canada. A former Minister of Education from Saskatchewan acknowledged that "in Western Canada, the relations among the ministers are more like an informal working group with irregular meetings and haphazard efforts. Our relations are simply not as formalized as those in Atlantic Canada."[82] A respondent from Alberta similarly noted that "there is not even a separate caucus dedicated exclusively to the education ministers of Western Canada."[83] Provincial education officials in western Canada thus lacked the essential organizational support that seems necessary for complete harmonization.

Interprovincial organizational bonds are partly a function of cultural ties among the provinces. The three Maritime provinces have long had close affinities with one another, and these have often manifested themselves in similar policy choices and a general tendency to look to one another when considering educational reform. The provinces of western Canada have never exhibited a comparable degree of cultural synergy, and this is exemplified by the variations in their educational regimes. During the wave of district consolidations in the 1940s, for example, the governments of BC and Alberta acted unilaterally, imposing amalgamations without local consent, while Manitoba and Saskatchewan engaged their respective publics and worked towards gaining the consent of those affected. Differences in the internal educational regimes of the western provinces that stem from contrasting political cultures may therefore have impeded the establishment of a meaningful intergovernmental organization.

Sources involved in the WCP also reported that contemporary ideological differences, particularly between Alberta and the other jurisdictions, further undermined harmonization. At the time, the Alberta government was pursuing an agenda for radical change in education; one prominent proposal involved strengthening choice in education by creating public–private partnerships and establishing charter schools in line with the somewhat more radical NPM prescriptions.[84] Many of these initiatives in Alberta failed to gain the necessary traction to inspire transformative change in the province; even so, these ideas became lightning rods in heated debates that expanded beyond Alberta's borders. Despite the emerging consensus around a variety of educational reform initiatives, the impulse towards privatization clashed with many of the ideas held by other signatories of the protocol, especially in Saskatchewan and Manitoba. Ideological distance between the affected parties reinforced the barriers to curriculum harmonization in western Canada.

Finally, since the late 1960s, politicians, bureaucrats, and academics in the Maritime provinces had been increasingly attuned to the benefits of collective action. On 26 March 1968, the premiers of New Brunswick, Nova Scotia, and Prince Edward Island called on Dr J.J. Deutsch to examine the state of political and economic affairs in the region. Arguing that the most serious challenge for people in the Maritime provinces was "the threat of slow economic growth and a continued inferior level of participation in the economic and political life of the nation," Deutsch outlined three basic approaches for ameliorating the situation: informal cooperation, formal cooperation, and some form of Maritime Union.[85] Provincial politicians and policy makers drew inspiration from Deutsch's proposals and created a series of formal councils, such as the Council of Maritime Premiers. Furthermore, following the approval of the Free Trade Agreement, which sent shock waves of concern in the eastern part of the country, eastern premiers like Frank McKenna reinvigorated the calls for Atlantic Canadian cooperation.[86] This type of acknowledged interdependency is not a feature in the western provinces, where there are far fewer incentives to collaborate so intensely – all of which contributed to the differences in the results of these regional initiatives.

A Pan-Canadian Agreement on Teacher Certification?

The idea of harmonizing teacher certification has waxed and waned on provincial policy agendas since the inception of elementary and secondary schooling in Canada. Piecemeal efforts at harmonization were made at CEA conventions, where delegates noted that variations in certification regimes were hindering teachers' mobility. They argued that the provinces should, at a minimum, attempt to reconcile all the terms used for classifying the different certificates. The Canadian Teachers' Federation sponsored various events to examine the problems teachers faced when they moved between provinces; in 1971, it called for "each province [to] recognize, on a reciprocal basis, the certification of persons with degree standing who hold permanent certificates."[87] Despite these efforts, it was not until the 1990s that the provincial governments made a more determined effort to eliminate – or at least systematically reduce – the barriers to teacher mobility and reconcile the relevant standards.

The growing political attention to teacher mobility was driven mainly by the 1994 Agreement on Internal Trade (AIT), which emerged after the Charter was enacted. Under Chapter Seven of the AIT, "any worker qualified for an occupation in the territory of a Party [should] be granted access to employment opportunities in that occupation in the territory of any other Party." This was to be achieved through harmonization and mutual recognition of standards and regulations. Unfortunately, the AIT did not immediately transform the Canadian labour market; sector-by-sector negotiations would be required to reach the necessary agreements.

Because teachers comprise one of the largest professions in Canada, political pressures have been growing for the education sector to achieve conformity under the AIT.[88] Because teachers are more heavily controlled by the state than other occupations, politicians and bureaucrats have stronger levers at their disposal to influence teacher certification. Political leaders, for their part, hope that an accord for teachers will set an example for other sectors. As one respondent noted: "The folks in the labour department have a big stake in the process and they really wanted a winner to serve as an example to the other professions. Since teachers are the largest profession, if we get an agreement, it puts more pressure on the other groups to work towards a collective agreement."[89] On 29 September 1999, the CMEC ratified an agreement-in-principle (AIP) in relation to the AIT's chapter on labour mobility. Like the AIT, this agreement provided only a general rubric for structuring negotiations to develop an agreement among all the provinces. Given the aforementioned political pressures, it seemed that all the pieces were in place for harmonization. To date, however, an agreement remains out of reach. The obstacles are threefold.

First, the definitions, terms, and basic requirements for certification are noticeably different across the jurisdictions. Teachers in Alberta, for example, are certified from K to 12 inclusive, while in other provinces, distinctions are made according to grade level. These variations in standards emerge in part from the considerable differences in labour markets, migration patterns, and student enrolments among the provinces. The Atlantic provinces, for example, often report an oversupply of teachers, while Alberta finds itself in constant need of them.[90] Consequently, there may be some incentives for Atlantic Canada to elevate its standards to restrict the job market even while Alberta moves to loosen its requirements to encourage new teachers to move to the province. Second, some members of the policy community perceive that a pan-Canadian agreement will end up harmonizing to the lowest common denominator, thereby reducing standards from coast to coast.[91] The third and final obstacle is the universities and the programs they are offering. As autonomous institutions, universities exercise considerable control over initial teacher education, and variations in these programs complicate the harmonization process.[92] Negotiating an effective compromise to address these three challenges presents a considerable test to provincial decision makers. To quote one respondent close to the initiative: "Everyone agrees to the idea of labour mobility, but the real issue across the country is that the way that we certify the teachers is really different – and we don't all agree on the components."[93]

There are, nonetheless, some indications that a pan-Canadian agreement is on the horizon. In 2006, frustrated with delays in the pan-Canadian AIT process, Alberta and BC ratified the Trade Investment Labour Mobility Agreement (TILMA); the two provinces also signed bilateral agreements to eliminate barriers to teacher mobility.[94] Teachers were the first profession to achieve compliance under the TILMA as provincial education officials, supported by administrative staff with expertise in labour market coordination, worked to find common ground between the two jurisdictions. It is significant that the negotiations were limited to the Alberta and BC registrars for certification, and left out other potential stakeholders such as the teachers' federations and the Deans of Education in the respective provinces. As expressed by one Alberta public servant:

> The deans and teachers do not play a formal or authoritative role in certification and so they were excluded from this part of the process. It was already difficult enough to get the authoritative parties to all agree – having additional voices at the table would have just made it that much harder.[95]

The agreement between BC and Alberta may accelerate the pan-Canadian process, for it provides a tangible example of successful harmonization. Also, there are now officials with expertise in negotiating such a deal. On 30 April 2010, the TILMA was transformed into the New West Partnership when BC and Alberta welcomed Saskatchewan into the agreement. In the 1960s, the "soft" influence of western strategies in teacher preparation had pioneered a new approach that gradually spread across the country; it is possible that the New West Partnership could now spearhead a new certification regime that will cover Canada as a whole.

Furthermore, key stakeholders that once opposed the idea of credential recognition have signalled their support for it. In 2006, the Association of Canadian Deans of Education (ACDE) issued a general statement on the common objectives of initial teacher education known as the Accord on Initial Teacher Education. If the universities voluntarily harmonize their programs, or at least reduce the variations, it will be easier to reach an agreement on certification standards. Teachers themselves strongly support the principle of labour mobility; it was the CTF that helped the CMEC Secretariat broker a multilateral pension agreement in 2003 to ensure that pensions could be carried across provincial borders.[96] Thus, a broad agreement for the teaching profession may soon be achieved.

Building the Theoretical Links

This chapter concludes my study of the evolution of Canadian elementary and secondary education. Over time, the pendulum has swung between centralization and decentralization of provincial education policies and practices. As the education enterprise was founded and expanded, policy actors in most provinces dedicated themselves to establishing public, (generally) secular control over schooling; this was overseen by provincial Departments of Education. In the 1960s and 1970s, provincial decision makers and education professionals attempted to craft individualized programs tailored to students' individual needs, abandoning the uniform and rigid practices of the past. In 1982, the pendulum began to swing again. Faced with mounting arguments that academic standards were in decline and that there was a glaring lack of accountability in the sector, provincial decision makers moved to regain control over public education.[97]

In a dramatic reversal from the previous period, provinces from coast to coast introduced policies to standardize practices and to recentralize government control over public schooling. Many of these reforms were motivated by the intense criticisms launched both in Canada and abroad against the practices of child-centred education. All of this dovetailed with the NPM paradigm that had captured the minds of decision makers everywhere. This new orthodoxy encouraged many of the features of education reform that pervaded the day. Beyond the changing ideational aspects of the policy climate, legal developments ushered in by the patriation of the Constitution and the entrenchment of the Charter of Rights and Freedoms had direct and indirect effects on provincial education policies. Furthermore, the reinforced commitment to interprovincial mobility and the drive for economic union stimulated developments in teacher certification. The provinces seem to be moving towards an increasingly integrated regime. Clearly, adjustments in the policy climate have had strong implications for provincial education.

As in the previous periods, policy diffusion was driven largely by interprovincial learning. Yet interprovincial convergence continued to be tempered as new ideas encountered internal policy contexts of each individual province. When an idea proved viable, provinces were likely to adopt it, possibly with some adjustments to ensure its compatibility with internal conditions. The circumstances surrounding full state funding support this analysis: prevailing conditions in Saskatchewan and Manitoba led those two provinces to resist that funding model. Cultural bonds, moreover, continued to influence and mediate policy diffusion, as reflected in the hesitation among some western provinces to fully harmonize curriculum with Alberta.

Yet it was during this period that we find the first clear evidence of cooperation as a motor of policy diffusion. This reinforces my argument that changes in the policy climate can strongly influence policy diffusion. Intergovernmental organizational innovations provided the essential means for facilitating formal collaboration, which manifested itself in a number of dimensions of the education sector. These interactions then contributed to policy exchanges as well as to the realization of convergence. This is neatly demonstrated by the dissemination and installation of universal assessments from coast to coast. Furthermore, changes in the legal bonds of interdependence fashioned by the renewed Canadian Constitution marshalled in new incentives for interprovincial collaboration, for the provinces needed to develop new curricula. This soon blossomed into sustained interactions, particularly in certain regions of the country.

It is worth recalling that throughout all these changes, the provinces remained generally committed to the basic principles of the Canadian education policy framework that had been consolidated in the 1960s. A policy framework that the provinces had managed to construct largely on their own, without the direct and sustained intervention of the federal government, as ideas on education policy diffused across permeable political boundaries, carried by the processes of learning and cooperation.

Conclusion: Learning to School

In a country so diverse as Canada, uniformity is the exception rather than the rule. This is particularly true in educational matters wherein, added to our manifest differences in historical and cultural backgrounds, in urbanization and industrialization, in topography and resources, what uniformity does exist comes more by diffusion than by invention. Education is a provincial matter; provinces may borrow and trade ideas among one another or from without, but in the final analysis the educational system of any one province is the working out of its own inventiveness.

A.F. Brown, 1959

I began with a puzzle. Without national standards, or any authoritative Leviathan, the Canadian provinces have developed highly similar systems of elementary and secondary education. This similarity was revealed when we examined the investments, achievements, and substantive policies currently at work in education across the ten jurisdictions. In effect, the ten provinces have installed a "pan-Canadian" policy framework that informally manages and oversees the education sector, providing Canadians with equal access to reasonably comparable programs, regardless of where in Canada they live.

For federalism scholars, the *de facto* policy framework in Canadian elementary and secondary education defies the odds. The division of powers between a central government and a series of constituent units is rarely regarded as a hospitable environment for the realization of country-wide similarity in public policy. Federal pessimists emphasize that autonomous actors – in this case, provinces – seldom work well together, particularly if they lack a strong central leader. Without strong central leadership, the pessimists continue, federations risk negative consequences such as intergovernmental bickering, pre-empted policy space, jurisdictional buck passing and blame avoidance for policy failures, incoherent activities as jurisdictions pursue different strategies, and races to the bottom as jurisdictions undercut one another. All of which may contribute to suboptimal policy outcomes. Federal optimists, by contrast, value the division of powers as a means to encourage policy diversity and experimentation, and to allow substates to act as "laboratories" of innovation, pioneering new strategies and cultivating new ideas separate from the country as a whole. Moreover, in multinational federations like Canada, the division of powers takes on new meaning, for the principle of self-rule offers jurisdictional autonomy for minority nations to pursue their own strategies and preserve their distinctive cultures, identities, and languages, further augmenting the potential for internal policy variation. Country-wide policy similarity, according to both pessimists and optimists, is thus unlikely in federations.

Poor outcomes and unfettered diversity can damage a federation, given that a modicum of coherence in policy activity is necessary for the preservation and success of a state. Perhaps nowhere is this more apparent than in the arena of social policy – which includes education – where the Marshallian notion of social citizenship calls for the equal treatment of all citizens regardless of where in the country they live.[1] Education is crucial to this project, for it helps hold together the various elements of a polity by inculcating and transmitting shared norms and values across generations, providing individuals with the tools for personal growth, and enabling people to participate fully in the economy and society. When deftly crafted, elementary and secondary schooling can redress inequalities among citizens, foster ideas of common citizenship, and contribute to the state's overall success. In fact, one could argue that education is one of the most important policy arenas of the day. Given its significance, how can the necessary equity and coherence be achieved if provinces are free to pursue different strategies that are uncoordinated by an overarching authority capable of imposing common standards and practices?

The Canadian provinces have achieved this seemingly Sisyphean feat, gradually crafting a *de facto* elementary and secondary education system without the direct intervention of the federal government as an authoritative overseer influencing choices, imposing standards, and mandating common practices. To be sure, differences appear in the nooks and crannies of the ten provincial education systems, and meaningful imperfections are scattered from coast to coast that policy makers must address; in the main, however, commonalities outweigh particularities and the provinces have created a remarkably effective system of elementary and secondary schooling. Before distilling the lessons to be learned from the case of Canadian education, it is important to consider the ways in which certain features of the education sector more broadly, and the attributes of the Canadian federation more specifically, may have expedited the achievement of the elementary and secondary education framework. To put it bluntly: Was the achievement of the education policy framework simply an accident?

The Pan-Canadian Education Framework: A Happy Accident?

Certain features of the education sector itself may have led to the achievement of substate policy similarity without central intervention. To start, much of the previous research on federalism and social policy has investigated areas of redistributive policy, such as social assistance. In areas such as these, substate governments have compelling reasons to make sure they are more tight-fisted than their neighbours in order to prevent undesirable citizens from moving into their territory and depleting their resources. Education, however, is an area of developmental policy, which involves investing in the general well-being of a population and providing the necessary infrastructure for economic growth. So, while areas of redistributive policy may be more likely to generate races to the bottom and thus require central intervention to avoid this outcome, areas of developmental policy demand investments, potentially spurring races to the top as substate governments work to create successful systems that are appealing to both investors and citizens.

Citizens, moreover, consistently demand high-quality education systems from their governments, and this keeps schooling high on policy agendas. The same cannot always be said for other policy areas such as income security, employment insurance, and social assistance. As discussed in chapter 1, during elections, education is almost always at the top of voter priorities, and citizens tend to have common expectations when it comes to public activities regardless of their place of residence. Furthermore, those employed in the education system are extremely well informed of their own working conditions and of those in other jurisdictions. Professional organizations such as teachers' unions and superintendents' associations track such things as salaries, benefits, and infrastructure investments both in their own province and across the country, using benchmarks to indicate when their jurisdiction might be lagging behind or when others are gaining ground. In other words, education has a highly organized policy community with powerful and mobilized stakeholders. Scholars of policy communities and policy networks have long implicated stakeholders as crucial stimulants of policy choices, and the findings of this book confirm that non-state stakeholders are significant players in education policy development. So perhaps the emergence of the policy framework is simply the result of the constellation of alternative incentives and interests surrounding education as an area of developmental policy. If so, the lessons we learn from the case of education cannot be transferred to other policy domains.

But interprovincial policy collaboration is not restricted to the education sector. To be sure, the scale and scope of activity in education is perhaps unrivalled, relative to what has happened in other sectors, but the diffusion of policies and the emergence of policy frameworks have both occurred in other arenas. The evidence of provincial collaboration in sectors that are not exclusively developmental suggests that analysing Canadian education can help us expose generalizable conditions and alternative processes for framework formulation in federations. Two brief examples here can help expose these dynamics: anti-smoking strategies and securities regulation.

Not long ago, Canadians could smoke almost anywhere – at work, in bars and restaurants, in front of offices, and even at schools. Today, due to increasingly strict regulations, smoking outside of one's own private residence is nearly impossible from coast to coast. The anti-smoking framework was not the result of Ottawa directly imposing national standards to regulate behaviour; instead, starting in the 1990s, some provinces and municipalities began experimenting with various measures designed to target smoking and gradually make the practice unacceptable. In 1994, Ontario became the first jurisdiction in North America to prohibit cigarette sales in pharmacies and drug stores and also made it illegal to sell cigarettes to people under the age of nineteen; this launched the first wave of policies designed to combat smoking.[2] Over the following decade, Ontario's program diffused across the country as the other provinces adopted comparable strategies to combat smoking. The second wave of anti-smoking legislation appeared in the 2000s, with each province gradually introducing broad-based anti-smoking acts that banned prominent displays of tobacco products, prohibited smoking in public areas, and eliminated smoking sections in restaurants, bars, clubs, bingo halls, and casinos. Today, all provinces except Quebec and Alberta even prohibit smoking in cars when children are present.[3] Put together, provincial action has put Canada at the forefront of anti-smoking legislation in the world – a result achieved largely without the central government imposing comparable regulations to ensure parity from coast to coast.[4] It seems that Canada as a whole has benefited from the various provinces experimenting with different ideas and copying one another's tactics to reduce smoking.

Another sector that has witnessed seemingly unexpected interprovincial collaboration is securities regulation, which includes the policies, practices, and rules that govern capital markets, protect investors from unfair or fraudulent practices, and stabilize the financial system. Securities regulations foster confidence among investors and consumers alike by steadying the markets. Banking comes under the purview of the federal government, whereas according to Section 92(13) of the Constitution Act, securities regulation comes under the provincial power over property and civil rights. As a result, among the 109 current members of the International Organization of Securities Commissions (IOSCO), Canada is the only country without a national securities regulator. Instead, the thirteen provincial and territorial governments manage Canada's securities industry, with a separate securities commission or equivalent authority operating in each jurisdiction. This decentralized and fragmented arrangement could have led to chaos, providing a haven for white-collar criminals. Instead, without federal intervention, the provinces have created an essentially pan-Canadian framework that manages the industry with remarkable success. Imperfections remain, and there have been calls from certain quarters – including the International Monetary Fund (IMF) – for Canada to create a national regulator overseen by Ottawa.[5] Yet a number of expert reports have reached a different conclusion: "The provinces have demonstrated an ability to effectively regulate securities activities, and a national system thwarting their authority could prove to be both inefficient and ineffective."[6]

Indeed, there is evidence of horizontal problem solving and interprovincial collaboration in a multitude of policy areas, including labour market regulation, environmental standards, occupational training, insurance harmonization, and procurement coordination. This does not mean that all of the provinces uniformly match one another's strategies in all of these fields. As we have seen in this book, the presence of a policy framework has not meant that provincial practices in elementary and secondary education are identical from coast to coast. The release of results on standardized assessments, for example, varies widely: at one end of the spectrum, some provinces expose the outcomes of individual schools; at the other, some only circulate province-level data. Moreover, whatever commonalities exist, the design and delivery of teacher preparation programs across the country are influenced by the choices of university administrators. The details of full state funding arrangements continue to vary, and implementation strategies for common policies exhibit important differences. All of this signals the magnitude of internal determinants of policy activity. When he was Chair of the Ontario Economic Council, Thomas Courchene's mantra was "for programs and policies to be national they need not be central."[7] This mantra holds true today. "Pan-Canadian" frameworks need not be synonymous with the central government, nor need they be accompanied by complete uniformity of practices.

Mechanisms of diffusion can carry policy ideas across the jurisdictions; these ideas can then be adapted by actors in the respective jurisdictions to suit the local context. These diffusion and adaptive processes, however, are neither immediate nor perfect, and they are accompanied by certain risks, for executing them can take considerable time and resources. As a result, the citizens of a federation must often accept degrees of policy incoherence, ineffectiveness, and inconsistency as those engaged in a particular sector work to find solutions to similar problems while simultaneously being influenced by internal material and ideational conditions that may encourage (or require) alternative policy tactics. Unfortunately, there is no clear answer for how much difference and potential incoherence either can be or should be accepted. Rather, it is by negotiating, managing, and overseeing policy frameworks achieved through interjurisdictional collaboration of state and non-state actors that such answers might be found as policy makers engage in the shared rule and self-rule of a federation.

While the incentives in the education arena that seem to encourage investments and collaborative policy action may have eased the achievement of interprovincial comparability, the incentives of the sector itself are not the lone explanatory variable. Policy demands for effective high-quality programming would go unmet if substate jurisdictions lacked, for example, the necessary autonomy or capacity to invest in education. The fact that some countries demonstrate greater internal variability in education than what we find in Canada suggests that specific features of the Canadian federation may also have contributed to the achievement of the *de facto* policy framework. So to simply assert that country-wide policy frameworks are more readily achievable in areas of developmental policy would be to miss other influential factors that play a role in the dynamics of policy making in federations. Which features more specific to the Canadian federation eased the achievement of interprovincial similarity in education?

It is here that we begin to discern the potential importance of the central government in the crafting and establishment of policy frameworks. A central government may lack jurisdictional authority to legislate or impose certain standards in particular policy arenas like education, but in most federations, it can intervene by deploying its spending power – a tactic with which Canadians are quite familiar if not universally comfortable. Perhaps our ambivalence to the federal spending power is a function of the potentially negative and positive consequences that can follow in its wake. The key seems to reside in how the central government executes its authority and the expectations that are held by the pertinent players that operate within a particular policy field.

A central government that unilaterally imposes policy mandates or alters intergovernmental agreements without consulting the substate jurisdictions may impede policy activity. The imposition of mandates can torque substate priorities away from locally defined needs and interests, thus sacrificing the federal principle of self-rule and compelling substate jurisdictions to invest in areas in ways that may not be suited to the conditions in their particular regions. This sort of unilateral action can also jeopardize trust and feed suspicion among the relevant players, contributing to dysfunctional relations while creating disincentives for provinces to act in policy areas. Why should substate decision makers attempt to develop programs if they are going to be overruled by a central government that suddenly decides to act? This is precisely the analysis of policy uncertainty in federations that Barry Rabe offers in his examination of substate activity in the climate change arena in the United States and Canada.

Observing that many American states are considerably ahead of their Canadian provincial counterparts in environmental regulation, Rabe concludes that part of the explanation for the paucity of Canadian provincial activity rests on the prolonged debate over the ratification of the Kyoto Accord and Ottawa's intermittent signals that it was going to act in the field.[8] Indeed, more recent work by Barry Rabe, Erick Lachapelle, and David Houle has pointed to a new burst of provincial activity in climate change policy coinciding with Ottawa's retreat from the sector.[9] Interestingly, except for a few instances (see below), the central government has rarely engaged with elementary and secondary education, which suggests that federal disengagement in a policy area may not be a bad thing if the substate governments show themselves willing and able to act in the field.

Policy certainty for the substates – and by this I simply mean clear jurisdictional control with a somewhat curtailed threat of unilateral central intervention – is nevertheless meaningless if the jurisdictions lack the fiscal capacity to act. This exposes the potentially positive consequences of the federal spending power in policy development. There is considerable research indicating that because fiscal resources are never evenly distributed across a country, it is critically important for the central government to act as an economic redistributor in order to ensure that substate governments have somewhat comparable levels of fiscal capacity to act in their respective policy areas. The devil, however, lies in the details of these arrangements.

The largely unconditional arrangements of the Canadian fiscal architecture developed by the federal government – including the equalization system and the semi-restricted large block grants for many social policy sectors – contributed to parity in educational investments among the provinces. As detailed in chapter 5, once Newfoundland joined Confederation and started receiving federal funds, its investments in education began climbing to meet those of the other provinces. Moreover, the disparities among the provinces have progressively narrowed overall since the 1950s (Appendices 6 and 8). Finally, in the 1990s, although it cut back funding in health and social policy, Ottawa left equalization alone, with the result that provincial parity in educational investments remained in place. It therefore appears that equalization contributed to the creation of a pan-Canadian system by mitigating fiscal disparities in the provinces' economic capacities, allowing them to "deliver comparable services at comparable rates of taxation."[10] While additional research is needed to conclusively link the fiscal architecture with central and substate spending patterns, the case of Canadian education illuminates the crucial yet indirect role the central government plays in the development of policy frameworks.[11]

Fiscal capacity is undeniably important when policies are being crafted and implemented. Similar investments in education, however, do not necessarily translate into comparable achievements. Using the insights of sociological institutionalism, I argued that other contextual factors particular to the Canadian case help us explain why the provinces record similar results. To start, the common commitment to destratify educational opportunities may have translated into high results on international tests and elevated graduation rates from coast to coast. Destratification in secondary schools seems to mitigate significant between-school variations in educational achievements, and this contributes to the comparability of results across the country as well as to shared educational norms and values. Thus, the selection of this particular policy option during the 1960s in one dimension of the education sector may have inadvertently fostered an active policy framework from coast to coast. What is more, as noted earlier, the absence of the federal government as a force in the policy sector may have helped iron out intergovernmental relations, which in Canada can be both tempestuous and hierarchical. In education, provinces meet and interact as equals, and this "socializes" them into a relationship that is more amenable to cooperation; they acknowledge one another as responsible for their own respective systems, which encourages constructive dialogue and eases the exchange of information and ideas among them.

Based on this final insight, we could speculate that any proposal to create a federal Department of Education or to ratify standards proposed by the federal government might upset the constructive balance that has emerged among the provinces. The ratification of national standards often requires the expenditure of significant political capital and can generate intense debates about national unity and legitimate authority; all of this, in turn, can distract policy actors from substantive policy issues. This sort of negative dynamics in intergovernmental relations is often exacerbated in multinational federations like Canada. Political leaders and members of the policy community should therefore tread cautiously when calling for central intervention and consider instead alternative routes to *de facto* policy frameworks of the sort that have been elaborated here.

We are now left with the mystery of how the provinces achieved substantive commonalities in their actual education policies. In chapter 2, having deconstructed the education sector into five dimensions, we saw that the process of building schooling systems involves selecting from a cornucopia of policy instruments, settings, and options, many of which have succeeded in countries around the world. There is no universal recipe for elementary and secondary education, and the provinces could have developed substantively different systems while still recording similar results and making similar investments. Unpacking the processes and conditions that led to the observed commonalities in education policy itself required the articulation of a new perspective on the dynamics of policy making in federations more broadly – a perspective that moved away from the emphasis on coercion and competition as the primary drivers of policy diffusion in favour of learning and cooperation.

Beyond Coercion and Competition

Scholars of federalism often implicate coercion as a powerful motor of policy diffusion and policy framework formulation. Yet as this book has demonstrated, coercion rarely played a role in the emergence of an active policy framework in Canadian education. As discussed in chapters 4 to 6, the federal government's piecemeal attempts to compel the provinces to pursue certain policy pathways in educational administration and curriculum enjoyed marginal success.

Ottawa's first foray into education came in the late 1800s, when it imposed religious trusteeship as the arrangement for educational administration in Manitoba. New immigrants from abroad and migrants from Ontario, however, rapidly changed Manitoba's population base and internal context. Unconvinced of the value of religious trusteeship, new policy actors who had experience of other models of educational administration decided to abolish the system imposed by Ottawa in favour of ministerial responsibility (which had been pioneered in neighbouring Ontario). The federal government's coercive tactics thus failed to establish a lasting policy legacy in Manitoba; provincial policy makers chose an alternative pathway, having drawn lessons from Ontario, and implemented an administrative arrangement more suited to their own values, needs, and interests.

The federal government also attempted to shape the direction of Canadian secondary education. Efforts at this began in the early twentieth century when Ottawa established the Royal Commission on Industrial Training and Technical Education.[12] Based on its recommendations, Ottawa offered the provinces a series of conditional grants to increase the number of technical training institutes that operated according to the model of partite schooling. These conditional grants were aligned with the dominant educational ideas of the time; however, they proved to be ineffective, for most of the provinces were unable to take advantage of them owing to the diminutive size and capacities of local school boards. Ottawa's policy had been inappropriately calibrated to the practical realities of the day.

In the 1960s, Ottawa again moved to influence secondary schooling, offering conditional grants to the provinces geared to the continuation of the partite and stratified high school model. This time, thanks to school board consolidations and general improvements in local administrative capacities, the provinces were able to use federal funds, and the number of secondary schools increased exponentially. But rather than preserving the partite model for high school, as Ottawa had intended, the provinces redeployed federal funds to suit their own policy agendas, which by this time had embraced the principles of composite schooling. So in this case, an arrangement favoured by federal policy makers was not ideationally congruent with the prevailing "progressive" educational paradigm that had coalesced both within and across the provincial education policy communities. Federal financial support had enabled the infrastructural expansion of secondary schooling, but hierarchical coercion had failed to impose a policy option preferred by the central government.

Coercion need not always come from above; it can also arise if some provinces call on the others to implement a policy against their will. This book, however, has offered little evidence of this actually occurring. Although it took an early lead in many dimensions of the education sector, Ontario never cajoled the other provinces to follow its policy choices. Rather, other jurisdictions independently decided to learn from Ontario's experience, adapted some of its practices, and benefited from the advances it had made. Similarly, Alberta took an early lead in university-led teacher education, which was rapidly adopted by its regional counterparts, but it did not impose the new approach on them, nor did it force the eastern provinces to transform their own regimes. All intergovernmental organizations and all collaborative activities in education, such as curriculum development and assessments, are premised on the principle of voluntary engagement – policy action cannot be compelled. This attribute of the Canadian educational landscape was succinctly captured in chapter 7, which described how Saskatchewan and Manitoba resisted overtures to fully harmonize course materials with the other two western provinces due to certain ideological differences with Alberta. Thus, even when collaborating, the provinces can still adhere to their own principles and goals, pursuing initiatives independently. Interprovincial collaborations do not require unanimity in order to advance.

Clearly, coercion was not the primary mechanism of policy diffusion that contributed to the emergence of an education framework in Canada. As the authors of the *Rowell–Sirois Report* sagely declared, a population of common origin and traditions, deeply habituated to think alike on fundamental issues, may be readily able to maintain the agreement necessary for collective action affecting the whole range of community life. Canada lacks that homogeneity and this, in turn, limits the extent of collective endeavours which can be effectively organized under Dominion control. That is why Canada is a federal state and must remain so. Deep, underlying differences cannot be permanently overcome by coercion.[13]

Hierarchical or vertical coercion may sometimes seem a useful strategy for achieving interjurisdictional policy similarity, as it can rapidly impose supposedly common practices, but the results may prove less than satisfactory. My comparative historical analysis of provincial elementary and secondary education reveals alternative routes to framework formulation that do not rely on coercion to achieve similar policies in a federation.

Scholars of federalism also implicate competition as a key driver of interjurisdictional policy diffusion. According to Tiebout, because citizens can "vote with their feet," moving to regions that provide more favourable policy packages, substate governments are constantly seeking ways to attract and keep both residents and investors.[14] Competition is thus thought to encourage policy diffusion as substate decision makers strive to see that their programs and strategies can rival those of their counterparts elsewhere. What role, then, did interjurisdictional competition play in the emergence of the Canadian education policy framework?

This book has shown that horizontal competition among the provinces contributed to substantive policy diffusion in only one dimension of the education sector: teacher education. Here, as detailed in chapters 5 and 6, the western provinces introduced a policy innovation imported from the United States – that is, they transferred teacher training from provincially run normal schools to universities. The eastern provinces resisted this approach and continued with the status quo, arguing that it better fit their ideational and managerial arrangements. They were opposed to "American" policy ideas, and in addition, eastern universities fought vehemently against offering teacher preparation programs, viewing teaching as a vocation rather than a profession. Within a decade, however, the eastern provinces had followed western Canada's lead and implemented university-led teacher education, citing in part a fear that the quality of their teachers was in decline relative to their western counterparts. Although they faced considerable resistance from key stakeholders, including the universities themselves, policy actors in Ontario, Quebec, New Brunswick, Nova Scotia, PEI, and Newfoundland gradually abandoned the normal school system and converged with the other provinces to ameliorate this perceived disparity. The eastern provinces did not want to risk compromising their reputation for providing high-quality education.

Other dimensions of the education sector, however, rarely saw competition drive policy diffusion. In teacher certification – an area where one might expect to see competitive pressures – the provinces continued with their own arrangements based on internal labour market conditions, irrespective of any adjustments their neighbours were making. Substate competition did not result in changes in mandatory testing, nor did it drive the spread of full state funding. Furthermore, even when the eastern provinces followed their western counterparts in teacher education driven in part by competition, they needed to learn about the practice through studies and information exchanges, capitalizing on the cross-provincial links that had been forged within the education policy community.

These findings fundamentally challenge the notion shared by many federal scholars that interjurisdictional competition is a key mechanism of policy diffusion. They also reinforce the conclusions reached recently by Kathryn Harrison that "provinces within the Canadian federation are not completely at the mercy of destructive provincial competition."[15] Instead, competitive pressures are countervailed because "ideas and knowledge also flow freely within a national political community"[16] as policy makers, stakeholders, and voters benchmark and learn from one another. Furthermore, Tiebout's competitive model is predicated on citizens moving to jurisdictions with more appealing policy packages, yet the history of provincial education policy suggests something quite different – citizens moved to new jurisdictions, brought their ideas with them, and thereby acted as carrier molecules for diffusion. It was not people moving to other provinces in pursuit of more attractive policies, as Tiebout's adherents posit; rather, diffusion happened as people moved to other provinces and worked to make their new home more attractive. In this way, policies were transplanted from one jurisdiction to the next. The image of competition propounded in the literature thus fails to capture all of the dynamics of policy development in federations.

Achieving Learning and Cooperation

Rather than coercion and competition, this book has documented the significance of learning and cooperation as mechanisms of diffusion across the provinces. The pattern of policy learning among the provinces in elementary and secondary education dates back to Confederation. Right from the outset of Canadian educational history, provincial policy actors demonstrated a strong commitment to take in and reflect upon the examples being set by their neighbours. Initially piecemeal and carried out through informal and irregular channels – such as the physical migration of policy entrepreneurs between former colonies – policy makers and other members of the policy community worked to establish an active policy network that would link the seemingly independent education systems. Organizations such as the Dominion Educational Association (DEA), which evolved into the Canadian Education Association (CEA), expedited this process by gathering and disseminating information on educational practices and policies in the different provinces. Stakeholder-specific groups like the Canadian School Trustees' Association (CSTA) and the Canadian Teachers' Federation (CTF) abetted the efforts of the omnibus organizations. Each era of education policy development also saw regional and pan-Canadian conferences sponsored by various stakeholders that brought policy actors together and exposed them to ideas from coast to coast. Periodic Royal Commissions at the provincial level also contributed to ideational exchanges among the epistemic community that transcended provincial borders. Over time, these initiatives created a dense and highly integrated education network that enabled the diffusion of ideas by linking state and non-state policy actors from the different provinces.

Two factors exerted the greatest influence on interprovincial learning: consistent engagement in the policy network, and the relative cohesion of the dominant cognitive and normative ideas that prevailed at a particular point in time. In each era of provincial education development, the integration and participation of the various provinces in the germinating education network varied, and those that remained somewhat outside or detached from the jurisdictions that were pursuing a certain initiative tended to exhibit the greatest differences from the rest. When the francophone contingent of the Quebec delegation withdrew from the DEA in the early nineteenth century, for example, it further isolated that component of the province's education system from the other Canadian jurisdictions, allowing greater fissures to appear in areas such as curriculum and teacher certification. In the meantime, the anglophone component of the Quebec education system continued to engage with the pan-Canadian organization, learned from its counterparts in the other provinces, and pursued policies that demonstrated greater affinities with the other provinces than with those at work in Quebec's francophone sector. Engagement with the broader policy network had similar effects in Newfoundland. Initially, the colony was excluded from the provincial education policy network, but once it joined with the CEA in the 1930s, the opportunity for education policy makers to learn from the experiences of the Canadian provinces increased and new ideas on educational administration began to percolate on the island. Clearly, the nurturing of associational bonds across a policy community to forge a sustained policy network is vital for interjurisdictional policy learning, which can then act as a key mechanism in policy framework formulation.

The nature of the ideas themselves proved to be the second factor in policy framework formulation. As ideas on education coalesced into clearer, more cohesive policy paradigms offering somewhat coherent programmatic directives to those engaged in the policy community, the ideas could be transferred more easily across jurisdictional boundaries. As ideas congeal, moreover, a clearer agenda may emerge that is shared across several types of knowledge-producing organizations that are active in the policy network and that contribute to the knowledge regime. As happens in many policy sectors, alternative educational paradigms ebb and flow over time. When there has been greater clarity and consensus on the components and perceived legitimacy of an educational paradigm, the flow of policies across the provinces has been expedited, leading to interprovincial similarities. The gradual transformation from universalizing to individualizing elementary and secondary education neatly illuminates the significance of paradigmatic and programmatic cohesion within and across the various jurisdictions; the transition from stratified partite schools to comprehensive or composite schools required a strong consensus and commitment across the education community. Ideas therefore play an important role in the dynamics of framework formulation in federations.

The importance of ideational coherence points to an interesting set of questions that cannot be answered here. How does a policy paradigm emerge, and who is involved in formulating a paradigm? What facilitates the spread and acceptance of a common paradigm by independent actors and jurisdictions in a federation? Is this expedited entirely through the domestic policy network, or do international actors also play a role? What factors precipitate the breakdown of an accepted paradigm? Is it a function of diminishing returns from existing practices as the conditions that precipitated the acceptance of a paradigm change? Or do the people involved in crafting policy paradigms attempt to be proactive and anticipate problems before they emerge? How important are such things as incubation periods and the support of pertinent members of the stakeholder community? And what role do political structures – such as parliamentary systems – and administrative styles play in the crafting of policy paradigms? The burgeoning literature on ideas and public policy has broken considerable ground in answering these types of questions, but until we know more about ideational coherence, our ability to understand the emergence of policy frameworks in federations will remain incomplete.

This book also exposed a new mechanism for policy diffusion in federations: cooperation. Chapter 7 chronicled a series of cooperative endeavours in different dimensions of the education sector. By working together, provincial decision makers gained new information and expertise, which they subsequently transferred to their respective jurisdictions. Events surrounding provincial assessments in PEI were particularly illuminative of this phenomenon. Working with the other provinces on the pan-Canadian assessment program under the auspices of the CMEC, PEI officials acquired the necessary experience to develop a comparable program for the province. Moreover, by participating in the pan-Canadian program, PEI officials were able to assuage the fears of professional educators and parents, assuring them that results would not be used to track and evaluate the accomplishments of individual teachers and students. Cooperation at the pan-Canadian level therefore contributed to the internal policy capacity of PEI while creating a by-product learning effect that facilitated the spread of a policy idea from coast to coast.

Students of diffusion have tended to view intergovernmental organizations as platforms for coercion, producers of particular policy paradigms, or passive venues for ideational exchanges. The potential impact of such organizations is considerably greater than this. They can create conditions whereby ostensibly independent policy actors can pursue collective action, ratify comprehensive agreements, and formally harmonize policies. For example, both the CMEC and the APEF provided the necessary support that brought about substate cooperation. To quote a former Minister of Education, "without the CMEC there, dare I say it, would be chaos – dragons in fact!"[17] The significance of these highly institutionalized organizations is further confirmed when the success of the regional initiatives in eastern Canada are contrasted with the limited success of the Western Canadian Protocol for Collaboration in Education. As one official from western Canada opined: "Without a permanent coordinative secretariat, it is really difficult to move beyond ratifying learning outcomes. Unlike our counterparts in Atlantic Canada, we in the west don't have the important institutional supports."[18] By providing a stable arena for exchange and collaboration supported by an administrative secretariat that can ensure some institutional memory, organizations like these offer support that is essential for interjurisdictional cooperation in federations.

Further research is nevertheless needed to unpack the factors and conditions that contribute to the effective construction and maintenance of intergovernmental organizations. Material from this study allows us to begin anticipating the factors that may have played a role in these results. With regard to the education sector, one such factor is the parallel administrative structures among the provinces. Because each of the ten jurisdictions gradually adopted individual ministerial responsibility as the preferred administrative model, all ten elementary and secondary systems are governed today by comparable authorities exercising similar powers and supported by highly capable bureaucracies that enjoy considerable autonomy from stakeholders in the policy community. In addition to this, policy choices made within each province, such as the initial choice to implement shared-cost financing before moving to full state funding for education, helped establish the clear authority of the state in education, thus reinforcing the autonomy of the bureaucracy and the ministers of education in the arena. As a result, when provincial policy makers act collaboratively, they have considerable assurances that their collective decisions will be implemented. Future studies can help us to better appreciate the potential role these factors and conditions play in the establishment of intergovernmental organizations and their subsequent influence on interjurisdictional framework formulation.

The Context, the Climate, and Policy Frameworks

The literature on federalism tends to focus on the diffusion processes of coercion and competition and to downplay the mechanisms of learning and cooperation. This has emerged from a proclivity for relying on the principles and tenets of rational choice theory to understand intergovernmental relations and policy development in federations. The problem is that the conditions of strict rational choice theory are not readily apparent in federations. As Elinor Ostrom wrote, the metaphors of rational choice, like those of collective action, are "special models that utilize extreme assumptions" and that can "successfully predict strategies and outcomes in fixed situations approximating the initial conditions of the models, but ... cannot predict outcomes outside that range."[19] When describing the international system, Peter Gourevitch laboured to dispel the image of anarchy and chaos that had been advanced by some of his peers. He argued that countries are interconnected through "structured links" and "that various elements of domestic society are linked to each other through international forces."[20] The same can be said of the constituent members of a federation. Rather than autonomous and independent, as a strict rational choice approach would hold, substate jurisdictions are interdependent and connected. By linking together the insights from rational choice, sociological and historical institutionalism, I crafted a new analytical architecture to give us a deeper and more complete understanding of federations. My central argument throughout this book has been that we have dramatically underestimated the importance of the interstitial tissues that evolve in a federation and the role they play in the development of policy frameworks.

Federalism inculcates four types of bonds among the constituent units: legal, economic, organizational, and cultural. Each type of bond binds the members of a federation in a structural network that enables the cross-pollination of policy ideas via multiple mechanisms of diffusion across territorial boundaries. While somewhat stable, these bonds are neither uniform nor immutable; they vary over space and time. Because certain configurations of structural bonds can privilege certain mechanisms of policy diffusion, changes to those bonds in a federation influence the diffusionary mechanisms as they unfold. Hierarchical configurations favour coercion and competition; horizontal configurations foster learning and cooperation. In addition, cultural connectivity – or more specifically, culture synergies – can lubricate interjurisdictional interactions, thus nurturing and enabling learning and cooperation. State and non-state stakeholder organizations also increase the potential for learning, while dedicated intergovernmental organizations ease formal collaboration. These structural bonds not only shape the frequency and density of the interactions among the jurisdictions, thereby influencing the degree to which interjurisdictional policy frameworks can be achieved, but they also establish opportunity structures that can trigger spillover effects, potentially generating new and ground-breaking innovations across a variety of fields.

Swirling around this structural network are the ideational, cognitive and normative constructs of the day. These ideational constructs may coalesce into a clear policy agenda that simultaneously shapes the ideas being exchanged and affects the probability that a common policy framework will emerge. During the individualizing of provincial schooling in the 1960s, for example, a clear consensus emerged across the education policy community not only with regard to the paradigm of progressive education but also regarding specific programmatic ideas that had became popular, and this contributed to highly similar policy development across the ten provincial systems. Each period of Canadian educational development, moreover, witnessed varying degrees of ideational coherence between the educational paradigm of the day and wider norms or government-wide policy agendas. This synergy was most apparent in the 1990s, when there was resonance between New Public Management and the drive to increase quality and accountability in education. Such dovetailing of sector-specific paradigms with broader societal norms and goals also shapes subsequent adoption of similar policies by different jurisdictions in a federation.

This book has attempted to uncover and specify the structural and ideational attributes of the policy climate in order to demonstrate that context and timing matter in the dynamics of policy making in federations. All of this builds on an approach advocated by Paul Pierson. In his words, for many in the social sciences, context has become "a bad word – a synonym for thick description, and an obstacle to social scientific analysis."[21] Here I have specified in great detail particular factors that have shaped social outcomes while drawing associations between the processes and the mechanisms that connected these contextual variables to the outcomes. The findings of this book thus propel the policy diffusion literature to better appreciate the types of bonds that appear among communities and the ways in which these bonds influence policy exchanges.

These features of the policy climate and the subsequent diffusion of policy ideas encounter the existing policy contexts of the receiving jurisdictions. Internal policy legacies and the active regime within a particular policy sector mediate the likelihood that similar practices will be implemented and thereby translate into a country-wide policy framework. Furthermore, the interactive effects of policy choices across the various dimensions of a particular sector carry significant implications for policy development writ large. Here we saw the centralizing and capacity-building implications for choices in administration, finance, curriculum, assessment, and the teaching profession. Prospective entrepreneurs must be sensitive to these internal features of the respective policy contexts as they work to translate novel ideas into existing conditions; in doing so, they must emphasize the relevance of the initiative to an identified problem, its compatibility with the existing administrative structures, and the political promise of the new strategy, program, or instrument, given the local institutional context.

By drawing on and integrating the collective explanatory power of the three institutionalisms while building bridges across and expanding on the diffusion and convergence literatures in public policy, this book has crafted a new analytical architecture for understanding the alternative dynamics of policy framework formulation in federations. In treating policy actors as important agents who are nested in temporally and structurally bound contexts, simultaneously motivated by the logic of consequences and the logic of appropriateness, and influenced by ideas, norms, and values, my goal has been to push the enterprise of institutional analysis forward, while injecting a much needed "ideational turn" into the study of federalism. Having explained how the provinces defied the odds in elementary and secondary education, I hope to have put forward a new framework that others find useful when they seek to investigate the intriguing ways that actors manage the challenges and opportunities that accompany the federal principles of shared-rule and self-rule.

Appendices

Appendix 1. Inter-school Equity: Odds ratios of the likelihood of students with the lowest socio-economic status to be lowest mathematics performers relative to the likelihood of students with the highest socio-economic status to be lowest mathematics performers (2003)

▲ – country odds ratio is significantly higher than the OECD average odds

▼ – country odds ratio is significantly lower than the OECD average odds

	Odds Ratio	S.E.	
Iceland	2.1	(0.23)	▼
Turkey	2.5	(0.31)	▼
Canada	2.7	(0.21)	▼
Japan	2.8	(0.32)	▼
Finland	2.8	(0.37)	
Greece	2.8	(0.32)	▼
Norway	2.9	(0.28)	▼
Spain	2.9	(0.28)	▼
Sweden	2.9	(0.27)	▼
Portugal	3.0	(0.29)	
Austria	3.1	(0.40)	
Italy	3.1	(0.27)	
Australia	3.2	(0.40)	
Poland	3.2	(0.31)	
Luxembourg	3.3	(0.40)	
United Kingdom	3.3	(0.32)	

Appendix 1 (*continued*)

▲ – country odds ratio is significantly higher than the OECD average odds
▼ – country odds ratio is significantly lower than the OECD average odds

	Odds Ratio	S.E.	
Korea	3.5	(0.40)	
Ireland	3.6	(0.44)	
New Zealand	3.6	(0.44)	
Netherlands	3.8	(0.70)	
United States	3.8	(0.34)	
Sweden	3.9	(0.27)	
Czech Republic	4.1	(0.44)	
Denmark	4.1	(0.37)	
Mexico	4.1	(0.52)	
France	4.3	(0.51)	
Germany	4.6	(0.50)	▲
Hungary	4.8	(0.56)	▲
Slovak Republic	5.1	(0.54)	▲
Belgium	5.4	(0.52)	▲
OECD Average	*3.5*	*(0.08)*	

Countries are ranking in ascending order.

Source: Adapted from OECD, *Education at a Glance,* 2006. Table A6.1. p. 91.

Appendix 2. Summary of Province-wide Examinations, as of 2008[1]

	Examination and level	Subjects and sources	Percentage of Final Grade	Marking
BC	Provincial examination program All Grade 10, 11, and 12 students enrolled in courses	Various core subjects and graduation requirements listed at http://www.bced.gov.bc.ca/exams/handbook/handbook_procedures.pdf (accessed on 18 March 2008)	40% of final grade	Marked centrally by teachers in a common location
AB	Diploma exams All Grade 12 students enrolled in course	Various core subjects and graduation requirements listed at http://education.alberta.ca/media/652175/guidetoed2007.pdf (accessed on 18 March 2008)	50% of final grade	Marked centrally
SK	Diploma exams All Grade 12 students enrolled in course not taught by an accredited teacher	Various core subjects and graduation requirements listed at http://www.sasked.gov.sk.ca/branches/aar/prov_exams/main/general_faq.shtml and http://www.sasked.gov.sk.ca/branches/aar/prov_exams/docs/pe_teacher_guide/teacherguide.pdf (accessed on 18 March 2008)	Blended 60% course grade and 40% exam grade	Approved local teachers
MB	Provincial Standards Test All students enrolled in 40S courses	Various core subjects and graduation requirements listed at http://www.edu.gov.mb.ca/k12/assess/docs/pol_proc/pol_proc_07.pdf (accessed on 19 March 2008)	30% of final grade	Locally graded

Appendix 2. (continued)

Examination and level	Subjects and sources	Percentage of Final Grade	Marking
ON Literacy Test Grade 10	Literacy Test administered by the Education Quality and Accountability Office designed to assess whether students have the literacy (reading and writing) skills needed to meet the requirements of the Ontario Secondary School Diploma Further information listed at http://www.eqao.com/pdf_e/08/Xe_Framework_07.pdf (accessed on 18 March 2008)	Must pass to receive diploma; opportunities to re-write	Centrally graded at EQAO
QU Uniform Ministry Exams All students in Secondary IV and V	Must pass two levels of languages (language of instruction and second language – FR/ENG), a history, a math, and a science course (From: www.maritamoll.ca)	50% of final mark, unless school mark is out of line with exam mark, in which case the exam mark has a higher value	Central grading for multiple choice items; remainder marked locally
NB Provincial Literacy Assessment Grade 9	English Language Proficiency Assessment French Immersion Literacy Assessment http://www.gnb.ca/0000/anglophone-e.asp#e (accessed on 19 March 2008)	Must pass to graduate; opportunities to re-write	Centrally graded
NS Diploma Exams All Grade 12 students enrolled in course	Various core subjects and graduation requirements listed at http://plans.ednet.ns.ca/documents/nse-policy_manual_2005.pdf (accessed on 19 March 2008) – tailored to the Atlantic Canada Curriculum	30% of final grade	Locally graded

Appendix 2. (*continued*)

	Examination and level	Subjects and sources	Percentage of Final Grade	Marking
PEI	No system	N/A	N/A	
NL	Public exams All students enrolled in 32 – level courses	Various subjects listed at http://www.ed.gov.nl.ca/edu/ k12/pub/sample.htm (accessed on 19 March 2008) Regulations listed at http://www.ed.gov.nl.ca/edu/pub/ reg.pdf (accessed on 19 March 2008)	50% of final grade	

Appendix 3. Summary of Provincial Assessment Programs

	Program and frequency	Grade level/students tested	Subjects	Marking	Purpose of tests
BC	Foundation Skills Assessment Annually	Grade 4	Reading Writing Numeracy	Centrally graded	Student assessment Accountability Individual student results released to parents School and district summaries are released
		Grade 7	Reading Writing Numeracy		
		All students			
AB	Achievement Testing Program Annually	Grade 3	English Math	Locally first graded and then centrally graded (both grades contribute to the student's final mark)	Student assessment Accountability Individual student results released to the local school and districts – not made available to parents
		Grade 6	English Math Science Social Studies		
		Grade 9	English Math Science		
		All Students	Social Studies Knowledge and Employability		

	Program	Grade	Subject	Grading	Notes
SK	Assessment for Learning Program – voluntary participation	Grade 5	Math	Locally graded	Locally determined improvement in learning
	Every two years	Grade 8	Math		Provincial averages released
		Regional samples			
		Grade 5	English/French	Locally graded	
		Grade 7	English/French		
		Regional samples			
MB	Provincial Assessment Program	Grade 3	Reading Lecture Numeracy	Locally graded	Student assessment
	Annually				Summative assessment to show student's attainment on each level of key competencies
		Grade 7	Math		
		Grade 8	Reading Writing		Schools must submit results to the department
		All students			
ON	Education Quality and Assessment Office	Grade 3	Reading Writing Math	Centrally graded at EQAO	Student assessment
	Student Achievement Exams	Grade 6	Reading Writing Math		Individual results released to parents
	Annually				Provincial, district, school level data publicly released
		Grade 9	Math		
		All students			

Appendix 3. (*continued*)

	Program and frequency	Grade level/students tested	Subjects	Marking	Purpose of tests
QU	Compulsory exams Annual	Grade 6 Grade 9	Language of instruction	Locally graded	System assessment – not for internal board evaluation
	Complementary exams Annual	Grade 3 Grade 6 All students	English English, Math	Locally graded	System assessment – not for internal board evaluation
NB	Provincial Assessments Annually	Grade 2 Grade 4 Grade 5 Grade 6 Grade 7 All students	Literacy Literacy Math Science Literacy	Centrally graded	Monitor student achievements Provincial averages released to the public Districts and schools provided provincial, district, and school level results in reading comprehension
NS	Program of Learning Assessment for Nova Scotia (PLANS) Annually	Grade 3 Grade 6 Grade 8 All students	Literacy Literacy Math	Centrally graded	Program assessment Grade 6 Literacy test results reported to parents
PEI	Provincial Assessment Annually	Grade 3 Grade 9 All students	Literacy Math	Centrally graded	Classroom and program assessment Provincial averages reported Principals learn classroom averages

	Provincial Assessment	Grade 3	English and Math	Centrally graded	Program assessment
NL	Annually	Grade 6	English and Science		Provincial averages reported
		Grade 9	French, English, Math, Science		
		All students			

Sources for Assessment Programs, as of 2008:

BC: http://www.bced.gov.bc.ca/assessment/welcome.htm (accessed on 19 March 2008)

AB: http://education.alberta.ca/media/671468/09_marking_&_results.pdf (accessed on 19 March 2008)

SK: http://www.learning.gov.sk.ca/adx/aspx/adxGetMedia.aspx?DocID=206,200,135,107,81,1,Documents&MediaID=733&Filename=2005update.pdf (accessed on 19 March 2008)

MB: http://www.edu.gov.mb.ca/k12/assess/docs/my_policy/my_policy_doc.pdf (accessed on 19 March 2008)

ON: http://www.eqao.com/pdf_e/04/04p027e.pdf (accessed on 19 March 2008)

QU: Marita Moll

NB: http://www.gnb.ca/0000/publications/eval/Grade2LiteracyAssessmentInformationBulletin2008.pdf (accessed on 19 March 2008)

NS: http://www.ednet.ns.ca/index.php?sid=8651725988t=sub_pages&cat=86 (accessed on 19 March 2008)

PEI: http://www.gov.pe.ca/educ/index.php3?number=1017793&lang=E (accessed on 19 March 2008)

NL: http://www.ed.gov.nl.ca/edu/pub/crt/pdf/crtassess-principal.pdf (accessed on 19 March 2008)

Appendix 4. Provincial Universities Offering an Education Degree[2]

Province	Universities	Degree type[3]
British Columbia	UBC	Concurrent and Consecutive
	UNBC	Concurrent and Consecutive
	Malaspina University College	Consecutive
	University of Victoria	Concurrent and Consecutive
	Simon Fraser	Consecutive
	Trinity Western University	Concurrent
	Thompson Rivers	Consecutive
Alberta	University of Alberta	Concurrent and Consecutive
	University of Lethbridge	Concurrent and Consecutive
	University of Calgary	Concurrent and Consecutive
	Concordia University	Consecutive
	King's University College	
Saskatchewan	University of Saskatchewan	Concurrent and Consecutive
	University of Regina	Concurrent and Consecutive
Manitoba	University of Brandon	Consecutive
	University of Manitoba	Concurrent and Consecutive
	University of Winnipeg	Concurrent and Consecutive
	Collège universitaire de Saint-Boniface	Consecutive
Ontario	Brock University	Concurrent and Consecutive
	Charles Sturt University	Consecutive
	Lakehead University	Concurrent and Consecutive
	Laurentian University	Concurrent and Consecutive (French)
	Niagara University	Consecutive
	Nipissing University	Concurrent and Consecutive
	University of Toronto	Concurrent and Consecutive
	Queen's University	Concurrent and Consecutive
	Redeemer University	Concurrent and Consecutive K–10
	Trent University	Consecutive
	University of Ontario Institute of Technology	Concurrent and Consecutive
	University of Ottawa	Consecutive

Province	Universities	Degree type[3]
	Western University	Concurrent and Consecutive
	University of Windsor	Concurrent and Consecutive
	Wilfrid Laurier University	Consecutive
	York University	Concurrent and Consecutive
Quebec	Bishop's University	Concurrent and Consecutive
	Concordia University	Concurrent and Consecutive**
	Université Laval	Concurrent
	McGill University	Concurrent
	Université de Montréal	Concurrent
	Université de Québec	Concurrent
	– Abitibi–Temiscamingue	Concurrent
	– Chicoutimi	Concurrent
	– Outaouais	Concurrent
	– Montréal	Concurrent
	– Rimouski	Concurrent
	– Trois-Rivières	Concurrent
New Brunswick	St Thomas University	Consecutive*
	University of New Brunswick	Concurrent and Consecutive
	Université de Moncton	Consecutive (French language only)
Nova Scotia	Acadia	Consecutive
	Mount Saint Vincent	Consecutive
	St Francis Xavier	Consecutive
	Université Sainte-Anne	Consecutive***
Prince Edward Island	University of Prince Edward Island	Consecutive
Newfoundland	Memorial University	Concurrent and Consecutive

* Two-year program completed in eleven months with students specializing in elementary, secondary, or French language
** Consecutive program open only to Concordia graduate students
*** Either two-year or one-year intensive
NOTE: Quebec universities tend to offer highly specialized programs with separate degrees for ECE, Special Education, French/English as a second language, mathematics, science and technology, history and geography, and social and cultural development. Moreover, consecutive programs have been effectively abandoned. So, an individual with a BA in history who wishes to become a teacher must return to university and complete the four-year Bachelor of Education program, as opposed to individuals in other provinces who can complete a one- or two-year consecutive program that centres on pedagogical training.

Appendix 5. Province of Residence of Native-Born Internal Migrants in Canada, Census Dates 1871 to 1971[4]

Year	Total	NL	PEI	NS	NB	QU	ON	MB	SK	AB	BC
1971	2470.0	16.8	13.1	90.3	72.0	256.3	785.8	135.0	105.7	342.5	631.8
1961	1892.1	9.8	8.0	74.1	56.3	223.2	577.6	118.8	111.0	255.1	445.1
1951	1382.4	4.1	5.6	52.7	26.1	161.0	410.0	97.3	107.0	161.0	349.3
1941	916.7	–	2.8	24.1	25.3	109.5	218.0	87.8	125.0	124.3	197.3
1931	783.5	–	2.5	15.8	23.6	79.4	145.4	89.2	160.0	125.0	140.7
1921	684.1	–	2.0	16.1	20.4	46.2	108.4	95.6	169.0	119.1	106.1
1911	537.3	–	1.7	11.7	13.5	28.8	77.5	92.4	140.1	86.4	83.1
1901	298.1	–	2.5	11.2	12.7	25.2	71.6	81.1		41.8	39.8
1891	210.1	–	3.3	8.7	12.2	19.3	68.6	57.4		20.6	20.2
1881	130.2	–	4.1	6.9	12.3	13.2	57.9	31.0		2.1	2.8
1871	67.8	–	–	4.0	7.9	8.8	47.2	–		–	–

Appendix 6. Average Government Expenditure per Pupil on Public Elementary and Secondary Schools, Selected School/Fiscal Years, 1900–01 to 1989–90[5]

School/fiscal year	Average expenditure per pupil in current dollars	Coefficient of variability	Average real expenditures per pupil in 1986 dollars	Average annual increase during preceding period (%)
1900	10	0.41	160	–
1915	31	0.50	314	6.4
1925	55	0.30	394	2.5
1935	51	0.31	458	1.6
1945	84	0.29	597	3.0
1950	137	0.33	684	2.9
1955	201	0.37	927	7.1
1960	305	0.30	1,283	7.7
1965	456	0.28	1,745	7.2
1970	814	0.19	2,587	9.7
1975	1,465	0.11	3,196	4.7
1980	2,915	0.17	4,085	5.6
1985	4,420	0.14	4,510	2.1
1989	5,484	0.10	4,697	1.0

Appendix 7. Historical Expansion of Teacher Qualifications – Public Elementary and Secondary Schools (Excluding Quebec)[6]

	Percentage of teachers with university degrees		
Province	1952	1973	Rate of Increase
Newfoundland	4.4	51.6	11.73
PEI	5.1	38.6	7.57
Nova Scotia	19.4	49.9	2.57
New Brunswick	11.4	52.3	4.59
Ontario	24.6	52.5	2.13
Manitoba	19.4	59.4	3.06
Saskatchewan	13.3	52.5	3.95
Alberta	35.5	73.8	2.08
British Columbia	36.2	66.9	1.85
9 provinces	21.8	57.0	2.61

Appendix 8. Government Expenditures on Public Elementary and Secondary Schools as Percentages of Total Provincial and Local Government Expenditures, Selected Fiscal Years 1913–14 to 1989–90[7]

Fiscal Year*	NL	PEI	NS	NB	QU	ON	MB	SK	AB	BC	CDA**
1913	–	34.5	28.6	27.4	17.1	26.1	20.8	22.7	14.7	8.5	18.6
1926	–	41.7	28.0	25.9	31.2	29.5	34.5	48.7	32.6	20.9	31.1
1937	–	17.3	15.5	14.0	14.1	20.3	19.5	10.9	27.1	16.6	17.3
1937	–	15.8	15.0	13.4	15.0	21.2	19.5	12.1	24.9	17.2	18.2
1950	18.2	15.1	20.1	21.0	17.1	22.2	24.5	26.2	22.5	17.2	20.9
1955	22.3	15.8	26.3	20.3	23.7	22.4	26.1	23.8	23.0	22.9	23.7
1960	24.2	20.2	25.8	22.4	24.5	24.8	24.3	27.9	25.5	23.4	25.5
1965	20.1	22.0	27.3	23.8	28.4	29.4	27.6	26.4	28.3	25.1	28.7
1965	14.4	17.1	21.0	18.8	23.1	24.9	23.0	21.2	21.7	21.7	23.6
1970	18.6	18.1	19.7	22.7	25.3	23.5	22.7	23.5	20.4	21.8	23.6
1975	17.4	16.1	19.1	18.1	20.6	18.7	17.3	17.6	16.5	16.7	19.0
1980	17.1	17.8	18.1	19.3	19.0	21.4	17.8	16.3	12.6	15.8	18.6
1985	17.7	15.2	17.3	18.2	15.4	18.2	15.9	14.2	12.9	14.1	16.2
1989	16.5	14.6	15.6	17.2	13.4	18.8	15.8	15.3	13.1	15.0	15.8

* The statistical series for provincial government expenditures is broken at 1937–8 and 1965–6. Hence, two sets of statistics are given for these fiscal years to permit comparison of long-term trends.
** Canada includes Yukon and the Northwest Territories and excludes Newfoundland before 1950–1.

Notes

Introduction: An Unexpected Policy Framework

1 Organisation for Economic Co-operation and Development, *Reviews of National Policies for Education: Canada* (Paris: 1976), 93.
2 Ibid., 102.
3 Canadian Council on Learning, "Lessons in Learning: Minority Francophone Education in Canada," accessed on 9 January 2012 at http://www.ccl-cca.ca/pdfs/LessonsInLearning/08_20_09-E.pdf; Jeffrey G. Reitz and Rupa Banerjee, "Racial Inequality, Social Cohesion, and Policy Issues in Canada," in *Belonging? Diversity, Recognition, and Shared Citizenship in Canada*, ed. Keith Banting, Thomas J. Courchene, and F. Leslie Seidle (Montreal: Institute for Research on Public Policy, 2007); Canadian Council on Learning, *The New Gender Gap: Exploring the "Boy Crisis" in Education* (Ottawa: Canadian Conference on Learning, 2011, accessed on 9 January 2012 at http://www.ccl-cca.ca/pdfs/OtherReports/Gendereport20110113.pdf; Canadian Council on Learning, "Lessons in Learning: The Rural-Urban Gap in Education" 1 March 2006, accessed on 9 January 2012 at http://www.ccl-cca.ca/pdfs/LessonsInLearning/10-03_01_06E.pdf.
4 Under the terms of the Constitution Act, 1867, the responsibility for the education of Aboriginal Peoples living on reserves falls to the federal government. There are critical gaps between the funding and infrastructure provided by the federal government for on-reserve schools and the funding allocated by the provinces to their own schools. According to the 2006 Census, more than 50 per cent of registered Indians living on-reserve fail to complete high school, compared to 29 per cent of registered Indians living off-reserve, who are therefore educated in the provincial systems, and 10 per cent of the non-Aboriginal population. See Council of

Ministers of Education, Canada, *Strengthening Aboriginal Success,* CMEC Summit on Aboriginal Education, 24–5 February 2009, accessed on 22 May 2012 at http://www.cmec.ca/publications/lists/publications/attachments/221/aboriginal_summit_report.pdf; Report of the Standing Senate Committee on Aboriginal Peoples, *Reforming First Nations Education: From Crisis to Hope,* December 2011, accessed on 22 May 2012 at http://www.parl.gc.ca/Content/SEN/Committee/411/appa/rep/rep03dec11-e.pdf.

5 John W. Meyer, John Boli, and George M. Thomas, "Ontology and Rationalization in the Western Cultural Account," in *Institutional Structure: Constituting State, Society, and the Individual,* ed. George M. Thomas, John W. Meyer, Francisco O. Ramirez, and John Boli (Beverly Hills: Sage, 1987), 12–37; John Boli and George M. Thomas, "World Culture in the World Polity: A Century of International Non-Governmental Organization," *American Sociological Review* 62(2) (1997): 171–90.

6 Peter A. Hall and Rosemary Taylor, "Political Science and the New Institutionalism," *Political Studies* 44(5) (1996): 936–57; John L. Campbell, *Institutional Change and Globalization* (Princeton: Princeton University Press, 2004); Paul Pierson and Theda Skocpol, "Historical Institutionalism in Contemporary Political Science," in *Political Science: State of the Discipline III,* ed. Ira Katznelson and Helen V. Milner (New York: W.W. Norton, 2002), 693–721; Wolfgang Streeck and Kathleen Thelen, *Beyond Continuity: Institutional Change in Advanced Political Economies* (Oxford: Oxford University Press, 2005); Daniel Béland, "Ideas and Social Policy," *Social Politics* 16(4) (2005): 558–81; James Mahoney and Kathleen Thelen, "A Theory of Gradual Institutional Change," in *Explaining Institutional Change: Ambiguity, Agency, and Power,* ed. James Mahoney and Kathleen Thelen (Cambridge: Cambridge University Press, 2010), 1–37.

7 Samuel L. Popkin, *The Rational Peasant: The Political Economy of Rural Society in Vietnam* (Berkeley: University of California Press, 1979); Douglass C. North, *Institutions, Institutional Change and Economic Performance* (Cambridge: Cambridge University Press, 1990); Russell Hardin, "The Social Evolution of Cooperation," in *The Limits to Rationality,* ed. Karen S. Cook and Margaret Levi (Chicago: University of Chicago Press, 1990), 358–77; Jack Knight, *Institutions and Social Conflict* (New York: Cambridge University Press, 1992); Kenneth A. Shepsle, "Rational Choice Institutionalism," in *Oxford Handbook of Political Institutions,* ed. S. Binder, R. Rhodes, and B. Rockman (Oxford: Oxford University Press, 2006), 23–39; Nicole Bolleyer, *Intergovernmental Cooperation: Rational Choices in Federal Systems and Beyond* (Oxford: Oxford University Press, 2009).

8   Colin Hay and Daniel Wincott, "Structure, Agency, and Historical Institutionalism," *Political Studies* 46(5) (1998): 951–7.

9   John W. Meyer and Brian Rowan, "Institutionalized Organizations: Formal Structures as Myth and Ceremony," *American Journal of Sociology* 83(2) (1977): 340–63; Benjamin Levin, "An Epidemic of Education Policy: (What) Can We Learn from Each Other?," *Comparative Education* 34(2) (1998); David Strang and Ellen M. Bradburn, "Theorizing Legitimacy or Legitimating Theory? Neoliberal Discourse and HMO Policy, 1970–1989," in *The Rise of Neoliberalism and Institutional Analysis*, ed. John L. Campbell and Ove K. Pedersen (Princeton: Princeton University Press, 2001), 129–58; Vivien A. Schmidt, "Discursive Institutionalism: The Explanatory Power of Ideas and Discourse," *Annual Review of Political Science* 11(1) (2008): 303–26.

10 Theda Skopol, *States and Social Revolutions: A Comparative Analysis of France, Russia, and China* (Cambridge: Cambridge University Press, 1979); Peter Hall, *Governing the Economy: The Politics of State Intervention in Britain and France* (Oxford: Oxford University Press, 1986); Sven Steinmo, Kathleen Thelen, and Frank Longstreth, eds., *Structuring Politics: Historical Institutionalism in Comparative Analysis* (Cambridge: Cambridge University Press, 1992); Paul Pierson, "When Effect Becomes a Cause: Policy Feedback and Political Change," *World Politics* 45(4) (1993): 123–63; Carolyn Hughes Tuohy, *Accidental Logics: The Dynamics of Change in the Health Care Arena in the United States, Britain, and Canada* (Oxford: Oxford University Press, 1999); Jacob Hacker, "The Historical Logic of National Health Insurance: Structure and Sequence in the Development of British, Canadian, and U.S. Medical Policy," *Studies in American Political Development* 12 (Spring 1998): 57–130; Miriam Smith, *Lesbian and Gay Rights in Canada: Social Movements and Equality-Seeking, 1971–1995* (Toronto: University of Toronto Press, 1999); Paul Pierson, *Politics in Time: History, Institutions, and Social Analysis* (Princeton: Princeton University Press, 2004); Jacob Hacker, "Privatizing Risk without Privatizing the Welfare State: The Hidden Politics of Social Policy Retrenchment in the United States," *American Political Science Review* 98(2) (2004): 243–60.

11 Campbell, *Institutional Change and Globalization*, 3, 4, 8.

12 Harold Laski, "The Obsolescence of Federalism," *New Republic* 98(3) (1939): 367.

13 Jeffrey L. Pressman and Aaron Wildavsky, *Implementation*, 3rd ed., expanded (Berkeley: University of California Press, 1984), 161.

14 Mancur Olson, Jr, *The Logic of Collective Action: Public Goods and the Theory of Groups* (Cambridge: Harvard University Press, 1971).

15 Ibid., 63.

16 Anthony Welch, *Australian Education: Reform or Crisis?* (St Leonards: Allen and Unwin, 1996), 3.

17 K.C. Wheare, *Federal Government*, 2nd ed. (London: Oxford University Press, 1951); Fritz W. Scharpf, "The Joint-Decision Trap: Lessons from German Federalism and European Integration," *Public Administration* 66(3) (1998): 239–78; William H. Riker, *Federalism: Origin, Operation, Significance* (Boston: Little, Brown, 1964); Paul Pierson, "Fragmented Welfare States: Federal Institutions and the Development of Social Policy," *Governance* 8(4) (1995): 449–78.

18 Milbrey McLaughlin, "Learning from Experience: Lessons from Policy Implementation," *Educational Management and Administration* 9(2)(1987): 139–50.

19 Jerome T. Murphy, "Title I of ESEA: The Politics of Implementing Federal Education Reform," *Harvard Educational Review* 41(60) (1971): 60.

20 J. Kim and G.L. Sunderman, *Large Mandates and Limited Resources: State Response to the No Child Left Behind Act and Implications for Accountability* (Cambridge: Civil Rights Project at Harvard, 2004); Edward B. Fiske and Helen F. Ladd, *Elusive Equity: Education Reform in Post-Apartheid South Africa* (Washington: Brookings Institution, 2004); Martha Minow, *In Brown's Wake: Legacies of America's Educational Landmark* (Oxford: Oxford University Press, 2010).

21 Tara Gibb and Judith Walker, "Educating for a High Skills Society? The Landscape of Federal Employment, Training, and Lifelong Learning Policy in Canada," *Journal of Education Policy* 26(3) (2011): 381.

22 Louis Brandeis, "Dissent," *New State Ice Co. v. Liebmann*, 285 U.S. 262 (1932), 52 S. Ct. 371, 76 L. Ed. 747.

23 Réjean Pelletier, *Le Québec et le Fédéralisme Canadien: Un Regard Critique* (Québec: Les Presses de l'Université Laval, 2008), 134.

24 Aaron Wildavsky, "Federalism Means Inequality: Political Geometry, Political Sociology, and Political Culture," in *The Costs of Federalism*, ed. Robert T. Golembiewski and Aaron Wildavsky (New Brunswick: Transaction Books, 1984), 57.

25 Charles Tiebout, "A Pure Theory of Local Expenditures," *Journal of Political Economy* 64(5) (1956): 416–24.

26 Kenneth Finegold, "The United States Federalism and Its Counterfactuals," in *Federalism and the Welfare State: New World and European Experiences*, ed. Herbert Obinger, Stephan Leibfried, and Francis G. Castles (Cambridge: Cambridge University Press, 2005), 139; Wallace Oates and R.M. Schwab, "The Allocative and Distributive Implications of Local Fiscal Competition," in *Competition among States and Local Governments:*

Efficiency and Equity in American Federalism, ed. Daphne A. Kenyon and John Kincaid (Washington: Urban Institute Press, 1991), 127–45; Therese J. McGuire, "Federal Aid to States and Localities and the Appropriate Competitive Framework," in *Competition among States and Local Governments*, ed. Kenyon and Kincaid, 153–66; Geoffrey Brennan and James M. Buchanan, *The Power to Tax: Analytical Foundations of a Fiscal Constitution* (Cambridge: Cambridge University Press, 1980).

27 Daniel Béland and André Lecours, "The Politics of Territorial Solidarity: Nationalism and Social Policy Reform in Canada, the United Kingdom, and Belgium," *Comparative Political Studies* 38(6) (2005): 676–703; Alain-G. Gagnon, "Le fédéralisme asymétrique au Canada," in *Le fédéralisme canadien contemporain: Fondements, traditions, institutions*, ed. Alain-G. Gagnon (Montréal: Les Presses de l'Université de Montréal, 2006), 288; Andrée Lajoie, "Le fédéralisme au Canada: provinces et minorités, même combat," in *Le fédéralisme canadien contemporain*, 183–210.

28 Alain-G. Gagnon, "The Moral Foundation of Asymmetrical Federalism: A Normative Exploration in the Case of Quebec and Canada," in *Multinational Democracies*, ed. Alain-G. Gagnon and James Tully (Cambridge: Cambridge University Press, 2001), 319–37.

29 Alain-G. Gagnon and Raffaele Iacovino, *Federalism, Citizenship, and Quebec: Debating Multinationalism* (Toronto: University of Toronto Press, 2007), 89.

30 Gérard Bélanger, "The Theoretical Defence of Decentralization," in *The Case for Decentralized Federalism*, ed. Ruth Hubbard and Gilles Paquet (Ottawa: University of Ottawa Press, 2010), 68–92; Wallace Oates, *Fiscal Federalism* (New York: Harcourt Brace Jovanovich, 1972); Vincent Ostrom, "Can Federalism Make a Difference?," *Publius: The Journal of Federalism* 3(2): 197–237; François Rocher and Marie-Christine Gilbert, "Re-Federalizing Canada: Refocusing the Debate on Centralization," in *The Case for Decentralized Federalism*, ed. Ruth Hubbard and Gilles Paquet (Ottawa: University of Ottawa Press, 2010), 116–55; Linda Cardinal and Marie-Joie Brady, "Citoyenneté et fédéralisme au Canada: une relation difficile," in *Le fédéralisme canadien contemporain: fondements, traditions, institutions*, ed. Alain-G. Gagnon (Montréal: Les Presses de l'Université de Montréal, 2006), 435–60.

31 T.H. Marshall, "Citizenship and Social Class," in *Class, Citizenship, and Social Development* (New York: Anchor Books, 1965), 72.

32 Keith Banting, "Social Citizenship and Federalism: Is a Federal Welfare State a Contradiction in Terms?," in *Territory, Democracy, and Justice: Regionalism and Federalism in Western Democracies*, ed. Scott L. Greer (New York: Palgrave Macmillan, 2006), 44.

33 Martin Diamond, "The Ends of Federalism," in *As Far as Republican Principles Will Admit: Essays by Martin Diamond*, ed. William A. Schambra (Washington: American Enterprise Institute, 1992), 145.

34 Bruno Théret, "Du principe fédéral à une typologie des fédérations: quelques propositions," in *Le fédéralisme dans tous ses États. Gouvernance identité et mythologie*, ed. Jean-François Gaudreault-Desbiens and Fabien Gélinas (Cowansville: Les Éditions Yvon Blais, 2005), 128.

35 Banting, "Social Citizenship and Federalism," 50.

36 Mark A. Luz and C. Marc Miller, "Globalization and Canadian Federalism: Implications of the NAFTA's Investment Rules," *McGill Law Journal* 47 (2002): 953.

37 John W. Meyer, John Boli, George M. Thomas, and Francisco O. Ramirez, "World Society and the Nation-State," *American Journal of Sociology* 103(1) (1997): 144–81.

38 Grace Skogstad, *Internationalization and Canadian Agriculture: Policy and Governing Paradigms* (Toronto: University of Toronto Press, 2008), 241.

39 Anja P. Jakobi, "International Organisations and Policy Diffusion: The Global Norm of Lifelong Learning," *Journal of International Relations and Development* 15(1) (2012): 31–64.

40 Ken Battle and Sherri Torjman, "Social Policy That Works: An Agenda," Caledon Institute of Social Policy, September 2002, 1. http://www.ontla.on.ca/library/repository/mon/5000/10309536.pdf.

41 In Norman M. Goble, "Education and the National Interest," in *Federal–Provincial Relations: Education Canada*, ed. J.W. George Ivany and Michael E. Manley-Casimir (Toronto: OISE Press, 1981), 67.

42 Bélanger, "The Theoretical Defence of Decentralization"; Barry Weingast, "The Economic Role of Political Institutions: Market-Preserving Federalism and Economic Development," *Journal of Law, Economics, and Organization* 11(1) (1995): 1–29; David R. Berman, *State and Local Politics*, 9th ed. (Armonk: M.E. Sharpe, 2000), 46.

43 Gagnon and Iacovino, *Federalism, Citizenship, and Quebec*, 2007.

44 Elinor Ostrom, *Governing the Commons: The Evolution of Institutions for Collective Action* (Cambridge: Cambridge University Press, 1990).

45 R. Kenneth Carty and W. Peter Ward, "The Making of a Canadian Political Citizenship," in *National Politics and Community in Canada*, ed. R. Kenneth Carty and W. Peter Ward (Vancouver: UBC Press, 1986), 75.

46 Christian Dufour, "Restoring the Federal Principle: The Place of Quebec in the Canadian Social Union," in *Forging the Canadian Social Union: SUFA and Beyond*, ed. Sarah Fortin, Alain Noël, and France St-Hilaire (Montreal: Institute for Research on Public Policy, 2003), 73–4.

47 Tiebout, "A Pure Theory of Local Expenditures," 416–24; Barry R.
    Weingast, "The Economic Role of Political Institutions," *Journal of Law
    Economics and Organization* 11(1) (1995): 1–31; Albert Breton, *Competitive
    Governments: An Economic Theory of Politics and Public Finance* (Cambridge:
    Cambridge University Press, 1996); Michael S. Greve, *Real Federalism:
    Why It Matters, How It Could Happen* (Washington: AIE Press, 1999); Craig
    Volden, "The Politics of Competitive Federalism: A Race to the Bottom
    in Welfare Benefits?," *American Journal of Political Science* 46(2) (2002):
    352–63; Kathryn Harrison, "Provincial Interdependence: Concepts and
    Theories," in *Racing to the Bottom? Provincial Interdependence in the Cana-
    dian Federation*, ed. Kathryn Harrison (Vancouver: UBC Press, 2006), 1–24.
48 Beth A. Simmons, Frank Dobbin, and Geoffrey Garrett, "Introduction:
    The International Diffusion of Liberalism," *International Organization* 60(4)
    (2006): 790.
49 Andrew Karch, "National Intervention and the Diffusion of Policy Inno-
    vations," *American Politics Research* 34(4) (2006): 403–26.
50 Tiebout, "A Pure Theory of Local Expenditures."
51 Harrison, "Provincial Interdependence."
52 Riker, *Federalism*, 155.
53 Alexis Bélanger, "Canadian Federalism in the Context of Combating
    Climate Change," *Constitutional Forum constitutionnel* 20(1) (2011): 26.
54 Barbara Carroll and Ruth J.E. Jones, "The Road to Innovation, Conver-
    gence, or Inertia: Devolution in Housing Policy in Canada," *Canadian
    Public Policy* 26(3) (2000): 277–93. See also Stephen McBride and Kathleen
    McNutt, "Devolution and Neoliberalism in the Canadian Welfare State:
    Ideology, National and International Conditioning Frameworks, and Pol-
    icy Change in British Columbia," *Global Social Policy* 7(2) (2007): 177–201.
55 David Cameron, "The Expansion of the Public Economy: A Comparative
    Analysis," *American Political Science Review* 72(4) (1978): 1243–61; Keith
    G. Banting, *The Welfare State and Canadian Federalism*, 2nd ed. (Montreal
    and Kingston: McGill–Queen's University Press, 1987); Paul Pierson,
    "Fragmented Welfare States: Federal Institutions and the Development
    of Social Policy," *Governance* 8(4) (1995): 449–78; Richard Simeon, *Federal–
    Provincial Diplomacy* (Toronto: University of Toronto Press, 1972); Antonia
    Maioni, *Parting at the Crossroads: The Emergence of Health Insurance in the
    United States and Canada* (Princeton: Princeton University Press, 1998).
56 Alain Noël, "Is Decentralization Conservative? Federalism and the Con-
    temporary Debate on the Canadian Welfare State," in *Stretching the Fed-
    eration: The Art of the State in Canada*, ed. Robert Young (Kingston: Institute
    of Intergovernmental Relations, 1999), 195–218.

57 Bolleyer, *Intergovernmental Cooperation*.
58 Ostrom, *Governing the Commons*, 25.
59 Harrison, "Provincial Interdependence," 12.
60 Keith G. Banting, George Hoberg, and Richard Simeon, "Globalization, Fragmentation, and the Social Contract," in *Degrees of Freedom: Canada and the United States in a Changing World*, ed. Keith G. Banting, George Hoberg, and Richard Simeon (Montreal and Kingston: McGill–Queen's University Press, 1997), 3-22.
61 Edward Alan Miller and Jane Banaszak-Holl, "Cognitive and Normative Determinants of State Policymaking Behavior: Lessons from the Sociological Institutionalism," *Publius* 35(2) (2005): 191–2.
62 Kieran Egan, *The Educated Mind: How Cognitive Tools Shape Our Understanding* (Chicago: University of Chicago Press, 1997).
63 Times Higher Education, "Finding the Glue That Can Fix Cracks in Our Society," *Times Higher Education*, 22 June 2001, accessed on 20 June 2011 at http://www.timeshighereducation.co.uk/story.asp?storyCode=162844&sectioncode=26 .
64 T.H. Marshall, "Citizenship and Social Class," in *Class, Citizenship, and Social Development* (New York: Anchor Books, 1965), 78.
65 T.H. Marshall, *Social Policy* (London: Hutchinson, 1965), 1.
66 Béland and Lecours, "The Politics of Territorial Solidarity," n3.
67 Carsten Jensen, "Worlds of Welfare Services and Transfers," *Journal of European Social Policy* 18(2) (2008), 160.
68 Peter Flora and Arnold J. Heidenheimer, "Introduction," in *The Development of the Welfare State in Europe and America*, ed. Peter Flora and Arnold J. Heidenheimer (New Brunswick: Transaction Books), 7.
69 Another sector that has been the subject of sustained investigation is the environment, which can be classified, albeit imperfectly, as an area of regulatory policy. See Kathryn Harrison, *Passing the Buck: Federalism and Canadian Environmental Policy* (Vancouver: UBC Press, 1996); Barry Rabe, "Federalism and Entrepreneurship: Explaining American and Canadian Innovation in Pollution Prevention and Regulatory Integration," *Policy Studies Journal* 27(2) (1999): 288–306. Furthermore, some American academics have begun looking at the relationship between federalism and education policy in the United States. See Paul Manna, *School's In: Federalism and the National Education Agenda* (Washington: Georgetown University Press, 2006).
70 Paul E. Peterson, *The Price of Federalism* (Washington: Brookings Institution, 1995), 30.
71 Margaret Phillip, "Alberta Driving Out Welfare Recipients," *Globe and Mail* (9 February 1995), A10.

72 Peterson, *The Price of Federalism*, 17.
73 Marshall, "Citizenship and Social Class."
74 Andy Green, John Preston, and Jan Germen Janmaat, *Education, Equality, and Social Cohesion: A Comparative Analysis* (Basingstoke: Palgrave Macmillan, 2006).
75 The battles to establish public education are a compelling focus for any study. However, the gory details of these conflicts are largely absent from the pages that follow. This is not to suggest that the creation of public education was bloodless in Canada – far from it. To try and address the conflicts that went on within each province, however, would move away from the central question that motivates this study: How did a *de facto* policy framework emerge in Canada without national intervention? As a result, more attention is paid to identifying and detailing the mechanisms and processes that can help us explain this puzzle and fashion a framework to inform our analysis of policy making in federal states.
76 Manzer, *Public Schools and Political Ideas*, 3.
77 Some researchers, nevertheless, characterize Canada as quite centralized. See Migué, "The Economic Absurdity of Equalization," in *Sharing the Wealth: For the Federation. CRIC Papers*, 19–20 September; Dufour, "Restoring the Federal Principle."
78 Gray, *Federalism and Health Policy*, 4.
79 Denis Meuret, *Decision-Making in 14 OECD Education Systems* (Paris: OECD, 1995).
80 Personal interview, 20 December 2007.
81 By 1967, the Australian Commonwealth had staked a major role in education and diminished the independence of state governments in the sector. This history has been documented in Alan Barcan, *A History of Australian Education* (Melbourne: Oxford University Press, 1980). See also *Country Education Profile: Australia* (Paris: OECD, 2006).
82 For analysis of the penetration of the US federal government into the educational affairs of the states, see Manna, *School's In*; Patrick McGuinn, *No Child Left Behind and the Transformation of Federal Education Policy, 1965–2005* (Lawrence: University Press of Kansas, 2006); Matthew Hirschland and Sven Steinmo, "Correcting the Record: Understanding the History of Federal Intervention and Failure in Securing U.S. Educational Reform," *Educational Policy* 17(3) (2003): 343–64.
83 Jennifer Wallner, "Political Structures, Social Diversity, and Public Policy: Comparing Mandatory Education in Canada and the United States," *Comparative Political Studies* 47(7) (2012): 850–74.

84 Terry Wotherspoon, ed., *The Political Economy of Canadian Schooling* (Toronto: Methuen, 1987); Jan Erk, "Uncodified Workings and Unworkable Codes: Canadian Federalism and Public Policy," *Comparative Political Studies* 39(4) (2006): 441–62; David J. Elkins and Richard Simeon, *Small Worlds: Provinces and Parties in Canadian Political Life* (Toronto: Methuen, 1980); Richard Simeon, "Regionalism and Canadian Political Institutions," in *The Canadian Political Process*, 3rd ed., ed. Richard Schultz et al. (Toronto: Holt, Rinehart and Winston, 1979); Nelson Wiseman, *In Search of Canadian Political Culture* (Vancouver: UBC Press, 2007).

85 David J. Elkins and Richard Simeon, *Small Worlds: Provinces and Parties in Canadian Political Life* (Toronto: Methuen, 1980); R. Young, Philippe Faucher, and André Blais, "The Concept of Province-Building: A Critique," *Canadian Journal of Political Science* 17(4) (1984): 783–818.

86 David J. Elkins, "The Sense of Place," in *Small Worlds: Provinces and Parties in Canadian Political Life*, ed. David J. Elkins and Richard Simeon (Toronto: Methuen, 1980), 1–30.

87 Labour market training and welfare benefits, for example, are areas where studies have revealed salient differences in both the structure and delivery of programs and in the benefits provided by the provinces. See, for example, Tom McIntosh, ed., *Federalism, Democracy, and Labour Market Policy in Canada* (Montreal and Kingston: McGill–Queen's University Press, 1998); Rodney Haddow and Thomas Klassen, *Partisanship, Globalization, and Canadian Labour Market Policy: Four Provinces in Comparative Perspective* (Toronto: University of Toronto Press, 2006); Gerard Boychuk, *Patchworks of Purpose: The Development of Social Assistance Regimes in Canada* (Montreal and Kingston: McGill–Queen's University Press, 1998); and Richard Simeon and E. Robert Miller, "Regional Variations in Public Policy," in *Small Worlds: Provinces and Parties in Canadian Political Life* (Toronto: Methuen, 1980): 242–84.

88 Quoted in Donald V. Smiley, *The Federal Condition in Canada* (Toronto: McGraw-Hill Ryerson, 1987), 31.

89 Daniel Béland and André Lecours, *Nationalism and Social Policy: The Politics of Territorial Solidarity* (Oxford: Oxford University Press, 2008).

90 Jan Erk, "Federal Germany and its Non-Federal Society: The Emergence of an All-German Educational Policy System of Exclusive Provincial Jurisdiction," *Canadian Journal of Political Science* 36(2) (2003): 295–317; Erk, "Uncodified Workings and Unworkable Codes."

91 Erk, "Uncodified Workings and Unworkable Codes," 451.

92 Karl Polanyi, *The Great Transformation: The Political and Economic Origins of Our Time*, 2nd ed. (Boston: Beacon Press, 2001), 195.

93 James Mahoney and Dietrich Rueschemeyer, "Achievements and Agendas in Comparative Historical Analysis," in *Comparative Historical Analysis in the Social Sciences*, ed. James Mahoney and Dietrich Rueschemeyer (Cambridge: Cambridge University Press, 2003), 10.

94 Jeffrey Haydu, "Making Use of the Past: Time Periods as Cases to Compare and as Sequences of Problem Solving," *American Journal of Sociology* 104(2) (1998): 339–71.

95 Jack A. Goldstone, "Comparative Historical Analysis and Knowledge Accumulation in the Study of Revolutions," in *Comparative Historical Analysis in the Social Sciences*, ed. James Mahoney and Dietrich Rueschemeyer (Cambridge: Cambridge University Press, 2003), 47.

96 Ibid., 47–8.

97 Tulia G. Falleti and Julia F. Lynch, "Context and Causal Mechanisms in Political Analysis," *Comparative Political Studies* 42(9) (2009): 1143–66.

98 Alexander L. George and Andrew Bennett, *Case Studies and Theory Development in the Social Sciences* (Cambridge: MIT Press, 2005), 215.

99 Ibid., 207.

100 Margaret Levi, "An Analytic Narrative Approach to Puzzles and Problems," in *Problems and Methods in the Study of Politics*, ed. Ian Shapiro, Rogers M. Smith, and Tarek E. Masood (Cambridge: Cambridge University Press, 2004), 202; Goldstone, "Comparative Historical Analysis," 41–90.

101 Sven Steinmo, *The Evolution of Modern States: Sweden, Japan, and the United States* (Cambridge: Cambridge University Press, 2010), 7.

102 Dietrich Rueschemeyer, Evelyne Huber Stephens, and John D. Stephens, *Capitalist Development and Democracy* (Chicago: University of Chicago Press, 1992), 4.

103 Richard Simeon, *Political Science and Federalism: Seven Decades of Scholarly Engagement* (Kingston: Institute of Intergovernmental Relations School, Queen's University, 2002), 8; see also Daniel Wincott, "Ideas, Policy Change, and the Welfare State," in *Ideas and Politics in Social Science Research*, ed. Daniel Béland and Robert Henry Cox (Oxford: Oxford University Press, 2011), 150–1.

104 Jal Mehta, "The Varied Role of Ideas in Politics," in *Ideas and Politics in Social Science Research*, ed. Daniel Béland and Robert Henry Cox (Oxford: Oxford University Press, 2011), 31.

1. Defying the Odds I: Investments and Achievements

1 Andrew Coyne, "The Case for Strengthening Federal Powers," *Policy Options* 18(3) (1997): 19–23; Robert Howse, "Federalism, Democracy, and Regulatory Reform: A Sceptical View of the Case for Decentralization," in *Rethinking Federalism: Citizens, Markets, and Governments in a Changing World*, ed. Karen Knop, Sylvia Ostry, Richard Simeon, and Katherine Swinton (Vancouver: UBC Press, 1995); M. McLaughlin, "Learning from Experience: Lessons from Policy Implementation," *Educational Management and Administration* 9 (2)(1987): 139–50; Anthony Haigh, *A Ministry of Education for Europe* (London: George G. Harrap, 1970).

2 Roy Romanow, Linda Silas, and Steven Lewis, "Why Medicare Needs Ottawa," *Globe and Mail*, 16 January 2012.

3 Anthony Harold Birch, *Federalism, Finance, and Social Legislation in Canada, Australia, and the United States* (Oxford: Clarendon Press, 1955), chs. 5–6; *Constitution Act, 1982*, Section 36 (1, 2).

4 Keith Banting, "The Welfare State as Statecraft: Territorial Politics and Canadian Social Policy," in *European Social Policy: Between Fragmentation and Integration*, ed. Stephan Leibfried and Paul Pierson (Washington: Brookings Institution, 1995), 269–300; Mollie Dunsmuir, "The Spending Power: Scope and Limitations," paper prepared by the Law and Government Division, Parliament of Canada, October 1991, accessed on 22 November 2013 at: http://www.parl.gc.ca/Content/LOP/researchpublications/bp272-e.htm.

5 Student–teacher ratios broken down to the regional level, for example, are not published by Australia or the United States. In Australia, state-level spending is only provided as dollar-value expenditures, not according to per pupil allocations or as percentages of gross state product.

6 Harold Laski, "The Obsolescence of Federalism," *New Republic* 98(3) (1939): 367–9; Keith Banting, *The Welfare State and Canadian Federalism*, 2nd ed. (Montreal and Kingston: McGill–Queen's University Press, 1987); Barry R. Weingast, "The Economic Role of Political Institutions," *Journal of Law Economics and Organization* 11(1) (1995): 1–31; Paul Pierson, "Fragmented Welfare States: Federal Institutions and the Development of Social Policy," *Governance* 8(4) (1995): 449–78; Anthony Welch, *Australian Education: Reform or Crisis* (St Leonards: Allen and Unwin, 1996); Michael Mintrom, "Policy Entrepreneurs and the Diffusion of Innovation," *American Journal of Political Science* 41(3) (1997): 738–70; Martha Friendly and Linda A. White, "From Multilateralism to Bilateralism to Unilateralism in Three Short Years: Child Care in Canadian Federalism, 2003–2006," in *Canadian Federalism: Performance, Effectiveness, and Efficiency*, 2nd ed., ed.

Herman Bakvis and Grace Skogstad (Toronto: Oxford University Press: 2008), 182–204.

7 Richard Simeon, "Federalism and Social Justice," in *Territory, Democracy, and Justice: Regionalism and Federalism in Western Democracies*, ed. Scott L. Greer (New York: Palgrave Macmillan, 2006), 23.

8 Francis G. Castles, *Comparative Public Policy: Patterns of Post-War Transformation* (Cheltenham: Edward Elgar, 1999).

9 Herbert Obinger et al., "Introduction: Federalism and the Welfare State," in *Federalism and the Welfare State*, ed. Herbert Obinger et al. (New York: Cambridge University Press, 2005), 4.

10 David Cameron, "The Expansion of the Public Economy: A Comparative Analysis," *American Political Science Review* 72(4) (1978): 1243–61.

11 Duane Swank, "Political Institutions and Welfare State Restructuring: The Impact of Institutions on Social Policy Change in Developed Democracies," in *The New Politics of the Welfare State*, ed. Paul Pierson (Oxford: Oxford University Press, 2001), 197–236.

12 Wallace Oates, "An Essay on Fiscal Federalism," *Journal of Economic Literature* 37(3) (1999): 1122; Jonathan Rodden, "The Dilemma of Fiscal Federalism: Grants and Fiscal Performance around the World," *American Journal of Political Science* 46(3) (2002): 671.

13 Keith Banting, "Social Citizenship and Federalism: Is a Federal Welfare State a Contradiction in Terms?," in *Territory, Democracy, and Justice: Regionalism and Federalism in Western Democracies*, ed. Scott L. Greer (New York: Palgrave Macmillan, 2006), 45.

14 Mark Carl Rom, "Policy Races in the American States," in *Racing to the Bottom? Provincial Interdependence in the Canadian Federation*, ed. Kathryn Harrison (Vancouver: UBC Press, 2006), 229.

15 The question of social citizenship and the explanation for its possible absence in the United States has been of great interest for numerous scholars. For an excellent analysis, see N. Fraser and L. Gordon, "Contract versus Charity: Why Is There No Social Citizenship in the United States?," in *The Citizenship Debates*, ed. G. Shafir (Minneapolis: University of Minnesota Press, 1998), 113–27.

16 William H. Riker, *Federalism, Origin, Operation, Significance* (Boston: Little, Brown, 1964); Paul E. Peterson, *The Price of Federalism* (Washington: Brookings Institution, 1995); Mark Carl Rom, Paul E. Peterson, and Kenneth F. Scheve, Jr, "Interstate Competition and Welfare Policy," *Publius: The Journal of Federalism* 28(3) (1998): 17–37.

17 K.C. Wheare, *Federal Government*, 2nd ed. (London: Oxford University Press, 1951); Fritz W. Scharpf, "The Joint-Decision Trap: Lessons from

German Federalism and European Integration," *Public Administration* 66(3) (1988): 239–78.

18 Banting, "Social Citizenship and Federalism," 50.

19 Francis Castles, "The Impact of Parties on Public Expenditure," in *The Impact of Parties: Politics and Policies in Democratic Capitalist States*, ed. F.G. Castles (London: Sage, 1982): 21–96; Marius R. Busemeyer, "Determinants of Public Education Spending in 21 OECD Democracies, 1980–2001," *Journal of European Public Policy* 14(4) (2007): 582–610.

20 Mark Carl Rom and James C. Garand, "Interstate Competition in K-12 Education Policy," unpublished paper presented at the Association for Policy Analysis and Management Annual Research Conference, Washington, 2001.

21 Beyond the practical consideration of data availability, these three jurisdictions offer a useful touchstone to assess the importance of national standards. All three jurisdictions have a national department dedicated to educational affairs, but the influence of Germany's national department is the weakest. The United States and Germany are formally federal, while a constituent unit of the United Kingdom, England, governs its own educational affairs and has local educational authorities that oversee the financing of the individual schools.

22 Stephan Liebfried, Francis G. Castles, and Herbert Obinger, "Old and New Politics in Federal Welfare States," in *Federalism and the Welfare State: New World and European Experiences* (Cambridge: Cambridge University Press, 2005), 318.

23 Dietmar Braun, *Fiscal Policies in Federal States* (Aldershot: Ashgate Publishing, 2003).

24 Statistics Canada, *Report of the Pan-Canadian Education Indicators Program*, 2003, Table B1.4.

25 US Census Bureau, *The 2008 Statistical Abstract: The National Data Book*, Table 248, accessed on 12 May 2008 at http://www.census.gov/compendia/statab/cats/education/elementary_and_secondary_education_staff_and_finances.html.

26 Jennifer Wallner, "Beyond National Standards: Reconciling the Tension between Federalism and the Welfare State" *Publius: The Journal of Federalism* 40(4): 646-71.

27 Ronald L. Watts, *The Spending Power in Federal Systems: A Comparative Study* (Kingston: Institute of Intergovernmental Relations, Queen's University, 1999); Jan Erk, "Federal Germany and Its Non-Federal Society: The Emergence of an All-German Educational Policy in a System of Exclusive Provincial Jurisdiction," *Canadian Journal of Political Science*

36(2) (2003): 295–317; Paul Manna, *"School's In"*: *Federalism and the National Education Agenda* (Washington: Georgetown University Press, 2006).

28 PISA is an OECD-led project designed to provide international indicators of the skills and knowledge of fifteen-year-old students in the subject domains of reading, mathematics, and science. In 2006, fifty-seven countries participated in the PISA science assessment, including all 30 OECD countries. In most countries, the sample ranges from 4,500 to 10,000. In Canada, approximately 22,000 students from 1,000 schools wrote the assessments to ensure that information could be provided at both the Canadian and provincial levels. Other countries, with the notable exception of the United States, also maintain large enough sample sizes to permit inter-regional differences in performance outcomes. Here, Canadian data will be compared with results from Germany.

29 S.J. Prais, "Cautions on OECD's Recent Educational Survey," *Oxford Review of Education* 29(2) (2003): 139–63; Albert E. Beaton et al., *The Benefits and Limits of International Educational Achievement Studies* (Paris: International Institute for Educational Planning, 1999).

30 Tamara Knighton, Pierre Brochu, and Tomasz Gluszynski, *Measuring Up: Canadian Results of the OECD PISA Study – the Performance of Canada's Youth in Science, Reading and Mathematics – 2006 First Results for Canadians Aged 15* (Ottawa: Minister of Industry, 2010).

31 OECD, *Education at a Glance* 2006, Table A1.2a, 38, accessed on 12 December 2013, http://www.oecd.org/education/skills-beyond-school/education-ataglance2006-home.htm.

32 OECD, *Education at a Glance* 2011, Table A1.3a, 39, accessed on 12 December 2013, http://www.oecd.org/education/skills-beyond-school/48631582.pdf.

33 OECD, *Education at a Glance* 2011, Table D6.4, 462, accessed on 12 December 2013, http://www.oecd.org/education/skills-beyond-school/48631582.pdf.

34 Daniel I. Rees and H. Naci Mocan, "Labor Market Conditions and the High School Dropout Rate: Evidence from New York State," *Economics of Education Review* 16(2) (1997): 103–9.

35 Ibid.

36 OECD, *Education at a Glance 2006*, 77.

37 Clem Brooks and Jeff Manza, *Why Welfare States Persist: The Importance of Public Opinion in Democracies* (Chicago: University of Chicago Press, 2007).

38 Banting, "Social Citizenship and Federalism," 61.

39 Charles Tiebout, "A Pure Theory of Local Expenditures," *Journal of Political Economy* 64(5) (1956): 416–24; Vincent Ostrom, "Can Federalism Make

a Difference?," *Publius: The Journal of Federalism* 3(2) (1973): 230; Vincent Ostrom and Elinor Ostrom, "Public Goods and Public Choices," in *Alternatives for Delivering Public Services: Toward Improved Performance*, ed. E.S. Savas (Boulder: Westview Press, 1977), 15.

40 Jan Erk, "Wat We Zelf Doen, Doen We Beter: Belgian Substate Nationalisms, Congruence, and Public Policy," *Journal of Public Policy* 23(2) (2003): 201–24; Daniel Béland and André Lecours, "The Politics of Territorial Solidarity: Nationalism and Social Policy Reform in Canada, the United Kingdom, and Belgium," *Comparative Political Studies* 38(6): 676–703.

41 Banting, "Social Citizenship and Federalism," 61.

42 See also Sébastien Bernard and Paul Saint-Arnaud, "More of the Same? The Position of the Four Largest Canadian Provinces in the World of Welfare Regimes," *Research Report F/49 Family Network Canadian Policy Research Networks*, November 2004; Richard Simeon and Donald E. Blake, "Regional Preferences: Citizens' Views of Public Policy," in *Small Worlds: Provinces and Parties in Canadian Political Life*, ed. David J. Elkins and Richard Simeon (Toronto: Methuen, 1980), 77–105.

43 Canadian Education Association, *Public Education in Canada: Facts, Trends, and Attitudes* (Toronto: 2007), 7.

44 In the 2000 Canadian Elections Study, the survey asked, "Which level of government do you think should have the primary responsibility for health, education and social welfare?" Of those surveyed, 57.5 per cent indicated that the federal government should have primary responsibility. Moreover, in a Public Opinion Trends Series, researchers surveyed from across the country over time and asked which level of government should have the primary responsibility for education. Significant numbers in each region indicated that they supported some role for the federal government in education.

45 Personal Interview, 20 December 2007.

46 Richard Simeon and Christina Murray, "Multi-Sphere Governance in South Africa: An Interim Assessment," *Publius: The Journal of Federalism* 31(4) (2001): 66.

47 Peterson, *The Price of Federalism*, 27; Paul E. Peterson and Mark Carl Rom, *Welfare Magnets: A New Case for National Standards* (Washington: Brookings Institution, 1990); Bruno Théret, "Regionalism and Federalism: A Comparative Analysis of the Regulation of Economic Tensions between Regions by Canadian and American Federal Intergovernmental Programmes," *International Journal of Urban and Regional Research* 23(3) (1999): 479–512.

48 Ronald Watts, *Comparing Federal Systems*, 1999, 45; Ronald Watts, "Equalization in Commonwealth Federations," *Regional and Federal Studies* 13(4) (2003): 112.

49 Théret, "Regionalism and Federalism," 1999.

50 Ronald L. Watts, *The Spending Power in Federal Systems: A Comparative Study* (Kingston: Institute of Intergovernmental Relations, Queen's University, 1999), 56.

51 John Kincaid, "From Cooperation to Coercion in American Federalism: Housing, Fragmentation, and Preemption, 1780–1992," *Journal of Law and Politics* 9(2) (1993): 333–430.

52 Timothy Conlan, "Between a Rock and a Hard Place: The Evolution of American Federalism," in *Intergovernmental Management for the Twenty-First Century*, ed. Timothy J. Conlan and Paul Posner (Washington: Brookings Institution Press, 2008), 27.

53 Watts, *The Spending Power in Federal Systems*.

54 Douglas Brown, "Fiscal Federalism: The New Equilibrium between Equity and Efficiency," in *Canadian Federalism: Performance, Effectiveness, and Legitimacy*, ed. Herman Bakvis and Grace Skogstad (Toronto: Oxford University Press, 2002), 59–86.

55 Jennifer M. Wallner and Gerard W. Boychuck, "Comparing Federations: Testing the Model of Market-Preserving Federalism on Canada, Australia, and the United States," in *Comparing Canada: Citizens, Government, and Policy*, ed. Luc Turgeon, Martin Papillon, Jennifer Wallner, and Stephen White (Vancouver: UBC Press, forthcoming).

56 For details of this program, see Expert Panel on Equalization and Territorial Formula Financing, *Achieving a National Purpose: Putting Equalization Back on Track*, May 2008, accessed on 19 December 2008 at http://www.eqtff-pfft.ca/english/EQTreasury/index.asp.

57 Rom, "Policy Races in the United States," 2006.

58 Peter Hall and Rosemary Taylor, "Political Science and the Three New Institutionalisms," *Political Studies* 44(5) (1996): 946.

59 Douglass North, *Institutions, Institutional Change, and Economic Performance* (New York: Cambridge University Press, 1990).

60 Walter W. Powell and Paul J. DiMaggio, eds., *The New Institutionalism in Organizational Analysis* (Chicago: University of Chicago Press, 1991); Mark Granovetter, "Economic Action and Social Structure," in *The Sociology of Economic Life*, ed. Mark Granovetter and Richard Swedberg (Boulder: Westview Press, 1992), 51–77; Martha Finnemore, "Norms, Culture, and World Politics: Insights from Sociology's Institutionalism," *International Organization* 50(2) (1996): 326.

61 Hall and Taylor, "Political Science and the Three New Institutionalisms,"
    948. See also Friedrich Kratochwil, *Rules, Norms, and Decisions* (Cam-
    bridge: Cambridge University Press, 1989).
62 John W. Meyer, Francisco O. Ramirez, Richard Subinson, and John Boli-
    Bennett, "The World Educational Revolution, 1950–1970," *Sociology of
    Education* 50(4) (1977): 242–58; John W. Meyer, Francisco O. Ramirez, and
    Yasemin Nuhoglu Soysal, "World Expansion of Mass Education, 1870–
    1980," *Sociology of Education* 65(2) (1992): 128–49.
63 Centre for Educational Research and Innovation, *Formative Assessment:
    Improving Learning in Secondary Classrooms* (Paris: OECD, 2005).
64 Ronald Manzer, *Public Schools and Political Ideas: Canadian Educational
    Policy in Historical Perspective* (Toronto: University of Toronto Press,
    1994).
65 Wolfgang Lehmann, "Is Germany's Dual System Still a Model for Ca-
    nadian Youth Apprenticeship Initiatives?," *Canadian Public Policy* 26(2)
    (2000): 225–40; Ludger Wöessmann, "Fundamental Determinants of
    School Efficiency and Equity: German States as a Microcosm for OECD
    Countries," PEPG/07-02, accessed on 13 May 2008 at http://www.hks.
    harvard.edu/pepg/PDF/Papers/PEPG07-02_Woessmann.pdf.
66 Manzer, *Public Schools and Political Ideas*, 189.
67 Hilda Neatby, *So Little for the Mind* (Toronto: Clarke, Irwin, 1953); Andrew
    Nikiforuk, *School's Out: The Catastrophe in Public Education and What We
    Can Do About It* (Toronto: Macfarlane, Walter and Ross, 1993).
68 Personal interview, 15 May 2008; phone interview, 16 May 2008.

2. Defying the Odds II: Provincial Education Policies

1 Ronald Manzer, *Public Schools and Political Ideas: Canadian Educational Policy
   in Historical Perspective* (Toronto: University of Toronto Press, 1994), 23.
2 Geoffrey Burkhardt and Milton March, "Educational Restructuring in
   the Act Government School System," in *Restructuring School Management:
   Recent Administrative Reorganization of Public School Governance in Australia,* ed. Grant Harman, Headley Beare, and George F. Berkley (Canberra:
   Australian College of Education, 1991), 77–94; Ronald Manzer, *Educational
   Regimes and Anglo-American Democracy* (Toronto: University of Toronto
   Press, 2003), 32–40.
3 Edward B. Fiske, *Decentralization of Education: Politics and Consensus*
   (Washington: World Bank, 1996), 16.
4 Jennifer Wallner, "Political Structures, Social Diversity, and Public
   Policy," *Comparative Political Studies* 45(7) (2012): 850–74.

5 Michael M. Atkinson and William D. Coleman, "Strong States and Weak States: Sectoral Policy Networks in Advanced Capitalist Economies," *British Journal of Political Science* 19(1) (1989): 47–67; William D. Coleman and Grace Skogstad, "Policy Communities and Policy Networks: A Structural Approach," in *Policy Communities and Public Policy in Canada: A Structural Approach*, ed. William D. Coleman and Grace Skogstad (Mississauga: Copp Clark Pitman, 1990), 14–33.

6 Coleman and Skogstad, "Policy Communities and Policy Networks," 16.

7 Ronald Manzer, *Educational Regimes*, 14.

8 Ronald Manzer, *Public Schools and Political Ideas*, 19.

9 Ronald Manzer, *Educational Regimes*, 15. See also Milton Friedman, *Capitalism and Freedom* (Chicago: University of Chicago Press, 1967), 93; Charles Bruce Sissons, *Church and State in Canadian Education: An Historical Study* (Toronto: Ryerson Press, 1959).

10 Manzer, *Educational Regimes*, 15.

11 Manzer, *Public Schools and Political Ideas*, 19.

12 Ibid., 19.

13 Ibid.

14 Stephen Lawton, *Financing Canadian Education* (Toronto: Canadian Education Association, 1996), 1.

15 Milton Friedmann, "The Role of Government in Public Education," in *Economics and the Public Interest*, ed. Robert A. Solo (New Brunswick: Rutgers University Press, 1955), 123–44; Friedmann, *Capitalism and Freedom*.

16 Herbert Spencer, *The Man versus the State* (Caldwell: Caxton Printers [1884]1940).

17 Wallner, "Political Structures, Social Diversity, and Public Policy," 864.

18 Jennifer Wallner, "Legitimacy and Public Policy: Seeing beyond Performance, Effectiveness, and Efficiency," *Policy Studies Journal: The Journal of the Policy Studies Organization* 36(3) (2008): 421–43.

19 Joseph Katz, "The Curriculum of the Elementary School," in *Elementary Education in Canada*, ed. Joseph Katz (London: McGraw-Hill Company, 1961), 115.

20 George A. Beauchamp, "Curriculum Organization and Development in Historical Perspective," *Review of Educational Research* 27(3) (1957): 241–9; Robert M. Stamp, *The Schools of Ontario, 1876–1976* (Toronto: University of Toronto Press, 1982).

21 Quoted in Ivor F. Goodson, *Studying Curriculum* (Toronto: OISE Press, 1994), 18.

22 Quoted in George S. Tompkins, *A Common Countenance: Stability and Change in the Canadian Curriculum* (Vancouver: Pacific Educational Press, 2008), 132.

23 Scott Davies, "The Paradox of Progressive Education: A Frame Analysis," *Sociology of Education* 75(4) (2002): 269.

24 Mauritz Johnson, Jr, "Definitions and Models in Curriculum Theory," *Educational Theory* 17(2) (1967): 130.

25 Manzer, *Educational Regimes*, ch. 2; Manzer, *Public Schools and Political Ideas*, ch. 6; David H. Hargreaves, *The Challenge for the Comprehensive School* (London: Routledge, 1982); OECD, *Completing the Foundation for Lifelong Learning: An OECD Survey of Upper Secondary Schools* (Paris: 2004).

26 Sharon O'Donnell, *International Review of Curriculum and Assessment Frameworks: Comparative Tables and Factual Summaries,* Eurydice Network, December 2004.

27 Colin Marsh, Christopher Day, Lynne Hannay, and Gail McCutcheon, *Reconceptualizing School-Based Curriculum Development* (London: Falmer Press, 1990), 5–6 and ch. 5.

28 O'Donnell, *International Review*, 3.

29 W. James Popham, *Test Better, Teach Better: The Instructional Role of Assessment* (Alexandria: Association for Supervision and Curriculum Development, 2003), 1.

30 Ross Traub, *Standardized Testing in Canada* (Toronto: Canadian Education Association), 5.

31 Lorna M. Earl, "Accountability and Assessment: Ensuring Quality in Ontario Schools," in *For the Love of Learning: Background Papers for the Royal Commission on Learning,* vol. 2, ed. Nancy Watson, Joyce Scane, and George Bedard (Ontario: Royal Commission on Learning, 1995), 411.

32 In recent years, the lines between tests and assessments are becoming increasingly blurred; some jurisdictions are using results on standardized assessments as a component of students' final grades. However, for the moment, the distinction between these two components of evaluation will be maintained, as not all jurisdictions are pursuing this particular policy adjustment.

33 Earl, "Accountability and Assessment," 407.

34 M.L. Smith and C. Rottenburg, "Unintended Consequences of External Testing in Elementary Schools," *Educational Measurement: Issues and Practice* 10(4) (1991): 7–11.

35 Canadian Teachers' Federation, "Teachers Know About Learning and Assessment" (pamphlet), accessed on 1 December 2009 at http://www.

ctf-fce.ca/publications/pd_newsletter/PD2008_Volume7-2English_Article11.pdf .

36 Additionally, practices pertaining to the teaching profession include such things as the regulations governing working conditions, labour laws, promotion and tenure, and professional development. However, because these elements bridge into the territory of industrial relations and pertain more specifically to teachers themselves, these aspects have been excluded from this study.

37 Douglas Myers and Fran Reid, eds., *Educating Teachers: Critiques and Proposals* (Toronto: OISE, 1974); Seymore Sarason, *A Critical Appraisal of Teacher Education* (Washington: American Association of Colleges for Teacher Education, 1995).

38 Lilian Katz and James D. Raths, eds., *Advances in Teacher Education*, vol. 4 (New Jersey: Ablex Publishing, 1991).

39 Michael Fullan and F. Michael Connelly, *Teacher Education in Ontario: Current Practice and Options for the Future – A Position Paper* (Toronto: OISE, 1987); D. Hopkins, "Drift and Change in Canadian Higher Education," *Higher Education Review* 16(2) (1984): 51–60; National Commission for Excellence in Teacher Education, *A Call for Change in Teacher Education* (Washington: American Association of Colleges for Teacher Education, 1985).

40 Frank McKinnon, *The Politics of Education: A Study of the Political Administration of the Public Schools* (Toronto: University of Toronto Press, 1960), 4.

41 Provinces do vary in terms of the policy scope of the departments, which are frequently altered to respond to the changing needs and priorities of governments and the public. Prince Edward Island and Saskatchewan merged K–12 and post-secondary education (PSE) under one umbrella; New Brunswick, Ontario, Alberta, and BC maintain separate departments for K–12 and PSE; Nova Scotia includes cultural affairs with education; Quebec ministry includes sports; Manitoba's contains citizenship and youth; and Newfoundland's ministry encompasses all stages of education from early childhood through PSE and adult education.

42 Canadian School Boards Association, *Education Governance in Canada: Provincial/Territorial Summaries*, February 1994 (updated March 1994); Alberta Home and School Councils' Association, *Alberta School Council Resource Manual*, accessed on 19 July 2008 at http://education.alberta.ca/media/464094/scm.pdf.

43 Alberta Home and School Councils' Association, *Alberta School Council Resource Manual*.

44 Wallner, "Legitimacy and Public Policy," 431–3.

45 Personal interview, 12 November 2007; personal interview, 15 May 2008; phone interview, 16 May 2008.

46 André Siegfried, *Le Canada: Les deux races* (Paris: Librairie Armand Colin, 1906); Michel Bastarache et al., eds., *Les droits linguistiques au Canada* (Montréal: Les editions Yvon Blais, 1986); Linda Cardinal, "Ruptures et fragmentations de l'identité francophone en milieu minoritaire; un bilan critique," *Sociologie et sociétés* 26(1) (1994): 71–86; Wilfrid B. Denis, "Ethnicité et conflits scolaires en Saskatchewan de 1905 à 1980," in *Une langue qui pense: La recherche en milieu minoritaire francophone,* ed. Linda Cardinal (Ottawa: Presses de l'Université d'Ottawa, 1993); Pierre Foucher, "Les droits scolaires des acadiens et la charte," *University of New Brunswick Law Journal* 33 (1984): 97–154; Chad Gaffield, *Language, Schooling, and Cultural Conflict: The Origins of the French Language Controversy in Ontario* (Montreal and Kingston: McGill–Queen's University Press, 1988); Gerald Friesen, "Bilingualism in Manitoba: The Historical Context," in *Essays on Manitoba and Prairie History* (Winnipeg: University of Manitoba Press, 1996), 23–8; Michael Macmillan, *The Practice of Language Rights in Canada* (Cambridge: Cambridge University Press, 1989).

47 Marilyn Barber, "The Ontario Bilingual Schools Issue: Sources of Conflict," In *Minorities, Schools, and Politics* (Toronto: University of Toronto Press, 1969), 66.

48 Michael D. Behiels, *Canada's Francophone Minority Communities: Constitutional Renewal and the Winning of School Governance* (Montreal and Kingston: McGill–Queen's University Press, 2004), 7.

49 *Royal Commission on Bilingualism and Biculturalism* (Ottawa: 23 October 1969), 102–6.

50 Provinces with larger and territorially defined minority-language populations, such as Alberta, created individual French-language school boards. Other provinces with smaller and dispersed communities, such as Nova Scotia, established a French-language school board for the entire province.

51 One notable sub-state policy difference emerges in the decision to provide public funds for private schools. Across western Canada and Quebec, many private schools are eligible to receive up to 50 per cent of the per pupil amount allocated to public schools. In return, private schools are obliged to adhere to provincial regulations, including hiring provincially certified teachers, using provincially approved curriculum, and administering provincial tests. Private schools in the remaining provinces are not eligible for public funds and rely instead on individual tuition fees. However, even with financial support in some provinces, private

schools only service approximately 5 per cent of Canadian school-aged children and will therefore not be assessed in the remainder of this study.

52 Phone interview, 11 November 2007.

53 CMEC, Canada *K to 12: Common Framework of Science Learning Outcomes* (Toronto: 1997), Introduction.

54 Saskatchewan, Ministry of Education, *A Curriculum Guide for the Elementary Level*, January 2002, accessed on 19 July 2008 at http://www.sasked.gov.sk.ca/docs/ela/index.html .

55 Ontario, Ministry of Education, *The Ontario Curriculum, Grades 1–8, Revised* (Toronto: 2006), 45–7.

56 Personal interview, 20 December 2007; personal interview, 1 February 2008; personal interview, 21 April 2008.

57 Personal interview, 1 February 2008.

58 Alice Collins and Rob Tierney, "Teacher Education Accord: Values and Ideals of the Teaching Profession in Canada," accessed on 27 November 2013 at http://www.cea-ace.ca/sites/default/files/EdCan-2006-v46-n4-Collins.pdf.

59 Nancy M. Sheehan and Michael Fullan, "Teacher Education in Canada: A Case Study of British Columbia and Ontario," in *Changing Times in Teacher Education: Restructuring or Reconceptualization?*, ed. Marvin F. Wideen and Peter P. Grimmett (London: Falmer Press, 1995), 89–104; Nancy M. Sheehan and J. Donald Wilson, "From Normal School to the University to the College of Teachers: Teacher Education in British Columbia in the Twentieth Century," in *Children, Teachers, and Schools in the History of British Columbia*, ed. Jean Barman, Neil Sutherland, and J. Donald Wilson (Calgary: Detselig Enterprises, 1995), 307–22. However, given that the BC College of Teachers was disbanded in 2012, it seems as if this experiment with external regulation is failing.

60 Colin Hay, "Globalization's Impact on States," in *Global Political Economy*, ed. John Ravenhill (Oxford: Oxford University Press, 2005), 236–62.

61 J.W Meyer, "Rationalized Environments," in *Institutional Environments and Organizations*, ed. W.R. Scott and J.W. Meyer (Newbury Park: Sage, 1994), 28–54; J.W. Meyer et al., "World Society and the Nation-State," *American Journal of Sociology* 103(1) (1997): 144–81; J. Boli and G.M. Thomas, *Constructing World Culture* (Stanford: Stanford University Press, 1999); J.W. Meyer, F.O. Ramirez, and Yasemin Nuhoglu Soysal, "World Expansion of Mass Education, 1870–1980," *Sociology of Education* 65(2) (1992): 128–49.

62 Meyer, Ramirez, and Soysal, "World Expansion of Mass Education," 128.

63 Andy Green, "Education and Globalization in Europe and East Asia: Convergent and Divergent Trends," *Journal of Education Policy* 14(1) (1999): 51.

64 Sven Steinmo, *The Evolution of Modern States: Sweden, Japan, and the United States* (Cambridge: Cambridge University Press, 2010); Kurt Weyland, "Theories of Policy Diffusion: Lessons from Latin American Pension Reform," *World Politics* 57 (January 2005): 262–95; Vivien Schmidt, *The Futures of European Capitalism* (Oxford: Oxford University Press, 2002); Margaret Weir, "Ideas and Politics: The Acceptance of Keynesianism in Britain and the United States," in *The Political Power of Economic Ideas: Keynesianism across Nations*, ed. Peter A. Hall (Princeton: Princeton University Press, 1989), 53–86.

65 John Campbell, "Ideas, Politics, and Public Policy," *Annual Review of Sociology* 28(1) (2002): 26.

66 Tom Burridge, "Why Do Finland's Schools Get the Best Results?," *BBC World News*, 7 April 2010, accessed on 10 March 2012 at http://news.bbc.co.uk/2/hi/8601207.stm.

67 Steven Bernstein and Benjamin Cashore, "Globalization, Four Paths of Internationalization, and Domestic Policy Change: The Case of EcoForestry in British Columbia, Canada," *Canadian Journal of Political Science* 33(1) (2000): 72.

68 Grace Skogstad, *Internationalization and Canadian Agriculture: Policy and Governing Paradigm* (Toronto: University of Toronto Press, 2008), 27.

69 Skogstad, *Internationalization and Canadian Agriculture*; Skogstad, "Internationalization, Democracy, and Food Safety Measures: The (Il)Legitimacy of Consumer Preferences," *Global Governance* 7(3) (2001): 293–316; Dennis Quinn, "The Correlates of Change in International Financial Regulation," *American Political Science Review* 91(3) (1997): 531–51; Bernstein and Cashore, "Globalization, Four Paths of Internationalization, and Domestic Policy Change," 67–99.

70 Sacha Garben, *EU Higher Education Law: The Bologna Process and Harmonization by Stealth* (Alphen an de Rijn: Kluwer Law International, 2011).

71 Mitchell A. Orenstein, *Privatizing Pensions: The Transnational Campaign for Social Security Reform* (Princeton: Princeton University Press, 2008), 57.

72 Ibid., 70.

73 Wade Jacoby, "Minority Traditions and Post-Communists Politics: How Do IGOs Matter?," in *Transnational Actors in Central and East European Transitions*, ed. Mitchell A. Orenstein, Stephen Bloom, and Nicole Mindstrom (Pittsburgh: University of Pittsburgh Press, 2008).

74 Jal Mehta, "The Varied Roles of Ideas in Politics: From 'Whether' to 'How,'" in *Ideas and Politics in Social Science Research*, ed. Daniel Béland and Robert Henry Cox (Oxford: Oxford University Press, 2011), 25.

75 Donald A. Schön and Martin Rein, *Frame Reflection: Toward the Resolution of Intractable Policy Controversies* (New York: Basic Books, 1994); Deborah Stone, "Causal Stories and the Formation of Policy Agendas," *Political Science Quarterly* 104(2) (1989): 281–300; Peter A. Hall, ed., *The Political Power of Economic Ideas: Keynesianism across Nations* (Princeton: Princeton University Press, 1989); Frank Fischer, *Reframing Public Policy: Discursive Politics and Deliberative Practices* (Oxford: Oxford University Press, 2003).

76 Campbell, *Institutional Change and Globalization* (Princeton: Princeton University Press, 2004), 96; see also John Kingdon, *Agendas, Alternatives, and Public Policy*, 2nd ed. (New York: Addison-Wesley, 1995).

77 Jack Knight and Douglass North, "Explaining Economic Change: The Interplay between Cognition and Institutions," *Legal Theory* 3(3) (1997): 211–26; see also Campbell, *Institutional Change and Globalization*, 94–5.

78 Peter Hall, "Policy Paradigms, Social Learning, and the State: The Case of Economic Policy Making in Britain," *Comparative Politics* 25(3): 275–96.

79 Judith Goldstein, *Ideas, Interests, and American Trade Policy* (Ithaca: Cornell University Press, 1993).

80 Daniel Béland and Robert Cox, "Introduction: Ideas and Politics," in *Ideas and Politics in Social Science Research,* ed. Daniel Béland and Robert Cox (Oxford: Oxford University Press, 2011), 12.

81 Alan M. Jacobs, "How Do Ideas Matter? Mental Models and Attention in German Pension Politics," *Comparative Political Studies* 42(2) (2009): 253.

82 Mark Blyth, *Great Transformations: Economic Ideas and Institutional Change in the Twentieth Century* (Cambridge: Cambridge University Press, 2002).

83 John L. Campbell and Ove K. Pedersen, "Knowledge Regimes and Comparative Political Economy," in *Ideas and Politics in Social Science Research,* ed. Daniel Béland and Robert Henry Cox (Oxford: Oxford University Press, 2011), 167.

84 Manzer, *Public Schools and Political Ideas*, 255.

85 Scott Davies and Neil Guppy, "Globalization and Educational Reforms in Anglo-American Democracies," *Comparative Education Review* 41(4) (1997): 435–59; Arthur Zilversmit, *Changing Schools: Progressive Education Theory and Practice, 1930–1960* (Chicago: University of Chicago Press, 1993); Scott Davies, "The Paradox of Progressive Education: A Frame Analysis," *Sociology of Education* 75(4) (2002): 269–86.

86 Daniel Béland and Jacob Hacker, "Ideas, Private Institutions, and American Welfare State 'Exceptionalism': The Case of Health and Old-Age Insurance in the United States, 1915–1965," *International Journal of Social Welfare* 13(1): 42–54.

87 Wolfgang Streeck and Kathleen Thelen, *Beyond Continuity: Institutional Change in Advanced Political Economies* (Oxford: Oxford University Press, 2005), 14.

3. Theorizing Policy Frameworks in Federations

1 For reviews of this research, see Frances Stokes Berry, "Sizing Up State Policy Innovation Research," *Policy Studies Journal* 22(3) (1994): 442–56; David Dolowitz and David Marsh, "Who Learns What from Whom: A Review of the Policy Transfer Literature," *Political Studies* 44(2) (1996): 343–87; and Edward Alan Miller, "Advancing Comparative State Policy Research: Toward Conceptual Integration and Methodological Expansion," *State and Local Government Review* 36(1) (2004): 35–58.

2 Jack Walker, "The Diffusion of Innovations among the American States," *American Political Science Review* 63(3) (1969): 880–99.

3 Virginia Gray, "Innovation in the States: A Diffusion Study," *American Political Science Review* 67(4) (1973): 1174–85; Frances Stokes Berry and William D. Berry, "State Lottery Adoptions as Policy Innovations: An Event History Analysis," *American Political Science Review* 84(2) (1990): 395–415; William D. Berry and Brady Baybeck, "Using Geographic Information Systems to Study Interstate Competition," *American Political Science Review* 99(4) (2005): 505–20; Michael Mintrom and Susan Vergari, "Policy Networks and Innovation Diffusion: The Case of State Education Reforms," *Journal of Politics* 60(1) (1998): 126–48; Craig Volden, "States as Policy Laboratories: Emulating Success in the Children's Health Insurance Program," *American Journal of Political Science* 50(2) (2006): 294–312.

4 Paul E. Peterson and Mark C. Rom, *Welfare Magnets: A New Case for a National Standard* (Washington: Brookings Institution, 1990); Andrew Karch, "National Intervention and the Diffusion of Policy Innovations," *American Politics Research* 34(4) (2006): 403–26; Keith G. Banting, *The Welfare State and Canadian Federalism*, 2nd ed. (Montreal and Kingston: McGill–Queen's University Press, 1987).

5 Daniel Wincott, "Ideas, Policy Change, and the Welfare State," in *Ideas and Politics in Social Science Research*, ed. Daniel Beland and Robert Henry Cox (Oxford: Oxford University Press, 2011), 146.

6 Everett Rogers, *The Diffusion of Innovations*, 3rd ed. (New York: Free Press, 1995).

7 Beth A. Simmons, Frank Dobbin, and Geoffrey Garrett, "Introduction: The International Diffusion of Liberalism," *International Organization* 60(4) (2006): 782.

8   Robert J. Franzese Jr, and Jude C. Hays, "Interdependence in Comparative Politics: Substance, Theory, Empirics, Substance," *Comparative Political Studies* 41(4–5) (2008): 771.

9   Kenneth W. Abbott and Duncan Snidal, "International "Standards" and International Governance," *Journal of European Public Policy* 8(3) (2001): 345–70.

10 Robert Keohane and Joseph S. Nye, *Power and Interdependence: World Politics in Transition* (Boston: Little, Brown, 1977).

11 Ernst B. Haas, "Words Can Hurt You; or, Who Said What to Whom about Regimes?," *International Organization* 36(2) (1982): 236.

12 Michael M. Barnett and Martha Finnemore, "The Politics, Power, and Pathologies of International Organizations," *International Organization* 53(4) (1999): 699–723.

13 David Strang and John W. Meyer, "Institutional Conditions for Diffusion," *Theory and Society* 22(4) (1993): 495.

14 Harold K. Jacobson, *Networks of Interdependence: International Organizations and the Global Political System* (New York: Alfred A. Knopf, 1979); Phillip Cerny, "Globalization and the Changing Logic of Collective Action," *International Organization* 49(4) (1995): 595–625; Martha Finnemore and Kathryn Sikkink, "International Norm Dynamics and Political Change," *International Organization* 52(4) (1998): 887–917; Daniel Drezner, "Globalization, Harmonization, and Competition: The Different Pathways to Policy Convergence," *Journal of European Public Policy* 12(5) (2005): 841–59; Geoffrey Garrett, "Global Markets and National Politics," *International Organization* 52(4) (1998): 787–825; Geoffrey Garret and Phillip Lange, "Political Responses to Interdependence: What's 'Left' for the Left?," *International Organization* 45(4) (1991): 539–64.

15 Paul Pross, *Group Politics and Public Policy* (Toronto: Oxford University Press, 1986), 98.

16 Grace Skogstad, "Policy Networks and Policy Communities: Conceptualizing State–Societal Relationships in the Policy Process," in *The Comparative Turn in Canadian Political Science*, ed. Linda A. White, Richard Simeon, Robert Vipond, and Jennifer Wallner (Vancouver: UBC Press, 2008), 208.

17 Paul Sabatier, "An Advocacy Coalition Framework of Policy Change and the Role of Policy-Oriented Learning Therein," *Policy Sciences* 21(2–3) (1988): 133.

18 Diane Stone, "Learning Lessons and Transferring Policy across Time, Space, and Disciplines," *Politics* 19(1) (1999): 55.

19 John Kingdon, *Agendas, Alternatives, and Public Policies*, 2nd ed. (New York: HarperCollins College, 1995); see also Michael Mintrom, "Policy

Entrepreneurs and the Diffusion of Innovation," *American Journal of Political Science* 41(3) (1997): 738–70.

20 Walker, "The Diffusion of Innovation among the American States," 849.

21 David Marsh and Martin Smith, "Understanding Policy Networks: Towards a Dialectical Approach," *Political Studies* 48(1) (2000): 4–21.

22 R.A.W. Rhodes, "Policy Network Analysis," *Oxford Handbook of Public Policy* (Oxford: Oxford University Press, 2004), 426.

23 Skogstad, "Policy Networks and Policy Communities," 206.

24 Ibid., 212.

25 Colin Hay and David Richards, "The Tangled Webs of Westminster and Whitehall: The Discourse, Strategy, and Practice of Networking within the British Core Executive," *Public Administration* 78(1) (2000): 1–2; see also Marsh and Smith, "Understanding Policy Networks."

26 Marsh and Smith, "Understanding Policy Networks," 8; see also John L. Campbell and Ove K. Pedersen, "Knowledge Regimes and Comparative Political Economy," in *Ideas and Politics in Social Science Research*, ed. Daniel Béland and Robert Henry Cox, (Oxford: Oxford University Press, 2011), 167–90.

27 Jennifer Smith, *Federalism* (Vancouver: UBC Press, 2004), ch. 3.

28 Miriam Smith, *Lesbian and Gay Rights in Canada: Social Movements and Equality-Seeking, 1971–1995* (Toronto: University of Toronto Press, 1999).

29 Ronald Watts, *Comparing Federal Systems*, 2nd ed. (Kingston and Montreal: McGill–Queen's University Press, 1999), ch. 1. However, it should not be presumed that federalism immediately fashions a perfect economic union with a completely open market among the jurisdictions. In Canada, barriers between the provinces have often been greater than barriers across national borders, and the rules governing the internal economic union have been the focus of intense political debates. See Royal Commission on the Economic Union and Development Prospects for Canada, *Commission on Canada's Future* (Ottawa: 1984).

30 This goal of regional economic redistribution and equalization is not a universal attribute of all federations' arrangements for fiscal federalism. For more on the significance of the design and execution of federal fiscal architectures, see Robin Boadway and Anwar Shah, *Fiscal Federalism: Principles and Practice of Multiorder Governance* (Cambridge: Cambridge University Press, 2009).

31 Strang and Meyer, "Institutional Conditions for Diffusion," 492.

32 Douglass C. North, *Institutions, Institutional Change, and Economic Performance* (Cambridge: Cambridge University Press, 1990).

33 Anthony Appiah, *The Ethics of Identity* (Princeton: Princeton University Press, 2005), 114.

34 Gabriel A. Almond and G. Bingham Powell, Jr, *Comparative Politics: A Developmental Approach* (Boston: Little, Brown, 1966), 51.

35 Alan Patten, "Rethinking Culture: The Social Lineage Account," *American Political Science Review* 105(4) (2011): 735–49.

36 My understanding of intersubjectivity is informed by such works as Charles Taylor, *Philosophical Papers*, vol. 1 (Cambridge: Cambridge University Press, 1985); Mark Bevir and R.A.W. Rhodes, "Interpretive Approaches to British Government and Politics," *British Politics* 1(1) (2006): 84–112; Daniel Little, *Varieties of Social Explanation: An Introduction to the Philosophy of Social Science* (Boulder: Westview Press, 1991); and Emanuel Adler and Vincent Pouliot, "International Practices," *International Theory* 3(1) (2011): 1–36.

37 Almond and Powell, *Comparative Politics*, 50, 57.

38 Beth Simmons and Zachary Elkins, "The Globalization of Liberalization: Policy Diffusion in the International Political Economy," *American Political Science Review* 98(1) (2004): 175.

39 Alexander Wendt, *Social Theory of International Relations* (Cambridge: Cambridge University Press, 1999), 188.

40 Brendan McSweeney, "Dynamic Diversity: Variety and Variation Within Countries," *Organization Studies* 30(9) (2009): 933–57.

41 Clifford Geertz, *The Social History of an Indonesian Town* (Cambridge: MIT Press, 1965), 145.

42 Beth Simmons and Zachary Elkins, "The Globalization of Liberalization," 175; Jeffrey Checkel, "Ideas, Institutions, and the Gorbachev Foreign Policy Revolution," *World Politics* 45(2) (1993): 271–300.

43 Strang and Meyer, "Institutional Conditions for Diffusion," 499.

44 Triadafilos Triadafilopoulos, *Becoming Multicultural: Immigration and the Politics of Citizenship in Canada and Germany* (Vancouver: UBC Press, 2012), 16.

45 Vivian Schmidt, "Discursive Institutionalism: The Explanatory Power of Ideas and Discourse," *Annual Review of Political Science* 11(1) (2008): 303–26. See also John L. Campbell, "Ideas, Politics, and Public Policy," *Annual Review of Sociology* 28(1) (2002): 21–38.

46 Campbell, "Ideas, Politics, and Public Policy"; Schmidt, "Discursive Institutionalism," 307.

47 Colin Hay, "The 'Crisis' of Keynesianism and the Rise of Neoliberalism in Britain," in *The Rise of Neoliberalism and Institutional Analysis*, ed. John L. Campbell and Ove K. Pedersen (Princeton: Princeton University Press,

2001), 193–218; Keith G. Banting, "Dis-embedding Liberalism? The New Social Policy Paradigm in Canada," in *Dimensions of Inequality in Canada*, ed. David A. Green and Jonathan R. Kesselman (Vancouver: UBC Press, 2006), 417–52; Jane Jenson, "Diffusing Ideas for after Neoliberalism: The Social Investment Perspective in Europe and Latin America," *Global Social Policy* 10(1) (2010): 59–84; see also Jane Jenson, "Redesigning Citizenship Regimes after Neoliberalism: Ideas about Social Investment," prepared for the meeting of RC 19, Florence, September 2007, available on-line at http://www.cccg.umontreal.ca/pdf/Jenson%20RC19%2007.pdf.

48 John L. Campbell and Ove K. Pedersen, "Introduction: The Rise of Neo-liberalism and Institutional Analysis," in *The Rise of Institutionalism and Institutional Analysis*, ed. John L. Campbell and Ove K. Pedersen (Princeton: Princeton University Press, 2001), 1–24.

49 Mark Blyth, *Great Transformations: Economic Ideas and Institutional Change in the Twentieth Century* (Cambridge: Cambridge University Press, 2002); Robert C. Lieberman, "Ideas, Institutions, and Political Order: Explaining Political Change," *American Political Science Review* 96(4) (2002): 697–712; Daniel Béland, "Ideas and Institutional Change in Social Security: Conversion, Layering, and Policy Drift," *Social Science Quarterly* 88(1) (2007): 20–38.

50 Jenson, "Redesigning Citizenship Regimes," 1.

51 Campbell, *Institutional Change and Globalization* (Princeton: Princeton University Press, 2004), 84.

52 Kurt Weyland, "Neoliberal Populism in Latin America and Eastern Europe," *Comparative Politics* 31(4) (1999): 382.

53 Donald A. Schön and Martin Rein, *Frame Reflection: Toward the Resolution of Intractable Policy Controversies* (New York: Basic Books, 1994), 8–9.

54 Strang and Meyer, "Institutional Conditions for Diffusion," 490.

55 Simmons, Dobbin, and Garrett, "Introduction"; Herbert Simon, "A Behavioural Model of Rational Choice," *Quarterly Journal of Economics* 69 (1955): 99–118; Sarah M. Brooks, "Interdependent and Domestic Foundations of Policy Change: The Diffusion of Pension Privatization around the World," *International Studies Quarterly* 49(2) (2005): 273–94.

56 There are a number of different conceptions of "learning" used in the literature. Peter Hall's emphasizes learning as a deliberate action, while Hugh Heclo sees learning as a less conscious activity that can occur as a response to a societal or environmental stimulus. For a useful analysis of these different conceptualizations, see Colin Bennett and Michael Howlett, "The Lessons of Learning: Reconciling Theories of Policy Learning and Policy Change," *Policy Sciences* 25(3) (1992): 275–94.

57 Simmons, Dobbin, and Garrett, "Introduction," 790; Erica R. Gould, "Money Talks: Supplementary Financiers and International Monetary Fund Conditionality," *International Organization* 57(3) (2006): 551–86.
58 Kathryn Harrison, "Provincial Interdependence: Concepts and Theories," in *Racing to the Bottom? Provincial Interdependence in the Canadian Federation,* ed. Kathryn Harrison (Vancouver: UBC Press, 2006); John Kincaid, "From Cooperation to Coercion in American Federalism: Housing, Fragmentation, and Preemption, 1780–1992" *Journal of Law and Politics* 9(2) (1993): 333–430; Mark Carl Rom, "Policy Races in the American States," in *Racing to the Bottom? Provincial Interdependence in the Canadian Federation,* ed. Kathryn Harrison (Vancouver: UBC Press, 2006), 229–56; Mark Carl Rom, Paul E. Peterson, and Kenneth F. Scheve, Jr, "Interstate Competition and Welfare Policy," *Publius: The Journal of Federalism* 28(4) (1998): 17–37.
59 Hugh Heclo, *Modern Social Politics in Britain and Sweden: From Relief to Income Maintenance* (New Haven: Yale University Press, 1974), 305.
60 Kurt Weyland, "Theories of Policy Diffusion: Lessons from Latin American Pension Reforms," *World Politics* 57 (January 2005): 270–1.
61 Duane Swank, "Tax Policy in an Era of Internationalization: An Assessment of a Conditional Diffusion Model of the Spread of Neoliberalism," *International Organization* 60 (Fall 2006): 859.
62 Barbara Levitt and James G. March, "Organizational Learning," *Annual Review of Sociology* 14(1) (1988): 320; see also Jon Forester, "Bounded Rationality and the Politics of Muddling Through," in *The Science of Public Policy: Essential Readings in Policy Science I,* ed. Tadao Miyakawa (London and New York: Routledge, 1999), 490–507.
63 Margaret Weir, "Ideas and the Politics of Bounded Innovation," in *Structuring Politics: Historical Institutionalism in Comparative Analysis,* ed. Sven Steinmo, Kathleen Thelen, and Frank Longstreth (Cambridge: Cambridge University Press, 1992), 188–216.
64 Peter Haas, "Introduction: Epistemic Communities and International Policy Coordination," *International Organization* 46(1) (1992): 1–35.
65 Campbell and Pedersen, "Knowledge Regimes," 171–2.
66 Margaret Keck and Kathrine Sikkink, *Activists beyond Borders: Advocacy Networks in International Politics* (Ithaca: Cornell University Press, 1998).
67 William D. Coleman and Grace Skogstad, "Policy Communities and Policy Networks: A Structural Approach," in *Policy Communities and Public Policy in Canada: A Structural Approach* (Toronto: Copp Clark Pitman, 1990), 25.

68 Chang Kil Lee and David Strang, "The International Diffusion of Public-Sector Downsizing: Network Emulation and Theory-Driven Learning," *International Organization* 60 (Fall 2006): 889.
69 Michael Howlett, "Beyond Legalism? Policy Ideas, Implementation Styles, and Emulation-Based Convergence in Canadian and US Environmental Policy," *Journal of Public Policy* 20(3) (2000): 308.
70 Frank Dobbin, Beth Simmons, and Geoffrey Garrett, "The Global Diffusion of Public Policies: Social Construction, Coercion, Competition, or Learning," *Annual Review of Sociology* 33(1) (2007): 451.
71 Simmons and Elkins, "The Globalization of Liberalization," 172.
72 Weyland, "Theories of Policy Diffusion," 270.
73 Simon, "A Behavioural Model of Rational Choice."
74 James G. March and Johan P. Olsen, *Rediscovering Institutions: The Organizational Basis of Politics* (New York: Free Press, 1989).
75 Blyth, *Great Transformations*; Wade Jacoby, *The Enlargement of the European Union and NATO: Ordering from the Menu in Central Europe* (Cambridge: Cambridge University Press, 2004); Mitchell Orenstein, *Privatizing Pensions: The Transnational Campaign for Social Security Reform* (Princeton: Princeton University Press, 2008).
76 Katerina Linos, "How Do Ideas Shape the Welfare State? Family Policy Developments in Greece and Spain," paper presented at the Internationalization and Public Policy Paradigm Change Workshop, University of Toronto, Canada, 11 April 2008, 9.
77 Simmons, Dobbin, and Garrett, "Introduction," 787–91; Zachary Elkins and Beth Simmons, "On Waves, Clusters, and Diffusion: A Conceptual Framework," *Annals, AAPSS* 598(1) (2005): 33–51; Martha Finnemore, *National Interests in International Society* (Ithaca: Cornell University Press, 1996).
78 Elinor Ostrom, *Governing the Commons: The Evolution of Institutions for Collective Action* (Cambridge: Cambridge University Press, 1990).
79 Ibid., 90.
80 Katharina Holzinger and Christoph Knill, "Causes and Conditions of Cross-National Policy Convergence," *Journal of European Public Policy* 12(5) (2005): 782; Janice Gross Stein, "International Co-operation and Loss Avoidance: Framing the Problem," in *Choosing to Co-operate: How States Avoid Loss* (Baltimore: Johns Hopkins University Press, 1991), 2–34.
81 Michael S. Greve, *Real Federalism: Why It Matters, How It Could Happen* (Washington: AIE Press, 1999), 2.
82 Harrison, "Provincial Interdependence," 7.
83 Ibid., 5.

84 Heclo, *Modern Social Politics*.

85 David J. Elkins and Richard Simeon, *Small Worlds: Provinces and Parties in Canadian Political Life* (Toronto: Methuen, 1980); Richard Simeon and Ian Robinson, *States, Society, and the Development of Canadian Federalism* (Toronto: University of Toronto Press, 1990).

86 Claudio Radaelli, "Diffusion without Convergence: How Political Context Shapes the Adoption of Regulatory Impact Assessment," *Journal of European Public Policy* 12(5) (2005): 924–43.

87 Clark Kerr, *The Future of Industrial Societies: Convergence or Continuing Diversity* (Cambridge: Harvard University Press, 1983), 3.

88 Colin Bennett, "What Is Policy Convergence and What Causes It?," *British Journal of Political Science* 12(2) (1991): 215–33; Stephan Heichel, Jessica Pape, and Thomas Sommerer, "Is There Convergence in Convergence Research? An Overview of Empirical Studies on Policy Convergence," *Journal of European Public Policy* 12(5) (2005): 817–40; Holzinger and Knill, "Causes and Conditions," 775–96.

89 Christopher Knill, "Introduction: Cross-National Policy Convergence: Concepts, Approaches, and Explanatory Factors," *Journal of European Public Policy* 12(5) (2005): 775.

90 James Mahoney, "Strategies of Causal Assessment in Comparative Historical Analysis," *Comparative Historical Analysis in the Social Sciences*, ed. James Mahoney and Dietrich Rueschemeyer (Cambridge: Cambridge University Press, 2003), 344.

91 Keith Banting, George Hoberg, and Richard Simeon, "Introduction," in *Degrees of Freedom: Canada and the United States in a Changing World*, ed. Keith Banting, George Hoberg, and Richard Simeon (Montreal and Kingston: McGill–Queen's University Press, 1997), 15–18.

92 Ibid., 16.

93 Peter Hall, *Governing the Economy: The Politics of State Intervention in Britain and France* (New York: Oxford University Press, 1986), 265.

94 Campbell and Pedersen, "Knowledge Regimes."

95 Ibid., 175; see also Beryl Radin and Joan Boas, "Federalism, Political Structure, and Public Policy in the United States and Canada," *Journal of Comparative Policy Analysis: Research and Practice* 2(1) (2000): 65–89; Jennifer Wallner, "Political Structures, Social Diversity, and Public Policy: Comparing Mandatory Education in Canada and the United States," *Comparative Political Studies* 45(7) (2012): 850–74.

96 Michael Atkinson and William Coleman, "Strong States and Weak States: Sectoral Policy Networks in Advanced Capitalist Economies," *British Journal of Political Science* 19(1) (1989): 49.

97   Peter Katzenstein, "Introduction: Alternative Perspectives and National Security," in *The Culture of National Security* (New York: Columbia University Press, 1996), 7.

98   Ronald Manzer, *Educational Regimes and Anglo-American Democracy* (Toronto: University of Toronto Press, 2003), 4.

99   Haas, "Words Can Hurt You," 211; see also Campbell and Pedersen, "Knowledge Regimes"; Sarah Babb, *Managing New Mexico* (Princeton: Princeton University Press, 2001); Stephen D. Krasner, "Structural Causes and Regime Consequences: Regimes as an Intervening Variable," *International Organization* 36(2) (1982): 185.

100 Kingdon, *Agendas, Alternatives, and Public Policies*, ch. 8.

101 Peter A. Hall, "Conclusion," in *The Political Power of Economic Ideas: Keynesianism across Nations*, ed. Peter A. Hall (Princeton: Princeton University Press, 1989), 369–75; David A. Rochefort and Roger W. Cobb's work on problem definition supports Hall's deconstruction of viability, while Neil Bradford has used the concept with great success in his analysis of the importance of Royal Commissions in Canadian economic policy. See Rochefort and Cobb, "Problem Definition: An Emerging Perspective," in *The Politics of Problem Definition: Shaping the Policy Agenda*, ed. David A. Rochefort and Roger W. Cobb (Lawrence: University Press of Kansas, 1994), 24–6; Neil Bradford, *Commissioning Ideas: Canadian National Policy Innovation in Comparative Perspective* (Toronto: Oxford University Press, 1998).

102 Paul Pierson, "When Effect Becomes Cause: Policy Feedback and Political Change," *World Politics* 45(4) (1993): 596.

103 Bradford, *Commissioning Ideas*, 20.

104 Schmidt, "Discursive Institutionalism," 303–26; see also Schön and Rein, *Frame Reflection*.

105 Kingdon, *Agendas, Alternatives, and Public Policies*, 140.

106 Mintrom, "Policy Entrepreneurs," 738–70.

107 Jacob Hacker, "The Historical Logic of National Health Insurance: Structure and Sequence in the Development of British, Canadian, and U.S. Medical Policy," *Studies in American Political Development* 12 (Spring 1998): 59; Paul Pierson, *Politics in Time: History, Institutions, and Social Analysis* (Princeton: Princeton University Press, 2004).

108 Charles Tilly, *Explaining Social Processes* (Boulder: Paradigm Publishers, 2008), 3.

109 Pierson, *Politics in Time*, 67–8.

110 Jacob S. Hacker, "Privatizing Risk without Privatizing the Welfare State: The Hidden Politics of Social Policy Retrenchment in the United States," *American Political Science Review* 98(2) (2004): 244.

111 See also Wolfgang Streeck and Katheleen Thelen, eds., *Beyond Continuity: Institutional Change in Advanced Political Economies* (Oxford: Oxford University Press, 2005); James Mahoney and Kathleen Thelen, eds., *Explaining Institutional Change: Ambiguity, Agency, and Power* (Cambridge: Cambridge University Press, 2010).

112 Carolyn Tuohy, *Accidental Logics: The Dynamics of Change in the Health Care Arena in the United States, Britain, and Canada* (New York and Oxford: Oxford University Press, 1999).

113 Jacob Hacker, "Dismantling the Health Care State? Political Institutions, Public Policies, and the Comparative Politics of Health Reform," *British Journal of Political Science* 34(4) (2004): 693–724.

4. Founding and Consolidating Provincial Schooling

1 John W. Meyer, Francisco O. Ramirez, and Yasemin Nuhglu Soysal, "World Expansion of Mass Education, 1870–1980," *Sociology of Education* 65(2) (1992): 128–49.

2 Alfred Marshall, "The Future of the Working Classes," in *Memorials of Alfred Marshall*, ed. A.C. Pigou (New York: Kelley and Millman, 1956), 101–18.

3 Manoly R. Lupul, "Educational Crisis in the New Dominion to 1917," in *Canadian Education: A History*, ed. J. Donald Wilson et al. (Toronto: Prentice-Hall, 1970), 267.

4 George M. Weir, *The Separate School Question in Canada* (Toronto: Ryerson Press, 1934), 27n1.

5 Garth Stevenson, *Unfulfilled Union: Canadian Federalism and National Unity*, rev. ed. (Toronto: Gage Publishing, 1982), 28–34.

6 Weir, *The Separate School Question in Canada*, 11.

7 Donald Smiley, "Canada and the Quest for a National Policy," *Canadian Journal of Political Science* 8(1) (1975): 42–6.

8 Royal Commission on Dominion–Provincial Relations, *Report*, Book I: *Canada 1867–1939* (hereafter Rowell–Sirois Report), 66.

9 Ibid., 130.

10 Quoted in G.E. Malcolm MacLeod and Robert E. Blair, *The Canadian Education Association: The First 100 Years, 1891–1991* (Toronto: CEA, 1992), 6.

11 Sir William Dawson, quoted in DEA, *The Minutes of Proceedings, with Addresses, Papers and Discussions of the First Convention of the Association*, Montreal, 5–8 July 1892 (Montreal: L. John Lovell and Son, 1893), 37.

12 *Constitution of the Dominion Educational Association*, Article III, Membership.

13 DEA, *The Minutes of the Proceedings, with Addresses and Papers of the Third Convention of the Association, Halifax, August 2–5, 1898* (Halifax: 1900), lxvi–lxxv.

14 Freeman K. Stewart, *Interprovincial Co-operation in Education: The Story of the Canadian Education Association* (Toronto: W.J. Gage, 1957), 32–3.

15 Delegates from Newfoundland attended the Quebec Confederation in 1864 and signed the original resolutions. However, anti-confederates fought hard against the idea of a union with the other colonies, capturing the sentiment in a song: "Her face turns to Britain, her Back to the Gulf / Come near at your peril, Canadian Wolf!" (http://www.heritage.nf.ca/law/song.html, accessed on 29 January 2012).

16 CNEA, *Proceedings of the Eighteenth Convention of the Association,* Halifax, St John, and Charlottetown, 15 to 19 August 1938.

17 Trustees in Alberta, for example, founded the Alberta School Trustees Association (ASTA) in 1907.

18 The CTF began as an initiative to gain closer cooperation between the teachers' alliances and federations of the four western provinces with an eye to pushing for the standardization of teachers' certificates and a uniform minimum salary for the region. Hearing of the idea, teachers from Ontario sent representatives to the first meeting of the Western Federation and promoted the idea of creating a national organization. The representatives from western Canada agreed, and the Canadian Teachers' Federation emerged. For more on this history, see Gerald Nason, "The Canadian Teachers' Federation: A Study of Its Historical Developments, Interest, and Activities from 1919 to 1960" (thesis, University of Toronto, 1964).

19 Dr Inch, Chief Superintendent of Education, New Brunswick. Quoted in DAE, *The Minutes of Proceedings,* xli.

20 These are lines from a famous anti-confederate song popular in Newfoundland toward the end of the nineteenth and into the twentieth century (for more on this legacy, see http://www.heritage.nf.ca/law/debate.html, accessed on 15 February 2012).

21 Educational development in France followed this pathway of centralization. Napoleon established a central administrative apparatus in 1806 and 1808 that took control of secondary education. Laws in 1816 then put elementary schools under the control of communal committees, which were also overseen by the central state. Prussian educational administration exhibited a similar propensity for centralization, with the marginalization of local control between 1780 and 1840. For more on this, see Andy Green, *Education and State Formation: The Rise of Education Systems in England, France, and the USA* (London: Macmillan, 1990).

22 Weir, *The Separate School Question in Canada,*1–2.

23 Ibid.

24 Frank Peters, "Tomorrow's School Boards: The Issue of Underlying Values," *Education Canada* 36(4) (1996): 16; R.D. Gidney and D.A. Lawr, "The Development of an Administrative System for the Public Schools: The First Stage, 1841–50," in *Egerton Ryerson and His Times,* ed. Neil McDonald and Alf Chaiton (Toronto: Macmillan, 1978), 160–84.

25 Ronald Manzer, *Public Schools and Political Ideas* (Toronto: University of Toronto Press, 1993).

26 Egerton Ryerson, quoted in Goldwin S. French, "Egerton Ryerson and the Methodist Model for Upper Canada," in *Egerton Ryerson and His Times,* ed. Neil McDonald and Alf Chaiton (Toronto: Macmillan, 1978), 56.

27 Charles Edward Phillips, *The Development of Education in Canada* (Toronto: Gage Publishing, 1957), 224.

28 R.D. Gidney and D.A. Lawr, "The Development of an Administrative System for the Public Schools: The First Stage, 1841–50," in *Egerton Ryerson and His Times,* 173.

29 Egerton Ryerson, *Report on a System of Public Elementary Instruction for Upper Canada* (Montreal: Lovell and Gibson, 1847), 22–3.

30 Manzer, *Public Schools and Political Ideas,* 55.

31 T.C. Bryne, "The Evolution of the Provincial Superintendent," *The Canadian Superintendent: Official Publication of the Canadian Association of School Superintendents and Inspectors* 5 (May 1957): 6.

32 Frederick W. Rowe, *Education and Culture in Newfoundland* (Toronto: McGraw-Hill Ryerson, 1976), 5.

33 Frederick W. Rowe, *The Development of Education in Newfoundland* (Toronto: Ryerson Press, 1964), 81.

34 Lionel Groulx, *L'enseignement français au Canada,* I (Montréal: Librairie d'Action Canadienne-Française, 1931), 283 (author's translation).

35 Jean-Pierre Charland, *L'entreprise educative au Québec, 1840–1900* (Québec: Les Presses de l'Université Laval, 2000), ch. 3.

36 Ronald Manzer, *Educational Regimes and Anglo-American Democracy* (Toronto: University of Toronto Press, 2003), 47.

37 Roger Magnuson, *A Brief History of Quebec Education: From New France to Parti Québécois* (Montreal: Harvest House, 1980), 49.

38 Pressured by his Quebec colleagues in Parliament, Prime Minister Macdonald fashioned the Manitoba Act to mirror the institutional arrangements in Quebec. Manitoba had a bicameral legislature, conducted all public business in French and English, and printed public proceedings in both official languages. For more information, see Charles Bruce Sissons,

Church and State in Canadian Education: An Historical Study (Toronto: Ryerson Press, 1959).

39 Tom Mitchell, "Forging a New Protestant Ontario on the Agricultural Frontier: Public Schools in Brandon and the Origins of the Manitoba School Question, 1881–1890," *Issues in the History of Manitoba Education*, ed. Rosa Bruno Jofré (Lewiston: Edwin Mellen Press, 1993), 19.

40 The proportion of Catholics to Protestants tipped from near equity in 1870 to a distribution of 12,000 to 50,000 by 1881. See Alexander Gregor and Keith Wilson, *The Development of Education in Manitoba* (Dubuque: Kendall-Hunt, 1984), 46.

41 Sissons, *Church and State in Canadian Education*, 177.

42 Ibid., 179.

43 T.C. Down, "The Story of the Manitoba Schools Question," *The Nineteenth Century*, July 1896, 117–27, accessed on 16 January 2012 at http://faculty.marianopolis.edu/c.belanger/quebechistory/docs/manitoba/down.htm.

44 *Manitoba School Question! French-Canadian Interference with Manitoba*, accessed on 16 January 2012 at http://ia700507.us.archive.org/11/items/cihm_30378/cihm_30378.pdf.

45 Down, "The Story of the Manitoba Schools Question."

46 Sissons, *Church and State in Canadian Education*, 190.

47 Quoted in ibid., 180.

48 Sissons, *Church and State in Canadian Education*, 181.

49 For more on this, see Donald Grant Creighton, *Minorities, Schools, and Politics* (Toronto: University of Toronto Press, 1969).

50 Agar Adamson, "Nova Scotia: The Wisdom of Their Ancestors Is Its Foundation," in *Provincial and Territorial Legislatures in Canada*, ed. Gary Levy and Graham White (Toronto: University of Toronto Press, 1989), 140.

51 Keith Fenwick and Peter McBride, *The Government of Education in Britain* (Oxford: M. Robertson, 1981), 8.

52 Katherine MacNaughton, *The Development of the Theory and Practice of Education in New Brunswick, 1784–1900: A Study in Historical Background* (MA thesis, University of New Brunswick, 1947), 190.

53 Fenwick and McBride, *The Government of Education in Britain*, 11.

54 Robert Gidney and Winnifred Millar, *Inventing Secondary Education: The Rise of the High School in Nineteenth-Century Ontario* (Montreal and Kingston: McGill–Queen's University Press, 1990), ch. 9.

55 J. George Hodgins, ed., *Documentary History of Education in Upper Canada, from the passing of the Constitutional Act of 1791, to the close of Rev. Dr. Ryerson's administration of the Education Department in 1876*, vol. 240 (Toronto: Warwick Bros. and Rutter, 1894–1910).

56   Robert Marleau and Eric Montpetit, eds., *House of Commons Procedure and Practice*, ch. 11, accessed on 7 March 2008 at http://www.parl.gc.ca/MarleauMontpetit/DocumentViewer.aspx?DocId=1001&Sec=Ch11&Seq=2&Lang=E.

57   Robert M. Stamp, *The Schools of Ontario, 1876–1976* (Toronto: University of Toronto Press, 1982), 5.

58   When justifying the chance, Premier Mowat argued that "the Chief Superintendent had hitherto been virtually a minister without a minister's responsibility ... If responsibility was essential to all other departments of the Government, surely it was to the Education Department." *The Globe,* 22 January 1876.

59   Under the *Common School Ordinance 1869*, educational governance in BC was entrusted to the Executive Council. However, according to the Dominion Statistician H. Marshall, education "thus regulated did not function effectively," and by 1891, the province followed Ontario and appointed a specific minister to preside over the Department of Education. H. Marshall, *The Organization and Administration of Public Schools in Canada*, Dominion Bureau of Statistics Reference Paper (Ottawa: 1952), 22.

60   Atlantic Institute of Education, *A Guide to Public Education in Nova Scotia* (Halifax: 1979).

61   Manzer, *Public Schools and Political Ideas*, 83.

62   New Brunswick, *Annual Report of the Department of Education of the Province of New Brunswick, 1936* (Fredericton: King's Printer, 1937), 9.

63   Dominion Bureau of Statistics, *Annual Survey of Education in Canada 1936* (Ottawa: J.O. Patenaude, 1937), xxx.

64   Charles Edward Phillips, *The Development of Education in Canada* (Toronto: Gage Publishing, 1957), 281.

65   E. Brock Rideout, *Alternatives for Education Finance within the Established Parameters* (Ottawa: Commission on Declining School Enrolments in Ontario, 1978), 3.

66   The Free Schools movement was not universally endorsed. Strong opposition was launched by political conservatives who saw education as the privilege of the elite and not as an individual right. Reverend John Roaf, for one, wrote a letter to *The Globe* declaring that free schooling amounted to "communism in education" and undermined private property and the privileges of elites. Roaf contested the idea of the working class enjoying the right to "educate their children at the expense of their more wealthy neighbours"; while "it is our duty to give this blessing to the poor, it does not follow that the poor should forcibly take from us." See Phillips, *The Development of Education in Canada*, 284.

67 Toronto Board of Education, quoted in ibid., 284.

68 J. Donald Wilson, "The Pre-Ryerson Years," in *Egerton Ryerson and His Times*, ed. Neil McDonald and Alf Chaiton (Toronto: Macmillan), 34–8.

69 J.H. Putnam and G.H. Weir, *Survey of the School System* (Victoria: BC Education Survey Commission, 1925), 30–1.

70 CNEA, *Trends in Education 1944: A Survey of Current Educational Developments in the Nine Provinces of Canada and Newfoundland* (Toronto: 1944), 17.

71 Quebec and Newfoundland were the exceptions to this trend. Religious trusteeship undermined uniformity of curriculum both within the two provinces and between them and the other provinces. Within the two provinces, each religious council maintained a firm grip on its curriculum and resisted any advances from its counterparts. The religious committees also maintained their isolation from developments in the other provinces, which reinforced certain interprovincial differences in the structure and direction of curriculum policy. The one exception to this pattern was the Protestant Committee in Quebec's Council for Public Instruction. The Protestant Committee intentionally drew its programs of study from the other anglophone provinces. As a result, anglophone children in Quebec received a education similar to that of other Canadian children.

72 Peter Sandiford, "Canada," in *Comparative Education: Studies of Educational Systems of Six Modern Nations*, ed. Peter Sandiford (London and Toronto: J.M. Dent and Sons, 1918), 364.

73 William F. Russell, "United States," in *Comparative Education*, ed. Peter Sandiford, 12–24.

74 Paul Axelrod, *The Promise of Schooling: Education in Canada, 1800–1914* (Toronto: University of Toronto Press, 1997), 18.

75 Egerton Ryerson, *A Special Report on the Systems of Popular Education on the Continent of Europe, on the British Isles, and the United States of America, with Practical Suggestions for the Improvement of Public Instruction in the Province of Ontario* (Toronto: Leader Steam Press, 1868), 171.

76 Phillips, *The Development of Education in Canada*, 252.

77 Sir William Dawson, *Addresses, Papers, and Discussions of the General Meetings of the Dominion Educational Association*, 5 July (Halifax: Dominion Educational Association 1892), 37.

78 One of the first resolutions of the DEA read: "The varied classification of the Schools of the different Provinces has been found to be a matter of considerable perplexity in dealing with the attainments of pupils who have changed their residence from one Province to another. Your Committee would therefore recommend the adoption of a uniform nomenclature in the designation of the Schools of the Province and the adoption

of a course of study for each class, so that pupils so moving from one Province to another may be conveniently allocated to the class which they are best qualified to enter." Dominion Education Association, *The Minutes of the Proceedings*, 29–30.

79 Manzer, *Public Schools and Political Ideas*, ch. 6.

80 DEA, *The Minutes of the Proceedings*, 88–107.

81 Sandiford, "Canada."

82 Royal Commission on Industrial Training and Technical Education, *Report* (Ottawa: King's Printer, 1913).

83 CNEA, *Trends in Education 1944*, 29.

84 Putnam–Weir Commission, *Survey of the School System*, 300; Saskatchewan, Department of Education, *Annual Report*, 1918, 16; CEA, *Minutes of the Proceedings 1938*, 118; New Brunswick, Vocational Education Board, *First Annual Report of the Vocational Education Board* (Fredericton: 1919).

85 William J. Smith and Helen M. Donahue, *The Historical Roots of Quebec Education*, 23; Henry Milner, *The Long Road to Reform: Restructuring Public Education in Quebec* (Kingston and Montreal: McGill–Queen's University Press, 1986), 15–16.

86 Louis-Philippe Audet, *Histoire du Conseil de L'Instruction Publique de la province de Québec 1856–1964* (Montréal: Éditions Leméac, 1964), 166.

87 Dominion Bureau of Statistics, *Student Progress through the Schools by Grade* (Ottawa: Queen's Printer, 1960), 28.

88 James Love, "The Professionalization of Teachers in the Mid-Nineteenth Century Upper Canada," in *Ryerson and His Times*, ed. Neil McDonald and Alf Chaiton (Toronto: Macmillan, 1978), 109–98.

89 Teacher education diverged between the two denominations. In general, teachers in the Protestant system received training in Normal Schools. Teachers in the Catholic system, however, were frequently excluded, as they tended to be members of the clergy. For more on this difference and the implications of it, see Smith and Donahue, *The Historical Roots of Québec Education*, and Magnuson, *A Brief History of Quebec Education*.

90 Ryerson himself was inspired by the training schools operating in Prussia, France, Great Britain, and Ireland when he made his educational tours in 1845. When he set up the Toronto School, he blended attributes from the German and Irish systems that, according to him, had "preeminence over all similar establishments in the British Dominions." Quoted in *Report of the Royal Commission on Education in Ontario, 1950* (Toronto: Baptist Johnston, 1950), 540). In some cases, Europeans themselves initiated the policy development. For example, a Scotsman named John M. Stark, who had been educated at a Normal School in Glasgow,

established the program in Prince Edward Island. For more on the history of teacher education in PEI, see, Willard Brehaut, *Teacher Education in Prince Edward Island: Report of a Study Undertaken at the Request of the Minister of Education of the Province of Prince Edward Island* (Toronto: OISE, 1972).

91 F. Henry Johnson, "Teacher Education in Historical Perspective," *Teacher Education at the University of British Columbia, 1956–1966* (Vancouver: UBC Faculty of Education), 18.

92 John Kingdon, *Agendas, Alternatives, and Public Policies*, 2nd ed. (New York: HarperCollins College, 1994).

93 John Jessop provides but one example of specific individuals who carried ideas between provinces. D.J. Goggin has been similarly credited with bringing Ryerson's ideas to the West. Born and raised in Ontario, Goggin taught in Ryerson's system before being appointed as principal in the Manitoba Normal School. Active in the education circles, he gained a strong reputation beyond the provincial borders. When the Council for Public Instruction of the Northwest Territories wanted to set up its own Normal Schools, it appointed Goggin as the first Director and Superintendent of Education for the territories. Goggin thus introduced the Ryersonian tradition into what would become Alberta and Saskatchewan. John W. Chalmers, *Schools of the Foothills Province: The Story of Education in Alberta* (Toronto: University of Toronto Press for the Alberta Teachers' Association, 1967), ch. 1; Alan H. Child, "The Ryerson Tradition in Western Canada, 1871–1906," in *Egerton Ryerson and His Times*, 279–301.

94 Manitoba's first Normal School opened in 1882, British Columbia's in 1901, Alberta's in 1905, and Saskatchewan's in 1911.

95 Chalmers, *Schools of the Foothills Province*, 32.

96 Johnson, "Teacher Education in Historical Perspective," 18.

97 Stewart, *Interprovincial Cooperation in Education*, 13.

98 At the third DEA conference, J.A. MacCabe observed: "We find that each province of the Dominion, in receiving at Confederation control over education within its own limits, has established for itself a system of licensing its teachers, and will not accept, without re-examination, a teacher licensed by another province." He argued that the ratification of a uniform teacher's licence system would help elevate the overall standards of the profession and ease interprovincial teacher mobility. Dominion Educational Association, *The Minutes of the Proceedings*, lxxix–lxxxvi.

99 The case of BC is instructive. Teachers were certified into four classes: Academic (for university degree plus teacher training); First Class (senior matriculation plus teacher training); Second Class (junior matriculation

plus teacher training); and Special Certificates (for teachers of manual training, domestic science, and commercial subjects).

5. Universalizing Provincial Schooling

1 Richard M. Titmuss, *Problems of Social Policy* (London: HMSO and Longmans, Green, 1950), 508.
2 The motivation that underpinned the establishment of the welfare state has been the subject of numerous lively academic debates. For more information, see T.H. Marshall, *Class, Citizenship, and Social Development* (New York: Anchor Books, 1965); Gosta Esping-Andersen, *Politics against Markets* (Princeton: Princeton University Press, 1985); R. Merton, *Social Theory and Social Structure* (Glencoe: Free Press, 1958); and Clause Offe, *Contradictions of the Welfare State* (Cambridge, MA: MIT Press, 1984).
3 Gary S. Becker, "Investments in Human Capital: A Theoretical Analysis," *Journal of Political Economy* 70(5) (1962): 9–49.
4 Scott Davies, "The Paradox of Progressive Education: A Frame Analysis," *Sociology of Education* 75(4) (2002): 271; Celine Mulhern, "Globalization and the Selective Permeability of Public Policy-Making: The Case of K–12 Education in Ontario, 1990–2003," PhD diss., University of Toronto, 2007.
5 Ontario, Royal Commission on Education in Ontario, *Report* (Toronto: 1950), 67 (hereafter the Hope Commission).
6 OECD, *Convention on the Organisation for Economic Co-operation and Development*, Paris, 14 December 1960. Accessed on 15 October 2008 at http://www.oecd.org/document/7/0,3343,en_2649_34483_1915847_1_1_1_1,00.html.
7 Because education was a provincial responsibility and Canada lacked a national Department of Education, the federal government could not effectively represent Canadian interests abroad in this policy area. Therefore, the federal Department of External Affairs fashioned agreements first with the Canadian Education Association and later with the Council of Ministers of Education, Canada, to represent Canada abroad. As a result, the provinces are directly involved in international meetings that pertain to education. For example, it is the provincial chair of the CMEC and/or its director general who attends international meetings sponsored by the OECD, not officials from the federal government. See LAC, Canadian Education Association Archives, series MG 28 I 472 vol. 13, file 131. Also, phone interview, 24 May 2007; personal interview, 20 December 2007.
8 R.H. Tawney, *Secondary Education for All*, quoted in T.H. Marshall, *Class, Citizenship, and Social Development* (London: Anchor Books, 1965), 113.

9 Quoted in Donald Smiley, "The Rowell–Sirois Report, Provincial and Post-War Canadian Federalism," *Canadian Journal of Economics and Political Science* 28(1) (1962): 56.
10 Ronald L. Watts, *The Spending Power in Federal Systems: A Comparative Study* (Kingston: Institute of Intergovernmental Relations, Queen's University, 1999), 2.
11 J. Stefan Dupré, David M. Cameron, Graeme H. McKechnie, and Theodore B. Rotenberg, *Federalism and Policy Development: The Case of Adult Occupational Training in Ontario* (Toronto: University of Toronto Press, 1973), 10.
12 Quebec, Royal Commission of Inquiry on Constitutional Problems, *Report of the Royal Commission of Inquiry on Constitutional Problems* (Quebec: 1956), 381 (hereafter the Tremblay Commission).
13 Donald Smiley, *The Federal Condition in Canada* (Toronto: McGraw-Hill Ryerson, 1987), ch. 6; see also Kenneth Norrie, Richard Simeon, and Mark Krasnick, *Federalism and the Economic Union in Canada* (Toronto: University of Toronto Press, 1986), ch. 12; and Alain-G. Gagnon and Raffaele Iacovino, *Federalism, Citizenship, and Quebec: Debating Multinationalism* (Toronto: University of Toronto Press, 2007), 28–32.
14 Freeman K. Stewart, *Interprovincial Co-operation in Education: The Story of the Canadian Education Association* (Toronto: W.J. Gage, 1957), 55.
15 Canada and Newfoundland Education Association, *Trends in Education 1944: A Survey of Current Educational Developments in the Nine Provinces of Canada and Newfoundland* (Toronto: 1944).
16 Canadian Education Association Archives, LAC, series MG 28 I472, vol. 13, File NACER Miscellaneous, 327.
17 George G. Croskery and Gerald Nason, eds., *Addresses and Proceedings of the Canadian Conference on Education*, Ottawa, 16–20 February 1958 (Ottawa: Mutual Press, 1958).
18 Reports of the Saskatchewan Program Commission, Canadian Conference on Education, Montreal, 4–8 March 1962, 1.
19 T.C. Routley, "Canadian Conference on Education," *Canadian Medical Association Journal* 82 (25 June 1960): 1324.
20 Letter from George Croskery (CTF) to Stewart (CEA), 23 October 1948, LAC, Canadian Education Association Archives, Series MG 28 I472, vol. 13, file CTF-CEA, 318.
21 British Columbia, Commission of Inquiry into Educational Finance, *Report* (Victoria: 1945) (hereafter the Cameron Commission [BC]); the Hope Commission; Alberta, Royal Commission on Education, *Report* (Edmonton: 1959) (hereafter the Cameron Commission [Alberta]); Manitoba,

Royal Commission on Education, *Report* (Winnipeg: 1959) (hereafter the MacFarland Commission); British Columbia, Royal Commission on Education, *Report* (Victoria: 1960) (hereafter the Chant Commission); Commission royale d'enquête sur l'enseignement dans la province de Quebec, *Report of the Royal Commission of Inquiry on Education in the Province of Quebec* (Quebec: 1963–6) (hereafter the Parent Commission).

22 This finding supports the works of Neil Bradford and Annis May Timpson, who implicate Royal Commissions as key venues for policy exchanges and as playing a significant role in the formulation of somewhat coherent ideas for responding to particular problems. See Bradford, *Commissioning Ideas*; and Timpson, *Driven Apart: Women's Employment Equality and Child Care in Canadian Public Policy* (Vancouver: UBC Press, 2001).

23 The changes were also part of a broader movement to renew the public sector by introducing a merit-based system in the bureaucracy and by modernizing the machinery of government in the province. For more on these reforms, see J. Murray Beck, *Politics of Nova Scotia*, vol. 2: *1896–1988* (Tantallon: Four East Publications, 1988), chs. 7–8.

24 Roger Magnuson, *A Brief History of Quebec Education: From New France to Parti Québécois* (Montreal: Harvest House, 1980), 43; Jean-Pierre Charland, *L'enterprise educative au Québec, 1840–1900* (Québec: Les Presses de L'Université Laval, 2000), ch. 3; Henry Milner, *The Long Road to Reform: Restructuring Public Education in Quebec* (Montreal and Kingston: McGill–Queen's University Press, 1986), 37; Andre Siegfried, *Le Canada: Les deux races* (Paris: Librairie Armand Colin, 1960).

25 The major structural difference between the two education systems in Quebec was that for Protestants, secondary school was provided for free by the public system, but for Catholics, secondary education was housed under the private sector in classical colleges operated by the clergy. These schools provided superior training in literature and philosophy but little in terms of technology, commerce, or science. Moreover, tuition rates often exceeded the means of individual families so that the rate of francophone participation in advanced education was dramatically lower than for anglophones in the province and throughout the rest of Canada. For more on this, see Norman Henchey and Donald A. Burgess, *Between Past and Future: Quebec Education in Transition* (Calgary: Detselig Enterprises, 1987).

26 In 1867–8, educational expenditures made up 23.5 per cent of the Quebec government's budget. By 1876, the figure had dropped below 10 per cent, where it remained for many years. See J.I. Gow, "L'administration

québécoise de 1867 à 1900: un Etat en formation," *Canadian Journal of Political Science* 12(3) (1979): 555–620.

27 Teacher qualifications varied in Quebec as only the laity were required to have an education diploma. Clergymen and women were exempted. See Milner, *The Long Road to Reform*, 15.

28 Magnuson, *A Brief History of Quebec Education*, 77.

29 Parent Commission, Pt I, 65.

30 Henry Milner and Sheilagh Hodgins Milner, *The Decolonization of Quebec: An Analysis of Left-Wing Nationalism* (Toronto: McClelland and Stewart, 1973), 139–93.

31 Parent Commission, vol. 1, iii.

32 Parent Commission, Pt I, ch. 3.

33 Ibid., 81.

34 Ibid., 82–3.

35 Canada and Newfoundland Education Association, *Trends in Education 1944*, 21.

36 Saskatchewan Teachers' Federation, "New Light on the Larger Unit," *Bulletin*, May 1939, 10–12; "What the Larger Unit Is," *Bulletin*, September 1939, 37–9; "The Problem of Finance" *Bulletin*, September 1939, 37–9; James M. Paton, *The Professional Status of Teachers*, Conference Study no. 2, Canadian Conference on Education, Montreal, 2–8 March 1962.

37 John West Chalmers, *Schools of the Foothills Province: The Story of Public Education in Alberta* (Toronto: University of Toronto Press, 1967), 28.

38 M.E. LaZerte, *School Finance in Canada, 1955* (Edmonton: Canadian Schools Trustees' Association, School Finance Research Committee, 1955), 215.

39 John Kingdon, *Agendas, Alternatives, and Public Policies*, 2nd ed. (New York: HarperCollins College, 1995), 1.

40 Cameron Commission (Alberta), 76.

41 British Columbia, *Survey of the School System* (Victoria: Charles F. Banfield, 1925), 300–2 (hereafter the Putnam and Weir Report).

42 Putman and Weir Report, 302.

43 J.F.K. English, "An Evaluation of the Reorganized System of Local School Administration in British Columbia," PhD diss., University of Toronto, 1956, 3.

44 Hope Commission, 261; Michael Owen, "Towards a New Day: The Larger School Unity in Saskatchewan 1935–1950," in *The History of Education in Saskatchewan: Selected Readings*, ed. Brian Noonan, Dianne Hallman, and Murray Scharf (Regina: Canadian Plains Research Center).

45 Hope Commission, 261.

46 Alexander Gregor and Keith Wilson, *The Development of Education in Manitoba* (Dubuque: Kendall-Hunt, 1984), 108.

47 Owen, "Towards a New Day," 44.

48 MacFarland Commission, ch. 2.

49 LAC, Canadian Education Association Archives, MG 28 I472, vol. 1, file 6, "Western Resource Workshop, Saskatoon."

50 Through an extended series of articles in its regular publication, the *Bulletin*, the Saskatchewan Teachers Federation, for example, actively educated its clientele and members on the benefits of larger administrative units as demonstrated by operational models in other provinces.

51 Hope Commission, 263.

52 Ibid., 253.

53 Ronald Manzer, *Public Schools and Political Ideas: Canadian Educational Policy in Historical Perspective* (Toronto: University of Toronto Press, 1994), 100–5; see also R.D. Gidney, *From Hope to Harris: The Reshaping of Ontario's Schools* (Toronto: University of Toronto Press, 1999), ch. 3; John Porter, *The Vertical Mosaic: An Analysis of Social Class and Power in Canada* (Toronto: University of Toronto Press, 1965); Committee on Educational Research, Faculty of Education, University of Alberta, *Composite High Schools in Canada*, University of Alberta Monographs in Education, no. 1 (Edmonton: Committee on Educational Research, 1958).

54 Canada and Newfoundland Education Association, *Trends in Education*, 29.

55 Ibid., 31.

56 A.F. Brown, "Composite High Schools in Canada: The Nature and Scope of the Study," in *Composite High Schools in Canada*, ed. John H.M. Andrews and Alan F. Brown (Edmonton: Committee on Educational Research, 1959), 2.

57 At the Conference on the Canadian High School held in 1963, all of the participants agreed that the composite model was the preferred policy option for secondary school. For more information, see Lawrence W. Downey and L. Ruth Godwin, eds., *The Canadian Secondary School: An Appraisal and a Forecast* (Toronto: Macmillan and W.J. Gage, 1963).

58 Saskatchewan, Department of Education, *Annual Report 1949–50*, 15.

59 Cameron Commission (Alberta), 91.

60 Chant Commission, 244.

61 Robert M. Stamp, *The Schools of Ontario, 1876–1976* (Toronto: University of Toronto Press, 1982), 205.

62 Manzer, *Public Schools and Political Ideas*, 109.

63 Harold S. Baker, "Changing Purposes and Programmes of the Canadian High School," in *The Canadian Secondary School: An Appraisal and a Forecast*

– A Collection of the Papers Delivered at the Conference on the Canadian High School Sponsored by the Department of Secondary Education, University of Alberta, ed. Lawrence W. Downey and L. Ruth Godwin (Toronto: Macmillan and W.J. Gage, 1963), 17.

64 W.G. Fleming, Ontario's Educative Society: Schools, Pupils, and Teachers (Toronto: University of Toronto Press, 1971), 95.

65 Harry Smaller, "Vocational Education in Ontario's Secondary Schools: Past, Present – and Future?," WIP#2000-04, Labour Education and Training Research Network, York University. Accessed on 2 August 2008 at www.yorku.ca/crws/network/english/Smaller.pdf.

66 Harry Pullen, quoted in Stamp, The Schools of Ontario, 204.

67 Committee on Educational Research, Composite High Schools in Canada, 97–8.

68 H.P. Moffatt, "An SOS from the Schools: Report of the Canadian Education Association's Committee on the Status of the Teaching Profession," Canadian Education Association, September 1949, Toronto.

69 Canadian School Trustees' Association, The Road Ahead (Edmonton: Hamly Press, 1955), 12.

70 In New Brunswick, for example, efforts to take advantage of federal grants and establish vocational education programs were delayed due in part to poorly trained teachers. According to the secretary and director of the Vocational Education Board, Fletcher Peacock, the "greatest single difficulty in the successful establishment of vocational education in New Brunswick is to procure competent teachers." New Brunswick, First Annual Report of the Vocational Education Board, 1919, 18.

71 Moffatt, "An SOS from the Schools."

72 G.P. Smith, Alberta's Minister of Education during the First World War and through the 1920s, often refused requests from the ATA to extend the initial training period for teachers, viewing it as an unnecessary burden on the province that would exacerbate rather than ameliorate teacher shortages there. For more on G.P. Smith's outlook, see Chalmers, Schools of the Foothills Province, ch. 23.

73 Herbert Coutts, "Some Personalities in Alberta Teacher Education," in Teacher Education in Alberta: The Record and the Future, ed. Dorothy Mary Lampard (Lethbridge: University of Lethbridge, 1976), 27–36.

74 Bernard Keeler, "Influence of the Profession in Teacher Education," in Teacher Education in Alberta: The Record and the Future, ed. Dorothy Mary Lampard, (Lethbridge: University of Lethbridge, 1976), 37–46.

75 Alberta, Speech from the Throne, 22 February 1945, in Journals of the Legislative Assembly of the Province of Alberta (Edmonton), vol. 46, 11.

76 Bernard Keeler, "Influence of the Profession in Teacher Education," in *Teacher Education in Alberta: The Record and the Future*, ed. Dorothy Mary Lampard (Lethbridge: University of Lethbridge, 1976), 41.

77 Western Canada Regional Conference on Teacher Education, University of Alberta, Edmonton, 20–22 May 1954.

78 In March 1956, for example, the University of British Columbia appointed Neville V. Scarfe, then Dean of the Faculty of Education of the University of Manitoba, as Dean of the new College of Education at UBC.

79 The Government of Saskatchewan had established a four-year undergraduate program for elementary and secondary teachers in cooperation with its universities in 1952, although it continued to operate Normal Schools until 1964. The BC government transferred the responsibility in 1954 and Manitoba in 1965.

80 Some universities in Nova Scotia, for example, offered education courses and later extended the programs to culminate in a Bachelor of Education degree. These programs, however, were not coordinated with the Department of Education's Normal Schools, nor were they effectively connected with the certification regime in the province. Consequently, the vast majority of prospective teachers in Nova Scotia continued under the Normal School system. For more on this, see Royal Commission on Education, Public Services, and Provincial Municipal Relations, *Report*, 1974, ch. 58.

81 Katharine MacNaughton, *The Development of the Theory and Practice of Education in New Brunswick, 1984–1900: A Study in Historical Background*, MA thesis, University of New Brunswick, 1947, 24–5.

82 Ryerson to Higginson, 30 April 1845, in J. George Hodgins, ed., *Documentary History of Education in Upper Canada, from the passing of the Constitutional Act of 1791, to the close of Rev. Dr. Ryerson's administration of the Education Department in 1876*, vol. 240 (Toronto: Warwick Bros. and Rutter, Printers, 1894–1910), 241.

83 Hope Commission, 571.

84 Michael Fullan and F. Michael Connelly, *Teacher Education in Ontario: Current Practice and Options for the Future: A Position Paper* (Toronto: OISE, 1987), 11.

85 Ibid., 11.

86 Canada and Newfoundland Education Association, *Trends in Canadian Education, 1944*; Hope Commission, ch. 21; Parent Commission, ch. 8, pt 4; George G. Croskery and Gerald Nason, *Addresses and Proceedings of the Canadian Conference on Education*, 523–35.

87 John Macdonald, C. Wayne Hall, H. Pullen, and Florence G. Irvine, *Four Viewpoints on Teacher Education* (Ottawa: Canadian Teachers' Federation,

1966); Canadian Teachers' Federation, *Foundations for the Future: A New Look at Teacher Education and Certification in Canada*, Proceedings of the 1966 Seminar on Teacher Education, Ottawa, 9–11 May 1966 (Ottawa: Canadian Teachers' Federation, 1967).

88 Glen Jones, "Sectors, Institutional Types, and the Challenges of Shifting Categories: A Canadian Commentary," *Higher Education Quarterly* 63(4) (2009): 375.

89 Dr W.H. Swift, Alberta Deputy Minister of Education, Closing Address to the Second Canada-Wide Work Conference of School Superintendents, 31 May 1954, LAC, CEA Archives, MG 28 I472, vol. 1, file 10, Notes and Reports CEA 1954 Short Course.

6. Individualizing Provincial Schooling

1 Pierre Berton, *1967: The Last Good Year* (Toronto: Doubleday, 1997), 364.

2 Diane Ravitch, *The Troubled Crusade: American Education, 1945–1980* (New York: Basic Books, 1983), 237.

3 Niall Byrne and Jack Quarter, *Must Schools Fail? The Growing Debate in Canadian Education* (Toronto: McClelland and Stewart, 1972).

4 Alberta, Commission on Educational Planning, *A Choice of Futures/A Future of Choices* (Edmonton: 1972) (hereafter the Worth Report); Ontario, Provincial Committee on Aims and Objectives in the Schools of Ontario, *Living and Learning* (Toronto: Newton Publishing, 1968) (hereafter the Hall-Dennis Report); Nova Scotia, Royal Commission on Education, Public Services, and Provincial–Municipal Relations, *Report* (Halifax: 1974) (hereafter the Graham Report); Canadian Education Association, *Education in Transition: A Capsule Review 1960 to 1975* (Toronto: 1975), 11–14.

5 *Decentralizing Decision-Making within School Systems*, Fifteenth Banff Regional Conference (Edmonton: Department of Education Administration, University of Alberta, 1974).

6 Robert A. Young, Philippe Faucher, and André Blais, "The Concept of Province-Building: A Critique," *Canadian Journal of Political Science* 17(4) (1984): 784.

7 David Cameron and Richard Simeon, "Intergovernmental Relations in Canada: The Emergence of Collaborative Federalism," *Publius: The Journal of Federalism* 32(2) (2002): 51.

8 Alan Cairns, "The Politics of Constitutional Renewal in Canada," in *Redesigning the State: The Politics of Constitutional Change in Industrial Nations*, ed. Keith G. Banting and Richard Simeon (Toronto: University of Toronto Press, 1985), 100.

9 Ian Robinson and Richard Simeon, "The Dynamics of Canadian Federalism," in *Canadian Politics*, 3rd ed., ed. James Bickerton and Alain-G.
   Gagnon (Peterborough: Broadview Press, 1999), 252.
10 David M. Cameron, "Collaborative Federalism and Post-Secondary
   Education: Be Careful What You Wish For," paper prepared for the John
   Deutsch Institute for the Study of Economic Policy, Queen's University,
   Kingston, February 2004, 4. Accessed on 16 December 2013 at http://jdi-
   legacy.econ.queensu.ca/Files/Conferences/PSEconferencepapers/Cam-
   eronconferencepaper.pdf.
11 Stefan Dupré et al., *Federalism and Policy Development: The Case of Adult Occupational Training in Ontario* (Toronto: University of Toronto Press, 1973),
   5.
12 LAC, Canadian Education Association Archives, MG 28, I472, vol. 33, file
   II-6, Standing Committee of Ministers Responsible for Education, 1961.
   Canadian Education Association Memorandum to Dr F.S. Rivers Re:
   Canada's External Aid Program in Education, 23 March 1961.
13 LAC, Canadian Education Association Archives, MG 28, I472, vol. 21,
   file VIII 10, Teachers' Federation, Unfair to Children: Our Educational
   Inequalities – pamphlet from the CTF, 1963.
14 Association of Universities and Colleges of Canada, *Financing Higher Edu-
   cation in Canada* (Toronto: AUCC with University of Toronto Press, 1965).
15 James Senter, "Education for Adults, VII: Achieving an Intellectual Elite,"
   Globe and Mail, 23 August 1960.
16 LAC, Canadian Education Association Archives, MG 28, I472, vol. 23, file
   II-6, Standing Committee of Ministers Responsible for Education, 1961,
   Letter from Freeman K. Stewart to Senator Donald Cameron, Alberta
   Royal Commissioner, 20 April 1961.
17 Economic Council of Canada, *Towards Sustained and Balanced Economic
   Growth: Second Annual Review of the Economic Council of Canada* (Ottawa:
   1965); J.E. Cheal, *Investment in Canadian Youth: An Analysis of Input–Output
   Differences among Canadian Provincial School Systems* (Toronto: Macmillan,
   1963), ch. 1.
18 Gary S. Becker, "Investment in Human Capital: A Theoretical Analysis,"
   Journal of Political Economy 70 (5) (1962): 9–49.
19 Malcolm MacLeod and Robert E. Blair, *The Canadian Education Association:
   The First 100 Years, 1891–1991* (Toronto: 1992), 36.
20 Donald V. Smiley, *The Federal Condition in Canada* (Toronto: McGraw-Hill
   Ryerson, 1987), 21.
21 Richard Simeon, *Federal–Provincial Diplomacy: The Making of Recent Policy
   in Canada* (Toronto: University of Toronto Press, 1973).

22 OECD, *Canada* (Paris: 1976); Canada and Council of Ministers of Education (Canada), *Review of Educational Policies in Canada* (Ottawa: 1975), vols. 1–5.

23 Canadian Education Association, *Reactions to the OECD Review – Canada 1976 Conference of the Canadian Education Association* (Toronto: 1976).

24 Mining and forestry industries expanded the size of certain communities and built educational facilities to meet the needs of the growing populations. Foreign investors, however, did not support the church-sponsored tradition of public schooling in Newfoundland and insisted on erecting interdenominational schools. Reports indicated that these nine amalgamated schools were generally larger, better equipped, and better staffed than even the most accomplished denominational schools. These developments, while limited, further confirm the importance of bonds of connectivity among the provinces. For more on this, see C. Robbins, "The Amalgamated Schools of Newfoundland," *Newfoundland Quarterly* 70(1) (1973): 15–30.

25 Quoted in Newfoundland, Royal Commission on Education and Youth, *Report*, vol. 1 (St John's: 1967), 54 (hereafter the Warren Commission).

26 Dominion Bureau of Statistics, *Student Progress trough the Schools by Grade* (Ottawa: 1960), 28.

27 Warren Commission, vol. 1, 60.

28 Phillip McCann, "The Politics of Denominational Education in the Nineteenth Century in Newfoundland," in *The Vexed Question: Denominational Education in a Secular Age,* ed. William A. McKim (St John's: Breakwater Books, 1988), 77.

29 Manzer, *Public Schools and Political Ideas*, 154–5.

30 Worth Commission, 28.

31 Ibid., 39.

32 In truth, a perfect form of composite education, where students remained entirely in control of their own course selection, remained out of reach in the different provincial systems. For more on the problems that faced the composite model, see Manzer, *Public Schools and Political Ideas*, ch. 9.

33 Parent Report, Pt II, vol. A, 126.

34 Ibid., 165.

35 For a statement of these differences, see ibid., 176–7.

36 Québec, Ministère de l'Education, *Statistiques de l'Éducation. Direction gérérale de la recherche et de la prospective* (Québec: 1985).

37 It is important to note that students who choose to pursue their studies in a vocational training institution in the *Cégep* system have the ability later on to transfer their credits into the university system if they choose to

alter their original pathway. As a result, even if the *Cégep* system resembles the partite model, it still adheres to the principles of the composite system. For more on this, see the Parent Report, Pt II, vol. A, ch. 6.

38 Roger Magnuson, *Education in the Province of Quebec* (Washington: US Department of Health, Education, and Welfare, 1969), 21.

39 *Dominion–Provincial Conference, 1960* (Ottawa: 1960), 130.

40 Onésime Gagnon, *Cultural Developments in the Province of Quebec: Minorities' Rights and Privileges under the Education System* (Toronto: University of Toronto Press, 1952), 11.

41 Parent Report, Pt II, vol. A, 47.

42 Joanna Tomkowicz and Tracey Bushnik, "Who Goes to Post-Secondary Education and When: Pathways Chosen by 20-Year-Olds," Education, Skills, and Learning Research Paper (Ottawa: Ministry of Industry, 2003), 14. Accessed on 20 February 2012 at http://publications.gc.ca/collections/Collection/Statcan/81-595-MIE/81-595-MIE2003006.pdf.

43 Cameron Commission (Alberta), 1959, 65.

44 Hope Commission, 1950, 95; Cameron Commission (Alberta), 1959, 65; Chant Commission, 1960.

45 Hall–Dennis Report, 12.

46 Prince Edward Island, Joint Review Committee, *Education Task Group: Elementary, Secondary, and Post-Secondary Sectors Report*, PEI Development Plan, 1971.

47 According to the commissioners, "the chastisement of pupils for not meeting set, rigid requirements, is almost a form of barbarism in our day" (Hall–Dennis Report, 62). Alberta's Worth Commission echoed these sentiments: "It would be tragic … if school jurisdictions, singly or collectively, were to replace obligatory provincial examinations with local or regional examinations. A new tyranny would merely replace the old … It would be equally tragic if colleges, institutes, and universities were allowed to administer their own entrance examinations. This would replace the present matriculation examinations with a set of externals unlikely to be compatible with the learning objectives of the schools. The cure would be worse than the disease" (Worth Report, 206).

48 The Hall–Dennis Report, 10.

49 Ibid., 62.

50 Parent Commission, Pt II, vol. A, 19.

51 Warren Commission, vol. 1, 147.

52 Warren Commission; Parent Commission, *The Structure of the Educational System at the Provincial Level.*

53 Warren Commission, vol. 1, 186.

54 Ontario, Department of Education, *Report of the Minister's Committee on the Training of Elementary School Teachers* (Toronto: 1966) (hereafter the MacLeod Report).

55 Ontario, Legislative Assembly, *Debates*, 27th Leg., 4th Session, 29 March 1966, 2010.

56 Michael Fullan and F. Michael Connelly, *Teacher Education in Ontario: Current Practice and Options for the Future: A Position Paper* (Toronto: OISE, 1987), 11.

57 The MacLeod Report emphasized that two conditions needed to be met: (1) demonstration of scholarship; and (2) distinguished and successful teaching experience. When devising its plan, however, the Ontario government made no reference to these conditions. Faculty associations issued statements declaring the proposal to be "potentially dangerous" and "an essential contradiction to the recommendations of the MacLeod Report" (quoted in Ontario Confederation of University Faculty Associations, "A Policy Statement on the Amalgamation of Elementary Teachers' Colleges with Universities," November 1968, 9–10).

58 Minister Davis sent signals to administrators that gave credence to their fears. He insisted that the universities needed to organize a specific college or faculty of education and rejected the idea of having a department of education nested within a faculty of arts – an arrangement common in the United States. Davis also indicated his strong preference for a consecutive program eschewing concurrent training. See Douglas Myers and Douglas Saul, "How Not to Reform a Teacher Education System: Ontario 1966–1971," in *Educating Teachings: Critiques and Proposals* (Toronto: OISE, 1974), 40.

59 Hall–Dennis Report, 169.

60 Nova Scotia, *Royal Commission on Education, Public Service, and Provincial– Municipal Relations*, vol. 1 (Halifax: 1974), 276.

61 Geraldine Channon, *Innovations in Teacher Education in Canada* (Toronto: Canadian Teachers' Federation, 1971); Canadian Teachers' Federation, *Interprovincial Conference on the Economic Status of the Teachers of Canada* (Toronto: 1970).

62 University of Prince Edward Island, Committee on Teacher Education, *Teacher Education: Perseverance or Professionalism* (published and printed in the Atlantic provinces, 1971), 19–20.

63 Canadian Teachers' Federation, *Interprovincial Conference on the Economic Status of the Teachers of Canada* (Toronto: 1970): Canadian Teachers' Federation, *Foundations for the Future: A New Look at Teacher Education and Certification in Canada*, Proceedings of the 1966 Seminar on Teacher

Education (Ottawa, 9–11 May 1966); James M. Paton, *The Professional Status of Teachers,* Conference Study no. 2, Canadian Conference on Education, Montreal, 2–8 March 1962.

64 In some cases, provincial commissions seconded experts from other provinces. The Warren Commission, for example, asked the Dean of Education from Alberta – Dr Herbert Coutts – to assess the state of teacher education in Newfoundland: "The Commission considers itself very fortunate that Dr. Coutts agreed to undertake the study. Much of what is contained in this chapter and the next one is based on his findings and recommendations" (Warren Commission, 109).

65 Manzer, *Public Schools and Political Ideas,* 118.

66 William J. McCordic, *Financing Education in Canada* (Ottawa: Canadian Conference on Education, 1961), 2.

67 Canadian Federation of Mayors and Municipalities, *The Financing of Education in Canada* (Ottawa: 1967).

68 M.E. LaZerte, *School Finance in Canada, 1955* (Edmonton: Canadian Schools Trustees' Association, School Finance Research Committee, 1955), ch. 18.

69 Wilfred J. Brown, *Financing Education in Canada,* 2nd ed. (Ottawa: Canadian Teachers' Federation, 1967), 24.

70 In 1963, teachers' salaries made up 69.8 per cent of the total school board operating costs. Dominion Bureau of Statistics, *Daily Bulletin,* vol. 35-181, 21 September 1966, Reference 5, 69.

71 P.J. Atherton, E.J. Hanson, and J.F. Berlando, *Quality Education: What Price?,* Research Monograph no. 16 (Edmonton: Alberta Teachers' Association, 1969), 3.

72 The CTF sponsored two conferences on education finance in 1965 and 1967. Prior to the conferences, the CTF commissioned Wilfred J. Brown (an expert on education finance in Canada) to prepare advance documentation that presented an analysis of trends and comparisons on various financial aspects of education from 1946 to 1962. See Wilfred J. Brown, *Financing Education in Canada,* 2nd ed. (Ottawa: Canadian Teachers' Federation, 1967). The Canadian Federation of Mayors and Municipalities similarly offered its own interpretation of the state of education finance in Canada and echoed the observations on the fiscal imbalance recorded by the CTF. See Canadian Federation of Mayors and Municipalities, *The Financing of Education in Canada* (Ottawa: June 1967).

73 New Brunswick, *Report of the Royal Commission on the Financing of Schools in New Brunswick* (Fredericton: Minister of Education, 1955).

74 W. Wynn Meldrum, *New Brunswick Legislative Debates,* 19 April 1967, 230.

75 New Brunswick, Department of Education, *Report of the Deputy Minister of Education, 1963–1964*, 7.

76 According to the Department of Education's Annual Report, in 1961, the average annual income for employed males across Canada was $3,999, while in New Brunswick is was $3,070. Moreover, the number of families in 1961 with an annual income of less than $1,000 as a percentage of the total number of families across Canada was 4.5 per cent, while in New Brunswick it was 7.3 per cent. New Brunswick, Department of Education, *Annual Report of the Department of Education, 1967* (Fredericton: 1968), 9.

77 Pierre Michaud, "Educational Finance in Quebec and New Brunswick: Similarities and Differences," *The Costs of Controlling the Costs of Education in Canada*, Proceedings of a Symposium on Educational Finance in Canada at the 1983 Meeting of the American Educational Research Association, Montreal, 12 April 1983 (Toronto: OISE, 1983), 49–64.

78 Robin Boadway and Ronald Watts, *Fiscal Federalism in Canada*. (Kingston: Institute of Intergovernmental Relations, July 2000), 47.

79 McCordic, *Financing Education in Canada*, 30.

80 Lawton, *The Price of Quality*, 59.

81 BC Teachers' Federation, *The Cost of Education: Who Should Pay and Why?* (Vancouver: 1967), 3.

82 Albert Moore, *Financing Education in British Columbia* (Vancouver: BC School Trustees Association, 1966).

83 Manitoba Teachers' Society, *A Study of Education Finance in Manitoba: Analysis, Projections, Priorities, Recommendations* (Winnipeg: 1970), 157.

84 New Brunswick, *Legislative Assembly Synoptic Report of the Proceedings of the Fifth Session of the Forty-Fifth Legislative Assembly of the Province of New Brunswick, 1967*, vol. 1, 64.

7. Standardizing Provincial Schooling

1 Tom R. William and Holly Millinoff, *Canada's Schools: A Report Card for the 1990s: A CEA Opinion Poll* (Toronto: Canadian Education Association, 1990).

2 Rosemary Speirs, "Schools Shortchanging Youth of Canada, Mulroney Says," *Toronto Star*, 26 August 1989, A2.

3 Canadian Business Task Force on Literacy, *Measuring the Costs of Illiteracy in Canada* (Toronto: Woods Gordon, 1988).

4 James E. Cote and Anton K. Allahar, *Ivory Tower Blues: A University System in Crisis* (Toronto: University of Toronto Press, 2007); John Ferri,

"Canadian Students Hit Books Less Than Europeans, Study Says," *Toronto Star*, 10 August 1986, A2.

5 Stephen J. Ball, "Big Policies/Small World: An Introduction to International Perspectives in Education Policy," *Comparative Education* 34(2) (1998): 122.

6 Neil Nevitte, *The Decline of Deference* (Peterborough: Broadview Press, 1996).

7 B. Guy Peters, *The Future of Governing*, 2nd ed. (Lawrence: University Press of Kansas, 2001), 1.

8 David Osborne and Ted Gabler, *Reinventing Government: How the Entrepreneurial Spirit Is Transforming the Public Sector* (New York: Plume, 1993); Peter Aucoin, *The New Public Management: Canada in Comparative Perspective* (Montreal: Institute for Research on Public Policy, 1995).

9 National Commission on Excellence in Education, *A Nation at Risk: The Imperatives for Educational Reform* (Washington: US GPO, April 1983).

10 OECD, *Education at a Glance* (Paris: 1993), 9.

11 Centre for Education Research and Innovation, *Education at a Glance: Analysis* (Paris: OECD, 1996), 7, 12.

12 Tamara Knighton, Pierre Brochu, and Tomasz Gluszynski, *Measuring Up: Canadian Results of the OECD PISA Study: The Performance of Canada's Youth in Reading, Mathematics, and Science 2009* (Ottawa: Minister of Industry, 2010), 10.

13 Christopher Hood, "The 'New Public Management' in the 1980s: Variations on a Theme," *Accounting, Organizations, and Society* 20(2–3) (1995): 95.

14 Grace Skogstad and Jennifer Wallner, "Transnational Ideas, Federalism, and Public Accountability: Food Safety and Mandatory Education Policies in Canada," in *From New Public Management to New Public Governance: Essays in Honour of Peter Aucoin*, ed. Herman Bakvis and Mark Jarvis (Montreal and Kingston: McGill–Queen's University Press, 2012), 242–67.

15 Peter Hogg, "Federalism Fights the Charter," in *Federalism and Political Community*, ed. David Shugarman and Reg Whitaker (Peterborough: Broadview Press, 1989), 250; Guy Laforest, *Trudeau and the End of a Canadian Dream* (Montreal and Kingston: McGill–Queen's University Press, 1995); James Kelly, "Reconciling Rights and Federalism during Review of the Charter of Rights and Freedoms: The Supreme Court of Canada and the Centralization Thesis, 1982–1999," *Canadian Journal of Political Science* 36(2) (2001): 321–55.

16 Michael D. Behiels, *Canada's Francophone Minority Communities: Constitutional Renewal and the Winning of School Governance* (Montreal and Kingston: McGill–Queen's University Press, 2004), ch. 3.

17 Ibid., 76.
18 Chantal Hébert, "Politique Stephen Harper Avait Raison!" *L'Actualité*, 15 December 2011, 35. Translation by the author.
19 Edgar Grande and Louis W. Pauly, "Reconstituting Political Authority: Sovereignty, Effectiveness, and Legitimacy in a Transnational Order," in *Complex Sovereignty: Reconstituting Political Authority in the Twenty-First Century*, ed. Edgar Grand and Louis W. Pauly (Toronto: University of Toronto Press, 2005); Grace Skogstad, "Canadian Federalism, International Trade, and Regional Market Integration in an Era of Complex Sovereignty," in *Canadian Federalism: Performance, Effectiveness, Legitimacy*, ed. Herman Bakvis and Grace Skogstad (Toronto: Oxford University Press, 2008).
20 Stephen Clarkson, *Uncle Sam and Us: Globalization, Neoconservatism, and the Canadian State* (Toronto: University of Toronto Press, 2002); Stephen McBride, "Quiet Constitutionalism in Canada: The International Political Economy of Domestic Institutional Change," *Canadian Journal of Political Science* 36(2) (2003): 251–73.
21 Reference Re Canada Assistance Plan (B.C.), [1991] 2 S.C.R. 525.
22 Department of Finance, *Budget Plan* (Ottawa: Department of Finance, 27 February 1995), 52.
23 Paul A.R. Hobson and France St-Hilaire, "The Evolution of Federal–Provincial Fiscal Arrangements: Putting Humpty Together Again," in *Canada: The State of the Federation 1999/2000 Towards a New Mission Statement for Canadian Fiscal Federalism*, ed. Harvey Lazar (Montreal and Kingston: McGill–Queen's University Press, 2000), 159–88.
24 Dan Perrins, "The Impact of Changes in Federal Provincial Block Transfers," in *Education Finance: Current Canadian Issues*, ed. Y.L. Jack Lam (Calgary: Detselig Enterprises), 25–34.
25 Doug Brown, "Fiscal Federalism: Searching for a Balance," in *Canadian Federalism: Performance, Effectiveness, Efficiency* (Toronto: Oxford University Press, 2008), 73.
26 While difficult to confirm in the Canadian context, my analysis finds support from research on other federations. Mark Carl Rom, for example, has argued that US states are often forced to cut from education because they lack the necessary funds and unconditional financial support from Washington in the form of an equalization program comparable to that of Canada. See Mark Carl Rom, "Policy Races in the American States," in *Racing to the Bottom? Provincial Interdependence in the Canadian Federation*, ed. Kathryn Harrison (Vancouver: UBC Press, 2006), 229–56.
27 Agreement on Internal Trade, ch. 1, art. 100, 2.

28 Katherine Swinton, "Law, Politics, and the Enforcement of the Agreement on Internal Trade," in *Getting There: An Assessment of the Agreement on Internal Trade*, ed. Michael J. Trebilcock and Daniel Schwanen, Policy Study no. 26 (Toronto: C.D. Howe Institute, 1995); Eugene Beaulieu, Jim Gaisford, and Jim Higginson, *Interprovincial Trade Barriers in Canada: How Far Have We Come? Where Should We Go?* (Calgary: Van Horne Institute, 2003).

29 Richard Simeon and Ian Robinson, *States, Society, and the Development of Canadian Federalism* (Toronto: University of Toronto Press, 1990), 251.

30 Nova Scotia, Royal Commission on Education, Public Services, and Provincial–Municipal Relations, *Report* (Halifax: 1974), 2.

31 Ibid.

32 Royal Commission on Public Education Finance, *Report* (Halifax: 1981), 21–42 (hereafter the Walker Report).

33 Stephen B. Lawton, *The Price of Quality: The Public Financing of Elementary and Secondary Education in Canada* (Toronto: CEA, 1987); see also Bargaining Division, BC Teachers' Federation, *1985 Education Finance in British Columbia* (Victoria: BCTF, 1985).

34 At the time, this RMC model was gaining ground in the United States, advocated by such experts as Chambers and Parrish, financial consultants from California. The RMC model had been adopted by a number of US states, but in Canada, it had only been considered by Manitoba and Ontario.

35 Sandford Borins, "New Public Management, North American Style," in *New Public Management: Current Trends and Future Prospects*, ed. Kate McLaughlin, Stephen P. Osborne, and Ewan Ferlie (London: Routledge, 2002), 185.

36 CMEC, *Annual Report 1989–1990*, 8.

37 Alberta Hansard, 12 April 1994, 1135.

38 Ibid.

39 Ibid., 1136.

40 Ontario, Royal Commission on Learning, *For the Love of Learning*, vol. 4 (Toronto: 1994), 126 (hereafter the Bégin Commission).

41 Ontario Hansard, 22 September 1997, 12252.

42 Reid Report, 1933, 24.

43 Seymore Martin Lipset, *Agrarian Socialism: The Co-operative Commonwealth Federation in Saskatchewan*, updated ed. (Toronto: Anchor Books, 1968).

44 Dick Henley and Jon Young, "School Boards and Education Finance in Manitoba: The Politics of Equity, Access, and Local Autonomy," *Canadian Journal of Educational Administration and Policy* 72 (April 2008), accessed

on 12 December 2008 at http://www.umanitoba.ca/publications/cjeap/articles/young_henley.html.

45 Benjamin Levin, *Governing Education* (Toronto: University of Toronto Press, 2005), 127.

46 Paul Samyn, "Man-Elect-95-NDP," *Winnipeg Free Press* (7 April 1995).

47 Levin, *Governing Education*, 127.

48 Henley and Young, "School Boards and Education Finance in Manitoba."

49 In opposition to Filmon's budget cuts, the MTS developed a position on school funding inspired by the policy changes in other provinces. The MTS encouraged the government to implement full state funding, similar to the other Canadian provinces. Manitoba Teachers' Society, *The Retreat from Equity: A Study of the Impact of the Public School Funding Model of the Government of Manitoba – The Schools Finance Program 1992–1999* (Winnipeg: 2000).

50 Levin, *Governing Education*, 134.

51 Personal interview, 12 November 2007.

52 Levin, *Governing Education*, 134.

53 Jennifer Wallner, "Legitimacy and Public Policy: Seeing Beyond Performance, Effectiveness, and Efficiency," *Policy Studies Journal: The Journal of the Policy Studies Organization* 36(3): 421–43.

54 Personal interview, 13 May 2008.

55 Andrew Nikiforuk, *School's Out: The Catastrophe in Public Education and What We Can Do about It* (Toronto: Macfarlane Walter and Ross, 1993), xi.

56 CMEC, *Annual Report 1989–1990*, 8.

57 Phone interview, 8 April 2008; phone interview, 10 April 2008.

58 Personal interview, 7 April 2006.

59 CMEC, *Annual Report, 1898–1990*, 8.

60 John Kingdon, *Agendas, Alternatives, and Public Policies*, 2nd ed. (New York: Longman, 2003), 1.

61 New Brunswick and the Commission on Excellence in Education, *Schools for a New Century* (Fredericton: 1992), 17.

62 Bégin Commission, *A Short Version*, 9.

63 Select Committee on Education, *Report*, vol. 1 (31 March 1992), 254–5.

64 Dennis Raphael, "Student Assessment: A Flawed Framework?," in *Ring Some Alarm Bells in Ontario: Reactions to the Report of the Royal Commission on Learning*, ed. Geoff Milburn (London: Althouse Press, 1996), 79–94; Marita Moll, ed., *Passing the Test: The False Promises of Standardized Testing* (Ottawa: Canadian Centre for Policy Alternatives, 2004); Bernie Froese-Germain, *Standardized Testing: Undermining Equity in Education* (Ottawa: Canadian Teachers' Federation, 1999).

65 Lenora Fagen and Dana Spurrell, *Evaluating Achievement of Senior High School Students in Canada: A Study of Policies and Practices of Ministries and School Boards in Canada* (Toronto: CEA, 1995), 51.

66 Phone interview, 9 May 2008.

67 Phone interview, 10 May 2008. Translated from French by the author.

68 New Brunswick and the Commission on Excellence in Education, *Schools for a New Century*, 17.

69 Phone interview, 10 April 2008.

70 CMEC, *Recent Trends in Curriculum Reform at the Elementary and Secondary Levels in Canada* (Toronto: 1988), ix.

71 Angus Reid Group, Inc. *B.C. Reid Report* (Summer 1993), 67.

72 Centre for Educational Research and Innovation, *Education at a Glance*, 39.

73 Atlantic Provinces Education Foundation, *Foundation for the Atlantic Canada Science Curriculum* (1996), accessed on 30 August 2008 at http://www.ednet.ns.ca/pdfdocs/curriculum/camet/foundations-science.pdf; Barry LeDrew, "Atlantic Canada Common Curriculum Development: Departments of Education in the Atlantic Provinces Work Together to Renew Curriculum for the K to 12 System," in *Prospects: The Journal of the Canada/Newfoundland COOPERATION Agreement on Human Resource Development* 3(3) (1996), accessed on 7 October 2008 at http://www.cdli.ca/Community/prospects/v3n3/acccd.htm.

74 CMEC, *Update* 2(1) (1997).

75 Phone interview, 25 June 2008.

76 Jennifer Lewington, "Joining Forces on the Three R's," *Globe and Mail*, 12 July 1994, A1.

77 Department of Education and Human Resources, Prince Edward Island, *Annual Report for the Year Ending June 30, 1993* (Charlottetown: 1993), 11.

78 Phone interview, 25 June 2008.

79 Phone interview, 14 May 2008.

80 CMEC, *Update* 1(1) (1996).

81 Phone interview, 14 May 2008.

82 Personal interview, 13 May 2008.

83 Phone interview, 16 May 2008.

84 Alison Taylor, *The Politics of Education Reform in Alberta* (Toronto: University of Toronto Press, 2001).

85 Maritime Union Study, *The Report on Maritime Union Commissioned by the Governments of Nova Scotia, New Brunswick, and Prince Edward Island* (Fredericton, Halifax, Charlottetown: Queen's Printer, 1970), 10.

86 Canadian Press, "Atlantic Premiers Seek Free-Trade Zone," *Toronto Star* (26 September 1989), C3.

87 Canadian Teachers' Federation, *The 1971 Conference on Teacher Certification,* proceedings of the meeting held in Vancouver, 7–8 June 1971, 2; see also Donald Roy Cameron, *Teacher Certification in Canada* (Ottawa: Canadian Teachers' Federation, Research Division Information Bulletin, 1960).

88 Personal interview, 12 November 2007; personal interview, 20 December 2007; personal interview, 1 February 2008; phone interview, 7 February 2008.

89 Phone interview, 7 February 2008.

90 Nova Scotia, Department of Education, *Nova Scotia Public Education: Teacher Supply and Demand,* update report (Halifax: 2004).

91 Personal interview, 20 December 2007; personal interview, 1 February 2008; phone interview, 7 February 2008; phone interview, 14 May 2008.

92 In Ontario, for example, the NDP government attempted to encourage the faculties of education to change their initial teacher education programs from the one-year model to the national norm of two years. The faculties successfully resisted the pressure, and most of the programs continue to be completed in one year. Ontario, Ministry of Education and Training, *New Foundation for Ontario Education* (Toronto: 1995), 7–8.

93 Phone interview, 14 May 2008.

94 Alberta, Ministry of Economic Development and the BC College of Teachers, "Alberta and B.C. Teachers Agree to Labour Mobility," news release, 17 December 2007, accessed on 11 December 2013, http://education.alberta.ca/media/741985/mobility%20fact%20sheet.pdf.

95 Phone interview, 7 February 2008.

96 Personal interview, 21 April 2008.

97 A number of education scholars have suggested that much of the child-centred movement proved to be more rhetorical than revolutionary as provincial policy makers paid lip service to the ethos. While significant, a detailed investigation of the extent to which the paradigm resulted in transformative change is beyond the reach of this study. Rather, what is important here involves identifying the degree of similarities and differences in the policies and practices of the ten provinces.

Conclusion: Learning to School

1 T.H. Marshall, "Citizenship and Social Class," in *Class, Citizenship, and Social Development* (New York: Anchor Books, 1965).

2 CBC Digital Archives, "Ontario Passes Tough New Anti-Smoking Legislation," accessed on 30 September at http://www.cbc.ca/archives/categories/

health/public-health/butting-out-the-slow-death-of-smoking-in-canada/
ontario-passes-tough-new-anti-smoking-legislation.html.
3 CBC News, "Anti-Smoking Efforts in Canada and Abroad," 30 September
2009, accessed on 30 September 2012 at http://www.cbc.ca/news/health/
story/2009/09/29/f-smoking-bans-tobacco.html.
4 Donley T. Studlar, "What Explains the Paradox of Tobacco Control Policy
under Federalism in the U.S. and Canada? Comparative Federalism
Theory versus Multi-Level Governance," *Publius* 40(3) (2010): 389–411.
5 Michael J. Trebilcock, *National Securities Regulator Report*, 20 May 2010;
Thomas Hockin, "One Securities Regulator against the Storm" *Globe and
Mail*, 17 July 2012, accessed on 2 October 2012 at http://www.theglobean-
dmail.com/commentary/one-securities-regulator-against-the-storm/arti-
cle4420856; Expert Panel on Securities Regulation, *Creating an Advantage in
Global Capital Markets: Final Report and Recommendations*, January 2009, accessed on 2 October 2012 at http://www.groupeexperts.ca/eng/documents/
Expert_Panel_Final_Report_And_Recommendations.pdf; International
Monetary Fund, *Canada: Financial System Stability Assessment – Update*,
IMF Country Report no. 08/59, February 2008, accessed on 2 October 2012
at http://www.imf.org/external/pubs/ft/scr/2008/cr0859.pdf.
6 Jonathan Macey, *An Analysis of the Canadian Federal Government's Initiative
to Create a National Securities Regulator*, 2010, 69. See also Cristie L. Ford,
"New Governance, Compliance, and Principles-Based Securities Regulation," *American Business Law Journal* 45(1) (2008): 1–60; Thomas Courchene,
"The Economic Integration Continuum and the Canadian Securities Industry: In Praise of the Status Quo," paper commissioned by the Government of Alberta and included in the record filed with the Supreme Court
of Canada, 2010, 10, accessed on 30 September 2012 at http://www.irpp.
org/miscpubs/archive/courchene_securities.pdf.
7 Courchene, "The Economic Integration Continuum," 10.
8 Barry Rabe, "Beyond Kyoto: Climate Change Policy in Multilevel Governance Systems," *Governance: An International Journal of Policy, Administration, and Institutions* 20(3) (2007): 423–44.
9 Barry Rabe, Erick Lachapelle, and David Houle, "Climate Compared:
Sub-Federal Dominance on a Global Issue," in *Canada Compared*, ed. Luc
Turgeon, Martin Papillon, Jennifer Wallner, and Stephen White (Vancouver: UBC Press, forthcoming).
10 Douglas M. Brown, "Fiscal Federalism: Searching for Balance," in *Canadian
Federalism: Performance, Effectiveness, and Legitimacy*, 2nd ed., ed. Herman
Bakvis and Grace Skogstad (Toronto: Oxford University Press, 2008), 69.

11 This finding reinforces Paul Peterson's assertion that central governments must use their power to move fiscal resources among the substate jurisdictions to further policy development and contribute to positive results in federations. See Peterson, *The Price of Federalism* (Washington: Brookings Institution, 1995).

12 Canada, Royal Commission on Industrial Training and Technical Education, *Report* (Ottawa: 1913).

13 "The Sirois Commission as Historians," *Canadian Forum*, November 1940, 118–19, quoted in *The Rowell–Sirois Report*, Bk 1, abridged version, ed. Donald V. Smiley (Toronto: McClelland and Stewart, 1963), 4.

14 Charles Tiebout, "A Pure Theory of Local Expenditures," *Journal of Political Economy* 64(5) (1956): 416–24.

15 Kathryn Harrison, "Are Canadian Provinces Engaged in a Race to the Bottom? Evidence and Implications," in *Racing to the Bottom? Provincial Interdependence in the Canadian Federation* (Vancouver: UBC Press, 2005), 257.

16 Ibid., 258.

17 Phone interview, 16 May 2008.

18 Phone interview, 23 May 2008.

19 Elinor Ostrom, *Governing the Commons: The Evolution of Institutions for Collective Action* (Cambridge: Cambridge University Press, 1990), 183.

20 Peter Gourevitch, "The Second Image Reversed: The International Sources of Domestic Politics," *International Organization* 32(4) (1978): 909.

21 Paul Pierson, *Politics in Time: History, Institutions, and Social Analysis* (Princeton: Princeton University Press, 2004), 167.

Appendices

1 Adapted from Ross Traub, *Standardized Testing in Canada: A Survey of Standardized Achievement Testing by Ministries of Education and School Boards* (Toronto: Canadian Education Association, 1994).

2 Information gathered from a Web-based scan of Canadian universities offering a Bachelor of Education program, searched by individual province and university. Cross-listed this scan with the members of the Association of Canadian Deans of Education. Because membership in the ACDE is not mandatory, it is possible that this list is not comprehensive, and the author apologies for any omissions. Table also does not cover differences in terms of the degree structure, such as generalist (K–12 inclusive) versus a specialist (ECE, Elementary, Middle School, High School, special education, languages, etc.) program.

3 Concurrent programs range between four and five years; consecutive programs are two years with the exception of the Ontario universities, and St Thomas University in New Brunswick, which only take one year to complete.

4 Source: Statistics Canada, *Historical Statistics of Canada*, 2nd ed., ed. F.H. Leacy, 1983. Series A327–388. Shows the number of persons living in each province who were born in another province.

5 Source: Manzer, *Public Schools and Political Ideas*, Table 7.9, 129 (all calculations from original author).

6 Source: *Historical Statistics of Canada*, Section W: Education. Accessed on 14 October 2012 at http://www.statcan.gc.ca/pub/11-516-x/sectionw/4147445-eng.htm#2.

7 Source: Manzer 1994, 122.

Bibliography

Abbott, Kenneth W., and Duncan Snidal. 2001. "International 'Standards' and International Governance." *Journal of European Public Policy* 8(3): 345–70. http://dx.doi.org/10.1080/13501760110056013.

Adamson, Agar. 1989. "Nova Scotia: The Wisdom of Their Ancestors Is Its Foundation." In *Provincial and Territorial Legislatures in Canada*, ed. Gary Levy and Graham White, 139–56. Toronto: University of Toronto Press.

Adler, Emanuel, and Vincent Pouliot. 2011. "International Practices." *International Theory* 3(1): 1–36. http://dx.doi.org/10.1017/S175297191000031X.

Almond, Gabriel A., and G. Bingham Powell, Jr. 1966. *Comparative Politics: A Developmental Approach*. Boston: Little, Brown.

Appiah, Anthony. 2005. *The Ethics of Identity*. Princeton: Princeton University Press.

Atkinson, Michael M., and William D. Coleman. 1989. "Strong States and Weak States: Sectoral Policy Networks in Advanced Capitalist Economies." *British Journal of Political Science* 19(1): 47. http://dx.doi.org/10.1017/S0007123400005317.

Aucoin, Peter. 1995. *The New Public Management: Canada in Comparative Perspective*. Montreal: Institute for Research on Public Policy.

Audet, Louis-Philippe. 1964. *Histoire du Conseil de L'Instruction Publique de la province de Québec 1856–1964*. Montréal: Éditions Leméac.

Avis, J., M. Bloomer, G. Esland, and P. Hodkinson. 1996. *Knowledge and Nationhood: Education, Politics, and Work*. London: Cassell.

Axelrod, Paul. 1997. *The Promise of Schooling: Education in Canada, 1800–1914*. Toronto: University of Toronto Press.

Babb, Sarah. 2001. *Managing New Mexico*. Princeton: Princeton University Press.

Ball, Stephen J. 1998. "Big Policies/Small World: An Introduction to International Perspectives in Education Policy." *Comparative Education* 34(2): 119–30. http://dx.doi.org/10.1080/03050069828225.

Banting, Keith. 1987. *The Welfare State and Canadian Federalism*. 2nd ed. Montreal and Kingston: McGill–Queen's University Press.

– . 1995. "The Welfare State as Statecraft: Territorial Politics and Canadian Social Policy." In *European Social Policy: Between Fragmentation and Integration*, ed. Stephen Leibfried and Paul Pierson, 269–300. Washington: Brookings Institution.

– . 2006. "Social Citizenship and Federalism: Is a Federal Welfare State a Contradiction in Terms?" In *Territory, Democracy, and Justice: Regionalism and Federalism in Western Democracies*, ed. Scott L. Greer, 44–66. New York: Palgrave Macmillan.

– . 2006. "Dis-embedding Liberalism? The New Social Policy Paradigm in Canada." In *Dimensions of Inequality in Canada*, ed. David A. Green and Jonathan R. Kesselman, 417–52. Vancouver: UBC Press.

Banting, Keith, George Hoberg, and Richard Simeon. 1997. "Globalization, Fragmentation and the Social Contract." In *Degrees of Freedom: Canada and the United States in a Changing World*, ed. Keith Banting, George Hoberg, and Richard Simeon, 3–22. Montreal and Kingston: McGill–Queen's University Press.

Barber, Marilyn. 1969. "The Ontario Bilingual Schools Issue: Sources of Conflict." In *Minorities, Schools, and Politics*, ed. Donald Grant Creighton, 63–84. Toronto: University of Toronto Press.

Barcan, Alan. 1980. *A History of Australian Education*. Melbourne: Oxford University Press.

Barnett, Michael M., and Martha Finnemore. 1999. "The Politics, Power, and Pathologies of International Organizations." *International Organization* 53(4): 699–732. http://dx.doi.org/10.1162/002081899551048.

Beauchamp, George A. 1957. "Curriculum Organization and Development in Historical Perspective." *Review of Educational Research* 27(3): 241–9.

Beaulieu, Eugene, Jim Gaisford, and Jim Higginson. 2003. *Interprovincial Trade Barriers in Canada: How Far Have We Come? Where Should We Go?* Calgary: Van Horne Institute.

Beck, J. Murray. 1988. *Politics of Nova Scotia*, Vol. 2: *1896–1988*. Tantallon: Four East Publications.

Becker, Gary S. 1962. "Investment in Human Capital: A Theoretical Analysis." *Journal of Political Economy* 70(S5): 9–49. http://dx.doi.org/10.1086/258724.

Behiels, Michael D. 2004. *Canada's Francophone Minority Communities: Constitutional Renewal and the Winning of School Governance*. Montreal and Kingston: McGill–Queen's University Press.

Béland, Daniel. 2005. "Ideas and Social Policy." *Social Politics* 16(4): 558–81. http://dx.doi.org/10.1093/sp/jxp017.

– . 2007. "Ideas and Institutional Change in Social Security: Conversion, Layering, and Policy Drift." *Social Science Quarterly* 88(1): 20–38. http://dx.doi.org/10.1111/j.1540-6237.2007.00444.x.

Béland, Daniel, and Robert Cox. 2011. "Introduction: Ideas and Politics." In *Ideas and Politics in Social Science Research*, ed. Daniel Béland and Robert Cox, 3–22. Oxford: Oxford University Press.

Béland, Daniel, and André Lecours. 2005. "The Politics of Territorial Solidarity: Nationalism and Social Policy Reform in Canada, the United Kingdom, and Belgium." *Comparative Political Studies* 38(6): 676–703. http://dx.doi.org/10.1177/0010414005275600.

– . 2008. *Nationalism and Social Policy: The Politics of Territorial Solidarity*. Oxford: Oxford University Press. http://dx.doi.org/10.1093/acprof:oso/9780199546848.001.0001.

Béland, Daniel, and Jacob Hacker. 2004. "Ideas, Private Institutions, and American Welfare State 'Exceptionalism': The Case of Health and Old-Age Insurance in the United States, 1915–1965." *International Journal of Social Welfare* 13(1): 42–54.

Bélanger, Alexis. 2011. "Canadian Federalism in the Context of Combating Climate Change." *Constitutional Forum constitutionnel* 20(1): 21–31.

Bélanger, Gérard. 2010. "The Theoretical Defence of Decentralization." In *The Case for Decentralized Federalism*, ed. Ruth Hubbard and Gilles Paquet, 68–92. Ottawa: University of Ottawa Press.

Bennett, Colin. 1991. "What Is Policy Convergence and What Causes It?" *British Journal of Political Science* 21(2): 215–33. http://dx.doi.org/10.1017/S0007123400006116.

Bennett, Colin, and Michael Howlett. 1992. "The Lessons of Learning: Reconciling Theories of Policy Learning and Policy Change." *Policy Sciences* 25(3): 275–94. http://dx.doi.org/10.1007/BF00138786.

Berman, David R. 2000. *State and Local Politics*. 9th ed. Armonk: M.E. Sharpe.

Bernard, Sébastien, and Paul Saint-Arnaud. 2004 (November). "More of the Same? The Position of the Four Largest Canadian Provinces in the World of Welfare Regimes." *Research Report F/49 Family Network Canadian Policy Research Networks*.

Bernstein, Steven, and Benjamin Cashore. 2000. "Globalization, Four Paths of Internationalization, and Domestic Policy Change: The Case of EcoForestry in British Columbia, Canada." *Canadian Journal of Political Science* 33(1): 67–99. http://dx.doi.org/10.1017/S0008423900000044.

Berry, Frances Stokes. 1994. "Sizing Up State Policy Innovation Research." *Policy Studies Journal: The Journal of the Policy Studies Organization* 22(3): 442–56. http://dx.doi.org/10.1111/j.1541-0072.1994.tb01480.x.

Berry, Frances Stokes, and William D. Berry. 1990. "State Lottery Adoptions as Policy Innovations: An Event History Analysis." *American Political Science Review* 84(2): 395–415. http://dx.doi.org/10.2307/1963526.

Berry, William D., and Brady Baybeck. 2005. "Using Geographic Information Systems to Study Interstate Competition." *American Political Science Review* 99(4): 505–20. http://dx.doi.org/10.1017/S0003055405051841.

Bevir, Mark, and R.A.W. Rhodes. 2006. "Interpretive Approaches to British Government and Politics." *British Politics* 1(1): 84–112. http://dx.doi.org/10.1057/palgrave.bp.4200001.

Birch, Anthony Harold. 1955. *Federalism, Finance, and Social Legislation in Canada, Australia, and the United States.* Oxford: Clarendon Press.

Black, Edwin R. 1975. *Divided Loyalties: Canadian Concepts of Federalism.* Montreal and Kingston: McGill–Queen's University Press.

Blyth, Mark. 2002. *Great Transformations: Economic Ideas and Institutional Change in the Twentieth Century.* Cambridge: Cambridge University Press. http://dx.doi.org/10.1017/CBO9781139087230.

Boadway, Robin, and Anwar Shah. 2009. *Fiscal Federalism: Principles and Practice of Multiorder Governance.* Cambridge: Cambridge University Press. http://dx.doi.org/10.1017/CBO9780511626883.

Boehmke, Frederick J., and Richard Witmer. 2004. "Disentangling Diffusion: The Effects of Social Learning and Economic Competition on State Policy Innovation and Expansion." *Political Research Quarterly* 57(1): 39–51.

Boli, John, and George M. Thomas. 1997. "World Culture in the World Polity: A Century of International Non-governmental Organization." *American Sociological Review* 62(2): 171–90. http://dx.doi.org/10.2307/2657298.

– . 1999. *Constructing World Culture.* Stanford: Stanford University Press.

Bolleyer, Nicole. 2009. *Intergovernmental Cooperation: Rational Choices in Federal Systems and Beyond.* Oxford: Oxford University Press. http://dx.doi.org/10.1093/acprof:oso/9780199570607.001.0001.

Borins, Sandford. 2002. "New Public Management, North American Style." In *New Public Management: Current Trends and Future Prospects,* ed. Kate McLaughlin, Stephen P. Osborne, and Ewan Ferlie, 181–94. London: Routledge.

Boychuck, Gerard. 1998. *Patchworks of Purpose: The Development of Social Assistance Regimes in Canada.* Montreal and Kingston: McGill–Queen's University Press.

Bradford, Neil. 1998. *Commissioning Ideas: Canadian National Policy Innovation in Comparative Perspectives.* Toronto: Oxford University Press.

Braen, Andre, Emmanuel Didier, Pierre Foucher, and Michel Bastarache, eds. 1986. *Les Droits linguistiques au Canada.* Montréal: Les editions Yvon Blais.

Brandeis, Louis. 1932. "Dissent," *New State Ice Co. v. Liebmann*, 285 U.S. 262 (1932), 52 S. Ct. 371, 76 L. Ed. 747.

Braun, Dietmar. 2003. *Fiscal Policies in Federal States.* Aldershot: Ashgate Publishing.

Brennan, Geoffrey, and James M. Buchanan. 1980. *The Power to Tax: Analytical Foundations of a Fiscal Constitution.* Cambridge: Cambridge University Press.

Breton, Albert. 1996. *Competitive Governments: An Economic Theory of Politics and Public Finance.* Cambridge: Cambridge University Press.

Brooks, Clem, and Jeff Manza. 2007. *Why Welfare States Persist: The Importance of Public Opinion in Democracies.* Chicago: University of Chicago Press. http://dx.doi.org/10.7208/chicago/9780226075952.001.0001.

Brooks, Sarah M. 2005. "Interdependent and Domestic Foundations of Policy Change: The Diffusion of Pension Privatization around the World." *International Studies Quarterly* 49(2): 273–94. http://dx.doi.org/10.1111/j.0020-8833.2005.00345.x.

Brown, Doug. 2008. "Fiscal Federalism: Searching for a New Balance." In *Canadian Federalism: Performance, Effectiveness, Efficiency*, 2nd ed., ed. Herman Bakvis and Grace Skogstad, 63–88. Toronto: Oxford University Press.

Burkhardt, Geoffrey, and Milton March. 1991. "Educational Restructuring in the Act Government School System." In *Restructuring School Management: Recent Administrative Reorganization of Public School Governance in Australia*, ed. Grant Harman, Headley Beare, and George F. Berkley, 77–94. Canberra: Australian College of Education.

Burridge, Tom. 2012. "Why Do Finland's Schools Get the Best Results?" *BBC World News*, 7 April. Accessed on 10 March 2012 at http://news.bbc.co.uk/2/hi/8601207.stm.

Burton, Pierre. 1997. *1967: The Last Good Year.* Toronto: Doubleday.

Busemeyer, Marius R. 2007. "Determinants of Public Education Spending in 21 OECD Democracies, 1980–2001." *Journal of European Public Policy* 14(4): 582–610. http://dx.doi.org/10.1080/13501760701314417.

Byrne, Niall, and Jack Quarter. 1972. "Must Schools Fail? The Growing Debate." In *Canadian Education*, ed. Niall Byrne and Jack Quarter, 47–68. Toronto: McClelland and Stewart.

Cairns, Alan. 1985. "The Politics of Constitutional Renewal in Canada" In *Redesigning the State: The Politics of Constitutional Change in Industrial Nations*, ed. Keith G. Banting and Richard Simeon, 95–145. Toronto: University of Toronto Press.

Cameron, David. 1978. "The Expansion of the Public Economy: A Comparative Analysis." *American Political Science Review* 72(4): 1234–61.

Campbell, John L. 2002. "Ideas, Politics, and Public Policy." *Annual Review of Sociology* 28(1): 21–38. http://dx.doi.org/10.1146/annurev. soc.28.110601.141111.

– . 2004. *Institutional Change and Globalization.* Princeton: Princeton University Press.

Campbell, John L., and Ove K. Pedersen. 2001. "Introduction: The Rise of Neoliberalism and Institutional Analysis." In *The Rise of Institutionalism and Institutional Analysis*, ed. John L. Campbell and Ove K. Pedersen, 1–24. Princeton: Princeton University Press.

– . 2011. "Knowledge Regimes and Comparative Political Economy." In *Ideas and Politics in Social Science Research*, ed. Daniel Béland and Robert Henry Cox, 167–90. Oxford: Oxford University Press.

Campbell, Richard. 1985. "Background for the Uninitiated." In *Paradoxes of Rationality and Cooperation*, ed. R. Campbell and L. Sowden, 3–44. Vancouver: UBC Press.

Canadian Press. 1989. "Atlantic Premiers Seek Free-Trade Zone." *Toronto Star,* 26 September, C3.

Cardinal, Linda. 1994. "Ruptures et fragmentations de l'identité francophone en milieu minoritaire; un bilan critique." *Sociologie et Sociétés* 26(1): 71–86. http://dx.doi.org/10.7202/001118ar.

Cardinal, Linda, and Marie-Joie Brady. 2006. "Citoyenneté et fédéralisme au Canada: une relation difficile." In *Le fédéralisme canadien contemporain: fondements, traditions, institutions*, ed. Alain-G. Gagnon, 435–60. Montréal: Les Presses de l'Université de Montréal.

Carroll, Barbara, and Ruth J.E. Jones. 2000. "The Road to Innovation, Convergence, or Inertia: Devolution in Housing Policy in Canada." *Canadian Public Policy* 26(3): 277–93.

Carty, R. Kenneth, and W. Peter Ward. 1986. "The Making of a Canadian Political Citizenship." In *National Politics and Community in Canada,* ed. R. Kenneth Carty and W. Peter Ward, 65–79. Vancouver: UBC Press.

Castles, Francis G. 1982. "The Impact of Parties on Public Expenditure." In *The Impact of Parties: Politics and Policies in Democratic Capitalist States*, ed. F.G. Castles, 21–96. London: Sage.

– . 1999. *Comparative Public Policy: Patterns of Post-War Transformation.* Cheltenham: Edward Elgar.

Cerny, Phillip. 1995. "Globalization and the Changing Logic of Collective Action." *International Organization* 49(4): 595–625. http://dx.doi.org/10.1017/S0020818300028459.

Chalmers, John W. 1967. *Schools of the Foothills Province: The Story of Public Education in Alberta.* Toronto: University of Toronto Press for Alberta Teachers' Association.

Charland, Jean-Pierre. 2000. *L'entreprise educative au Québec, 1840–1900*. Québec: Les Presses de l'Université Laval.

Cheal, J.E. 1963. *Investment in Canadian Youth: An Analysis of Input-Output Differences among Canadian Provincial School Systems*. Toronto: Macmillan.

Checkel, Jeffrey. 1993. "Ideas, Institutions, and the Gorbachev Foreign Policy Revolution." *World Politics* 45(2): 271–300. http://dx.doi.org/10.2307/2950660.

Child, Alan H. 1978. "The Ryerson Tradition in Western Canada, 1871–1906." In *Egerton Ryerson and His Times*, ed. Neil McDonald and Alf Chaiton, 279–301. Toronto: Macmillan.

Clarkson, Stephen. 2002. *Uncle Sam and Us: Globalization, Neoconservatism, and the Canadian State*. Toronto: University of Toronto Press.

Coleman, William D., and Grace Skogstad. 1990. "Policy Communities and Policy Networks: A Structural Approach." In *Policy Communities and Public Policy in Canada: A Structural Approach*, ed. William D. Coleman and Grace Skogstad, 14–33. Mississauga: Copp Clark Pitman.

Conlan, Timothy. 2008. "Between a Rock and a Hard Place: The Evolution of American Federalism." In *Intergovernmental Management for the Twenty-First Century*, ed. Timothy J. Conlan and Paul Posner, 26–41. Washington: Brookings Institution Press.

Cote, James E., and Anton L. Allahar. 2007. *Ivory Tower Blues: A University System in Crisis*. Toronto: University of Toronto Press.

Coutts, Herbert. 1976. "Some Personalities in Alberta Teacher Education." In *Teacher Education in Alberta: The Record and the Future*, 27–36. Lethbridge: University of Lethbridge.

Coyne, Andrew. 1997. "The Case for Strengthening Federal Powers." *Policy Options* 18(3): 19–23.

Creighton, Donald Grant. 1969. *Minorities, Schools, and Politics*. Toronto: University of Toronto Press.

Davies, Scott. 2002. "The Paradox of Progressive Education: A Frame Analysis." *Sociology of Education* 75(4): 269. http://dx.doi.org/10.2307/3090279.

Davies, Scott, and Neil Guppy. 1997. "Globalization and Educational Reforms in Anglo-American Democracies." *Comparative Education Review* 41(4): 435–59. http://dx.doi.org/10.1086/447464.

Denis, Wilfrid B. 1993. "Ethnicité et conflits scolaires en Saskatchewan de 1905 à 1980" In *Une langue qui pense: La recherche en milieu minoritaire francophone*, ed. Linda Cardinal, 77–100. Ottawa: Presses de l'Université d'Ottawa.

Diamond, Martin. 1992. "The Ends of Federalism." In *As Far as Republican Principles Will Admit: Essays by Martin Diamond*, ed. William A. Schambra. Washington: American Enterprise Institute.

Dobbin, Frank, Beth Simmons, and Geoffrey Garrett. 2007. "The Global Diffusion of Public Policies: Social Construction, Coercion, Competition,

or Learning." *Annual Review of Sociology* 33(1): 449–72. http://dx.doi.
org/10.1146/annurev.soc.33.090106.142507.

Dolowitz, David, and David Marsh. 1996. "Who Learns What from Whom:
A Review of the Policy Transfer Literature." *Political Studies* 44(2): 343–57.
http://dx.doi.org/10.1111/j.1467-9248.1996.tb00334.x.

Down, T.C. 1986. "The Story of the Manitoba Schools Question." *The Nineteenth Century* (July): 117–27. Accessed on 16 January 2012 at http://faculty.
marianopolis.edu/c.belanger/quebechistory/docs/manitoba/down.htm.

Downey, Lawrence W., and L. Ruth Godwin, eds. 1963. *The Canadian Secondary School: An Appraisal and a Forecast.* Toronto: Macmillan and W.J. Gage.

Drezner, Daniel. 2005. "Globalization, Harmonization, and Competition: The
Different Pathways to Policy Convergence." *Journal of European Public Policy*
12(5): 841–59. http://dx.doi.org/10.1080/13501760500161472.

Dufour, Christian. 2003. "Restoring the Federal Principle: The Place of Quebec
in the Canadian Social Union." In *Forging the Canadian Social Union: SUFA
and Beyond*, ed. Sarah Fortin, Alain Noël, and France St-Hilaire, 69–92. Montreal: Institute for Research on Public Policy.

Dupré, Stefan, David M. Cameron, Graeme H. McKechnie, and Theodore B.
Rotenburg. 1973. *Federalism and Policy Development: The Case of Adult Occupational Training in Ontario.* Toronto: University of Toronto Press.

Egan, Kieran. 1997. *The Educated Mind: How Cognitive Tools Shape Our Understanding.* Chicago: University of Chicago Press. http://dx.doi.org/10.7208/
chicago/9780226190402.001.0001.

Elkins, David J. 1980. "The Sense of Place." In *Small Worlds: Provinces and Parties in Canadian Political Life*, ed. David J. Elkins and Richard Simeon, 1–30.
Toronto: Methuen.

Elkins, David J., and Richard Simeon. 1980. *Small Worlds: Provinces and Parties
in Canadian Political Life.* Toronto: Methuen.

Elkins, Zachary, and Beth Simmons. 2005. "On Waves, Clusters, and Diffusion: A Conceptual Framework." *Annals, AAPSS* 598(1): 33–51. http://dx.doi.
org/10.1177/0002716204272516.

Erk, Jan. 2003. "Federal Germany and Its Non-Federal Society: The Emergence
of an All-German Educational Policy System of Exclusive Provincial Jurisdiction." *Canadian Journal of Political Science* 36(2): 295–317. http://dx.doi.
org/10.1017/S0008423903778640.

–. 2003. "Wat We Zelf Doen, Doen We Beter: Belgian Substate Nationalisms,
Congruence, and Public Policy." *Journal of Public Policy* 23(2): 201–24.

–. 2006. "Uncodified Workings and Unworkable Codes: Canadian Federalism
and Public Policy." *Comparative Political Studies* 39(4): 441–62. http://dx.doi.
org/10.1177/0010414005276665.

Esping-Andersen, Gosta. 1985. *Politics against Markets*. Princeton: Princeton University Press.

Falleti, Tulia G., and Julia F. Lynch. 2009. "Context and Causal Mechanisms in Political Analysis." *Comparative Political Studies* 42(9): 1143–66. http://dx.doi.org/10.1177/0010414009331724.

Fenwick, Keith, and Peter McBride. 1981. *The Government of Education in Britain*. Oxford: Wiley and Sons, Incorporated.

Fernandez, Raquel, and Richard Rogerson. 2003. "Equity and Resources: An Analysis of Education Finance Systems." *Journal of Political Economy* 111(4): 858–97. http://dx.doi.org/10.1086/375381.

Ferri, John. 1986. "Canadian Students Hit Books Less Than Europeans, Study Says." *Toronto Star*, 10 August, A2.

Finegold, Kenneth. 2005. "The United States Federalism and Its Counterfactuals." In *Federalism and the Welfare State: New World and European Experiences*, ed. Herbert Obinger, Stephan Leibfried, and Francis G. Castles, 138–78. Cambridge: Cambridge University Press. http://dx.doi.org/10.1017/CBO9780511491856.006.

Finnemore, Martha. 1996. *National Interests in International Society*. Ithaca: Cornell University Press.

– . 1996. "Norms, Culture, and World Politics: Insights from Sociology's Institutionalism." *International Organization* 50(2): 325. http://dx.doi.org/10.1017/S0020818300028587.

Finnemore, Martha, and Kathryn Sikkink. 1998. "International Norm Dynamics and Political Change." *International Organization* 52(4): 887–917. http://dx.doi.org/10.1162/002081898550789.

Fischer, Frank. 2003. *Reframing Public Policy: Discursive Politics and Deliberative Practices*. Oxford: Oxford University Press. http://dx.doi.org/10.1093/019924264X.001.0001.

Fiske, Edward B. 1996. *Decentralization of Education: Politics and Consensus*. Washington: World Bank.

Fiske, Edward B., and Helen F. Ladd. 2004. *Elusive Equity: Education Reform in Post-Apartheid South Africa*. Washington: Brookings Institution.

Fleming, W.G. 1971. *Ontario's Educative Society: Schools, Pupils, and Teachers*. Toronto: University of Toronto Press.

Flora, Peter, and Arnold J. Heidenheimer. 1981. "Introduction." In *The Development of the Welfare State in Europe and America*, ed. Peter Flora and Arnold J. Heidenheimer, 1–16. New Brunswick: Transaction Books.

Ford, Cristie L. 2008. "New Governance, Compliance, and Principles-Based Securities Regulation." *American Business Law Journal* 45(1): 1–60. http://dx.doi.org/10.1111/j.1744-1714.2008.00050.x.

Forester, Jon. 1999. "Bounded Rationality and the Politics of Muddling Through." In *The Science of Public Policy: Essential Readings in Policy Sciences I*, ed. Tadao Miyakawa, 490–507. London and New York: Routledge.

Fortin, Sarah, Alain Noël, and France St-Hilaire, eds. 2003. *Forging the Canadian Social Union: SUFA and Beyond*. Montreal: Institute for Research on Public Policy.

Foucher, Pierre. 1984. "Les droits scolaires des acadiens et la charte." *University of New Brunswick Law Journal* 33: 97–154.

Franzese, Jr, Robert J., and Jude C. Hays. 2008. "Interdependence in Comparative Politics: Substance, Theory, Empirics, Substance." *Comparative Political Studies* 41(4–5): 742–80.

Fraser, N., and L. Gordon. 1998. "Contract versus Charity: Why Is There No Social Citizenship in the United States?" In *The Citizenship Debates*, ed. G. Shafir, 113–27. Minneapolis: University of Minnesota Press.

French, Goldwin S. 1978. "Egerton Ryerson and the Methodist Model for Upper Canada." In *Egerton Ryerson and His Times*, ed. Neil McDonald and Alf Chaiton, 45–58. Toronto: Macmillan.

Friedman, Milton. 1955. "The Role of Government in Public Education." In *Economics and the Public Interest*, ed. Robert A. Solo, 123–44. New Brunswick: Rutgers University Press.

– . 1967. *Capitalism and Freedom*. Chicago: University of Chicago Press.

Friendly, Martha, and Linda A. White. 2008. "From Multilateralism to Bilateralism to Unilateralism in Three Short Years: Child Care in Canadian Federalism, 2003–2006." In *Federalism: Performance, Effectiveness, and Efficiency*, 2nd ed., ed. Herman Bakvis and Grace Skogstad, 182–204. Oxford: Oxford University Press.

Friesen, Gerald. 1996. "Bilingualism in Manitoba: The Historical Context." In *Essays on Manitoba and Prairie History*, ed. Gerald Friesen, 23–28. Winnipeg: University of Manitoba Press.

Gaffield, Chad. 1988. *Language, Schooling, and Cultural Conflict: The Origins of the French Language Controversy in Ontario*. Montreal and Kingston: McGill–Queen's University Press. http://dx.doi.org/10.1177/036319908801300126.

Gagnon, Alain-G. 2001. "The Moral Foundation of Asymmetrical Federalism." In *Multinational Democracies*, ed. Alain-G. Gagnon and James Tully, 319–37. Cambridge: Cambridge University Press. http://dx.doi.org/10.1017/CBO9780511521577.019.

– . 2006. "Le fédéralisme asymétrique au Canada." In *Le fédéralisme canadien contemporain: Fondements, traditions, institutions*, ed. Alain-G. Gagnon. Montréal: Les Presses de l'Université de Montréal.

Gagnon, Alain-G., and Raffaele Iacovino. 2007. *Federalism, Citizenship, and Quebec: Debating Multinationalism.* Toronto: University of Toronto Press.

Gagnon, Onésime. 1952. *Cultural Developments in the Province of Quebec: Minorities' Rights and Privileges under the Education System.* Toronto: University of Toronto Press.

Garben, Sacha. 2011. *EU Higher Education Law: The Bologna Process and Harmonization by Stealth.* Aphen aan de Rijn: Kluwer Law International.

Garrett, Geoffrey. 1998. "Global Markets and National Politics: Collision Course or Virtuous Circle." *International Organization* 52(4): 787–824. http://dx.doi.org/10.1162/002081898550752.

Garrett, Geoffrey, and Phillip Lange. 1991. "Political Responses to Interdependence: What's 'Left' for the Left?" *International Organization* 45(4): 539–64. http://dx.doi.org/10.1017/S0020818300033208.

Geertz, Clifford. 1965. *The Social History of an Indonesian Town.* Cambridge: MIT Press.

Gibb, Tara, and Judith Walker. 2011. "Educating for a High Skills Society? The Landscape of Federal Employment, Training, and Lifelong Learning Policy in Canada." *Journal of Education Policy* 26(3): 381–98.

Gidney, R.D. 1999. *From Hope to Harris: The Reshaping of Ontario's Schools.* Toronto: University of Toronto Press.

Gidney, R.D., and D.A. Lawr. 1978. "The Development of an Administrative System for the Public Schools: The First Stage, 1841–50." In *Egerton Ryerson and His Times,* ed. Neil McDonald and Alf Chaiton, 160–84. Toronto: Macmillan.

Gidney, Robert, and Winnifred Millar. 1990. *Inventing Secondary Education: The Rise of the High School in Nineteenth-Century Ontario.* Montreal and Kingston: McGill–Queen's University Press.

Goble, Norman M. 1981. "Education and the National Interest." In *Federal–Provincial Relations: Education Canada,* ed. J.W. George Ivany and Michael E. Manley-Casimir, 43–68. Toronto: OISE Press.

Goldstein, Judith. 1993. *Ideas, Interests, and American Trade Policy.* Ithaca: Cornell University Press.

Goldstone, Jack A. 2003. "Comparative Historical Analysis and Knowledge Accumulation in the Study of Revolutions." In *Comparative Historical Analysis in the Social Sciences,* ed. James Mahoney and Dietrich Rueschemeyer, 41–90. Cambridge: Cambridge University Press.

Goodson, Ivor F. 1994. *Studying Curriculum.* Toronto: OISE Press.

Gould, Erica R. 2006. "Money Talks: Supplementary Financiers and International Monetary Fund Conditionality." *International Organization* 57(3): 551–86.

Gourevitch, Peter. 1978. "The Second Image Reversed: The International Sources of Domestic Politics." *International Organization* 32(4): 881–912. http://dx.doi.org/10.1017/S002081830003201X.

Gow, J.L. 1979. "L'administration quebecoise de 1867 a 1900: un Etat en formation." *Canadian Journal of Political Science* 12(3): 555. http://dx.doi.org/10.1017/S0008423900051751.

Granovetter, Mark. 1992. "Economic Action and Social Structure." In *The Sociology of Economic Life*, ed. Mark Granovetter and Richard Swedberg, 51–77. Boulder: Westview Press.

Gray, Gwendolyn. 1991. *Federalism and Health Policy: The Development of Health Systems in Canada and Australia*. Toronto: University of Toronto Press.

Gray, Virginia. 1973. "Innovation in the States: A Diffusion Study." *American Political Science Review* 67(4): 1174–85. http://dx.doi.org/10.2307/1956539.

Green, Andy. 1990. *Education and State Formation: The Rise of Education Systems in England, France, and the USA*. London: Macmillan.

– . 1997. *Education, Globalization, and the Nation State*. New York: St Martin's Press. http://dx.doi.org/10.1057/9780230371132.

– . 1999. "Education and Globalization in Europe and East Asia: Convergent and Divergent Trends." *Journal of Education Policy* 14(1): 55–71. http://dx.doi.org/10.1080/026809399286495.

Green, Andy, John Preston, and Jan Germen Janmaat. 2006. *Education, Equality, and Social Cohesion: A Comparative Analysis*. Basingstoke: Palgrave Macmillan. http://dx.doi.org/10.1057/9780230207455.

Gregor, Alexander, and Keith Wilson. 1984. *The Development of Education in Manitoba*. Dubuque: Kendall-Hunt.

Greve, Michael S. 1999. *Real Federalism: Why It Matters, How It Could Happen*. Washington: AIE Press.

Groulx, Lionel. 1931. *L'enseignement français au Canada, I*. Montréal: Librairie d'Action Canadienne-Française.

Haas, Ernst B. 1982. "Words Can Hurt You; or, Who Said What to Whom about Regimes." *International Organization* 36(2): 207. http://dx.doi.org/10.1017/S0020818300018932.

– . 1992. "Introduction: Epistemic Communities and International Policy Coordination." *International Organization* 46(1): 1–35. http://dx.doi.org/10.1017/S0020818300001442.

Hacker, Jacob. 1998. "The Historical Logic of National Health Insurance: Structure and Sequence in the Development of British, Canadian, and US Medical Policy." *Studies in American Political Development* 12 (Spring): 57–130.

– . 2004. "Dismantling the Health Care State? Political Institutions, Public Policies, and the Comparative Politics of Health Reform." *British Journal of Political Science* 34(4): 693–724. http://dx.doi.org/10.1017/S0007123404000250.

– . 2004. "Privatizing Risk without Privatizing the Welfare State: The Hidden Politics of Social Policy Retrenchment in the United States." *American Political Science Review* 98(2): 243–60. http://dx.doi.org/10.1017/S0003055404001121.

Haddow, Rodney, and Thomas Klassen. 2006. *Partisanship, Globalization, and Canadian Labour Market Policy: Four Provinces in Comparative Perspective.* Toronto: University of Toronto Press.

Haigh, Anthony. 1970. *A Ministry of Education for Europe.* London: George G. Harrap.

Hall, Peter. 1986. *Governing the Economy: The Politics of State Intervention in Britain and France.* New York: Oxford University Press.

– . 1989. "Conclusion." In *The Political Power of Economic Ideas: Keynesianism across Nations,* ed. Peter A. Hall, 361–91. Princeton: Princeton University Press.

– , ed. 1989. *The Political Power of Economic Ideas: Keynesianism across Nations.* Princeton: Princeton University Press.

– . 1993. "Policy Paradigms, Social Learning, and the State: The Case of Economic Policy Making in Britain." *Comparative Politics* 25(3): 275–96. http://dx.doi.org/10.2307/422246.

Hall, Peter, and Rosemary Taylor. 1996. "Political Science and the Three New Institutionalisms." *Political Studies* 44(5): 936–57. http://dx.doi.org/10.1111/j.1467-9248.1996.tb00343.x.

Hardin, Russell. 1990. "The Social Evolution of Cooperation." In *The Limits to Rationality,* ed. Karen S. Cook and Margaret Levi, 358–77. Chicago: University of Chicago Press.

Hargreaves, David H. 1982. *The Challenge for the Comprehensive School.* London: Routledge.

Harrison, Kathryn. 1996. *Passing the Buck: Federalism and Canadian Environmental Policy.* Vancouver: UBC Press.

– , ed. 2006. *Racing to the Bottom? Provincial Interdependence in the Canadian Federation.* Vancouver: UBC Press.

– . 2006. "Provincial Interdependence: Concepts and Theories." In *Racing to the Bottom? Provincial Interdependence in the Canadian Federation,* ed. Kathryn Harrison, 1–24. Vancouver: UBC Press.

Hay, Colin. 2001. "The 'Crisis' of Keynesianism and the Rise of Neoliberalism in Britain." In *The Rise of Neoliberalism and Institutional Analysis,* ed. John L.

Campbell and Ove K. Pedersen, 193–218. Princeton: Princeton University Press.

– . 2005. "Globalization's Impact on States." In *Global Political Economy*, ed. John Ravenhill, 236–62. Oxford: Oxford University Press.

Hay, Colin, and David Richards. 2000. "The Tangled Webs of Westminster and Whitehall: The Discourse, Strategy, and Practice of Networking within the British Core Executive." *Public Administration* 78(1): 1–28. http://dx.doi.org/10.1111/1467-9299.00190.

Hay, Colin, and Daniel Wincott. 1998. "Structure, Agency, and Historical Institutionalism." *Political Studies* 46(5): 951–7. http://dx.doi.org/10.1111/1467-9248.00177.

Haydu, Jeffrey. 1998. "Making Use of the Past: Time Periods as Cases to Compare and as Sequences of Problem Solving." *American Journal of Sociology* 104(2): 339–71. http://dx.doi.org/10.1086/210041.

Hébert, Chantal. 2011. "Politique Stephen Harper Avait Raison!" *L'Actualité* 15 (décembre): 35.

Heclo, Hugh. 1974. *Modern Social Politics in Britain and Sweden: From Relief to Income Maintenance*. New Haven: Yale University Press.

Heichel, Stephan, Jessica Pape, and Thomas Sommerer. 2005. "Is There Convergence in Convergence Research? An Overview of Empirical Studies on Policy Convergence." *Journal of European Public Policy* 12(5): 817–40. http://dx.doi.org/10.1080/13501760500161431.

Henchey, Norman, and Donald A. Burgess. 1987. *Between Past and Future: Quebec Education in Transition*. Calgary: Detselig Enterprises.

Henley, Dick, and Jon Young. 2008. "School Boards and Education Finance in Manitoba: The Politics of Equity, Access, and Local Autonomy." *Canadian Journal of Educational Administration and Policy* 72 (April). Accessed on 12 December 2008 at http://www.umanitoba.ca/publications/cjeap/articles/young_henley.html.

Hirschland, Matthew, and Sven Steinmo. 2003. "Correcting the Record: Understanding the History of Federal Intervention and Failure in Securing U.S. Educational Reform." *Educational Policy* 17(3): 343–64. http://dx.doi.org/10.1177/0895904803017003003.

Hobson, Paul A.R., and France St-Hilaire. 2000. "The Evolution of Federal–Provincial Fiscal Arrangements: Putting Humpty Together Again." In *Canada: The State of the Federation 1999/2000: Towards a New Mission Statement for Canadian Fiscal Federalism*, ed. Harvey Lazar, 159–88. Kingston and Montreal: McGill–Queen's University Press.

Hockin, Thomas. 2012. "One Securities Regulator against the Storm." *Globe and Mail*, 17 July. Accessed on 2 October 2012 at http://www.theglobeandmail.com/commentary/one-securities-regulator-against-the-storm/article4420856.

Hogg, Peter. 1989. "Federalism Fights the Charter of Rights." In *Federalism and Political Community*, ed. David Shugarman and Reg Whitaker, 249–66. Peterborough: Broadview Press.

Holzinger, Katharina, and Christoph Knill. 2005. "Causes and Conditions of Cross-National Policy Convergence." *Journal of European Public Policy* 12(5): 775–96. http://dx.doi.org/10.1080/13501760500161357.

Hood, Christopher. 1995. "The 'New Public Management' in the 1980s: Variations on a Theme." *Accounting, Organizations, and Society* 20(2–3).

Hopkins, D. 1984. "Drift and Change in Canadian Higher Education." *Higher Education Review* 16(2): 51–60.

Howlett, Michael. 2000. "Beyond Legalism? Policy Ideas, Implementation Styles, and Emulation-Based Convergence in Canadian and U.S. Environmental Policy." *Journal of Public Policy* 20(3): 305–29. http://dx.doi.org/10.1017/S0143814X00000866.

Howse, Robert. 1995. "Federalism, Democracy, and Regulatory Reform: A Skeptical View of the Case for Decentralization." In *Rethinking Federalism: Citizens, Markets, and Governments in a Changing World*, ed. Karen Knop, Sylvia Ostry, Richard Simeon, and Katherine Swinton, 273–93. Vancouver: UBC Press.

Jacobs, Alan M. 2009. "How Do Ideas Matter? Mental Models and Attention in German Pension Politics." *Comparative Political Studies* 42(2): 252–79. http://dx.doi.org/10.1177/0010414008325283.

Jacobson, Harold K. 1979. *Networks of Interdependence: International Organizations and the Global Political System*. New York: Alfred A. Knopf.

Jacoby, Wade. 2004. *The Enlargement of the European Union and NATO: Ordering from the Menu in Central Europe*. Cambridge: Cambridge University Press.

–. 2008. "Minority Traditions and Post-Communists Politics: How Do IGOs Matter?" In *Transnational Actors in Central and East European Transitions*, ed. Mitchell A. Orenstein, Stephen Bloom, and Nicole Mindstrom, 56–76. Pittsburgh: University of Pittsburgh Press.

Jakobi, Anja P. 2012. "International Organisations and Policy Diffusion: The Global Norm of Lifelong Learning." *Journal of International Relations and Development* 15(1): 31–64. http://dx.doi.org/10.1057/jird.2010.20.

Jensen, Carsten. 2008. "Worlds of Welfare Services and Transfers." *Journal of European Social Policy* 18(2): 151–62. http://dx.doi.org/10.1177/0958928707087591.

Jenson, Jane. 2010. "Diffusing Ideas for after Neoliberalism: The Social Investment Perspective in Europe and Latin America." *Global Social Policy* 10(1): 59–84. http://dx.doi.org/10.1177/1468018109354813.

Johnson, F. Henry. 1966. "Teacher Education in Historical Perspective." In *Teacher Education at the University of British Columbia*, 1–25. Vancouver: Faculty of Education, University of British Columbia.

Johnson, Jr, Mauritz. 1967. "Definitions and Models in Curriculum Theory." *Educational Theory* 17(2): 127–40. http://dx.doi.org/10.1111/j.1741-5446.1967.tb00295.x.

Jones, Glen. 2009. "Sectors, Institutional Types, and the Challenges of Shifting Categories: A Canadian Commentary." *Higher Education Quarterly* 63(4): 371–83. http://dx.doi.org/10.1111/j.1468-2273.2009.00439.x.

Karch, Andrew. 2006. "National Intervention and the Diffusion of Policy Innovations." *American Politics Research* 34(4): 403–26. http://dx.doi.org/10.1177/1532673X06288202.

Katz, Joseph. 1961. "The Curriculum of the Elementary School." In *Elementary Education in Canada*, ed. Joseph Katz, 114–34. London: McGraw-Hill.

Katz, Lilian, and James D. Raths, eds. 1991. *Advances in Teacher Education*, vol. 4. New Jersey: Ablex.

Katzenstein, Peter. 1996. "Introduction: Alternative Perspectives and National Security." In *The Culture of National Security*, ed. Peter Katzenstein, 1–32. New York: Columbia University Press.

Keck, M.E., and K. Sikkink. 1998. *Activists beyond Borders: Advocacy Networks in International Politics*. Ithaca: Cornell University Press.

Keeler, Bernard. 1976. "Influence of the Profession in Teacher Education." In *A Monograph on Teacher Education in Alberta: The Record and the Future*, ed. Dorothy Mary Lampard, 37–46. Lethbridge: University of Lethbridge.

Kelly, James. 2001. "Reconciling Rights and Federalism during Review of the Charter of Rights and Freedoms: The Supreme Court of Canada and the Centralization Thesis, 1982–1999." *Canadian Journal of Political Science* 36(2): 321–55.

Keohane, Robert O., and Joseph S. Nye. 1977. *Power and Interdependence: World Politics in Transition*. Boston: Little, Brown.

Kerr, Clark. 1983. *The Future of Industrial Societies: Convergence of Continuing Diversity*. Cambridge: Harvard University Press.

Kim, J., and G.L. Sunderman. 2004. *Large Mandates and Limited Resources: State Response to the No Child Left Behind Act and Implications for Accountability*. Cambridge: Civil Rights Project at Harvard.

Kincaid, John. 1993. "From Cooperation to Coercion in American Federalism: Housing, Fragmentation, and Preemption, 1780–1992." *Journal of Law and Politics* 9(2): 333–430.

Kingdon, John. 1995. *Agendas, Alternatives, and Public Policies*. 2nd ed. New York: Longman.

Knight, Jack. 1992. *Institutions and Social Conflict*. New York: Cambridge University Press. http://dx.doi.org/10.1017/CBO9780511528170.

Knight, Jack, and Douglass North. 1997. "Explaining Economic Change: The Interplay between Cognition and Institutions." *Legal Theory* 3(3): 211–26. http://dx.doi.org/10.1017/S1352325200000768.

Knill, Christoph. 2005. "Introduction: Cross-National Policy Convergence: Concepts, Approaches, and Explanatory Factors." *Journal of European Public Policy* 12(5): 764–74. http://dx.doi.org/10.1080/13501760500161332.

Krasner, Stephen D. 1982. "Structural Causes and Regime Consequences: Regimes as Intervening Variables." *International Organization* 36(2): 185. http://dx.doi.org/10.1017/S0020818300018920.

Kratochwil, Friedrich. 1989. *Rules, Norms, and Decisions*. Cambridge: Cambridge University Press. http://dx.doi.org/10.1017/CBO9780511559044.

Laforest, Guy. 1995. *Trudeau and the End of a Canadian Dream*. Montreal and Kingston: McGill–Queen's University Press.

Lajoie, Andrée. 2006. "Le fédéralisme au Canada: provinces et minorités, même combat." In *Le fédéralisme canadien contemporain: Fondements, traditions, institutions*, ed. Alain-G. Gagnon, 183–210. Montréal: Les Presses de l'Université de Montréal.

Laski, Harold. 1939. "The Obsolescence of Federalism." *New Republic* 98(3): 367–79.

Lee, Chang Kil, and David Strang. 2006. "The International Diffusion of Public-Sector Downsizing: Network Emulation and Theory-Driven Learning." *International Organization* 60 (Fall): 883–909.

Lehmann, Wolfgang. 2000. "Is Germany's Dual System Still a Model for Canadian Youth Apprenticeship Initiatives?" *Canadian Public Policy* 26(2): 225–40. http://dx.doi.org/10.2307/3552557.

Levi, Margaret. 2004. "An Analytic Narrative Approach to Puzzles and Problems." In *Problems and Methods in the Study of Politics*, ed. Ian Shapiro, Rogers M. Smith, and Tarek E. Masood, 201–26. Cambridge: Cambridge University Press. http://dx.doi.org/10.1017/CBO9780511492174.010.

Levin, Benjamin. 1998. "An Epidemic of Education Policy: (What) Can We Learn from Each Other?" *Comparative Education* 34(2): 131–41. http://dx.doi.org/10.1080/03050069828234.

– . 2005. *Governing Education*. Toronto: University of Toronto Press.

Levitt, Barbara, and James G. March. 1988. "Organizational Learning." *Annual Review of Sociology* 14(1): 319–40. http://dx.doi.org/10.1146/annurev.so.14.080188.001535.

Lewington, Jennifer. 1994. "Joining Forces on the Three R's." *Globe and Mail,*
12 July, A1.

Lieberman, Robert C. 2002. "Ideas, Institutions, and Political Order: Explaining Political Change." *American Political Science Review* 96(4): 697–712.
http://dx.doi.org/10.1017/S0003055402000394.

Leibfried, Stephan, Francis G. Castles, and Herbert Obinger. 2005. "Old and
New Politics in Federal Welfare States." In *Federalism and the Welfare State:
New World and European Experiences,* ed. Herbert Obinger, Stephan Leibfried, and Francis G. Castles, 307–55. Cambridge: Cambridge University
Press. http://dx.doi.org/10.1017/CBO9780511491856.010.

Lipset, Seymore Martin. 1968. *Agrarian Socialism: The Co-operative Commonwealth Federation in Saskatchewan,* updated edition. Toronto: Anchor Books.

Little, Daniel. 1991. *Varieties of Social Explanation: An Introduction to the Philosophy of Social Science.* Boulder: Westview Press.

Love, James. 1978. "The Professionalization of Teachers in the Mid-Nineteenth
Century Upper Canada." In *Egerton Ryerson and His Times,* ed. Neil McDonald and Alf Chaiton, 109–98. Toronto: Macmillan.

Lupul, Monoly L. 1970. "Educational Crisis in the New Dominion to 1917." In
Canadian Education: A History, ed. J. Donald Wilson et al., 266–89. Scarborough: Prentice-Hall.

Luz, Mark A., and C. Marc Miller. 2002. "Globalization and Canadian Federalism: Implications of the NAFTA's Investment Rules." *McGill Law Journal /
Revue de Droit de McGill* 47: 951–97.

MacLeod, G.E. Malcolm, and Robert E. Blair. 1992. *The Canadian Education
Association: The First 100 Years: 1891–1991.* Toronto: Canadian Education
Association.

Macmillan, Michael. 1989. *The Practice of Language Rights in Canada.* Cambridge: Cambridge University Press.

MacNaughton, Katherine. 1947. *The Development of the Theory and Practice of
Education in New Brunswick, 1784–1900: A Study in Historical Background.* MA
thesis, University of New Brunswick.

Magnuson, Roger. 1980. *A Brief History of Quebec Education: From New France to
Parti Québécois.* Montreal: Harvest House.

Mahoney, James. 2003. "Strategies of Causal Assessment in Comparative
Historical Analysis." In *Comparative Historical Analysis in the Social Sciences,*
ed. James Mahoney and Dietrich Rueschemeyer, 337–72. Cambridge: Cambridge University Press.

Mahoney, James, and Kathleen Thelen. 2010. "A Theory of Gradual Institutional Change." In *Explaining Institutional Change: Ambiguity, Agency, and*

Power, ed. James Mahoney and Kathleen Thelen, 1–37. Cambridge: Cambridge University Press.

– , eds. 2010. *Explaining Institutional Change: Ambiguity, Agency, and Power*. Cambridge: Cambridge University Press.

Maioni, Antonia. 1998. *Parting at the Crossroads: The Emergence of Health Insurance in the United States and Canada*. Princeton: Princeton University Press.

Manna, Paul. 2006. *School's In: Federalism and the National Education Agenda*. Washington: Georgetown University Press.

Manzer, Ronald. 2003. *Educational Regimes and Anglo-American Democracy*. Toronto: University of Toronto Press.

– . 1994. *Public Schools and Political Ideas: Canadian Educational Policy in Historical Perspective*. Toronto: University of Toronto Press.

March, James G., and Johan P. Olsen. 1984. "The New Institutionalism: Organizational Factors in Political Life." *American Political Science Review* 78(3): 734–49. http://dx.doi.org/10.2307/1961840.

– . 1989. *Rediscovering Institutions: The Organizational Basis of Politics*. New York: Free Press.

Marsh, Colin, Christopher Day, Lynne Hannay, and Gail McCutcheon. 1990. *Reconceptualizing School-Based Curriculum Development*. London: Falmer Press.

Marsh, David, and Martin Smith. 2000. "Understanding Policy Networks: Towards a Dialectical Approach." *Political Studies* 48(1): 4–21. http://dx.doi.org/10.1111/1467-9248.00247.

Marshall, Alfred. 1956. "The Future of the Working Classes." In *Memorials of Alfred Marshall*, ed. A.C. Pigou, 101–18. New York: Kelley and Millman.

Marshall, T.H. 1965. *Class, Citizenship, and Social Development*. New York: Anchor Books.

– . 1965. *Social Policy*. London: Hutchinson.

McBride, Stephen. 2003. "Quiet Constitutionalism in Canada: The International Political Economy of Domestic Institutional Change." *Canadian Journal of Political Science* 36(2): 251–73. http://dx.doi.org/10.1017/S0008423903778603.

McBride, Stephen, and Kathleen McNutt. 2007. "Devolution and Neoliberalism in the Canadian Welfare State: Ideology, National and International Conditioning Frameworks, and Policy Change in British Columbia." *Global Social Policy* 7(2): 177–201. http://dx.doi.org/10.1177/1468018107078161.

McCann, Phillip. 1988. "The Politics of Denominational Education in the Nineteenth Century in Newfoundland." In *The Vexed Question: Denominational Education in a Secular Age*, ed. William A. McKim, 30–59. St John's: Breakwater Books.

McGuinn, Patrick. 2006. *No Child Left Behind and the Transformation of Federal Education Policy, 1965–2005*. Lawrence: University Press of Kansas.

McGuire, Therese. J. 1991. "Federal Aid to States and Localities and the Appropriate Competitive Framework." In *Competition among States and Local Governments: Efficiency and Equity in American Federalism*, ed. Daphne A. Kenyon and John Kincaid, 153–66. Washington: Urban Institute Press.

McIntosh, Tom, ed. 2000. *Federalism, Democracy, and Labour Market Policy in Canada*. Montreal and Kingston: McGill–Queen's University Press.

McKinnon, Frank. 1960. *The Politics of Education: A Study of the Political Administration of the Public Schools*. Toronto: University of Toronto Press.

McLaughlin, M. 1987. "Learning from Experience: Lessons from Policy Implementation." *Educational Management and Administration* 9(2): 139–50.

McSweeney, Brendan. 2009. "Dynamic Diversity: Variety and Variation Within Countries." *Organization Studies* 30(9): 933–57. http://dx.doi.org/10.1177/0170840609338983.

Mehta, Jal. 2010. "The Varied Roles of Ideas in Politics: From 'Whether' to 'How.'" In *Ideas and Politics in Social Science Research*, ed. Daniel Béland and Robert Henry Cox, 23–46. Oxford: Oxford University Press. http://dx.doi.org/10.1093/acprof:oso/9780199736430.003.0002.

Merton, R. 1958. *Social Theory and Social Structure*. Glencoe: Free Press.

Meyer, John W. 1994. "Rationalized Environments." In *Institutional Environments and Organizations*, ed. W.R. Scott and J.W. Meyer, 28–54. Newbury Park: Sage.

Meyer, John W., Francisco O. Ramirez, Richard Subinson, and John Boli-Bennett. 1977. "The World Educational Revolution, 1950–1970." *Sociology of Education* 50(4): 242–58.

Meyer, John W., and Brian Rowan. 1977. "Institutionalized Organizations: Formal Structures as Myth and Ceremony." *American Journal of Sociology* 83(2): 340–63. http://dx.doi.org/10.1086/226550.

Meyer, John W., John Boli, and George M. Thomas. 1987. "Ontology and Rationalization in the Western Cultural Account." In *Institutional Structure: Constituting State, Society, and the Individual*, ed. George M. Thomas, John W. Meyer, Francisco O. Ramirez, and John Boli, 12–37. Beverly Hills: Sage.

Meyer, John W., Francisco O. Ramirez, and Yasemin Nuhglu Soysal. 1992. "World Expansion of Mass Education, 1879–1980." *Sociology of Education* 65(2): 128–49. http://dx.doi.org/10.2307/2112679.

Meyer, John W., John Boli, George M. Thomas, and Francisco O Ramirez. 1997. "World Society and the Nation-State." *American Journal of Sociology* 103(1): 144–81. http://dx.doi.org/10.1086/231174.

Migué, Jean-Luc. 2002. "The Economic Absurdity of Equalization." In *Sharing the Wealth: For the Federation*. CRIC Papers, September: 19–20.

Miller, Edward Alan. 2004. "Advancing Comparative State Policy Research: Toward Conceptual Integration and Methodological Expansion." *State and Local Government Review* 36(1): 35–58. http://dx.doi.org/10.1177/01603 23X0403600103.

Miller, Edward Alan, and Jane Banaszak-Holl. 2005. "Cognitive and Normative Determinants of State Policymaking Behavior: Lessons from the Sociological Institutionalism." *Publius* 35(2): 191–216. http://dx.doi.org/10.1093/publius/pji008.

Milner, Henry. 1986. *The Long Road to Reform: Restructuring Public Education in Quebec*. Montreal and Kingston: McGill–Queen's University Press.

Milner, Henry, and Sheilagh Hodgins Milner. 1973. *The Decolonization of Quebec: An Analysis of Left-Wing Nationalism*. Toronto: McClelland and Stewart.

Minow, Martha. 2010. *In Brown's Wake: Legacies of America's Educational Landmark*. Oxford: Oxford University Press.

Mintrom, Michael. 1997. "Policy Entrepreneurs and the Diffusion of Innovation." *American Journal of Political Science* 41(3): 738–70. http://dx.doi.org/10.2307/2111674.

Mintrom, Michael, and Susan Vergari. 1998. "Policy Networks and Innovation Diffusion: The Case of State Education Reforms." *Journal of Politics* 60(1): 126–48. http://dx.doi.org/10.2307/2648004.

Mitchell, Tom. 1993. "Forging a New Protestant Ontario on the Agricultural Frontier: Public Schools in Brandon and the Origins of the Manitoba School Question, 1881–1890." In *Issues in the History of Manitoba Education*, ed. Rosa Bruno Jofré, 19–46. Lewiston: Edwin Mellen Press.

Moll, Marita, ed. 2004. *Passing the Test: The False Promises of Standardized Testing*. Ottawa: Canadian Centre for Policy Alternatives.

Murphy, Jerome T. 1971. "Title I of ESEA: The Politics of Implementing Federal Education Reform." *Harvard Educational Review* 41(60): 35–63.

Myers, Douglas, and Fran Reid, eds. 1974. *Educating Teachers: Critiques and Proposals*. Toronto: Ontario Institute for Studies in Education.

Myers, Douglas, and David Saul. 1974. "How Not to Reform a Teacher Education System: Ontario 1966–1971." In *Educating Teachers: Critiques and Proposals*, ed. Douglas Myers and Fran Reid, 33–51. Toronto: Ontario Institute for Studies in Education.

Nason, Gerald. 1964. "The Canadian Teachers' Federation: A Study of Its Historical Developments, Interests, and Activities from 1919 to 1960." Unpublished thesis submitted to the University of Toronto.

Neatby, Hilda. 1953. *So Little for the Mind*. Toronto: Clarke, Irwin.

Nevitte, Neil. 1996. *The Decline of Deference*. Peterborough: Broadview Press.

Nikiforuk, Andrew. 1993. *School's Out: The Catastrophe in Public Education and What We Can Do about It*. Toronto: Macfarlane, Walter and Ross.

Noël, Alain. 1999. "Is Decentralization Conservative? Federalism and the Contemporary Debate on the Canadian Welfare State." *Stretching the Federation: The Art of the State in Canada*, ed. Robert Young, 195–218. Kingston: Institute of Intergovernmental Relations.

Noël, Alain, France St-Hilaire, and Sarah Fortin. 2003. "Learning from the SUFA Experience." In *Forging the Canadian Social Union: SUFA and Beyond*, ed. Sarah Fortin, Alain Noël, and France St. Hilaire, 1–30. Montreal: Institute for Research on Public Policy.

Norrie, Kenneth, Richard Simeon, and Mark Krasnick. 1986. *Federalism and Economic Union in Canada*. Toronto: University of Toronto Press.

North, Douglass C. 1990. *Institutions, Institutional Change, and Economic Performance*. New York: Cambridge University Press. http://dx.doi.org/10.1017/CBO9780511808678.

Oates, Wallace. 1972. *Fiscal Federalism*. New York: Harcourt Brace Jovanovich.

– . 1999. "An Essay on Fiscal Federalism." *Journal of Economic Literature* 37(3): 1120–49. http://dx.doi.org/10.1257/jel.37.3.1120.

Oates, Wallace, and R.M. Schwab. 1991. "The Allocative and Distributive Implications of Local Fiscal Competition." In *Competition among States and Local Governments: Efficiency and Equity in American Federalism*, ed. Daphne A. Kenyon and John Kincaid, 127–45. Washington: Urban Institute Press.

Obinger, Herbert, Stephan Leibfried, and Francis G. Castles. 2005. "Introduction: Federalism and the Welfare State." In *Federalism and the Welfare State*, ed. Herbert Obinger, Stephan Leibfried, and Francis G. Castles, 1–46. New York: Cambridge University Press. http://dx.doi.org/10.1017/CBO9780511491856.003.

Offe, Clause. 1984. *Contradictions of the Welfare State*. Cambridge: MIT Press.

Olson, Jr, Mancur. 1971. *The Logic of Collective Action: Public Goods and the Theory of Groups*. Cambridge: Harvard University Press.

Orenstein, Mitchell A. 2008. *Privatizing Pensions: The Transnational Campaign for Social Security Reform*. Princeton: Princeton University Press.

Osbourn, David, and Ted Gaebler. 1992. *Reinventing Government: How the Entrepreneurial Spirit Is Transforming the Public Sector*. Reading: Addison-Wesley.

Ostrom, Elinor. 1990. *Governing the Commons: The Evolution of Institutions for Collective Action*. Cambridge: Cambridge University Press. http://dx.doi.org/10.1017/CBO9780511807763.

Ostrom, Vincent. 1973. "Can Federalism Make a Difference?" *Publius: The Journal of Federalism* 3(2): 197–237.

Ostrom, Vincent, and Elinor Ostrom. 1977. "Public Goods and Public Choices." In *Alternatives for Delivering Public Services: Toward Improved Performance*, ed. E.S. Savas, 7–49: Boulder: Westview Press.

Owen, Michael. "Towards a New Day: The Larger School Unit in Saskatchewan, 1935–1950." In *History of Education in Saskatchewan: Selected Readings*, ed. Brian Noonan, Dianne Hallman, and Murray Scharf, 33–50. Regina: Canadian Plains Research Center.

Patten, Alan. 2011. "Rethinking Culture: The Social Lineage Account." *American Political Science Review* 105(4): 735–49. http://dx.doi.org/10.1017/S000305541100030X.

Pauly, Louis W., and Edgar Grande. 2005. "Reconstituting Political Authority: Sovereignty, Effectiveness, and Legitimacy in a Transnational Order." In *Complex Sovereignty: Reconstituting Political Authority in the Twenty-First Century*, ed. Edgar Grand and Louis W. Pauly, 3–21. Toronto: University of Toronto Press.

Pelletier, Réjean. 2008. *Le Québec et le Fédéralisme Canadien: Un Regard Critique.* Québec: Les Presses de l'Université Laval.

Perrins, Dan. 1998. "The Impact of Changes in Federal Provincial Block Transfers." In *Education Finance: Current Canadian Issues*, ed. Y.L. Jack Lam, 25–34. Calgary: Detselig Enterprises.

Peters, B. Guy. 2001. *The Future of Governing.* 2nd ed. Lawrence: University Press of Kansas.

Peters, Frank. 1996. "Tomorrow's School Boards: The Issue of Underlying Values." *Education Canada* 36(4): 16–23.

Peterson, Paul E. 1995. *The Price of Federalism.* Washington: Brookings Institution.

Peterson, Paul E., and Mark C. Rom. 1990. *Welfare Magnets: A New Case for a National Standard.* Washington: Brookings Institution.

Phillip, Margaret. 1995. "Alberta Driving Out Welfare Recipients." *Globe and Mail,* 9 February, A10.

Phillips, Charles Edward. 1957. *The Development of Education in Canada.* Toronto: Gage Publishing.

Pierson, Paul. 1993. "When Effect Becomes Cause: Policy Feedback and Political Change." *World Politics* 45(4): 595–628. http://dx.doi.org/10.2307/2950710.

– . 1995. "Fragmented Welfare States: Federal Institutions and the Development of Social Policy." *Governance* 8(4): 449–78.

– . 2004. *Politics in Time: History, Institutions, and Social Analysis.* Princeton: Princeton University Press.

Pierson, Paul, and Theda Skocpol. 2002. "Historical Institutionalism in Contemporary Political Science." In *Political Science: State of the Discipline III*, ed. Ira Katznelson and Helen V. Milner, 693–721. New York: W.W. Norton.

Polanyi, Karl. 2001. *The Great Transformation: The Political and Economic Origins of Our Time*. 2nd ed. Boston: Beacon Press.

Popham, W. James. 2003. *Test Better, Teach Better: The Instructional Role of Assessment*. Alexandria: Association for Supervision and Curriculum Development.

Popkin, Samuel L. 1979. *The Rational Peasant: The Political Economy of Rural Society in Vietnam*. Berkeley: University of California Press.

Porter, John. 1965. *The Vertical Mosaic: An Analysis of Social Class and Power in Canada*. Toronto: University of Toronto Press.

Powell, Walter W., and Paul J. DiMaggio, eds. 1991. *The New Institutionalism in Organizational Analysis*. Chicago: University of Chicago Press.

Prais, S.J. 2003. "Cautions on OECD's Recent Educational Survey." *Oxford Review of Education* 29(2): 139–63. http://dx.doi.org/10.1080/03054980320000 80657.

Pressman, Jeffrey L., and Aaron Wildavsky. 1984. *Implementation*. 3rd ed., expanded. Berkeley: University of California Press.

Pross, Paul. 1986. *Group Politics and Public Policy*. Toronto: Oxford University Press.

Quinn, Dennis. 1997. "The Correlates of Change in International Financial Regulation." *American Political Science Review* 91(3): 531–51. http://dx.doi.org/10.2307/2952073.

Rabe, Barry. 1999. "Federalism and Entrepreneurship: Explaining American and Canadian Innovation in Pollution Prevention and Regulatory Integration." *Policy Studies Journal: The Journal of the Policy Studies Organization* 27(2): 288–306. http://dx.doi.org/10.1111/j.1541-0072.1999.tb01969.x.

– . 2007. "Beyond Kyoto: Climate Change Policy in Multilevel Governance Systems." *Governance: An International Journal of Policy, Administration, and Institutions* 20(3): 423–44. http://dx.doi.org/10.1111/j.1468-0491.2007.00365.x.

Rabe, Barry, Erick Lachapelle, and David Houle. Forthcoming. "Climate Compared: Sub-Federal Dominance on a Global Issue." In *Canada Compared*, ed. Luc Turgeon, Martin Papillon, Jennifer Wallner, and Stephen White. Vancouver: UBC Press.

Radaelli, Claudio M. 2005. "Diffusion without Convergence: How Political Context Shapes the Adoption of Regulatory Impact Assessment." *Journal of European Public Policy* 12(5): 924–43. http://dx.doi.org/10.1080/13501760500161621.

Radin, Beryl, and Joan Boas. 2000. "Federalism, Political Structure, and Public Policy in the United States and Canada." *Journal of Comparative Policy Analysis: Research and Practice* 2(1): 65–89.

Ravitch, Diane. 1983. *The Troubled Crusade: American Education, 1945–1980.* New York: Basic Books.

Rees, Daniel I., and H. Naci Mocan. 1997. "Labor Market Conditions and the High School Dropout Rate: Evidence from New York State." *Economics of Education Review* 16(2): 103–9. http://dx.doi.org/10.1016/S0272-7757(96)00037-4.

Reitz, Jeffrey G., and Rupa Banerjee. 2007. "Racial Inequality, Social Cohesion, and Policy Issues in Canada." In *Belonging? Diversity, Recognition, and Shared Citizenship in Canada,* ed. Keith Banting, Thomas J. Courchene, and F. Leslie Seidle. Montreal: Institute for Research on Public Policy.

Rhodes, R.A.W. 2004. "Policy Network Analysis." In *Oxford Handbook of Public Policy,* ed. Michael Moran, Martin Rein, and Robert E. Goodin, 425–47. Oxford: Oxford University Press.

Riker, William H. 1964. *Federalism: Origin, Operation, Significance.* Boston: Little, Brown.

Robbins, C. 1973. "The Amalgamated Schools of Newfoundland." *Newfoundland Quarterly* 70(1): 15–30.

Robinson, Ian, and Richard Simeon. 1999. "The Dynamics of Canadian Federalism" In *Canadian Politics,* 3rd ed., ed. James Bickerton and Alain-G. Gagnon, 239–62. Peterborough: Broadview Press.

Rochefort, David A., and Roger W. Cobb. 1993. "Problem Definition, Agenda Access, and Policy Choice." *Policy Studies Journal: The Journal of the Policy Studies Organization* 21(1): 56–71. http://dx.doi.org/10.1111/j.1541-0072.1993.tb01453.x.

– . 1994. "Problem Definition: An Emerging Perspective." In *The Politics of Problem Definition: Shaping the Policy Agenda,* ed. David A. Rochefort and Roger W. Cobb, 1–31. Lawrence: University Press of Kansas.

Rocher, François, and Marie-Christine Gilbert. 2010. "Re-Federalizing Canada: Refocusing the Debate on Centralization." In *The Case for Decentralized Federalism,* ed. Ruth Hubbard and Gilles Paquet, 116–55. Ottawa: University of Ottawa Press.

Rodden, Jonathan. 2002. "The Dilemma of Fiscal Federalism: Grants and Fiscal Performance around the World." *American Journal of Political Science* 46(3): 670. http://dx.doi.org/10.2307/3088407.

Rogers, Everett. 1995. *The Diffusion of Innovations.* 3rd ed. New York: Free Press.

Rom, Mark Carl. 2006. "Policy Races in the American States." In *Racing to the Bottom? Provincial Interdependence in the Canadian Federation*, ed. Kathryn Harrison, 229–56. Vancouver: UBC Press.

Rom, Mark Carl, Paul E. Peterson, and Kenneth F. Scheve, Jr. 1998. "Interstate Competition and Welfare Policy." *Publius: The Journal of Federalism* 28(3): 17–37. http://dx.doi.org/10.1093/oxfordjournals.pubjof.a029977.

Romanow, Roy, Linda Silas, and Steven Lewis. 2012. "Why Medicare Needs Ottawa." *Globe and Mail*, 16 January.

Rowe, Frederick W. 1964. *The Development of Education in Newfoundland*. Toronto: Ryerson Press.

– . 1976. *Education and Culture in Newfoundland*. Toronto: McGraw-Hill Ryerson.

Routley, T.C. 1960. "Canadian Conference on Education." *Canadian Medical Association Journal* 82 (25 June): 1324.

Rueschemeyer, Dietrich, Evelyne Huber Stephens, and John D. Stephens. 1992. *Capitalist Development and Democracy*. Chicago: University of Chicago Press.

Russell, William F. 1918. "United States." In *Comparative Education: Studies of Educational Systems of Six Model Nations*, ed. Peter Sandiford, 12–24. London and Toronto: J.M. Dent.

Sabatier, Paul. 1988. "An Advocacy Coalition Framework of Policy Change and the Role of Policy-Oriented Learning Therein." *Policy Sciences* 21(2–3): 129–68. http://dx.doi.org/10.1007/BF00136406.

Sale, Tim, and Benjamin Levin. 1991. "Problems in the Reform of Educational Finance: A Case Study." *Canadian Journal of Education* 16(1): 32–47. http://dx.doi.org/10.2307/1495215.

Samyn, Paul. 1995. "Man-Elect-95-NDP." *Winnipeg Free Press*, 7 April.

– . 1995. "Manness Puts Kids to the Test." *Winnipeg Free Press*, 25 January.

Sandiford, Peter. 1918. "Canada." In *Comparative Education: Studies of Educational Systems of Six Modern Nations*, ed. Peter Sandiford. London and Toronto: J.M. Dent.

Santin, Aldo. 1995. "Panel Focused on Inequities." *Winnipeg Free Press*, 4 February.

Sarason, Seymore. 1995. *A Critical Appraisal of Teacher Education*. Washington: American Association of Colleges for Teacher Education.

Scharpf, Fritz W. 1988. "The Joint-Decision Trap: Lessons from German Federalism and European Integration." *Public Administration* 66(3): 239–78. http://dx.doi.org/10.1111/j.1467-9299.1988.tb00694.x.

Schmidt, Vivien. 2002. *The Futures of European Capitalism*. Oxford: Oxford University Press. http://dx.doi.org/10.1093/0199253684.001.0001.

– . 2008. "Discursive Institutionalism: The Explanatory Power of Ideas and Discourse." *Annual Review of Political Science* 11(1): 303–26. http://dx.doi.org/10.1146/annurev.polisci.11.060606.135342.

Schön, Donald A., and Martin Rein. 1994. *Frame Reflection: Toward the Resolution of Intractable Policy Controversies.* New York: Basic Books.

Schulz, Richard, and Alan Alexandroff. 1985. *Economic Regulation and the Federal System.* Toronto: University of Toronto Press.

Senter, James. 1960. "Education for Adults, VII: Achieving and Intellectual Elite." *Toronto Globe and Mail,* August 23.

Sergiovanni, Thomas J. 1984. "Leadership and Excellence in Schooling." *Educational Leadership* 41(5): 6–13.

Sheehan, Nancy M., and Michael Fullan. 1995. "Teacher Education in Canada: A Case Study of British Columbia and Ontario." In *Changing Times in Teacher Education: Restructuring or Reconceptualization?,* ed. Marvin F. Wideen and Peter P. Grimmett, 89–104. London: Falmer Press.

Sheehan, Nancy M., and J. Donald Wilson. 1995. "From Normal School to the University to the College of Teachers: Teacher Education in British Columbia in the Twentieth Century." In *Children, Teachers, and Schools in the History of British Columbia,* ed. Jean Barman, Neil Sutherland, and J. Donald Wilson, 307–22. Calgary: Detselig Enterprises.

Shepsle, Kenneth A. 2006. "Rational Choice Institutionalism." In *Oxford Handbook of Political Institutions,* ed. S. Binder, R. Rhodes, and B. Rockman, 23–39. Oxford: Oxford University Press.

Siegfried, André. 1906. *Le Canada: Les deux races.* Paris: Librairie Armand Colin.

Simeon, Richard. 1973. *Federal–Provincial Diplomacy: The Making of Recent Policy in Canada.* Toronto: University of Toronto Press.

– . 2002. *Political Science and Federalism: Seven Decades of Scholarly Engagement.* Kingston: Institute of Intergovernmental Relations, Queen's University.

– . 2006. "Federalism and Social Justice." In *Territory, Democracy, and Justice: Regionalism and Federalism in Western Democracies,* ed. Scott L. Greer, 18–43. New York: Palgrave Macmillan.

Simeon, Richard, and Donald E. Blake. 1980. "Regional Preferences: Citizens' Views of Public Policy." In *Small Worlds: Provinces and Parties in Canadian Political Life,* ed. David J. Elkins and Richard Simeon, 77–105. Toronto: Methuen.

Simeon, Richard, and E. Robert Miller. 1980. "Regional Variations in Public Policy." In *Small Worlds: Provinces and Parties in Canadian Political Life,* ed. David J. Elkins and Richard Simeon, 242–84. Toronto: Methuen.

Simeon, Richard, and Christina Murray. 2001. "Multi-Sphere Governance
in South Africa: An Interim Assessment." *Publius: The Journal of Federalism*
31(4): 65–92.

Simeon, Richard, and Ian Robinson. 1990. *States, Society, and the Development of
Canadian Federalism*. Toronto: University of Toronto Press.

Simmons, Beth. 2001. "The International Politics of Harmonization: The Case
of Capital Market Regulation." *International Organization* 55(3): 589–620.
http://dx.doi.org/10.1162/00208180152507560.

Simmons, Beth A., Frank Dobbin, and Geoffrey Garrett. 2006. "Introduction:
The International Diffusion of Liberalism." *International Organization* 60(4):
787–91. http://dx.doi.org/10.1017/S0020818306060267.

Simmons, Beth A., and Zachary Elkins. 2004. "The Globalization of Liberalization: Policy Diffusion to the International Political Economy." *American
Political Science Review* 98(1). http://dx.doi.org/10.1017/S0003055404001078.

Simon, Herbert. 1955. "A Behavioral Model of Rational Choice." *Quarterly
Journal of Economics* 69: 99–118.

Sissons, Charles Bruce. 1959. *Church and State in Canadian Education: An Historical Study*. Toronto: Ryerson Press.

Skocpol, Theda. 1979. *States and Social Revolutions: A Comparative Analysis of
France, Russia, and China*. Cambridge: Cambridge University Press.

Skocpol, Theda, and John Ikenberry. 1983. "The Political Formulation of the
American Welfare State in Historical and Comparative Perspective." *Journal
of Theoretical Politics* 1: 131–47.

Skogstad, Grace. 2001. "Internationalization, Democracy, and Food Safety
Measures: The (Il)Legitimacy of Consumer Preferences." *Global Governance*
7(3): 293–316.

– . 2008. "Canadian Federalism, International Trade, and Regional Market
Integration in an Era of Complex Sovereignty." In *Canadian Federalism: Performance, Effectiveness, Legitimacy*, ed. Herman Bakvis and Grace Skogstad,
223–45. Toronto: Oxford University Press.

– . 2008. *Internationalization and Canadian Agriculture: Policy and Governing Paradigms*. Toronto: University of Toronto Press.

– . 2008. "Policy Networks and Policy Communities: Conceptualizing State–
Societal Relationships in the Policy Process." In *The Comparative Turn in Canadian Political Science*, ed. Linda A. White, Richard Simeon, Robert Vipond,
and Jennifer Wallner, 205–20. Vancouver: UBC Press.

Skogstad, Grace, and Jennifer Wallner. 2012. "Transnational Ideas, Federalism,
and Public Accountability: Food Safety and Mandatory Education Policies
in Canada." In *From New Public Management to New Public Governance: Essays*

in Honour of Peter Aucoin, ed. Herman Bakvis and Mark Jarvis, 242–67. Montreal and Kingston: McGill–Queen's University Press.

Smiley, Donald V. 1962. "The Rowell–Sirois Report, Provincial Autonomy, and Post-War Canadian Federalism." *Canadian Journal of Economics and Political Science* 28(1): 54. http://dx.doi.org/10.2307/139263.

– . 1975. "Canada and the Quest for a National Policy." *Canadian Journal of Political Science VIII* 1(8): 40–62. http://dx.doi.org/10.1017/S0008423900045224.

– . 1987. *The Federal Condition in Canada.* Toronto: McGraw-Hill Ryerson.

– , ed. 1963. *The Rowell–Sirois Report Book One, Abridged Version.* Toronto: McClelland and Stewart.

Smith, Jennifer. 2004. *Federalism.* Vancouver: UBC Press.

Smith, Miriam. 1999. *Lesbian and Gay Rights in Canada: Social Movements and Equality-Seeking, 1971–1995.* Toronto: University of Toronto Press.

Smith, M.L., and C. Rottenberg. 1991. "Unintended Consequences of External Testing in Elementary Schools." *Educational Measurement: Issues and Practice* 10(4): 7–11. http://dx.doi.org/10.1111/j.1745-3992.1991.tb00210.x.

Smith, William J., and Helen M. Donahue. 1999. *The Historical Roots of Quebec Education.* Montreal: Office of Research on Educational Policy, McGill University.

Speirs, Rosemary. 1989. "Schools Shortchanging Youth of Canada, Mulroney Says." *Toronto Star,* 26 August, A2.

Spencer, Herbert. [1884]1940. *The Man versus the State.* Caldwell: Caxton Printers.

Stamp, Robert M. 1982. *The Schools of Ontario, 1876–1976.* Toronto: University of Toronto Press.

Stein, Janice Gross. 1991. "International Co-operation and Loss Avoidance: Framing the Problem." In *Choosing to Co-operate: How States Avoid Loss,* ed. Janice Gross Stein and Louis Pauly, 2–34. Baltimore: Johns Hopkins University Press.

Steinmo, Sven. 2010. *The Evolution of Modern States: Sweden, Japan, and the United States.* Cambridge: Cambridge University Press. http://dx.doi.org/10.1017/CBO9780511762185.

Steinmo, Sven, Kathleen Thelen, and Frank Longstreth, eds. 1992. *Structuring Politics: Historical Institutionalism in Comparative Analysis.* Cambridge: Cambridge University Press. http://dx.doi.org/10.1017/CBO9780511528125.

Stevenson, Garth. 1982. *Unfulfilled Union: Canadian Federalism and National Unity.* Revised ed. Toronto: Gage.

Stewart, Freeman K. 1957. *Interprovincial Co-operation in Education: The Story of the Canadian Education Association.* Toronto: W.J. Gage.

Stone, Deborah. 1989. "Causal Stories and the Formation of Policy Agendas." *Political Science Quarterly* 104(2): 281–300. http://dx.doi.org/10.2307/2151585.

Stone, Diane. 1999. "Learning Lessons and Transferring Policy across Time, Space, and Disciplines." *Politics* 19(1): 51–59. http://dx.doi. org/10.1111/1467-9256.00086.

Strang, David, and Ellen M. Bradburn. 2001. "Theorizing Legitimacy or Legitimating Theory? Neoliberal Discourse and HMO Policy, 1970–1989." In *The Rise of Neoliberalism and Institutional Analysis*, ed. John L. Campbell and Ove K. Pedersen, 129–58. Princeton: Princeton University Press.

Strang, David, and John W. Meyer. 1993. "Institutional Conditions for Diffusion." *Theory and Society* 22(4): 487–511. http://dx.doi.org/10.1007/ BF00993595.

Streeck, Wolfgang, and Kathleen Thelen. 2005. *Beyond Continuity: Institutional Change in Advanced Political Economies*. Oxford: Oxford University Press.

Studlar, Donley T. 2010. "What Explains the Paradox of Tobacco Control Policy under Federalism in the U.S. and Canada? Comparative Federalism Theory versus Multi-Level Governance." *Publius* 40(3): 389–411. http:// dx.doi.org/10.1093/publius/pjq003.

Swank, Duane. 2001. "Political Institutions and Welfare State Restructuring: The Impact of Institutions on Social Policy Change in Developed Democracies." In *The New Politics of the Welfare State*, ed. Paul Pierson, 197–233. Oxford: Oxford University Press. http://dx.doi.org/10.1093/0198297564.003.0008.

– . 2006. "Tax Policy in an Era of Internationalization: An Assessment of a Conditional Diffusion Model of the Spread of Neoliberalism." *International Organization* 60(4): 847–82.

Swinton, Katherine. 1995. "Law, Politics, and the Enforcement of the Agreement on Internal Trade." In *Getting There: An Assessment of the Agreement on Internal Trade*, ed. Michael J. Trebilcock and Daniel Schwanen, 196–210. Toronto: C.D. Howe Institute.

Taylor, Alison. 2001. *The Politics of Education Reform in Alberta*. Toronto: University of Toronto Press.

Taylor, Charles. 1985. *Philosophical Papers*, vol. 1. Cambridge: Cambridge University Press.

Théret, Bruno. 1999. "Regionalism and Federalism: A Comparative Analysis of the Regulation of Economic Tensions between Regions by Canadian and American Federal Intergovernmental Transfer Programmes." *International Journal of Urban and Regional Research* 23(3): 479–512. http://dx.doi. org/10.1111/1468-2427.00209.

– . 2005. "Du principe fédéral à une typologie des fédérations: quelques propositions." In *Le fédéralisme dans tous ses États. Gouvernance identité et mythologie*, ed. Jean-François Gaudreault-Desbiens and Fabien Gélinas, 99–133. Cowansville: Les Éditions Yvon Blais.

Tiebout, Charles. 1956. "A Pure Theory of Local Expenditures." *Journal of Political Economy* 64(5): 416–24. http://dx.doi.org/10.1086/257839.

Tilly, Charles. 2008. *Explaining Social Processes*. Boulder: Paradigm Publishers.

Times Higher Education. "Finding the Glue That Can Fix Cracks in Our Society." *Times Higher Education*, 22 June 2001. Accessed 13 December 2013 at http://www.timeshighereducation.co.uk/162844.article.

Timpson, Annis May. 2001. *Driven Apart: Women's Employment Equality and Child Care in Canadian Public Policy*. Vancouver: UBC Press.

Titmus, Richard M. 1950. *Problems of Social Policy*. London: HMSO and Longmans, Green.

Tompkins, George S. 2008. *A Common Countenance: Stability and Change in the Canadian Curriculum*. Vancouver: Pacific Educational Press.

Trebilcock, Michael J. 2010. *National Securities Regulator Report*, 20 May.

Triadafilopoulos, Triadafilos. 2012. *Becoming Multicultural: Immigration and the Politics of Citizenship in Canada and Germany*. Vancouver: UBC Press.

Tuohy, Carolyn Hughes. 1999. *Accidental Logics: The Dynamics of Change in the Health Care Arena in the United States, Britain, and Canada*. Oxford: Oxford University Press.

Volden, Craig. 2002. "The Politics of Competitive Federalism: A Race to the Bottom in Welfare Benefits?" *American Journal of Political Science* 46(2): 352–63. http://dx.doi.org/10.2307/3088381.

– . 2006. "States as Policy Laboratories: Emulating Success in the Children's Health Insurance Program." *American Journal of Political Science* 50(2): 294–312. http://dx.doi.org/10.1111/j.1540-5907.2006.00185.x.

Walker, Jack. 1969. "The Diffusion of Innovations among the American States." *American Political Science Review* 63(3): 880–99.

Wallner, Jennifer. 2008. "Legitimacy and Public Policy: Seeing beyond Effectiveness, Efficiency, and Performance." *Policy Studies Journal: The Journal of the Policy Studies Organization* 36(3): 421–43. http://dx.doi.org/10.1111/j.1541-0072.2008.00275.x.

– . 2010. "Beyond National Standards: Reconciling the Tension between Federalism and the Welfare State." *Publius: The Journal of Federalism* 40(4): 646–71. http://dx.doi.org/10.1093/publius/pjp033.

– . 2012. "Political Structures, Social Diversity, and Public Policy: Comparing Mandatory Education in Canada and the United States." *Comparative Political Studies* 45(7): 850–74. http://dx.doi.org/10.1177/0010414011428590.

Wallner, Jennifer, and Gerard W. Boychuck. Forthcoming. "Comparing Federations: Testing the Model of Market-Preserving Federalism on Canada,

Australia, and the United States" In *Canada Compared*, ed. Luc Turgeon, Martin Papillon, Jennifer Wallner, and Stephen White. Vancouver: UBC Press.

Watts, Ronald L. 1999. *Comparing Federal Systems*. 2nd ed. Kingston: Institute for Intergovernmental Relations.

– . 2003. *Comparing Federal Systems*. 3rd ed. Montreal and Kingston: McGill–Queen's University Press.

– . 2003. "Equalization in Commonwealth Federations." *Regional and Federal Studies* 13(4): 111–29. http://dx.doi.org/10.1080/13597560308559448.

– . 1999. *The Spending Power in Federal Systems: A Comparative Study*. Kingston: Institute of Intergovernmental Relations, Queen's University.

Weber, Max. 1948. "The Social Psychology of the World Religions." In *From Max Weber: Essays in Sociology*, ed. and trans. H.H. Gerth and C. Wright Mills, 267–301. London: Kegan Paul, Trench, Trubner.

Weingast, Barry. 1995. "The Economic Role of Political Institutions." *Journal of Law Economics and Organization* 11(1): 1–31.

– . 1995. "The Economic Role of Political Institutions: Market-Preserving Federalism and Economic Development." *Journal of Law Economics and Organization* 11 (April): 1–29.

Weir, George M. 1934. *The Separate School Question in Canada*. Toronto: Ryerson Press.

Weir, Margaret. 1989. "Ideas and Politics: The Acceptance of Keynesianism in Britain and the United States." In *The Political Power of Economic Ideas: Keynesianism across Nations*, ed. Peter A. Hall, 53–86. Princeton: Princeton University Press.

– . 1992. "Ideas and the Politics of Bounded Innovation." In *Structuring Politics: Historical Institutionalism in Comparative Analysis*, ed. Sven Steinmo, Kathleen Thelen, and Frank Longstreth, 188–216. Cambridge: Cambridge University Press. http://dx.doi.org/10.1017/CBO9780511528125.008.

Weir, Margaret, and Theda Skocpol. 1985. "State Structures and the Possibilities for 'Keynesian' Responses to the Great Depression in Sweden, Britain, and the United States." In *Bringing the State Back*, ed. Peter Evans et al., 107–64. New York: Cambridge University Press. http://dx.doi.org/10.1017/CBO9780511628283.006.

Weiss, Linda. 1997. "Globalization and the Myth of the Powerless State." *New Left Review* 225: 3–27.

Welch, Anthony. 1996. *Australian Education: Reform or Crisis*. St Leonards: Allen and Unwin.

Wendt, Alexander. 1999. *Social Theory of International Relations*. Cambridge: Cambridge University Press.

Weyland, Kurt. 1999. "Neoliberal Populism in Latin America and Eastern Europe." *Comparative Politics* 31(4): 379. http://dx.doi.org/10.2307/422236.

– . 2005. "Theories of Policy Diffusion: Lessons from Latin American Pension Reforms." *World Politics* 57(2): 262–95.

Wildavsky, Aaron. 1984. "Federalism Means Inequality: Political Geometry, Political Sociology, and Political Culture." In *The Costs of Federalism*, ed. Robert T. Golembiewski and Aaron Wildavsky, 55–69. New Brunswick: Transaction Books.

Wincott, Daniel. 2010. "Ideas, Policy Change, and the Welfare State." In *Ideas and Politics in Social Science Research*, ed. Daniel Béland and Robert Henry Cox, 143–51. Oxford: Oxford University Press. http://dx.doi.org/10.1093/acprof:oso/9780199736430.003.0008.

– . 2005. "Theories of Policy Diffusion: Lessons from Latin American Pension Reforms." *World Politics* 57 (January): 262–95. http://dx.doi.org/10.1353/wp.2005.0019.

Wheare, K.C. 1951. *Federal Government.* 2nd ed. London: Oxford University Press.

Wilson, J. Donald. 1978. "The Pre-Ryerson Years." In *Egerton Ryerson and His Times,* ed. Neil McDonald and Alf Chaiton, 9–42. Toronto: Macmillan.

Wiseman, Nelson. 2007. *In Search of Canadian Political Culture.* Vancouver: UBC Press.

Wotherspoon, Terry, ed. 1987. *The Political Economy of Canadian Schooling.* Toronto: Methuen.

– . 1987. "Introduction: Conflict and Crisis in Canadian Education." In *The Political Economy of Canadian Schooling*, ed. Terry Wotherspoon, 1–18. Toronto: Methuen.

Young, R., Philippe Faucher, and André Blais. 1984. "The Concept of Province-Building: A Critique." *Canadian Journal of Political Science* 17(4): 783. http://dx.doi.org/10.1017/S0008423900052586.

Zilversmit, Arthur. 1993. *Changing Schools: Progressive Education Theory and Practice, 1930–1960.* Chicago: University of Chicago Press.

Government Documents, Archives, and Publications from Non-Government Organizations

Agreement on Internal Trade. Accessed on 16 December 2013 at http://www.ait-aci.ca/index_en/ait.htm.

Alberta, Commission on Educational Planning. 1972. *A Choice of Futures/A Future of Choices.* Edmonton: Queen's Printer for the Province of Alberta.

Alberta Home and School Councils' Association. *Alberta School Council Resource Manual.* Accessed on 19 July 2008 at http://education.alberta.ca/media/464094/scm.pdf.

Alberta, Ministry of Economic Development and the BC College of Teachers. 2007. "Alberta and B.C. Teachers Agree to Labour Mobility." *News Release.* Accessed on 16 December 2013 at http://education.alberta.ca/media/741985/mobility%20fact%20sheet.pdf.

Alberta, Royal Commission on Education. 1959. *Report.* Edmonton: Queen's Printer.

Alberta, 1945. "Speech from the Throne," 22 February. *Journals of the Legislative Assembly of the Province of Alberta.* Edmonton: King's Printer, Volume 46.

Angus Reid Group. 1993. *B.C. Reid Report.* Angus Reid Group.

Association of Universities and Colleges of Canada. 1965. *Financing Higher Education in Canada.* Toronto: Association of Universities and Colleges of Canada by University of Toronto Press.

Atherton, P.J., E.J. Hanson, and J.F. Berlando. 1969. *Quality Education: What Price?* Research Monograph Number 16. Edmonton: Alberta Teachers' Association.

Atlantic Institute of Education. 1979. *A Guide to Public Education in Nova Scotia.* Halifax: Atlantic Institute of Education.

Atlantic Provinces Education Foundation. 1996. *Foundation for the Atlantic Canada Science Curriculum.* Accessed on 30 August 2008 at www.ednet.ns.ca/pdfdocs/curriculum/camet/foundations-science.pdf.

Australian Government. 2006. *Country Education Profile: Australia.* Paris: OECD.

Baker, Harold S. 1963. "Changing Purposes and Programmes of the Canadian High School." In *The Canadian Secondary School: An Appraisal and a Forecast – a Collection of the Papers Delivered at the Conference on the Canadian High School Sponsored by the Department of Secondary Education, University of Alberta,* ed. Lawrence W. Downey and L. Ruth Godwin, 11–34. Toronto: Macmillan and W.J. Gage, 1963.

Battle, Ken, and Sherri Torjman. 2002. "Social Policy That Works: An Agenda." Caledon Institute of Social Policy. September. Accessed on 12 May 2011 at http://www.ontla.on.ca/library/repository/mon/5000/10309536.pdf.

Beaton, Albert E., et al. 1999. *The Benefits and Limits of International Educational Achievement Studies.* International Institute for Educational Planning.

Boadway, Robin, and Ronald Watts. 2000. *Fiscal Federalism in Canada.* July. Kingston: Institute of Intergovernmental Relations.

Brehaut, Willard. 1972. *Teacher Education in Prince Edward Island: Report of a Study Undertaken at the Request of the Minister of Education of the Province of Prince Edward Island.* Toronto: OISE.

British Columbia, Commission of Inquiry into Educational Finance. 1945. *Report*. Victoria: King's Printer.

British Columbia, Ministry of Education, Skills and Training. 1997. *Moving On, Secondary to Post-Secondary Transition: A Report*. Victoria: Ministry of Education, Skills, and Training.

British Columbia, Royal Commission on Education. 1960. *Report*. Victoria: McDiarmid, Queen's Printer.

British Columbia Teachers' Federation. 1967. *The Cost of Education: Who Should Pay and Why?* Vancouver: BC Teachers' Federation.

– . Bargaining Division. 1985. *1985 Education Finance in British Columbia*. Vancouver: BC Teachers' Federation.

Brown, A.F. 1959. "Composite High Schools in Canada: The Nature and Scope of the Study." In *Composite High Schools in Canada*, eds. John H.M. Andrews and Alan F. Brown, 1–10. Edmonton: Committee on Educational Research.

Brehaut, Willard. 1972. *Teacher Education in Prince Edward Island: Report of a Study Undertaken at the Request of the Minister of Education of the Province of Prince Edward Island*. Toronto: OISE.

Bryne, T.C. 1957. "The Evolution of the Provincial Superintendent." In *The Canadian Superintendent: Official Publication of the Canadian Association of School Superintendents and Inspectors*. 5 (May).

Cameron, David M. 2004. "Collaborative Federalism and Post-Secondary Education: Be Careful What You Wish For." Paper prepared for the John Deutsch Institute for the Study of Economic Policy, Queen's University, Kingston, February. Accessed on 9 January 2009 at http://jdi.econ.queensu.ca/Files/Conferences/PSEconferencepapers/Cameronconferencepaper.pdf.

Cameron, Donald Roy. 1960. *Teacher Certification in Canada*. Ottawa: Canadian Teachers' Federation, Research Division Information Bulletin.

Canada and Council of Ministers of Education (Canada). 1975. *Review of Educational Policies in Canada*, vols. 1–5. Ottawa: Council of Ministers of Education Canada.

Canada and Newfoundland Education Association. 1938. *Proceedings of the Eighteenth Convention of the Association*. Halifax, St John's, and Charlottetown, 15 to 19 August.

– . 1944. *Trends in Education 1944: A Survey of Current Educational Developments in the Nine Provinces of Canada and Newfoundland*. Toronto.

Canada. 1969. *Royal Commission on Bilingualism and Biculturalism*. Ottawa: The Secretary of State Department, and Information Canada. 23 October.

– . Royal Commission on Dominion–Provincial Relations. 1940. *Report of the Royal Commission on Dominion–Provincial Relations, Book 1: Canada 1867–1939*. Ottawa: E. Cloutier, Queen's Printer.

– . Royal Commission on Industrial Training and Technical Education. 1913. *Report*. Ottawa: King's Printer.

– . Royal Commission on the Economic Union and Development Prospects for Canada. 1984. *Commission on Canada's Future*. Ottawa.

Canadian Business Task Force on Literacy. 1988. *Measuring the Costs of Illiteracy in Canada*. Toronto: Woods Gordon.

Canadian Council on Learning. 2006. "Lessons in Learning: The Rural-Urban Gap in Education." 1 March (Available on-line) http://www.ccl-cca.ca/pdfs/ LessonsInLearning/10-03_01_06E.pdf (accessed on 9 January 2012).

– . 2008. *State of Learning in Canada: Toward a Learning Future*. Ottawa: Canadian Council on Learning. Accessed on 16 December 2013 at http://www. ccl-cca.ca/pdfs/SOLR/2008/SOLR_08_English_final.pdf.

– . 2009. "Lessons in Learning: Minority Francophone Education in Canada." 20 August (Available on-line) http://www.ccl-cca.ca/pdfs/ LessonsInLearning/08_20_09-E.pdf (accessed on 9 January 2012).

– . 2011. *The New Gender Gap: Exploring the "Boy Crisis" in Education*. Ottawa: Canadian Conference on Learning. (Available on-line) http://www.ccl-cca.ca/ pdfs/OtherReports/Gendereport20110113.pdf (accessed on 9 January 2012).

Canadian Education Association. 1975. *Education in Transition: A Capsule Review 1960 to 1975*. Toronto: Canadian Education Association.

– . 1976. *Reactions to the OECD Review – Canada 1976 Conference of the Canadian Education Association*. Toronto: Canadian Education Association.

– . 2007. *Public Education in Canada: Facts, Trends, and Attitudes*. Toronto.

Canadian Federation of Mayors and Municipalities. 1967. *The Financing of Education in Canada*. Ottawa: Canadian Federation of Mayors and Municipalities.

Canadian School Boards Association. 1994. Education Governance in Canada: Provincial/Territorial Summaries, February (Updated March 1994).

Canadian School Trustees' Association. 1955. *The Road Ahead*. Edmonton: Hamly Press.

Canadian Teachers' Federation. 1967. *Foundations for the Future: A New Look at Teacher Education and Certification in Canada*. Proceedings of the 1966 Seminar on Teacher Education, Chateau Laurier Hotel, Ottawa, May 9–11, 1966. Ottawa: Canadian Teachers' Federation.

– . 1970. *Interprovincial Conference on the Economic Status of the Teachers of Canada*. Toronto: Canadian Teachers' Federation.

– . 1971. *The 1971 Conference on Teacher Certification*. Proceedings of the meeting held in Vancouver, BC, 7–8 June.

– . "Teachers Know About Learning and Assessment." On-line pamphlet, accessed on 20 July 2008 at http://www.ctf-fce.ca/e/programs/pd/ assessment_evaluation/AssessmentBrochure_Teacher_EN_lo.pdf.

CBC Digital Archives. "Ontario Passes Tough New Anti-Smoking Legislation." Accessed on 30 September 2012 at http://www.cbc.ca/archives/catego-
ries/health/public-health/butting-out-the-slow-death-of-smoking-in-canada/
ontario-passes-tough-new-anti-smoking-legislation.html.
CBC News. "Anti-Smoking Efforts in Canada and Abroad." Accessed on 30
September 2012 at http://www.cbc.ca/news/health/story/2009/09/29/f-smok-
ing-bans-tobacco.html.
Centre for Educational Research and Innovation. 1995. *Schools Under Scrutiny*.
Paris: OECD.
–. 1996. *Education at a Glance: Analysis*. Paris: OECD.
–. 2005. *Formative Assessment: Improving Learning in Secondary Classrooms*.
Paris: OECD.
Channon, Geraldine. 1971. *Innovations in Teacher Education in Canada*. Ottawa:
Canadian Teachers' Federation.
Collins, Alice, and Rob Tierney. n.d. "Teacher Education Accord: Values and
Ideals of the Teaching Profession in Canada." Accessed on 27 November 2013
at http://www.cea-ace.ca/sites/default/files/EdCan-2006-v46-n4-Collins.pdf.
Commission on Public Education Finance. 1981. *Report of the Commission on
Public Education Finance*. Halifax.
Commission royale d'enquête sur l'enseignement dans la province de Quebec.
1963–66. *Report of the Royal Commission of Inquiry on Education in the Province
of Quebec*. Québec: Pierre Des Marais Inc., Printer for the Government of the
Province of Quebec.
Committee on Educational Research, Faculty of Education, University of
Alberta. 1958. *Composite High Schools in Canada*. *University of Alberta Mono-
graphs in Education*, no. 1. Edmonton.
Committee on Teacher Education, University of Prince Edward Island. 1971.
Teacher Education: Perseverance or Professionalism. Published and printed in
the Atlantic Provinces.
Conseil supérieur de l'éducation. 2008. "Mission." Accessed on 4 August 2008
at http://www.cse.gouv.qc.ca/EN/Mandat/index.html.
–. 2008. "Organisation." Accessed on 19 July 2008 at http://www.cse.gouv.
qc.ca/FR/Organisation/index.html.
Council of Atlantic Premiers. *CMP Background*. Accessed on 29 July 2008 at
http://www.cap-cpma.ca/default.asp?mn=1.62.4.27.
Council of Ministers of Education. Canada. 1988. *Recent Trends in Curriculum
Reform at the Elementary and Secondary Levels in Canada*. Toronto.
–. Canada. 1991. *Annual Report 1989–1990*. Toronto.
–. Canada. 1996. *Update* 1, 1 (March). Accessed on 28 August 2008 at http://
www.cmec.ca/science/v0101en.htm.

– . Canada. 1996. *Update* 1, 2 (July). Accessed on 28 August 2008 at http://www.cmec.ca/science/v0102en.htm.

– . Canada. 1997. *Update* 2(1) (September). Accessed on 30 August 2008 at http://www.cmec.ca/science/v0201en.htm.

– . Canada. 1997. *K to 12: Common Framework of Science Learning Outcomes.* Toronto. Accessed on 4 July 2008 at http://www.cmec.ca/science/framework/pages/english/1.html.

– . Canada. 2009. *Strengthening Aboriginal Success.* CMEC Summit on Aboriginal Education, 24–5 February. Accessed on 22 May 2012 at http://www.cmec.ca/publications/lists/publications/attachments/221/aboriginal_summit_report.pdf.

Courchene, Thomas. 2010. "The Economic Integration Continuum and the Canadian Securities Industry: In Praise of the Status Quo." Paper commissioned by the Government of Alberta and included in the record filed with the Supreme Court of Canada. Accessed on 30 September 2012 at http://www.irpp.org/miscpubs/archive/courchene_securities.pdf.

Croskery, George G., and Gerald Nason, eds. 1958. *Addresses and Proceedings of the Canadian Conference on Education* held at Ottawa, 16–20 February. Ottawa: Mutual Press.

Department of Education Administration. University of Alberta. 1974. *Decentralizing Decision-Making within School Systems.* Fifteenth Banff Regional Conference. Edmonton.

Department of Finance. *Budget Plan.* Ottawa: Department of Finance, 27 February 1995.

Dominion Bureau of Statistics. 1937. *Annual Survey of Education in Canada 1936.* Ottawa: J.O. Patenaude, Printer to the King's Most Excellent Majesty.

– . 1960. *Student Progress through the Schools by Grade.* Ottawa: Queen's Printer.

– . 1966. *Daily Bulletin,* vols. 35–181 (September 21). Reference 5.

Dominion Educational Association. 1892. *Constitution of the Dominion Educational Association 1892.*

– . 1893. *The Minutes of Proceedings, with Addresses, Papers, and Discussions of the First Convention of the Association.* Montreal. 5–8 July 1892. Montreal: John Lovell and Son, Printers.

– . 1900. *The Minutes of Proceedings, with Addresses and Papers of the Third Convention of the Association, Halifax, August 2–5, 1898.* Halifax.

Dunsmuir, Mollie. 1991. "The Spending Power: Scope and Limitations." Paper prepared by the Law and Government Division, Parliament of Canada, October 1991. Accessed on 16 December 2013 at http://www.parl.gc.ca/Content/LOP/researchpublications/bp272-e.htm.

Earl, Lorna M. 1995. "Accountability and Assessment: Ensuring Quality in Ontario Schools." In *For the Love of Learning: Background Papers for the Royal Commission on Learning*, ed. Nancy Watson, Joyce Scane, and George Bedard, vol. 2, 399–430. Ontario: Royal Commission on Learning.

Economic Council of Canada. 1965. *Towards Sustained and Balanced Economic Growth: Second Annual Review of the Economic Council of Canada*. Ottawa: Queen's Printer.

English, J.F.K. 1956. "An Evaluation of the Reorganized System of Local School Administration in British Columbia." PhD diss., University of Toronto.

Expert Panel on Equalization and Territorial Formula Financing. 2008. *Achieving a National Purpose: Putting Equalization Back on Track*. May. On-line publication, accessed on 19 December 2008 at http://www.eqtff-pfft.ca/english/EQTreasury/index.asp.

Expert Panel on Securities Regulation. 2009. *Creating an Advantage in Global Capital Markets: Final Report and Recommendations*. January. Accessed on 2 October 2012 at http://www.groupeexperts.ca/eng/documents/Expert_Panel_Final_Report_And_Recommendations.pdf.

Fagen, Lenora Perry, and Dana Spurrell. 1995. *Evaluating Achievement of Senior High School Students in Canada: A Study of Policies and Practices of Ministries and School Boards in Canada*. Toronto: Canadian Education Association.

Froese-Germain, Bernie. 1999. *Standardized Testing: Undermining Equity in Education*. Ottawa: Canadian Teachers' Federation.

Fullan, Michael, and F. Michael Connelly. 1987. *Teacher Education in Ontario: Current Practice and Options for the Future: A Position Paper*. Toronto: OISE.

Hodgins, J. George, ed. 1894–1910. *Documentary History of Education in Upper Canada, from the passing of the Constitutional Act of 1791, to the close of Rev. Dr. Ryerson's administration of the Education Department in 1876*. Vol. 240. Toronto: Warwick Bros. and Rutter, Printers.

International Monetary Fund. 2008. *Canada: Financial System Stability Assessment – Update*. IMF Country Report No. 08/59, February. Accessed on 2 October 2012 at http://www.imf.org/external/pubs/ft/scr/2008/cr0859.pdf.

Jenson, Jane. 2007. "Redesigning Citizenship Regimes after Neoliberalism: Ideas about Social Investment." Prepared for the meeting of RC 19, Florence, September. Accessed on 16 December 2013 at http://www.cccg.umontreal.ca/pdf/Jenson%20RC19%202007.pdf.

Knighton, Tamara, Pierre Brochu, and Tomasz Gluszynski. 2010. *Measuring Up: Canadian Results of the OECD PISA Study: The Performance of Canada's Youth in Reading, Mathematics, and Science 2009*. Ottawa: Minister of Industry.

Lawton, Stephen B. 1987. *The Price of Quality: The Public Financing of El-ementary and Secondary Education in Canada.* Toronto: Canadian Education Association.

– . 1996. *Financing Canadian Education.* Toronto: Canadian Education Association.

LaZerte, M.E. 1955. *School Finance in Canada, 1955.* Edmonton: Canadian Schools Trustees' Association, Finance Research Committee.

LeDrew, Barry. 1996. "Atlantic Canada Common Curriculum Development: Departments of Education in the Atlantic Provinces Work Together to Renew Curriculum for the K to 12 System." *Prospects: Journal of the Canada/Newfoundland COOPERATION Agreement on Human Resource Development* 3, 3 (Fall). Accessed on 7 October 2008 at http://www.cdli.ca/Community/prospects/v3n3/acccd.htm.

Library and Archives Canada. Canadian Education Association Archives, Series MG 28 I472, vol. 1, File 6, *Western Resource Workshop, Saskatoon.*

– . 1954. *File 10, Notes and Reports CEA*, vol. 1. Canadian Education Association Archives, Series MG 28 I472. Short Course.

– . Canadian Education Association Archives, Series MG 28 I 472, vol. 13, File 131.

– . Canadian Education Association Archives, Series MG 28 I 472, vol. 13, File 318, CTF-CEA Relations with (official statement).

– . Canadian Education Association Archives, Series MG 28 I 472, vol. 13, File 326, Research Council, Miscellaneous.

– . Canadian Education Association Archives, Series MG 28 I 472, vol. 13, File 327, NACER Miscellaneous.

– . Canadian Education Association Archives, Series MG 28 I 472, vol. 21, File VIII 10, Teachers' Federation. "Unfair to Children: Our Educational Inequal-ities – pamphlet from the CTF, 1963."

– . Canadian Education Association Archives, Series MG 28 I 472, vol. 23, File II-6, Standing Committee of Ministers Responsible for Education, 1961. Letter from Freeman Stewart to Senator Donald Cameron, Alberta Royal Commissioner, 20 April 1961.

– . Canadian Education Association Archives, Series MG 28 I 472, vol. 24, File X II, Teacher Federation, "Teacher Bids Canada Unify Education."

– . Canadian Education Association Archives, Series MG 28 I 472, vol. 33, File II-6, Standing Committee of Ministers Responsible for Education, 1961, "The Canadian Education Association Memorandum to Dr F.S. Rivers Re: Canada's External Aid Program in Education," 23 March 1961.

Linos, Katarina. 2008. "How Do Ideas Shape the Welfare State? Family Policy Developments in Greece and Spain." Paper presented at "Internationalization and Public Policy Paradigm Change Workshop." University of Toronto, 11 April 2008.

Macdonald, John C., Wayne Hall, H. Pullen, and Florence G. Irvine. 1966. *Four Viewpoints on Teacher Education*. Ottawa: Canadian Teachers' Federation.

Macey, Jonathan. 2010. *An Analysis of the Canadian Federal Government's Initiative to Create a National Securities Regulator*.

Manitoba School Question! French-Canadian Interference with Manitoba. Accessed on 16 January 2012 at http://ia700507.us.archive.org/11/items/cihm_30378/cihm_30378.pdf.

Manitoba. Department of Youth and Education. 1968. *Annual Report*. Winnipeg: R.S. Evans, Queen's Printer for Manitoba.

– . Royal Commission on Education. 1959. *Report*. Winnipeg: Queen's Printer.

Manitoba Teachers' Society. 1970. *A Study of Education Finance in Manitoba: Analysis, Projections, Priorities, Recommendations*. Winnipeg.

– . 2000. *The Retreat from Equity: A Study of the Impact of the Public School Funding Model of the Government of Manitoba – the Schools Finance Program, Reviews of National Policies, 1992–1999*. Winnipeg.

Maritime Union Study. 1970. *The Report on the Maritime Union Commissioned by the Governments of Nova Scotia, New Brunswick, and Prince Edward Island*. Halifax.

Marleau, Robert, and Eric Montpetit, eds. *House of Commons Procedure and Practice*. Accessed on 7 March 2008 at http://www.parl.gc.ca/MarleauMontpetit/DocumentViewer.aspx?DocId=1001&Sec=Ch11&Seq=2&Lang=E.

Marshall, H. 1952. *The Organization and Administration of Public Schools in Canada. Dominion Bureau of Statistics Reference Paper*. Ottawa: King's Printer.

McCordic, William J. 1961. *Financing Education in Canada*. Ottawa: Canadian Conference on Education.

Meuret, Denis. 1995. *Decision-Making in 14 OECD Education Systems*. Paris: OECD.

Michaud, Pierre. 1983. "Educational Finance in Quebec and New Brunswick: Similarities and Differences." In *The Costs of Controlling the Costs of Education in Canada*. Proceedings of a Symposium on Educational Finance in Canada at the 1983 Meeting of the American Educational Research Association, Montreal, 12 April. 23–32. Toronto: OISE.

Moffatt, H.P. 1949. "An SOS from the Schools: Report of the Canadian Education Association's Committee on the Status of the Teaching Profession." In *September*. Toronto: Canadian Education Association.

Moore, Albert, and British Columbia School Trustees Association. 1966. *Financing Education in British Columbia*. Vancouver: BC School Trustees Association.

Mulhern, Celine. 2007. "Globalization and the Selective Permeability of Public Policy-Making: The Case of K–12 Education in Ontario, 1990–2003." PhD diss., University of Toronto.

National Commission on Excellence in Education. 1983. *A Nation at Risk: The Imperatives for Educational Reform*. Report to the Nation and the Secretary of Education, US Department of Education. Washington: US GPO, April 1983. Accessed on 16 December 2013 at http://datacenter.spps.org/uploads/sotw_a_nation_at_risk_1983.pdf.

National Commission for Excellence in Teacher Education. 1985. *A Call for Change in Teacher Education*. Washington: American Association of Colleges for Teacher Education.

New Brunswick. 1937. *Annual Report of the Department of Education of the Province of New Brunswick, 1936*. Fredericton: King's Printer.

– . 1955. *Report of the Royal Commission on the Financing of Schools in New Brunswick*. Fredericton: C.D. Taylor, Minister of Education.

– . 1967. *New Brunswick Legislative Debates*, 19 April.

– . 1968. *Legislative Assembly Synoptic Report of the Proceedings of the Fifth Session of the Forty-Fifth Legislative Assembly of the Province of New Brunswick, 1967*, vol. 1.

– . Vocational Education Board. 1919. *First Annual Report of the Vocational Education Board*. Fredericton.

New Brunswick and the Commission on Excellence in Education. 1992. *Schools for a New Century*. Fredericton.

New Brunswick and the Department of Education. 1964. *Report of the Deputy Minister of Education, 1963–1964*. Fredericton.

– . 1968. *Annual Report of the Department of Education, 1967*. Fredericton, NB: Department of Education.

Newfoundland. Royal Commission on Education and Youth. 1967. *Report*. St John's.

Nova Scotia. Department of Education. 2004. *Nova Scotia Public Education: Teacher Supply and Demand* (Update Report).

Nova Scotia and the Royal Commission on Education, Public Services, and Provincial–Municipal Relations. 1974. *Report*. Halifax: Queen's Printer.

Nova Scotia Teachers' Union. 1971. *Initial Statement of Position to the Royal Commission on Education, Public Services, and Provincial–Municipal Relations*. Halifax.

O'Donnell, Sharon. 2004. *International Review of Curriculum and Assessment Frameworks: Comparative Tables and Factual Summaries*. Brussels: Eurydice Network, December.

Ontario. Department of Education. 1966. Report of the Minister's Committee on the Training of Elementary School Teachers. Toronto.

– . Legislative Assembly. 2010. *Debates, 27th Leg., 4th Session, 29 March 1966.*

– . Ministry of Education. 2006. *The Ontario Curriculum, Grades 1–8: Language.* Revised. Toronto: Queen's Printer.

– . Ministry of Education and Training. 1995. *New Foundations for Ontario Education.* Toronto.

– . Provincial Committee on Aims and Objectives in the Schools of Ontario. 1968. *Living and Learning.* Toronto: Newton Publishing.

– . Royal Commission on Education in Ontario. 1950. *Report.* Toronto: King's Printer.

– . Royal Commission on Learning. 1994. *For the Love of Learning: Report of the Royal Commission on Learning.* Toronto: Queen's Printer for Ontario.

Ontario Confederation of University Faculty Associations. 1968. "A Policy Statement on the Amalgamation of Elementary Teachers' Colleges with the Universities." November.

Organisation for Economic Co-operation and Development. 1960. *Convention on the Organisation for Economic Co-operation and Development.* Paris. 14 December. Accessed on 15 October 2008 at http://www.oecd.org/document/7/0,3343,en_2649_34483_1915847_1_1_1_1,00.html.

– . 1976. *Reviews of National Policies for Education: Canada.* Paris.

– . 1993. *Education at a Glance.* Paris.

– . 2004. *Completing the Foundation for Lifelong Learning: An OECD Survey of Upper Secondary Schools.* Paris.

– . 2006. *Education at a Glance.* Paris

– . 2011. *Education at a Glance.* Paris.

Ottawa. *Dominion–Provincial Conference 1960.* Ottawa: Queen's Printer.

– . Department of Finance. 1995. *Budget Plan.*

Paton, James M. 1962. *The Professional Status of Teachers.* Conference Study no. 2. Canadian Conference on Education. Montreal, 2–8 March.

Prince Edward Island. Joint Review Committee. 1971. *Education Task Group: Elementary, Secondary, and Post-Secondary Sectors Report PEI Development Plan.*

– . Task Force on Student Achievement. 2005. *Excellence in Education: A Challenge for Prince Edward Island.* Accessed on 12 December 2008 at http://www.upei.ca/studentachievement/Reporta.pdf.

Prince Edward Island and Department of Education and Human Resources. 1993. *Annual Report for the Year Ending June 30, 1993.* Charlottetown.

Province of British Columbia. 1925. *Survey of the School System.* Victoria: Charles F. Banfield.

Quebec. Royal Commission of Inquiry on Constitutional Problems. 1956.
Report.

Québec. Ministère de l'Education. 1985. *Statistiques de l'Education. Direction
générale de la recherché et de la prospective.*

Raphael, Dennis. 1996. "Student Assessment: A Flawed Framework?" In *Ring
Some Alarm Bells in Ontario: Reactions to the Report of the Royal Commission on
Learning,* ed. Geoff Milburn, 79–94. London: Althouse Press.

Reference Re Canada Assistance Plan (B.C.), [1991] 2 S.C.R. 525.

Report of the Standing Senate Committee on Aboriginal Peoples. 2011 (December). *Reforming First Nations Education: From Crisis to Hope.* Accessed on
22 May 2012 at http://www.parl.gc.ca/Content/SEN/Committee/411/appa/
rep/rep03dec11-e.pdf.

Rideout, E. Brock. 1978. *Alternatives for Education Finance within the Established Parameters.* Ottawa: Commission on Declining School Enrolments in
Ontario.

Rom, Mark Carl, and James C. Garand. 2001. "Interstate Competition in K–12
Education Policy." Unpublished paper presented at the Association for Policy Analysis and Management Annual Research Conference, Washington.

Royal Commission on the Economic Union and Development Prospects for
Canada. 1984. *Commission on Canada's Future.* Ottawa.

Ryerson, Egerton. 1847. *Report on a System of Public Elementary Instruction for
Upper Canada.* Montreal: Lovell and Gibson.

– . 1896. *A Special Report on the Systems of Popular Education on the Continent
of Europe, on the British Isles, and the United States of America, with Practical
Suggestions for the Improvement of Public Instruction in the Province of Ontario.*
Toronto: Leader Steam Press.

Sarson, Seymore. 1995. *A Critical Appraisal of Teacher Education.* Washington:
American Association of Colleges for Teacher Education.

Saskatchewan. Department of Education. *Annual Report, 1918.*

– . Department of Education. *Annual Report, 1949–50.*

– . Ministry of Education. 2002. *A Curriculum Guide for the Elementary Level*
(January). Accessed on 19 July 2008 at http://www.sasked.gov.sk.ca/docs/
ela/index.html.

Saskatchewan Program Commission. 1962. Reports of the Canadian Conference on Education, Montreal, 4–8 March.

Saskatchewan School Boards Association. 1997. *School Trustee* 2, no. 1
(January).

Saskatchewan Teachers' Federation. 1939. "New Light on the Larger Unit."
Bulletin, May: 10–12.

– . 1939. "What the Larger Unit Is." *Bulletin,* September: 37–9.

Select Committee on Education, Nova Scotia. 1992. *Report,* vol. 1 (31 March).

Smaller, Harry. n.d. "Vocational Education in Ontario's Secondary Schools: Past, Present – and Future?" WIP#2000-04, Labour Education and Training Research Network, York University. Accessed on 2 August 2008 at www.yorku.ca/crws/network/english/Smaller.pdf.

Spady, William G. 1994. *Outcomes-Based Education: Critical Issues and Answers.* Arlington: American Association of School Administrators.

Statistics Canada. 1983. *Historical Statistics of Canada.* 2nd ed., ed. F.H. Leacy. A327–A388 Series.

– . 2003. *Report of the Pan-Canadian Education Indicators Program.* Ottawa. Statistics Canada.

Stokes, Janice. 2003. *Demographic Trends and Socio-Economic Sustainability in Saskatchewan: Some Policy Considerations.* Saskatchewan Institute of Public Policy. Paper no. 19 (October). Accessed on 5 December 2008 at http://www.uregina.ca/sipp/documents/pdf/PPP19_Demographics.pdf.

Tomkowicz, Joanna, and Tracey Bushnik. 2003. *Who Goes to Post-Secondary Education and When: Pathways Chosen by 20 Year Olds.* Education, skills and learning Research Paper. Ottawa: Ministry of Industry. On-line publication, accessed on 20 February 2012 at http://publications.gc.ca/collections/Collection/Statcan/81-595-MIE/81-595-MIE2003006.pdf.

Traub, Ross. 1994. *Standardized Testing in Canada.* Toronto: Canadian Education Association.

University of Alberta. *Western Canada Regional Conference on Teacher Education.* Edmonton. 20–22 May 1954.

US Census Bureau. 2008. *The 2008 Statistical Abstract: The National Data Book.* Accessed on 12 May 2008 at http://www.census.gov/compendia/statab/cats/education/elementary_and_secondary_education_staff_ and_finances.html.

"Western and Northern Canadian Protocol for Collaboration in Education." Accessed on 4 August 2008 at http://www.wncp.ca.

William, Tom R., and Holly Millinoff. 1990. *Canada's Schools: A Report Card for the 1990s: A CEA Opinion Poll.* Toronto: Canadian Education Association.

Wöessmann, Ludger. 2002. "Fundamental Determinants of School Efficiency and Equity: German States as a Microcosm for OECD Countries." PEPG/07–02. Accessed on 13 May 2008 at http://www.hks.harvard.edu/pepg/PDF/Papers/PEPG07-02_Woessmann.pdf.

Index

Studies in Comparative Political Economy and Public Policy